CRITICAL ISSUES IN EDUCATION

CRITICAL ISSUES IN EDUCATION

Jack L. Nelson
Rutgers University

Stuart B. Palonsky
University of Missouri

Kenneth Carlson
Rutgers University

McGRAW-HILL PUBLISHING COMPANY

New York   St. Louis   San Francisco   Auckland   Bogotá   Caracas
Hamburg   Lisbon   London   Madrid   Mexico   Milan   Montreal   New Delhi
Oklahoma City   Paris   San Juan   São Paulo   Singapore   Sydney   Tokyo   Toronto

This book was developed by Lane Akers, Inc.

This book was set in Times Roman by General Graphic Services, Inc.
The editors were Lane Akers and Laura D. Warner;
the production supervisor was Janelle S. Travers.
The cover was designed by Carla Bauer.
R. R. Donnelley & Sons Company was printer and binder.

CRITICAL ISSUES IN EDUCATION

1 2 3 4 5 6 7 8 9 0 DOC   DOC 8 9 4 3 2 1 0 9

ISBN   0-07-557235-4

Library of Congress Cataloging-in-Publication Data

Nelson, Jack L.
    Critical issues in education / Jack L. Nelson, Stuart B. Palonsky,
  Kenneth Carlson.
        p.   cm.
    Includes bibliographical references.
    ISBN 0-07-557235-4
        1. Education—United States.   2. Teaching.   3. Educational
  evaluation—United States.   4. Critical thinking—United States.
  I. Palonsky, Stuart B.   II. Carlson, Kenneth.   III. Title.
  LA217.N439   1990
  370'.973—dc20   89-39304

ABOUT THE AUTHORS

JACK L. NELSON is currently professor of education at Rutgers University. After earning his doctorate at the University of Southern California, he taught at California State University, Los Angeles, at the State University of New York at Buffalo, at San Jose State University, and at Cambridge University in England. A prolific writer, he has authored or edited fourteen books and more than a hundred articles and reviews. He has served as editor of *Social Science Record* and of *Theory and Research in Social Education,* and as book review editor for *Social Education.*

STUART B. PALONSKY is professor of education at the University of Missouri at Columbia. A former public school teacher in New York and New Jersey, he earned his doctorate at Michigan State University before teaching for several years at Rutgers University. Among his publications is *900 Shows a Year,* a book-length study of high school teaching from a teacher's perspective.

KENNETH CARLSON is an associate professor of education at Rutgers University, where he has developed such equity-related courses as "Sexism in Education" and "Liberty vs. Equality in Education." He was principal investigator on a three-year National Institute of Education study, done in conjunction with the Greater Newark Urban Coalition, of state compensatory education in New Jersey. He has been associate dean for teacher education, chairman of the Rutgers University Senate, and president of the New Jersey Conference of the American Association of University Professors.

979/3

CONTENTS

PREFACE

Critical Issues in Education is designed for courses in the undergraduate or graduate education curriculum that are devoted wholly or partly to a critical examination of current issues in education. The book presumes that education is a matter of great significance in modern society, and that a dialectic regarding its principal issues will eventually lead to new ideas and improvements.

Specifically, the book has two major goals. The first is simply to inform the reader about the most important issues on the current educational scene. To be informed about issues is a necessary step for any professional. Individual issues, however, never exist in a sociopolitical vacuum and, consequently, their in-depth examination broadens into an analysis of underlying themes (for example, liberty versus equality) that tie certain issues together. Some of these underlying themes are identified in the introduction to each of the four parts of the book, along with other background information that helps clarify the issues chapters that follow those introductions.

In addition to providing information about specific issues and underlying themes, this book also intends to whet the appetite for intellectual debate and the critical thinking that should accompany such debate. Thus, we have chosen to examine each issue from two divergent viewpoints, each one written in the form of an advocate to express that position. There are many possible divergent views on each issue, and we hope to stimulate consideration of those ideas by starting with the two provided in each issues chapter. Chapter 1 suggests the general framework of criticism and reform for examining issues contained in the book, and indicates our view of critical thinking. Each issues chapter concludes with some discussion questions, selected information on that issue, and references for further examination.

The issues were selected on the basis of (1) survey responses from professional colleagues across the country and (2) our own judgment of the significance and the staying power of specific issues. Most of those selected, we think, will prove to be perennial issues that students just beginning their study of education will still be pondering as they become the educational leaders of the twenty-first century. The issue arrangement in this text has roughly followed a macro to micro scheme, that is, moving from a consideration of the overarching school-society relationship to the curriculum, teaching, and evaluation considerations that flow out of that relationship.

It may be useful to know which author took major responsibility for which portions of the book; the breakdown is as follows: Nelson: Introduction to Part 2, and Chapters 1, 6, 8, 9, 10, 13, 16, 17. Palonsky: Introductions to Parts 3 and 4, and Chapters 11, 12, 14, 15. Carlson: Introduction to Part 1, and Chapters 2, 3, 4, 5, 7.

At this point we would like to acknowledge our great intellectual debt to those who have taken seriously the relation of education to society, and who have expressed divergent views in the extensive literature available. We are also indebted to students, colleagues, and the following reviewers who provided criticism and assistance: Leo Anglin, Kent State University; Nicholas Appleton, Arizona State University; Hal Burbach, University of Virginia; Marvin Grandstaff, Michigan State University; B. Edward McClelland, Indiana University; James Noll, University of Maryland; Susanne Shafer, Arizona State University; Gerald Unks, University of North Carolina; and George Wood, Ohio University. In particular, we express appreciation to Lane Akers, our effectively critical editor, and to Nancy and Gwen for forbearance and encouragement. We further dedicate this effort to Megan, Jordan, Jonathan, Kirsten, Tom, and others of the generation of students and teachers who will be the core of education in the twenty-first century.

Jack L. Nelson
Stuart B. Palonsky
Kenneth Carlson

CRITICAL ISSUES IN EDUCATION

CHAPTER 1

CRITICISM AND REFORM
IN EDUCATION

Schools are controversial. While virtually everyone agrees that schools are necessary, we disagree strongly on such matters as how schools should be organized, operated, financed, and controlled. These are political as well as educational issues. We disagree on the extent to which religious ideologies should exert influence on public schooling, and the relation of private religious education to secular schooling. We have disagreements over the role of the school in providing education on sexual matters, and we disagree on the function of the school as an agency which reproduces cultural biases for or against males or females. These, of course, are not all of the disagreements we have over schooling. They are mentioned here to illustrate that politics, religion, and sex are not only controversial topics in and of themselves, but practical issues in our children's schooling.

We also disagree on some of the purposes for schools, and how they should be translated into practice. There may be some commonly assumed school purposes, such as distributing knowledge and providing opportunity, but there are many controversies over what knowledge should be distributed, which children should get which opportunities, and who should be in charge of deciding.

Human societies, for over 3,000 years, have recognized the value of education—and have argued about it (Ulich, 1954). For hundreds of years, succeeding generations of people in America have agreed on the importance of education, but have disagreed over what it should be, who should get it, and how it should be organized.

There is no shortage of critics and reformers. Although they are interrelated, criticism and reform can be differentiated. Criticism highlights divergent views of the purposes and practices of schools; reform is an attempt to make changes toward one view or another. Criticism is the basis for reform efforts and reform efforts are the subject of criticism.

Critics and reformers present a bewildering array of educational ideas. Some would limit schools to classical knowledge taught to elite academic students, while others would create schools that teach contemporary ideas to students of all abilities and talents. Some would allow considerable latitude for students to choose what and how they study, while others would mandate certain information for all to master. Some would target social problems that schooling should solve, while others would keep school separate from the real world. Some would expect schools to emancipate students from oppressive aspects of the society and the economy, while others would have schools be training grounds for industry and patriotism. These views do not exhaust the diversity of educational criticism and reform, and each position incorporates ideological concepts that its advocates use as a measure of what they think schooling should be.

INDIVIDUAL CRITICISM AND PERVASIVE ISSUES

Although Gallup Polls show general public support of schools, most of us can identify one or more areas that need correction, such as poor cafeteria food, a weak teacher, a cloddish administrator, an ignorant counselor, or outdated textbooks. School is an easy target for criticism because it is one of the rare social institutions that virtually everyone has experienced over a long period of time. Most of us know the beauty as well as the warts and blemishes of schools from direct personal experience. The frequent school-bashing which takes place in backyard conversations or in the media is of interest because it indicates the level or focus of individual discontents. Some backyard critics propose quick and efficient reforms to improve schools: "Get rid of the deadwood." "Quit using standardized tests." "Stop dumping on kids; let them have fun." "Make them learn the basics or no graduation." "Cut the waste." "Fire the superintendent." Fortunately, most understand that change in schooling is more complex, and that the potential consequences of change need more thought.

Educational criticism may range from mild discontent with some temporary problem in school to pervasive and fundamental disagreement with the purposes and practices of schooling. Reforms may also range from slight modifications of current practice to radical or revolutionary alterations in the nature of schools. Successful revolutions are very rare (Johnson, 1966; Useem, 1975), but protests about social institutions and efforts at reform are common (Smelser, 1962; Gurr, 1970).

Reform of education suggests a much more complex and extensive agenda than a group of individual criticisms; it includes more general agreement on the defects of schools and broader support for proposed changes. Such movements take time to generate and to establish a base for action. They also need a setting that is conducive to reform, usually a period in history where other social institutions have been criticized, or where important social values have been challenged.

There needs to be a responsive public for a reform movement to attain influence. News media are very important in developing this public responsiveness. The sporadic newspaper story reporting tests that show how ignorant students are about math or American history has limited impact. However, the accumulation of these stories—along with stories about declining SAT scores, school principals sending ungrammatical or silly letters to parents, high school graduates unable to read or write, studies showing low math or science test scores compared with those of students in other countries, and similar features—develop a public perception that schools are defective and need remediation. That can provide the opportunity for politicians or leading critics of schools to galvanize opinion around educational reform. Advocates of the reform gain an agenda and a platform.

In this book we cite many thoughtful and cogent individual critics of education, but we are more concerned with pervasive disagreements and critical educational issues than with a particular critic or criticism. Pervasive disputes include divergent views on such matters as individual liberties and social rights; control by church, state, or profession; domination by mass or elite ideologies; values based on tradition or change; and the relative significance of authority or responsibility. Who should be educated, for how long, about what, and why are current questions about schools in America that reflect old arguments about what a good society should be, and how schools can be used to attain it.

Reformers see schools as either the cause of some problem or part of the cure. We are led to believe that schools are at fault when American business fails to remain competitive with the German or Japanese. We are also led to believe that schools can solve major social problems such as racism, sexism, automobile accidents, AIDS, teenage pregnancy, and drugs.

Schools are a battleground where the future of the society is at stake. Although we can't predict the future with a high degree of certainty, we can try to develop a preferred future society by teaching selected social values to the next generations. The issue here is that we don't agree on which social values should be taught.

There are two major frameworks for reform in society and education: functionalist and critical. Functionalist reform is more modest, with change seen as a natural, ongoing process within the evolution of social institutions. This view assumes that the social order is basically stable and that we share a commonly agreed set of social values. A critical framework proposes more radical or revolutionary change, seeking dramatic alteration in social institutions. This view sees social classes as being in conflict, with a dominant class of elites controlling the society and imposing a false sense of agreement on social values (Gouldner, 1970; Besag and Nelson, 1984). Reform movements, whether modest or dramatic, seem to follow a cyclic pattern.

REFORM MOVEMENTS: CYCLES OF PROGRESSIVISM AND TRADITIONALISM

Divergent views of schooling and politics can be understood in terms of an ideological continuum: from elitist positions on the extreme right to egalitarian positions on the extreme left, with mainstream conservative and liberal positions in the center. Radical views are important to the disputes, since they present stark and clearly defined differences between egalitarian and elitist ideologies. But mainstream conservative and liberal ideas govern most reform movements because of their general popularity and their immense influence over the media and government. Liberals, conservatives, and radicals differ in their views of which mainstream position has the schools in its grip, as the following two selections show.

James Watt, the former controversial secretary of the interior, began *The Courage of a Conservative* (1985) with the comment, "There is an intense battle raging in this land. It can be described in political terms, theological expressions or economic equations. . . . Its outcome will determine how we and our children will be governed in the twenty-first century. . . . The contest between liberals and conservatives is a moral battle" (pp. 17, 29). The moral battleground, in Watt's version, includes the schools, which he claims are "controlled by the liberal Establishment" as illustrated by such actions as abolishing the moral teachings of the McGuffey's *Readers,* substituting the doctrine of evolution for the biblical idea of creation, eliminating school prayers, insinuating "Humanism" into the school textbooks and curriculum, providing sex education and contraceptives that promote sexual promiscuity, and teaching that abortion and homosexuality are acceptable (pp. 104–123).

Conversely, in the introduction to David Purpel's book, *The Moral and Spiritual Crisis in Education* (1989), Henry Giroux and Paulo Freire describe a "volatile debate in social theory" where "now, as before, the debate over the reform of public schooling in the United States is being principally set by the right wing. The emphasis on character education and moral fundamentalism currently trumpeted by the New Right critics . . . served primarily to legitimate forms of authority and social discipline that undermine the very principles of democratic community and social responsibility" (pp. xii, xiv, xv). The right-wing agenda identified by Giroux and Freire includes ignoring basic social conflict to return to a mythical past portrayed in such books as McGuffey's *Readers,* elitist cultural uniformity, imposition of a rigid view of authority, and the reshaping of curriculum in the interests of industrialists.

Fred Kerlinger (1984), after several years studying political attitudes, proposes that "liberalism and conservatism seem to be general ideologies that pervade most social beliefs and attitudes. . . . Conservative and liberal beliefs are evidently not opposites. They are simply different. The person who espouses liberal beliefs does not necessarily condemn conservative beliefs" (pp. 222, 238). The main factors Kerlinger found that distinguished a conservative ideology were religion, economic conservatism, tradition and authority, and morality. The main factors among liberals were civil rights, social liberalism, sexual freedom, human warmth and feeling, and progressivism. He argues that these clusters are not bipolar opposites—for example, liberals may not be opposed to morality; they just don't see it as central to their view. The differences between conservatives and liberals, as they relate to social, economic, and political issues, are significant, but Kerlinger believes that it is improper to see these ideologies as simple opposites. There are many variations, and some shared attitudes. In regard to educational views, Kerlinger's studies suggest that the terms "traditionalism" and "progressivism" are more common, and that these are subsets of general political conservatism and liberalism. When liberal-progressive ideas become more popular, as in the presidency of Franklin Roosevelt, or when conservative-traditional ideas begin to dominate, as in that of Ronald Reagan, the schools are among the public institutions that are subject to reform toward that view. Schools are part of the political climate, and that climate typically shifts between conservative and liberal visions of the good society.

After noting that "education is rich in potential conflict" (p. 94), Kerlinger states that research shows "individuals tend to be basically progressive or traditional, but not both" (p. 117). Progressivism includes a set of ideas emphasizing the needs and interests of students; freedom of the teacher and student; permissiveness; life experience as important education; democratic citizenship; and concern for physical, emotional, and social development. Traditionalism incorporates an emphasis on ultimate truths and principles, intellectual standards, subject matter, spiritual and moral values, tradition, discipline, authority of the teacher, and school as preparation for life in the society (p. 23).

It is clear that many "progressives" favor such traditional school views as solid learning of basic knowledge and tougher grading, and that many "traditionalists" favor the integration of knowledge and giving students more freedom. In general, however, liberal and conservative school ideas are patterned after mainstream social ideas. On any important educational issue, there are at least two popular positions with an unlimited number of variations that could develop support. This book presents divergent positions on educational issues, not necessarily polar-opposite views.

The ideas of liberals in one time period may be seen as conservative in another, and vice versa. Recently, the labels "neo-conservative" and "neo-liberal" have been introduced to separate and identify those advocates who do not fit well under the more traditional labels, but these are also loose terms (Steinfels, 1979; Rothenberg, 1984). Although definitions of "conservative" and "liberal" may be slippery, these terms are very commonly applied to ideas and people in each time period. Various responses to contemporary educational issues are no less labeled as conservative or liberal.

Such shifts in the nomenclature of criticism and reform are common in American educational history (Cremin, 1961; Welter, 1962; Tyack, 1967; Karier, 1967; Katz, 1971), but the schools actually change only modestly. The traditional and progressive agendas differ, but the response of the schools to each reform movement seems to be to move very gradually in the direction proposed, with a few widely publicized examples of reform, and to await the next movement. Carl Kaestle (1985), discussing the impact of school reforms, states that the "real school system is more like a huge tanker going down the middle of a channel, rocking a bit from side to side as it attends to one slight current and then to another" (p. 423).

Schools, as social organizations, have the same resistance to change as any bureaucracy. There is often some surface alteration, like new textbooks or teacher workshops stressing the latest fad, but longer-lasting reform of education takes considerable effort and time.

As David Purpel described the 1980s school reform movement, "Despite all the hoopla and passion of the educational reform movement, I believe that the differences in classroom curriculum and pedagogy between the public educational system of the 1980s and that of the recent past reflect modest differences in emphasis and cannot be said to be fundamental" (1989, p. 14). He considers much of the reform to be "trivialization" of education. The mainstream reforms are mere window dressing while the schools remain relatively undisturbed. Trivializing concerns, such as test scores as measures of excellence, become popular causes while the serious crisis in education is overlooked. The serious critiques of education, according to Purpel, come from the extreme right and extreme left. The right identifies the underlying school ideology as godlessness and materialism, in a form that they call "secular humanism." The left identifies the school ideology as conformist, racist, sexist, and elitist.

BEYOND THE CONSERVATIVE-LIBERAL MAINSTREAM: RADICAL CRITIQUE

There are deeper ideological roots of discord beyond the popular mainstream liberal-conservative dialogue. These include a variety of radical positions on what the society, and its schools, should be. Critical positions are often expressed early in the radical literature of a time, then filter into the liberal and conservative rhetoric (Nelson, Carlson, and Linton, 1972). Those mainstream views sound much more reasonable at any point in history as bases for reform, but the radical ideas contain the seeds for longer-term and more significant change. In the age when kings were presumed to rule by divine right, and were not subject to challenge by the people, democracy was a radical view. In a dictatorship, individual freedom is considered radical. In a free-enterprise capitalistic society, socialism is considered radical.

Radical positions, from the right or left, offer highly divergent answers to pervasive educational issues. The more democracy, the more need for widespread and equal distribution of knowledge to the masses, since democracy requires a knowledgeable people. But, compulsory attendance at state-controlled schools doesn't fit well with the concepts of individual enterpreneurship and lack of governmental intervention in radical libertarian views of laissez-faire economics.

Radical critiques come from both the left- and right-wing extremes. They influence the general debate by providing clear polarities that allow liberals and conservatives to take more popular positions in the center. Radical ideas tend to have limited credibility in mainstream discussions, but liberals and conservatives draw from those ideas in making reform proposals.

Radical right-wing ideas about schooling come from different special interest groups. Some promote the teaching of fundamentalist religious dogma. Some seek to censor all teaching materials that deal with sex, socialism, athesim, or anything that they think is "anti-American." And some want to abolish public-supported schools in favor of elite schooling for a select group of students. The right wing has been articulate in the 1980s attack on schools. As Henry Giroux (1988b) characterizes the right wing:

> It has mounted a massive attack against feminism and against abortion rights. . . . it has launched an increasingly successful attack on "secular humanism" in the schools in order to attempt to promote either the teaching of religious fundamentalism or what it calls "character education". . . . [they] have become quite aggressive in pushing a program for schools to address and teach a particular set of moral values and virtues. (p. 42)

The radical left wing also has some disparate views of school. Some see education as the way for the masses to uncover the evils of capitalism and the corporate state. Some advocate free schools where everyone studies whatever he or she wants to study. And some propose education as the means for revolution, where all the institutions of society are subject to critique.

Conservative, liberal, and radical views of society and education provide different rationales for criticism of school and different proposals for reform. They are the general frameworks on which individual and group discontent with school practices can be placed. While we would like to include in this volume all possible viewpoints on each educational issue, that is obviously impossible. We have, instead, limited the presentation of perspectives to ones that can illustrate the issue in the current society; some draw from liberal-progressive ideas, some from conservative-traditional, and some from radical critiques. We have included some references to additional conservative, liberal, and radical literature, and we encourage the reader to explore those highly divergent views.

EDUCATIONAL REFORM OVER TIME

Reform in education is not a new phenomenon. Advocates of educational reform have existed for so long that it is impossible to identify the first one. Perhaps the first educational reformer, a member of a prehistoric group, rose up to protest that children in the group were not learning the basics the way he had. Or it could have been another member with a radical new plan to improve children's hunting and gathering skills. All we can tell is that dramatic changes occurred in civilization and schools over a long period of time. Presumably, reformers were involved in the shaping of those changes. Also, we can presume that there were many divergent views of the purposes and practices of education throughout prehistory, even though we have no written records to consult. There are probably some bashed skulls lying about—the results of arguments over education.

In our written records, there is considerable evidence of efforts to use education to alter society, and thus the recognition that divergent ideas about education can be very controversial. One of the two accusations leveled against Socrates in the indictment that brought him to trial, and to his death by taking hemlock, was "corruption of the young." Educational activities as a public critic of the Greek democracy and teacher of Alcibiades and Critias, considered enemies of the Greek democracy, made Socrates notorious. He may have paid the ultimate price for being an educational reformer in a political setting that was not ready for his reforms.

We know of Socrates through the writings of Plato, who also identified education as a central element in establishing and maintaining the good society. Lawrence Cremin (1965) considers Plato's *Republic:*

> . . . the most penetrating analysis of education and politics ever undertaken. Recall Plato's argument: In order to talk about the good life, we have to talk about the good society; and in order to talk about the good society, we have to talk about the kind of education that will bring that society into existence and sustain it. (p. 4)

Despite some ideas that were progressive for his time, Plato remains a prime examplar of the conservative view we now identify as "traditionalism" or "essentialism" in education. This view holds that there is essential or traditional knowledge which students must learn, that the teacher is the authority, that "wrong" ideas should be censored, and that the cultural heritage should be exalted. It is a very static view of knowledge and truth, rooted in the past.

Interpretations of Plato's ideas have been used to justify school practices that Plato might not have actually supported. We doubt that Plato would have liked joyless schools run by stern teachers who would not permit deviation from the lesson, and where rote memorization and recitation of useless information was the standard. We are not sure that Plato would have liked the excessive use of such measures as the SAT scores to determine who should be educated beyond a certain point; but we know that he did not have in mind that only the wealthy should have an elite education.

In *The Republic* Plato identifies two classes of citizens: ordinary ones who do the work of the society, and a military class from whom the rulers or guardians of the state will be drawn. Plato wanted different education for different classes, a form of tracking, in the ideal society he described in *The Republic*. The ordinary citizens (those of brass and iron) are what we think of as the working class; today, this would include merchants, industrialists, and professionals along with wage earners. And those in the existing slave class in Greece were not educated at all.

For Plato these classes of people are based on merit and ability, not on the chance of birth. Testing, in one form or another, would determine those fit for continuing education. He advocates a program of schooling starting at a very young age for those of the silver or gold (the military class), who will be trained to come to know truth with which they might develop into wise rulers. This education would be aimed at providing "right" ideas to help the young child begin to see the truth in his soul.

The program requires censorship to keep out "wrong" ideas, and includes early and continuing study of such subjects as music, literature, calculation, and physical education, with later (at age 20 to 30) study of science, and a higher education in dialectic forms of reasoning, where questioning and refutation are employed to determine truth. This schooling would be followed by about fifteen years of further education in the practical experience of administration of the state. This was to combine philosophic disposition with good practice to produce a philosopher-king, very much like a grand teacher for all of society.

On what we now consider the more liberal side, Plato was not a feminist, but he argued that the kind of education that develops men into good rulers also develops women. Thus, although men are considered by Plato to be more suitable than women for government and war, women should receive the same opportunity through education to attain those positions. This was not standard Greek practice at the time.

The Republic describes Plato's ideal for a state, but *The Laws,* written in his old age, conveys his view of the best possible state, since he had then recognized that the ideal was not possible. In *The Laws,* where Plato is much more practical, we find some surprisingly progressive educational ideas. He advocates free and natural play as an educative part of childhood, and indicates that some children will innovate with their games in ways that may influence them in later life to "desire a different sort of life," and "other institutions and laws" (*The Laws,* p. 798). That concept has potential for developing revolutionaries. He also proposes a carefully planned system of schools with specially prepared teachers who are paid a salary. At that time there were no such schools for students older than 10, and the professionalism suggested by Plato in his plan for teacher education and teacher salaries was opposite the Greek view.

JOHN DEWEY AND SCHOOL REFORM

In the long history of western thought since Plato, the schools have received extensive consideration by politicians, philosophers, writers, and others. Since this is not a treatise on the philosophy of education, we will not examine the many and diverse views expressed by such notables as Quintilian, St. Thomas Aquinas, Comenius, John Locke, Rousseau, Kant, Wordsworth, Pestalozzi, Herbart, Whitehead, Bertrand Russell, and characters in Doonesbury cartoons. References to some standard works which discuss competing philosophies of education are cited at the end of this chapter.

John Dewey, however, deserves some mention here as a contrast with Plato.

Dewey is credited with being the most influential philosopher on education in the twentieth century, and with being one of the founders of progressive education. It is Dewey who has earned the admiration or the hostility of contemporary battlers over the turf of schools.

Dewey shares with Plato an understanding of education as a broader concern than schooling, and a clear recognition of the interrelationship between the desired society and the nature of education. However, Dewey departs from Plato in his view of the purposes and practices of schooling. Dewey's book *Democracy and Education* (1916) challenges Plato's concept of a fixed ideal for school and for society; Dewey argues that society is dynamic, with change dominant. Dewey disputes Plato's notion that the social classes are separable according to some basic natural differences; he makes a case for individual rather than group differences. And Dewey places schools at the center of democratic development of society:

> The devotion of democracy to education is a familiar fact. . . . Since a democratic society repudiates the principle of external authority, it must find a substitute in voluntary disposition and interest; these can be created only by education. . . . Obviously, a society to which stratification into separate classes would be fatal, must see to it that intellectual opportunities are accessible to all on equable and easy terms. . . . Plato subordinated the individual to the social whole. . . . Progress in knowledge has made us aware of the superficiality of Plato's lumping of individuals and their original powers into a few sharply marked-off classes; it has taught us that original capacities are indefinitely numerous and variable. . . . Although his (Plato's) educational philosophy was revolutionary, it was none the less in bondage to static ideals. (1916, pp. 87–91)

Dewey, in a career spanning over fifty years, also challenged traditional educational ideas such as faculty psychology, mental discipline, and the separation of thought from action and knowing from doing. His writings and speeches provided the grounds for a host of educational innovations, including some he did not support. Although Dewey did argue that the child's individual social activities are the "true center" of the curriculum, rather than literature, science, or other subjects, he was opposed to giving unlimited freedom to students. He was also very concerned to find that some progressives had eliminated the traditional classical curriculum, but not replaced it with anything of substance. Still, Dewey is popularly associated with child-centeredness, and freedom from the traditional subject-oriented school.

Dewey also dissociated himself from what were considered the radical ideas of George Counts on reconstructionism in schools. Reconstructionism, a term Dewey had used in a more moderate sense, takes the view that schools should be used to change and improve society, not merely to reflect it (Counts, 1932; Brameld, 1956). This view would expect schools to educate youth to criticize the evils in society, and to develop social action to correct, or reconstruct, society. Reconstructionism developed some thoughtful advocates, and remains an intriguing reform movement that places schools even more in the center of social controversy (Stanley, 1981).

Examples from Plato and Dewey illustrate that wise thinkers can have thoughtful but divergent views on society and schools. They also provide rationales for a variety of criticisms and agendas for reform of schools. These two examples can be considered conservative and liberal views, with reconstructionism as one example of a radical critique. There are many other and more current examples of divergent views of pervasive educational issues, and there are innumerable implications of these views for school practice.

SCHOOL REFORM IN
EARLY TWENTIETH-CENTURY AMERICA

The United States has a long tradition of innovation in education, stemming from its pioneer role in providing popular education to large numbers of students at public expense. There are some major failures in this history, most notably in the lack of equal educational opportunities for blacks, native Americans, women, immigrants, and those of the lower classes. We have had, however, an expanding view of education as a major means for developing democracy and for offering some social mobility. We may not realize these ambitions, and the real intentions may be less altruistic (Katz, 1968). But the idealization of democratic reform through education is in the traditional American rhetoric.

In the early twentieth century, compulsory education laws became a primary reform agenda for schools, which were a part of a larger social reform movement. Urbanization and industrialization had created the need for different forms of school services. Large numbers of children from the working classes were now in schools in urban areas, and the traditional classical curriculum, teaching methods, and leisure-class approach to school were criticized by many.

In her striking analysis of the Progressive Education Association, Patricia Albjerg Graham identifies the extensive development of vocational and technical courses as the most dominant change in schooling before World War I. She also notes the broadening of the schools' activities to include medical exams, health instruction, free lunch programs, schools being kept open during vacation periods to assist in child care for working parents, and other community services. These reforms fit with the evolving sense of social progressivism. But, Graham contends, there were serious "discontinuities" in that school progressivism. These discontinuities include a prewar movement to expand the public schools to permit the children of the working class "full participation in American life," and a postwar progressive education centered mainly in the private schools, based on newer ideas in the experimental nature of "scientific" education, and appealing to the middle and upper classes (Graham, 1967).

The progressive education movement, from about 1920 to World War II, incorporated severe criticisms of traditional schooling ideas and practices. Schools where students were given corporal punishment, where rigid discipline existed, where rote memorization and drill were commonplace, where the classics were stressed without regard to student interests, and where failure rates were high received negative comments. The progressives offered a positive program of involving students in decisions about what was studied, in practical experiences and projects, in community activities, in the study of opposing opinions on controversial topics, in practicing democracy in the school, and in organizing the school as an embryonic society.

Opposition to progressive education was constant during this period, but public distrust of it took a long time to develop. Graham, summarizing the shift, states:

> Sometime between 1919 and 1955 the phrase "progressive education" shifted from a term of praise to one of opprobrium. To the American public of 1919, progressive education meant all that was good in education; thirty-five years later nearly all the ills in American education were blamed on it. (1967, p. 145)

The ascendancy of progressive education in the early part of the century paralleled social and political progressivism through the Depression and into World War II. The schools became more open to more students of all classes, and the curriculum moved from more esoteric studies to courses with current social application, such as drivers' education, home economics, business and vocational education, current events, health, sociology, sex education, and consumer math. There were sporadic and severe criticisms of progressive thought throughout that time, but a major reform movement from the right gained more public interest near the end of the Depression and again following the war. As Gurney Chambers notes:

> Soon after the market crash of 1929, the American people began to lose faith in the power of education to create the good life for all. . . . Teachers were rebuked for their complacency and inertia, and the schools, surprisingly enough, were blamed for the increasing crime and divorce rates and political corruption. The press charged the schools with trying to usurp the functions of the church, home, and policeman, while neglecting their true function of teaching reading, writing and arithmetic. . . . Thus, whether justly or not, education was charged with being largely responsible for the social and economic problems of the nation. (1948, in Hahn and Bidna, 1970, pp. 142–143)

RECENT CYCLES OF EDUCATIONAL REFORM

Attacks on the schools increased in intensity and frequency during the late 1940s and 1950s. The great school debates of this time involved many pervasive issues.

Church-state issues, including those of school prayer and the use of public funds for religious school busing and other school services, were significant. Racial issues, with the implications of the landmark Supreme Court decision in *Brown v. Board of Education of Topeka* (1954) on desegregation, were another focus of school controversy. Rapidly increasing tax burdens, to pay for new schools and teachers required by the baby boom, created many school critics. Rising expectations for education, exemplified by the thousands of "non-college prep" veterans who went to college on the GI Bill, were applied to the lower schools. Curricular issues, including disputes over the proper way to teach reading and the occasional story about test scores that showed students did not know enough history or math or science or English, filled the popular press. The McCarthy Period, another "Red Scare," produced rampant public fear of a creeping communistic influence in American life, and created suspicions that schools were likely places for "communal" and progressive thought. These and other factors led to renewed criticism of schools. For many, there was simply a lingering sense that the schools were not doing their job.

Two books illustrate the criticisms: Albert Lynd's *Quackery in the Public Schools* (1950, 1953) and Arthur Bestor's *Educational Wastelands* (1953) each attacked progressive education, and the "educationists" who advocated it, for turning schools away from traditional discipline and subject knowledge toward "felt needs" of children. As historian Clarence Karier notes in his discussion of the impact of Bestor's book, "the educationist who spoke out for 'progressive education,' and 'life adjustment education' appeared increasingly out of place in the postwar, cold war period" (Karier, in Bestor, 1985, p. 238).

Major foundations began to examine America's schools. The Ford Foundation stated that education had emerged as the focal point of its work. Grants were made to the Educational Testing Service to improve measures of student performance. The Carnegie Foundation asked James Bryant Conant, former president of Harvard and U.S. ambassador to West Germany, to conduct a series of studies of public education. There was much public criticism of academic failures of American schools. Then came the Soviet launch of Sputnik in 1957, ahead of the United States, and a new focus developed for educational reform. Sputnik was a highly visible catalyst for conservative critics who had been responding to what they considered excessive progressive reforms in schools during the pre–World War II period. They blamed the "permissive" atmosphere in schools for this deficiency in international space competition.

Acidic comments about progressive education came from Max Rafferty, the elected California state superintendent of schools during the 1960s:

> Despite what these spreaders of the gospel according to St. John Dewey have been drip-dripping into your ears and minds for 30 years and more, I say to you that the purpose of school is not to make pupils more popular or well-adjusted or universally approved. . . . Do those who run your schools believe that "life adjustment" should be the main goal of instruction? If they do, this is Progressive Education. Do they teach things like "social studies" and "social living" and "language arts" instead of history and geography and English? Do your school people tell you that report cards are old-fashioned? Do they teach reading predominantly through the "look-say" Egyptian-hieroglyphic method instead of through the phonics method? All these are the brand and trademark of Progressive Education. And Progressive Education, regardless of what your educational apologists are currently calling it, is bad education. (1968, pp. 5, 6)

Rafferty's views represent a strand of criticism that had arisen previously and remains in more recent attacks on the schools.

THE RECURRENCE OF EXCELLENCE

This post-Sputnik reform in the late 1950s was toward a reinstitution of rigor, discipline, traditional subject teaching, and standards. The theme, to be repeated again, was "excellence." In fact, there are some remarkable similarities in the language and rationales used in this reform movement and current efforts to return the schools to traditional work. International competition, advancing technology, and the needs of business are rationales found in the literature of both periods.

"Excellence," ill-defined and excessively used, is a main cue word that shows up in many reports and statements. John Gardner's prominent document for the Rockefeller Brothers Fund, *The Pursuit of Excellence: Education and the Future of America* (1958), is only one illustration. Another term common to both periods is "mediocrity," a threat suggested in the title of Mortimer Smith's book, *The Diminished Mind: A Study of Planned Mediocrity in Our Public Schools* (1955). The Conant Report, *The American High School Today* (1958), was a moderate book which proposed a standard secondary school curriculum, tracking by ability group, special courses for gifted students, improvements in English composition, better counseling, and other recommendations. It became a guide for many schools.

Dramatic improvements occurred in federal funds to support education. The National Defense Education Act (NDEA) was passed because of pleas that the schools were key to providing "national defense," and that Sputnik showed that the United States was vulnerable. Funds became available to improve teaching in science and math, foreign languages, social studies, and English. These curricular projects were primarily devoted to having university scholars in the subject fields determine better ways for conveying the subject matter, and many projects attempted to "teacher-proof" the material to avoid having classroom teachers teach it in a "wrong" way. Teacher education came in for its share of criticism, with blasts at the teachers' colleges, the progressive techniques advocated, and the quality of students going into teaching. All of this may sound hauntingly familiar to those who read current educational criticism.

Within the next decade after Sputnik an opposing liberal reform movement had developed as a response to the rote memorization and lockstep schooling that had increased school dropout and failure rates. As the public trend toward conservative educational ideas developed support and school practice turned back to standards and "rigor," criticism from the left began to emerge. A number of writers, including Paul Goodman, George Dennison, Edgar Z. Friedenberg, A. S. Neill, Nat Hentoff, John Holt, Herbert Kohl, and Jonathan Kozol, attacked the schools. Their targets were such things as sterility, bureaucracy, boredom, lack of creativity, rigidity, powerlessness of students and teachers, and inadequacy in educating disadvantaged youth. Holt (1964) stated:

> Most children in school fail. . . . They fail because they are afraid, bored, and confused. . . . They are bored because the things they are given and told to do in school

are so trivial, so dull, and make such limited and narrow demands on the wide spectrum of their intelligence, capabilities, and talents. . . . Schools should be a place where children learn what they want to know, instead of what we think they ought to know. (pp. xiii, xiv, 174)

This 1960s reform from the left rebelled against the schools' dehumanization and conservative authoritarianism. The liberal reforms included open education, nongraded schools, more student freedom, more electives, less reliance on standardized tests, abolition of dress codes and rigid rules, and more teacher-student equality. The Vietnam war and student demonstrations provided political issues that stimulated much of the late-1960s educational reform literature on the left.

As critics have shown (Bastian, et al., 1985; Giroux, 1988; Presseisen, 1985), the recent 1980s school reform movement has been dominated by thinking from mainstream conservatives. This conservative agenda seems to include more testing, more rigor in school, a return to basics, the imparting of more patriotic values, more homework for students, fewer electives, less student freedom, renewed emphasis on dress codes and socially acceptable behavior for students and teachers, stricter discipline, and merit pay for teachers.

In the 1980s, the agenda for change in schooling was similar to that of the post-Sputnik period almost thirty years before. The key term, "excellence," suggests the competitive nature of schooling and the demand for increased standards.

Discontented with falling scores on SAT and reading tests, and alarmed about stories showing drug abuse, vandalism, and chaos in the schools, the public's receptivity to reform increased. Nervousness about international competition, the resurgence of business and technology as dominant features of society, and questions about shifting morality and values provided a political setting where the schools could be blamed for inadequacies. Student protest had died and a negative reaction set in. Yuppies became the models for student style. There was an increasing perception of disarray in the American family, and a large-scale return to religion. And there was a recurrence of open confrontation with communism in various parts of the world. Schools could not only be blamed—and they were—they could also provide resolution to these strains in American life by becoming "excellent."

The focal document was an emotional report of the presidentially appointed National Commission on Excellence in Education, *A Nation at Risk* (1983), which claimed that there was a "rising tide of mediocrity" in the schools. The ensuing public debate produced a flurry of legislation to develop "excellence" and raise the quality of schools. Foundations and individual critics once again undertook the study of schools and produced volumes. These include the more liberal work of John Goodlad's *A Place Called School* (1983) and Theodore Sizer's *Horace's Compromise* (1984), as well as the moderate Ernest Boyer's *High School* for the Carnegie Foundation (1983), the conservative Mortimer Adler's *The Paideia Proposal* (1982), and generally conservative reports from the Twentieth Century Fund (1983), the College Entrance Examination Board (1983), the National Science Foundation (1983), and the Carnegie Foundation (1986).

The last decade of the twentieth century and the first of the twenty-first may be placid for schools, another period of recuperation from the last reforms, but a number of educational issues are sure to arise that will cause alarm and enflame passions. Some of these will be the core of the new school reforms.

The critique of schools, however, is not a futile waste of energy. Over the long haul schooling has improved and civilization has been served by the debates over education. More people get more education of a better quality across the world now than in previous generations. While there are lapses and declines, the debates force reconsideration of schooling ideas and permit increased sophistication about schools and society.

It is appropriate that schools are criticized; of all social institutions, the school should be the most ready for examination. Education rests upon critical assessment and reassessment. That does not mean that all criticism is justified, or even useful. Some of it is simplistic, mean-spirited, or wrongheadedly arrogant. But much of it is thoughtful and cogent. A skeptical orientation, where one rejects the idea of being a true believer, provides for the examination of evidence and its sources.

SOME OF THE SCHOOL QUESTIONS

Should schools be places of rigorous discipline and authority, where students learn what adults consider basic information and proper behavior? Or should schools be permissive places, where students are free to learn those things they recognize as valuable to their own self-development? Should schools be used to fit people into a capitalistic economy by training them to be "good workers" and making them docile? Or should schools be used to develop revolutionary ideas by exposing the oppressions of capitalism? Should schools emphasize nationalistic ideals or world citizenship? Should schools present a fundamental religion-based morality or secular values? Should schools separate students by social class background, by test scores, by race and gender, by religious preference, by teacher choice, or not at all? Should we rate schools by the level of student happiness, test scores, college admissions, or dropouts? Should everyone be required to learn basic skills, and only in English? Should we mandate that all students must study American history, science, and math? Should all students study useful trades and vocations? Should there be special classes for gifted children, or slow ones?

ON THE STUDY OF ISSUES: CRITICAL THINKING

School and educational issues are not resolved by the publication of extensive studies, or the passing of state laws requiring excellence or equality. Those pervasive issues remain because there are ideological and fundamental differences of view on what constitutes the good society and the good school, and there may be no permanent answer to education problems. There is always a need to improve, to reconsider, to develop. The difficulty is that the meaning of "improvement" differs according to which side one is on. The conflict between these differences provides the setting in which contemporary educational issues are debated.

This conflict is worthy of study for those interested in education. The proper process of education requires examination of opposing views, and willingness to subject previously held ideas to critical scrutiny. In this study it should be recognized that there are always more than two views possible and that there are underlying ideologies that bear consideration.

Critical thinking is advocated by virtually all educated people. Being against critical thinking is, for those with education, akin to being against ice cream or apple pie. There are some people who oppose critical thinking; they accept truth by divine revelation or dictatorial ideology. For them the truth is known, so why engage in questioning and skepticism?

Those who oppose critical thinking, however, are a small minority. If a large group of American citizens were asked, "Should students be taught how to do critical thinking?" the response would likely be overwhelming support. And, most school districts have documents, such as school policies or curriculum guides, containing a statement that critical thinking is to be taught in the school. Yet, if we asked those American citizens, and those teachers in schools where it is supposed to happen, "Is there much evidence that most people actually do critical thinking?" there might not be much agreement. Critical thinking is widely supported and typically expected in schools, but it is a fuzzy concept, shadowy and vague.

Differing presumptions about the results of critical thinking are part of the reason that there can be widespread agreement that it should be taught, but little agreement that people practice it. One misleading presumption is that critical thought is any reasoning which leads to conclusions that are already believed. This is simply rationalizing. Another defective presumption is that critical thinking should lead to conclusions already held by those in authority, such as parents, teachers, or political leaders. This may be popular thinking, but it is not necessarily critical. And a third improper presumption is that critical thinking must lead to negative views on everything. That is better defined as cynicism, and is not consistent with the ideas of progress and improvement which underlie much critical examination.

Part of the reason critical thinking is not practiced more is that it often challenges the status quo, and people learn when very young that it is not considered nice to raise certain questions. Many parents don't enjoy having children question their authority. Teachers do not always reward students for persistence in logic or inquiry that doesn't conform to the teachers' views. Bosses are not known for their patience with employees who seek explanations or better evidence of reasoning in the bosses' decisions. And, those who engage in critical thinking and collide with social norms may be subject to social ostracism or worse.

Part of the problem with education for critical thinking is that it is often defined in schools as a technical skill that is to be taught separately to students. Critical thinking, also known as "problem-solving" or "inquiry," is taught as a process made up of a series of steps that are expected to be used. This instruction is often conducted as though the steps had no relation to life situations or social issues. Students are expected to learn in sequence how to (1) define a problem, (2) state hypotheses and counterhypotheses, (3) find and evaluate evidence, and (4) draw conclusions. These techniques may be learned as separate steps, but students see little in them that helps in resolving human and social problems. Taught in isolation from existing social problems, the steps lead students to consider critical thinking as a cumbersome and difficult process that most people do not use and do not appreciate.

Developing critical thinking, a kind of thinking which expects deeper examination of issues, requires more than a list of steps or techniques. It is more complex than a simple skill, and it needs to be developed in the context of problems or issues. Mathematical problems, for some people, stimulate critical thinking. Moral and ethical problems stimulate it for some. Personal problems provide the reason for critical thought for some. Economic issues, personal or social, are the grounds for critical thinking for many. And political or social issues can be provocative for large numbers of people. We think that educational issues are suitable contexts for critical thinking about schools.

Of course, it is entirely possible to avoid critical thinking, and respond to issues with knee-jerk reactions or raw emotion. Immediate anger, crying, automatic rejection of different ideas, or the hurling of memorized slogans illustrate this response. Critical thinking, however, incorporates emotion, since values are at stake in any important issue, but it also requires thoughtful consideration of evidence, of opposing ideas, and of consequences. Values, like justice, equality, or democracy, undergird critical thinking. That is the reason that critical thinking includes the consideration of potential consequences of differing decisions. Values are used as criteria against which we can evaluate possible consequences.

Intuition can also be an appropriate avenue to understanding and a useful corollary to critical thinking. John Dewey in *How We Think* (1933) and Nel Noddings in her recent book *Awakening the Inner Eye: Intuition in Education* (1984) demonstrated that many intuitive insights have been the source of new and sound ideas in solving scientific, mathematical, personal, and social problems. Jerome Bruner identified intuitive thinking as among the most important of ways for scientists and mathematicians to solve problems. He notes that the "formalism of school learning has somehow devalued intuition," and that much work is needed to "develop the intuitive gifts of our students from the earliest grades onward" (Bruner, 1960, pp. 58–60). Bruner wisely counsels that intuitive, inductive, and analytic thinking are companions, one checking on the other, and that we need to encourage the improvement of each.

Critical thinking, as we understand and advocate it, involves what John Dewey described as the "active, persistent, and careful consideration of any belief or supposed form of knowledge in light of the grounds which support it and the further conclusions to which it tends'' (1933, p. 9). In addition to examination of the grounds, or evidence, which support beliefs, we think that critical thinking requires thoughtful consideration of views and evidence which differ. This consideration is more than merely acknowledging that different views exist, but requires ''putting yourself into the shoes of the other'' to fully understand the grounds for that difference. That is the basis for ''dialectic'' or ''dialogic'' reasoning. Dialectic reasoning allows the critique of views already held (a thesis) in light of divergent views (an antithesis), with the idea that a more refined view (a synthesis) can result. For that reason we include examples of divergent essays in this volume. There are, as noted, more than two sides to each issue, but examining two divergent ideas helps to focus the dialogue of critical thinking.

To summarize, critical thinking has several interrelated components: (1) It is wholistic, not a series of separated steps or atomistic skills, (2) it is most effectively done in the context of problems or issues, (3) it requires evaluation of available evidence, and the sources of that evidence, (4) it involves solid understanding of divergent evidence and viewpoints, (5) it can incorporate insights from intuition, and (6) it includes consideration of the potential consequences of decisions and actions.

SKEPTICISM AND CRITICAL THINKING

In the pursuit of critical thinking we propose the development of a skeptical perspective, a questioning orientation and suspended judgment. This does not mean that everything must be seen skeptically, but that skepticism might be the initial response in those social and personal issues that are important. Nonexperts need not be skeptical about the date on a calendar, the identification of strata in rock formations, or a mathematical formula. As Bertrand Russell noted in an essay on the value of scepticism, ''The scepticism that I advocate amounts only to this: (1) that when the experts are agreed, the opposite opinion cannot be held to be certain; (2) that when they are not agreed, no opinion can be regarded as certain by a non-expert; and (3) that when they all hold that no sufficient grounds for a positive opinion exist, the ordinary man would do well to suspend his judgment'' (1928, p. 10).

The issues discussed in this volume are ones about which there is no universal agreement among the experts. There are no ''certain'' opinions, although there are experts who are certain of their opinions. And suspending judgment is good advice. We agree with Russell that, under any circumstance, skepticism is an appropriate beginning, followed by critical examination of the issue.

REFERENCES

Adler, M. (1982). *The Paideia Proposal.* New York: Macmillan.
Apple, M., and Weis, L., eds. (1983). *Ideology and Practice in Schooling.* Philadelphia: Temple University Press.

Aronowitz, S., and Giroux, H. (1983). *Education Under Siege: The Conservative, Liberal, and Radical Debate over Schooling.* Granby, Mass.: Bergin & Garvey.

Baron, J. B., and Sternberg, R. J., eds. (1987). *Teaching Thinking Skills: Theory and Practice.* New York: Freeman.

Basseches, M. (1984). *Dialectical Thinking and Adult Development.* Norwood, N.J.: Ablex.

Bastian, A., et al. (1985). *Choosing Equality: The Case for Democratic Schooling.* San Francisco: New World Foundation.

Besag, F., and Nelson, J. (1984). *The Foundations of Education: Stasis and Change.* New York: Random House.

Bestor, A. (1953). *Educational Wastelands.* Urbana, Ill.: University of Illinois Press.

Boyer, E. (1983). *High School.* New York: Harper & Row.

Brameld, Theodore (1956). *Toward a Reconstructed Philosophy of Education.* New York: Holt.

Brown v. Board of Education of Topeka, Shawnee County, Kansas et al. (1954). 74 Sup. Ct. 686.

Chambers, G. (1948). "Educational Essentialism Thirty Years After." In *Secondary Education: Origins and Directions,* edited by R. Hahn and D. Bidna (1970). New York: Macmillan.

College Board (1983). *Academic Preparation for College.* New York: The College Board.

Conant, J. B. (1959). *The American High School Today.* New York: McGraw-Hill.

Counts, G. S. (1932). *Dare the Schools Build a New Social Order?* New York: John Day.

Cremin, L. (1961). *The Transformation of the School.* New York: Random House.

——— (1965). *The Genius of American Education.* New York: Random House.

de Rugierro, G. (1959). *The History of European Liberalism.* Translated by R. G. Collingwood. Boston: Beacon Press.

Dennison, G. (1969). *The Lives of Children.* New York: Random House.

Dewey, J. (1916). *Democracy and Education.* New York: Macmillan.

——— (1933). *How We Think.* Boston: Heath.

Freire, P. (1973). *Education for Critical Consciousness.* New York: Continuum.

Friedenberg, E. Z. (1965). *Coming of Age in America.* New York: Random House.

Gardner, J. (1958). *The Pursuit of Excellence: Education and the Future of America.* New York: Rockefeller Brothers Fund.

Giroux, H. (1988a). *Teachers as Intellectuals: Toward a Critical Pedagogy of Learning.* Granby, Mass.: Bergin & Garvey.

——— (1988b). *Schooling and the Struggle for Public Life.* Granby, Mass.: Bergin & Garvey.

Goodlad, J. I. (1983). *A Place Called School: Prospects for the Future.* New York: McGraw-Hill.

Goodman, P. (1964). *Compulsory Miseducation.* New York: Horizon Press.

Gouldner, A. (1970). *The Coming Crisis of Western Sociology.* New York: Basic Books.

Graham, P. A. (1967). *Progressive Education: From Arcady to Academe.* New York: Teachers College Press.

Gurr, T. (1970). *Why Men Rebel.* Princeton: Princeton University Press.

Hentoff, N. (1977). *Does Anybody Give a Damn?* New York: Knopf.

Holt, J. (1964). *How Children Fail.* New York: Pitman.

Hullfish, H., and Smith, P. G. (1961). *Reflective Thinking: The Method of Education.* New York: Dodd, Mead.

Johnson, C. (1966). *Revolutionary Change.* Boston: Little, Brown.

Kaestle, C. F. (1985). "Education Reform and the Swinging Pendulum." *Phi Delta Kappan,* **66,** 410–415.

Karier, C. (1967). *Man, Society and Education.* Chicago: Scott, Foresman.

―――― (1985). "Retrospective One." In A. Bestor, ed., *Educational Wastelands,* 2d ed. Urbana, Ill.: University of Illinois Press.

Katz, M. (1968). *The Irony of Early School Reform.* Cambridge, Mass.: Harvard University Press.

―――― (1971). *Class, Bureaucracy, and Schools: The Illusion of Educational Change in America.* New York: Praeger.

Kerlinger, F. (1984). *Liberalism and Conservatism.* Hillsdale, N.J.: Erlbaum.

Kohl, H. (1967). *36 Children.* New York: New American Library.

Kohlberg, L. (1981). *The Meaning and Measurement of Moral Development.* Worcester, Mass.: Clark University Press.

Kohlberg, L., and DeVries, R. (1987). *Child Psychology and Childhood Education.* New York: Longmans.

Kozol, J. (1967). *Death at an Early Age.* Boston: Houghton Mifflin.

Kristol, I. (1983). *Reflections of a Neoconservative.* New York: Basic Books.

Lloyd, T. (1988). *In Defense of Liberalism.* Oxford: Basil Blackwell.

Lynd, A. (1950). *Quackery in the Public Schools.* Boston: Little, Brown.

National Commission on Excellence in Education (1983). *A Nation at Risk.* Washington D.C.: U.S. Government Printing Office.

National Science Board. (1983). *Educating Americans for the 21st Century.* Washington, D.C.: National Science Foundation.

Neill, A. S. (1966). *Summerhill: A Radical Approach to Child Rearing.* New York: Hart.

Noddings, N. (1984a). *Awakening the Inner Eye: Intuition and Education.* New York: Teachers College Press.

―――― (1984b). *Caring: A Feminine Approach to Ethics and Moral Education.* Berkeley: University of California Press.

Parker, W. C. (1987). "Teaching Thinking: The Pervasive Approach." *Journal of Teacher Education,* **38,** 50–56.

Piaget, J. (1950). *The Psychology of Intelligence.* London: Routledge.

Plato. *The Works of Plato.* Edited by Irwin Erdman (1930). New York: Modern Library.

Presseisen, B. (1985). *Unlearned Lessons.* Philadelphia: Falmer.

Purpel, D. (1989). *The Moral and Spiritual Crisis in Education: A Curriculum for Justice and Compassion in Education.* Granby, Mass.: Bergin & Garvey.

Rafferty, M. (1968). *Max Rafferty on Education.* New York: Devin-Adair.

Rickover, H. (1959). *Education and Freedom.* New York: Dutton.

Rothenberg, R. (1984). *The Neoliberals.* New York: Simon & Schuster.

Russell, B. (1928). *Sceptical Essays.* London: George Allen & Unwin.

Sizer, T. (1984). *Horace's Compromise: The Dilemma of the American High School.* Boston: Houghton Mifflin.

Smelser, N. (1962). *Theory of Collective Behavior.* New York: Free Press.

Smith, M. (1954). *The Diminished Mind.* New York: Regnery.

Stanley, W. (1981). "Toward a Reconstruction of Social Education." *Theory and Research in Social Education,* **9,** 67–89.

Steinfels, P. (1979). *The Neoconservatives.* New York: Simon & Schuster.

Sternberg, R. J. (1985). *Beyond I.Q.: A Triarchic Theory of Human Intelligence.* New York: Cambridge University Press.

Tawney, R. H. (1964). *The Radical Tradition.* London: George Allen & Unwin.

Towns, E. L. (1974). *Have the Public Schools "Had It"?* New York: Nelson.

Twentieth Century Fund. (1983). *Making the Grade.* New York: Twentieth Century Fund.

Tyack, D. (1967). *Turning Points in American Educational History.* Waltham, Mass.: Blaisdell.

Ulich, R. (1954). *Three Thousand Years of Educational Wisdom.* 2d ed. Cambridge, Mass.: Harvard University Press.

Useem, M. (1975). *Protest Movements in America.* Indianapolis: Bobbs-Merrill.

Watt, J. (1985). *The Courage of a Conservative.* New York: Simon & Schuster.

Welter, R. (1962). *Popular Education and Democratic Thought in America.* New York: Columbia University Press.

PART ONE

WHAT INTERESTS SHOULD SCHOOLS SERVE?

This section presents opposing viewpoints on the general theme of liberty versus equality.

You may think it strange to see these two values cast in competition with each other. After all, aren't they both basic American values? Liberty and equality were clarion calls of the American Revolution. The colonists thought they were not being treated equally to the people in England because they had greater restraints on their liberty. Thus, liberty and equality are the values for which our nation was founded. The U.S. Constitution says that our government was formed to "promote the general Welfare, and secure the blessings of Liberty." Ask almost any American whether he or she believes in liberty and you will get a positive answer. Even children like to remind each other that "it's a free country, ain't it?" Ask the same people whether they believe in equality, and you will get the same "of course" kind of answer. Better yet, ask yourself these questions.

The difficulty is that liberty and equality lie along the same continuum. At one end of the continuum is pure liberty, and at the other pure equality. Very few people wish to go all the way out on either of these limbs. They try to have it both ways by dancing back and forth from the center of the line.

The people whose steps take them more often toward the liberty (or right) end of the continuum are called "Republicans" or "conservatives" or "libertarians," in the order of their distance from the center, with libertarians being the most distant. Sometimes the people in these categories get the generic label of "right-winger." The people who incline more often to the equality (or left) side of the continuum are "Democrats" or "liberals" or "egalitarians," with the egalitarians being the farthest out. The generic label for these groups is "left-winger."

Presidential elections are reminders of how skittish politicians can be about these terms, since most people pride themselves on their moderation and don't want to seem too far out in either direction. And the labels really are misleading, since most of us are an amalgam of conflicting urges: sometimes right-leaning, sometimes left, and with a pendulumlike behavior depending on the particular issue or the context, or just the mood we're in at the moment. That explains why we can have such otherwise oxymoronic terms as "liberal Republican" and "conservative Democrat."

The reason why right- and left-wingers get into such bitter wrangles is that each wing believes that what it values is imperiled by the efforts of the other side to promote its values. Right-wingers see liberty weakened with each increase in equality among Americans. That is because equality—even equality of opportunity—is produced by government actions that reduce our individual freedom and may hinder us in rising above the herd. Left-wingers, on the other hand, see equality—including equality of opportunity—diminished when there is so much individual freedom that some people can rise up to exploit and oppress other people.

Education is a good place to observe the liberty-equality battle. Education involves us all and has momentous consequences for our lives. Its pervasive influence commands the attention of both wings of the political spectrum. There is so much at stake if education is made more equal for students of different backgrounds or if it is left more to the varying fortunes of students' families. Because the stakes are so high, both the left and the right try to steer the government's education policies in their direction.

THE "LIBERTY" POSITION

In general, the right subscribes to the notion of the less government, the better. Parents should be free to find or develop the kind of education they want for their children. Parents can do this in cooperation with others who share their views, and most often they do so by living in communities with people who are like themselves. The government's role is to *allow* this to happen, to guarantee this freedom.

This position of the right in the matter of education is echoed in its attitude toward all the other areas of social policy. It fuels the centuries-old furor about the extent to which government should interfere in people's lives to promote the welfare of the less fortunate. Those on the right argue that government's attempts to help the disadvantaged do more harm than good to the very people who are supposed to benefit. The handouts these people receive, be they in the form of educational benefits or any other kind, sap initiative. As Irving Kristol puts it, "dependency tends to corrupt and absolute dependency corrupts absolutely" (Kristol, 1978, p. 242). Ira Glasser, himself a liberal and the executive director of the American Civil Liberties Union, examined the process by which well-intentioned government officials end up imprisoning the people they had set out to help, and concluded: "Because their motives were benevolent, their ends good, and their purpose caring, *they assumed the posture of parents* toward the recipients of their largesse. . . . As a result, they infantilized those they intended to help, and denied them their rights" (Glasser, 1978, p. 107). Charles Murray argues that welfare benefits and the way they are apportioned cause lower-class women to stay single but still have children, and this is the primary cause of family disintegration among America's poor (Murray, 1984). Lawrence Mead says that "no real progress in welfare is imaginable until government obligates needy adults to assume greater responsibility for their condition" (Mead, 1988, p. 52).

Moreover, the handouts the government provides do not materialize from thin air. The government pries them from the pockets of hardworking, productive people, and that discourages these people in their industriousness. "The egalitarian seeks a collective equality, not of opportunity, but of *results*. He wishes to wrest the rewards away from those who have earned them and give them to those who have not" (Simon, 1978, p. 200). It should be noted that one of the rewards which the right believe people in our society earn is the wherewithal to give their children a good education. If the children cannot benefit from their parents' effort, or can benefit no more than other people's children, a powerful work incentive has been taken from the parents.

Those on the right are therefore telling us of the signal advantage to inequality: that it makes us all work harder and realize ourselves more fully. When we do so, we not only help ourselves; we automatically advance the whole of society. This is the "invisible hand" described by Adam Smith, the eighteenth-century Scottish economist.

> As every individual, therefore, endeavours as much as he can both to employ his capital in the support of domestic industry, and so to direct that industry that its produce may be of the greatest value; every individual necessarily labours to render the annual revenue of the society as great as he can. . . . he intends only his own gain, and he is in this, as in many other cases, led by an invisible hand to promote an end which was no part of his intention. (Smith, 1976, p. 477)

Thus, each of us by his or her own labors helps those less fortunate simply by the sum we add to the *national* welfare. The ones who help the most are the rich, because they have money to invest in job-creating industries. George Gilder goes so far as to say that this is *the* function of the rich: "fostering opportunities for the classes below them in the continuing drama of the creation of wealth and progress" (Gilder, 1981, p. 82). Indeed, Gilder asserts that in order for the poor to get richer the rich must first get richer so they will have more to invest in opportunities for the poor (Gilder, 1981, p. 86).

These several aspects of the "liberty" position have been captured in a single paragraph written in 1835 by Alexis de Tocqueville, the French statesman and author famous for his insightful analyses of American society:

> Any permanent, regular, administrative system whose aim will be to provide for the needs of the poor will breed more miseries than it can cure, will deprave the population that it wants to help and comfort, will in time reduce the rich to being no

more than the tenant-farmers of the poor, will dry up the sources of savings, will stop the accumulation of capital, will retard the development of trade, will benumb human industry and activity, and will culminate in bringing about a violent revolution in the State, when the number of those who receive alms will have become as large as those who give it, and the indigent, no longer being able to take from the impoverished rich the means of providing for his needs, will find it easier to plunder them of all their property at one stroke than to ask for their help. (de Tocqueville, 1968, p. 25)

THE "EQUALITY" POSITION

Those on the left do not want a hands-off government content merely to guarantee the freedom of the powerful. They demand a government that will guarantee that children everywhere have equally good schooling regardless of their parents' circumstances. This means taking power away from parents and giving it to the government, which is to act as a benevolent parent to all our children (Keniston and The Carnegie Council on Children, 1977, p. 204).

The purpose of government, as far as those on the left are concerned, was expressed eloquently by Abraham Lincoln in his first annual message to the Congress: "to lift artificial weights from all shoulders; to clear the paths of laudable pursuit; to afford all an unfettered start, and a fair chance in the race of life" (quoted in Grant Commission, 1988, p. 118).

This, of course, is a classic exhortation to equality of *opportunity*. As such, it invokes the approval of those on the right as well. However, those on the right disagree with those on the left about the extent to which equality of opportunity is synonymous with equality of *condition*. To those on the left, being poor means the same thing as having little opportunity. It means poor prenatal and neonatal care, poor early childhood development, poor homes, poor schools, and ultimately poor jobs or no jobs. Conversely, "the children of the rich [tend] to grow up rich and powerful far more often than mere talent or energy or morality could have guaranteed. . . . power, privilege and prosperity [are] transmitted not only by the direct inheritance of wealth but also by the subtler route of acquired manners, learned skills, and influential friends" (Keniston and The Carnegie Council on Children, 1977, p. 40). "If we Americans wish children to reap the equality of opportunity that is so honored a goal of our society, we must address an issue that has, ironically, been obscured by our focus on equality of opportunity; we must attempt to create greater equality of social condition directly, not indirectly through children" (deLone, 1979, p. 25). In short, the distinction between opportunity and condition is not nearly as clear to those on the left as it is to those on the right.

Furthermore, the left see governmental attempts to give the poor more opportunity by equalizing their condition to that of better-off people as being much too feeble. Ever since modern welfare reforms were begun in the sixteenth century, the purpose has been to keep the poor miserable enough that they would remain dependent on the niggardliness of employers to improve their condition beyond a subsistence level. "Efforts to shape relief arrangements so they would not intrude on market relations virtually define the history of social welfare" (Block et al., 1987, p. 12). Equal opportunity is not provided, only continuing vulnerability to exploitation. That governmental relief is offered at all is to keep the poor from rioting, according to analysts on the left. Welfare is "a mechanism of social control, designed to pacify the poor and [serve] the interests of the business elite" (Block et al., 1987, p. 168).

How well the American welfare system has succeeded is now being seriously questioned in state legislatures and the Congress (where a major welfare reform bill was passed in the fall of 1988), as well as in reports from research groups of both the left and the right. The Ford Foundation has developed a series of booklets as part of its Project on Social Welfare and the American Future. The impetus to this project was articulated in a statement by Mitchell Sviridoff, vice president of the Ford Foundation:

> There is a segment of the nation's poor, small and sometimes invisible, that does not seem to be touched by . . . any sort of traditional outreach. For all our best efforts, this sector of the population is just about where we found them twenty years ago. . . . Their isolation and concentration have only exacerbated the frustration and hopelessness of their life and made their condition the most dangerous and intractable problem facing the cities in which they live. Numerically this group is relatively small, but it is extraordinarily destructive, and its behavior reflects intense anger, with consequences on a scale that mocks its size. (Quoted in Paterson, 1986, p. 216)

It has to be noted that this group is intergenerational, meaning that the plight of the parents has been visited upon their children, with the schools having been unable to prevent this. William Julius Wilson has documented the causes of this situation in enormous detail and thereby made a strong case for increased government action (Wilson, 1987).

Those on the left are not convinced that redistributing the wealth in America in such a way as to improve the living and educational conditions of the disadvantaged will backfire. They see the situation described above as such social dynamite that more, not less, redistribution is imperative to defuse it. Naturally, they would like to see the redistribution schemes administered more wisely than in the past so that the intended beneficiaries do not suffer unintended consequences. The left also believe that equalizing the educational *conditions* of children from different social classes is a good public investment. "Our primary concern should be with the acute failure to provide a vast number of low-income and minority students with decent schools and skills" (Bastian et al., 1985, p. 117).

Finally, the left are not persuaded that the rich always invest their money in ways that benefit the rest of society. In recent years especially, tremendous wealth has been invested in stock speculation and corporate takeovers that have benefited rich insiders at the expense of everyone else (Bruck, 1988). How rich the insiders got is demonstrated by the fact that one brokerage house, Drexel Burnham Lambert, could afford to pay a $650 million fine for its confessed felonies.

Perhaps the most significant difference between those on the right and the left is in the matter of *psychological* needs. Karl Marx had always thought that socialism could not come about until there was a technology of abundance to take care of our *material* needs. Such a technology was "an absolutely necessary practical precondition [of socialism], for without it one can only generalize *want*, and with such pressing needs, the struggle for necessities would begin again and all the old crap would come back again" (quoted in Harrington, 1973, p. 33). The United States now has a technology of abundance capable of satisfying everyone's basic material needs. The difficulty is that some people have a psychological need for more material goods than their neighbors. This is often referred to as "conspicuous consumption," the practice of acquiring and flaunting material possessions. This psychological dynamic can be observed even in the kinds of schools that parents "purchase" for their children, and it is resistant to equalization efforts (Thurow, 1980, p. 198).

Let us now get a preliminary sense of how the theme of liberty versus equality is played out in the chapters of this section.

FAMILY CHOICE/VOUCHERS

Chapter 2 presents arguments for and against allowing parents to pick the school their child(ren) will attend. The traditional American pattern has been for children to attend the school in their neighborhood. Where you live determines where you will be educated.

Giving parents choices beyond the traditional nonoption approach certainly enhances their liberty. The choices can be made possible in a variety of ways. Parents could have a choice among all the schools—public, private, and parochial—in a large geographic area, perhaps the size of a county. Or the choice could be limited to public schools only. The choice could be limited still further to the public schools within an existing school district. The choice could even be restricted to mini-schools within the same building, what are sometimes known as "schools-within-schools." The more limited the choice, the less liberty there is, but limited-choice plans have the advantage of being more administratively manageable.

The administration of President Reagan gave a lot of rhetorical support to the idea of choice in education, but did nothing significant to bring this about. President-elect Bush, in the days before his inauguration, came out strongly in support of choice. He asserted that "choice has worked," and that he intended "to provide every feasible assistance to the states and districts interested in further experimentation with choice plans" (Weinraub, 1988, p. B28). After becoming president, Bush asked Congress to appropriate $100 million for magnet schools that will increase parental choice of schools (Cohen, 1989, p. 23). In 1986, the National Governors Association went on record in favor of choice within the public school sector (NGA, 1986, p. 13). By the end of 1988 there were twenty-three states that either had choice plans or were considering them (Esposito, 1988, p. vi). The state that has gone the furthest is Minnesota, which by the 1990–91 school year will allow interdistrict choice of schools for all students (Eagleton, 1988, p. 16).

Cities too can create choice plans. The city of Chicago intends to have a public school choice plan in operation by 1991 (Snider, 1988, p. 6). Smaller cities have had choice plans for some time now, and these provide for a choice among "magnet" or theme schools, where students can focus on their particular interests in schools that are centered on those interests. Even one of the community school districts within New York City—District 4, in the area commonly known as "Spanish Harlem"—has had a magnet school plan, with fifty different schools in twenty school buildings. These included a bilingual school, a music academy, an environmental science school, and a communication arts school (Esposito, 1988, p. 75).

All of this should suggest to you that "choice" is an idea that has taken firm root in education and is likely to sprout lots of shoots over the next several years. This can be attributed to the way in which choice plans invoke the value of liberty. Their relationship to the value of equality is not so clear-cut, however. Choice plans can increase equality, but they can also decrease it.

Equality is increased when people who previously had no choice are given some say about the school where their children are to be educated. Choice plans thereby make these people more equal to people who can afford to send their children to private or parochial schools, or who can afford to live in communities that have good public schools.

Equality is decreased if the particular choice plan gives the same amount of benefit to both the rich and the poor, thereby augmenting the advantage which the rich already have. For example, if both rich and poor families are guaranteed a modest amount of government financial support to seek out schools to their liking, the rich can add this amount to that which they are already spending on good private schools and get even better ones. The poor might only be able to afford the kind of schools they are getting under the present no-choice system. Voucher proposals like that of the Friedmans (1980), which would give the same amount to all families regardless of wealth, threaten to have this *disequalizing* effect. So, too, do tuition tax credit plans which grant all families the same tax credit for tuition they pay for their children's schooling. Only parents who can afford to pay tuition in the first place are eligible for the tax credit. Even more disequalizing would be a plan that allows parents a tax credit in the amount they actually pay for tuition, since the wealthiest people tend to send their children to the schools that charge the highest tuitions.

Choice plans can also reduce equality if schools are allowed to refuse certain kinds of pupils. The "choice" in this situation is only that of trying to get into a desired school, and could result in finally having no choice left but the kind of school one had been attending previously. A variation on this possibility is the case where a student gets into the desired school only to be segregated into a *program* that is itself like the old school had been. Some magnet schools segregate pupils according to ability, and the low-ability youngsters get less attractive programs (Moran, 1987).

Christopher Jencks and his colleagues at Harvard once designed a choice system that had safeguards against the above kinds of inequalities (Jencks, 1970). For instance, poor families would get larger amounts of money than rich ones; schools could not demand more in tuition than the amount of money a family got from the government; schools would be limited in their latitude to refuse admission to applicants.

Ironically, the Jencks kind of system provokes claims of another kind of inequality. If the poor are guaranteed as much choice as the rich, they have been equalized up to the level of the rich. That means that the rich have lost in terms of *relative* equality. Their hard-earned wealth no longer entitles them to purchase greater liberty on behalf of their children than the poor can enjoy. By being made more equal to the poor, the rich are made less equal than their previous status.

PRIVATE SCHOOLS/PUBLIC SCHOOLS

Private schools (including parochial schools) have existed on the American mainland for longer than public schools. Indeed, private schools were *the* school system during the early years of the republic. They still serve a large portion of the elementary and secondary students in the United States, approximately 5 million students (Levine and Havighurst, 1989, p. 476).

Private schools serve as alternatives to a public school system that, until recently, has not had much element of choice built into it (as the previous section discusses). They therefore offer educational liberty that Americans would not otherwise have. However, since this liberty is available only to those who can afford to pay for it, private schools are institutions that foster inequality. Albeit, since the vast preponderance of private school enrollment is in parochial schools, roughly 85 percent, it can be argued that private schools serve another American value: religious freedom.

Americans are willing to have private schools, and many would like to see them receive public subsidies. A 1986 Gallup poll revealed that 43 percent of those questioned wished to see some tax dollars diverted to private schools (Gallup, 1986, p. 57). This is a much higher percentage of the population than that which actually patronizes private schools.

One reason for the significant degree of public support for private schools is the perception that private schools take a heavy burden off the public schools. Private school advocates have historically painted a grim picture of what would happen if suddenly all the private schools shut down. As Richard Nixon said when he was President, "If the nonpublic schools were ever permitted to go under in the major cities in America, many public schools might very well go under with them, because they simply couldn't undertake the burden" (quoted in Reischauer and Hartman, 1973, pp. 113–114). A standard retort to this traditional argument has been to claim that there would be greater public support for the public schools if people could not avoid using the public school system.

The increased support would include that from rich and powerful families who are not now dependent on the public schools.

In 1981, the researchers James Coleman, Thomas Hoffer, and Sally Kilgore aroused a storm of controversy by reporting that private (including parochial) high schools were more effective than public high schools. The gist of the report was that private high schools, when working with the same kinds of students as those in the public high schools, get better results in terms of student academic achievement. The main reasons cited for this greater effectiveness were the greater amount of homework and attendance in private high schools, as well as a more disciplined student body, an orderly environment and a cohesive school climate (Coleman et al., 1981).

The critics of this report were quick to point out that the students in private and public high schools are really not comparable. A major difference is that the parents of private school students support their education to the extent of paying tuition, whereas public school parents do not. This parental outlay of cash could well reflect a greater parental solicitude and encouragement toward private school students. The critics also found that the private and public school pupils in the Coleman study were already different in academic ability at the time they entered high school (Goldberger and Cain, 1982).

What is most noteworthy about this debate is that Coleman never contended that what private schools did could only be done by schools that were private. In fact, even before the critical responses appeared in print, Coleman himself wrote that the elements for successful education are: "a pluralistic conception of education, based on communities defined by interests, values, and educational preferences rather than residence; a commitment of parent and student that can provide the schools a lever for extracting from students their best efforts; and the educational choice for all that is now available only to those with money" (Coleman, 1981, p. 164). Coleman was making a case not for private schools as opposed to public schools but for conditions conducive to good education in both sets of schools. It happens that these conditions are more prevalent in private than in public schools.

Coleman's conclusion about the importance of school climate confirmed the findings of British researchers in an elaborate study of twelve London secondary schools. The British researchers found that student achievement was greater in those schools which had a climate, or ethos, characterized by such features as orderliness, high staff expectations of students, active engagement of the students in learning tasks, and staff cooperation in decision making (Rutter et al., 1979). This constellation of features is now commonly believed to characterize effective schools generally, be they private or public.

Further support for the variable of school climate is to be found in a recent report from the Brookings Institution. The researchers found that schools in which students do well academically tend to be run more democratically and collegially than other schools, even when there is no difference in the backgrounds of the pupils. "[S]chool organization emerges as the factor with the second largest impact on total test-score gains, trailing only . . . student aptitude. In importance it leads parental influence by a little, and school resources and peer pressure by a lot" (Chubb, 1988, p. 36).

It has been suggested repeatedly, and it is obvious, that these desirable features are easier to produce in small, independent schools than in large schools that are part of a big bureaucratic system. Public schools tend to be of the second kind. However, there are now attempts to decentralize them and give them more independence, which should blur the difference between them and private schools. In the meantime, the question remains as to whether parents who can afford to do so should be allowed to send their children to good private schools when other people's children are stuck in poor public schools. Should one group be allowed to exercise liberty when another group is not equally able to do so?

SCHOOL FINANCE EQUITY

The longstanding practice in America has been for the public schools to get their financial support from the communities in which they are located. The schools in Chicago are supported by the people of Chicago; the schools in suburban Winnetka, Illinois, by the people in Winnetka. And the most common means the local residents have used to pay for their public schools is a tax on their property (Goertz et al., 1982, pp. 9, 44).

Over time this system of school finance has led to two kinds of disparities. The first is that people in poor communities who have low incomes (property tax is paid out of income) bear a heavier tax burden than people in rich communities. A larger proportion of their income is spent on their property tax than is true for wealthier people. Since poor people don't have much income to begin with, this hits them especially hard. The second disparity is that even when poor people make the extra effort to support their schools, they come up with less money per pupil than people in wealthier communities. The amount spent on each public school child in a wealthy community can be two or three times the amount spent per pupil in a poor community.

States have reduced these spending gaps by giving more aid to poor communities than to richer ones. For some poor communities, the state actually covers 75 percent or more of the school budget, since the local residents cannot afford to pay for more than a small portion. Even with all this state assistance, poor communities still spend less on their students than richer communities elsewhere in the state (Lefelt, 1988).

There are two further complications to this picture: educational overburden and municipal overburden. Educational overburden exists when a school has an unusually high number of students who require special services. These are students who are handicapped or disadvantaged in some way. City schools typically have educational overburden and suburban schools typically do not. Municipal overburden occurs when there are a lot of public services the taxpayers have to support in addition to the schools. These can be police and fire departments, welfare offices, housing authorities (Jordan and McKeown, 1980,

p. 81; Levine and Havighurst, 1989, p. 302). Cities are much more likely to have municipal overburden than are suburbs. What all this amounts to is the fact that cities in America, especially the large cities, have high educational costs but not good revenue bases. And even when states try to help, the children in poor communities get a less expensive education than the children in rich communities.

The observable consequences of this situation in the cities are large class sizes, run-down buildings, beat-up and outdated textbooks, inexperienced and emergency-certificated teachers, and inadequate supplies and space all across the board. As scandalous as these conditions may sound to you on first reading about them, they beg a very basic question: How bad must things be before there is a legal obligation for the government to do something? How large a class size is too large? How beat-up a textbook is too beat-up? How inexperienced and unqualified is it permissible for teachers to be? When does inadequate become unacceptable? To put these questions another way, how identical must the schools of poor students be to those of rich students?

These questions have been brought before state and federal courts in a rash of litigation over the past two decades. The answers have been wide-ranging. Generally, the courts decline to deal with the questions in terms of specific school components. Judges do not feel competent to rule on such specifics as class size, textbook quality, and teacher qualifications. Moreover, the educational experts who appear before the courts contradict each other, and this leaves the judges even less inclined to get into these thickets. When they do, as Judge Skelly Wright did in the *Hobson v. Hansen* case, they have to withstand a barrage of criticism accusing them of going beyond their ability to comprehend the issues (Spring, 1988, pp. 161–166). Instead, the courts construe the issue in the simplest possible terms: dollars. That is, how equal is the amount of money spent per pupil in one school district to the amount spent in another district? Is the difference too large to be legally permissible?

The California Supreme Court ruled that the amount spent on a student could *not* be based on the wealth of the student's family or the community in which the student lived. This meant that there had to be statewide equalization in California (*Serrano v. Priest*, 1971). It did not mean that the same amount had to be spent on every pupil, but only that the tax base from which education was funded had to be the same for all school districts. A district had some say about how much it wanted to draw on this base in the amount it was willing to tax itself. The New Jersey Supreme Court ruled that there did not have to be complete tax base equalization, but rather a large reduction in the amount of the inequality (*Robinson v. Cahill*, 1973). The Georgia Supreme Court decided that the disparities in Georgia were not in violation of that state's constitution, so nothing had to be changed (*Thomas v. Stewart*, 1981).

A case was brought before the United States Supreme Court on the basis of the U.S. Constitution. The Supreme Court ruled that the spending inequalities in the state of Texas did not violate the "equal protection" guarantee of the Fourteenth Amendment to the Constitution. This ruling obviously implied that such inequalities are constitutionally tolerable in other states as well. However, this did not mean that the justices approved of these inequalities, only that they could find no constitutional justification for acting against them. Justice Potter Stewart wrote in his concurring opinion that the inequalities were "chaotic and unjust," but not illegal (*San Antonio Independent School District v. Rodriguez,* 1973). Since there was no U.S. Supreme Court ruling against the inequalities, each state, through its judicial and legislative branches, will continue to decide how much inequality it will permit. A Texas court of appeals has considered the kind of evidence the U.S. Supreme Court ruled on in 1973, and decided that the Texas inequalities should be allowed to continue because education is not a "fundamental right" and the inequalities are "rationally related to effectuating local control of education" (Mathis, 1989).

Even if a state decides that it will not tolerate differences in the taxable wealth available per pupil, it still has to decide whether it will allow the taxpayers in different communities to tax themselves so differently that one community raises a lot of money for its schools and another raises very little. In other words, states still have to decide how equal they want the *spending* to be. The state of Hawaii is one single school district so it does not have this problem. A problem it does have in common with other states, however, is deciding how much additional money should be spent on students in each special category. For example, how much extra is needed for the education of a blind student, or a mentally retarded student, or a socially maladjusted student?

It is hoped that the foregoing overview of school finance issues has given you a good enough sense of them to see how the values of liberty and equality come into play. If complete liberty were to exist for each school district, the rich districts could raise large amounts of money and have lavish education programs. Poor districts might have the theoretical liberty to do this, but they would not have the practical liberty because they simply cannot raise much money from their limited resources.

> The shortage of funds in some districts actually minimizes local discretion in programming and in the ability to compete for the services of good teachers. School boards in poor districts cannot opt to institute special services when their budgets do not include adequate funds even for essentials. In this sense local control is illusory. It is control for the wealthy, not for the poor. (*Robinson v. State of New Jersey,* 1972, p. 64)

A state can increase the liberty of a poor school district by equalizing its resources up to the level of richer districts. The more it does of this, the more it will cost the state. That means the state will have to collect tax money in rich communities and give it to poor communities. This brings equality to the poor at the expense of the rich. There is no other way. The rich can then claim correctly that the state has intruded on their liberty by confiscating their wealth, denying them the freedom to spend it as they see fit.

The major public policy question in school finance is: How much dollar liberty should be reserved for the rich and how much dollar equality conferred on the poor?

INTEGRATION: COMPULSORY/VOLUNTARY

One of the truly epochal events in American judicial history was the 1954 decision of the U.S. Supreme Court in the case of *Brown v. Board of Education of Topeka*. That decision began the long, turbulent, and still unfinished dismantling of racial segregation in America. It said that government could no longer require that the education of blacks take place in schools separate from those of whites. Richard Kluger, in his definitive history of the *Brown* decision, expressed its significance thus:

> At a moment when the country had just begun to sense the magnitude of its global ideological conquest with Communist authoritarianism and was quick to measure its own worth in megaton power, the opinion of the Court said that the United States still stood for something more than material abundance, still moved to an inner spirit, however deeply it had been submerged by fear and envy and mindless hate. (1976, p. 710)

Most of you who are now reading this are likely to have been born after 1954 and to have come of age after government segregation ceased to be taken for granted as part of the American way of life. It may therefore be difficult for you to understand how the land of the free could ever have been officially racist. It may help to trace the judicial history of desegregation since 1954.

How determined people were to maintain a segregated society can be seen in the fact that there was not just one *Brown* decision; rather, there was also what has come to be known as "*Brown II*." This decision was issued a year after the first one to direct local governments to eliminate their segregated schools "with all deliberate speed" (*Brown v. Board of Education*, 1955). There had been no speed after the first *Brown* decision, and the Court's vague exhortation hardly sped things up at all. The vast majority of black students in the south continued to attend all-black schools.

For thirteen years after *Brown II*, southern school districts found ways to continue segregation while appearing to be in compliance with the Court's directive. The most common way was to have "schools of choice," whereby black and white students were free to go to whatever school they wanted. Predictably, the black students stayed in their black schools and the white students in their white schools. So in 1968 the Supreme Court declared that the time for "all deliberate speed" had run out (*Green v. County School Board of New Kent County*, 1968). Three years later the Court began allowing lower federal courts to impose remedies to rid the south of segregation, and the most controversial remedy was forced busing (*Swann v. Charlotte-Mecklenburg Board of Education*, 1971).

After that the Court turned its attention to northern school districts. It found that even though these systems had not been segregated explicitly by law, they had been so through the deliberate actions of local officials (*Keyes v. School District No. 1, Denver, Colorado*, 1973).

The Supreme Court decision most directly related to the chapter you will be reading was issued in 1974. This decision said, in effect, that the suburbs of Detroit did not have to participate in a desegregation plan with the city of Detroit since it could not be shown that the racial segregation practiced within the Detroit city limits caused segregation throughout the whole metropolitan area. Detroit would have to desegregate its schools without the suburbs being forced to help (*Milliken v. Bradley*, 1974).

When Detroit and other northern cities tried to desegregate their schools, this provoked "white flight" to the suburbs, leaving the prospect of desegregating a system that had become mostly black. (White flight was inhibited in the south by the fact that many southern school districts are countywide, and include both a city and its suburbs.)

In several cases in the north, the lower federal courts have found that an entire metropolitan region had, in fact, been segregated deliberately by state housing policies. The first such case was in the Wilmington, Delaware, area (*Evans v. Buchanan*, 1976). In these cases the courts ordered desegregation plans involving both the cities and their suburbs.

One of the most bitter and protracted cases of court-ordered school desegregation took place in the cradle of American liberty, Boston. It pitted the Irish working class, who were intent on preserving their ethnic enclaves in South Boston and Charlestown, against the blacks in Roxbury, who wanted schools that would give their children a chance to escape the ghetto. When the federal court tried to impose cross-neighborhood busing at the opening of school in 1974, years of violence began. Some children stayed out of school for three years (Wilkinson, 1979, p. 208). There was even an ironic sidelight: school officials from Boston traveling to Charlotte, North Carolina, for advice on how to handle racial integration.

J. Harvie Wilkinson has traced five stages in the desegregation of America: absolute defiance, token compliance, modest integration, massive integration, and resegregation (Wilkinson, 1979, p. 78). We are well into the last stage now. The proportion of the minority population in large cities is growing daily, and many large cities are now overwhelmingly minority in population. The public schools of these cities are even more racially isolated than the cities themselves. Resegregation even has the endorsement of the federal circuit court for Norfolk, Virginia, which has ruled that since the Norfolk schools succeeded in abolishing segregation through busing, they were free to stop the busing and return to the practice of neighborhood schools, even though these schools would be racially segregated (*Riddick v. School Board of Norfolk*, 1986). A federal district court has issued a similar ruling in Oklahoma City (*Dowell v. Board of Education of Oklahoma City*, 1988). The U.S. Supreme Court has yet to rule on this form of resegregation.

At the same time that this resegregation is taking place, there are still attempts at desegregation elsewhere in the nation. The most recent explosion over school desegregation has occurred in the city of Yonkers, New York. The federal court for that jurisdiction ruled that Yonkers officials enacted policies with the clear but unannounced intention of segregating both the schools and the housing of the city. Yonkers was ordered to desegregate its housing as well as its schools. The city officials refused to comply until the judge assessed fines that would soon have brought the city to bankruptcy. The Yonkers crisis too had the school officials of a northern city going to the south for advice on successful integration (Foderaro, 1988).

Once the court battles and the public tumult have ended, and integrated schools have been established, scholars set about measuring the effects of the integration. Their main concern is with the consequences of integration for the children involved. How has it affected their academic performance? How has it affected their attitudes?

Unfortunately, the answers to these questions are not clear-cut or consistent. For example, Nancy St. John found in reviewing the studies that integration produced better academic performance the younger the black students are and the more middle-class they are. She also found, however, that integration had a negative effect on the self-esteem and the aspirations of black students (St. John, 1975).

Laurence and Gifford Bradley reviewed twenty-nine desegregation studies and found that all of them had methodological weaknesses, limiting the faith that one could put in their findings. The better-designed studies were divided between those that showed improved academic performance for the black students and those that did not (Bradley and Bradley, 1977).

More recently, David Armor, in a major study for the National Institute of Education, reached this conclusion:

> The very best studies available demonstrate no significant and consistent effects of desegregation on Black achievement. There is virtually no effect whatsoever for math achievement, and for reading achievement the very best that can be said is that only a handful of grade levels from the 19 best available studies show substantial positive effects, while the large majority of grade levels show small and inconsistent effects that average out to about 0. (Armor, 1984)

One of the most interesting studies in terms of attitude toward integration was done by Leroy McCloud. He was the black principal of the black school in Englewood, New Jersey, when the Englewood schools were integrated in 1963, at which time he himself opposed the integration. In the late 1970s, he contacted his former pupils to assess the impact that integration had had on them and their current opinions about integration. He hypothesized that both the impact and the opinions would be negative, given the turmoil and acrimony of the integration process. His findings clearly show the opposite to be true. His former students, who had since become young adults, overwhelmingly considered the integration experience to have been worth the pain and disruption with which it began. They felt that they were much better equipped to survive and thrive in a multiracial world than they would have been had their education remained segregated (McCloud, 1980).

Those who believe that integration has positive effects for blacks, in terms either of academic gains or of improved attitudes, and either short-term or long-term, are willing to intrude on the liberty of the opponents to bring these benefits about. They are convinced that blacks deserve this equalization upward even if it has to be forced upon an unwilling white community by court edict. To the extent that blacks themselves are reluctant to have their children integrated, the court edict would be seen as a violation of their liberty, too. For people who see integration as necessary for a more just society, the advantages that black children would reap not only would make them more equal, but would give them resources to be used in the exercise of their liberty. Greater equality means greater liberty for those who are being equalized upward. Alas, one person's gain is another person's loss in a competitive society with a finite number of opportunities. This reality is what pits caring parents against each other in the matter of school integration.

REFERENCES

Armor, D. (1984). *The Evidence on Desegregation and Black Achievement*. Washington, D.C.: National Institute of Education.

Bastian, A., et al. (1985). *Choosing Equality: The Case for Democratic Schooling*. New York: New World Foundation.

Block, F., et al. (1987). *The Mean Season: The Attack on the Welfare State*. New York: Pantheon.

Bradley, L., and Bradley, G. (1977). "Academic Achievement of Black Students." *Review of Educational Research*, **47**, 399–449.

Brown v. Board of Education (1955). 349 U.S. 294.

Bruck, C. (1988). *The Predators' Ball*. New York: Simon & Schuster.

Chubb, J. E. (1988). "Why the Current Wave of School Reform Will Fail." *The Public Interest*, **90**, 28–49.

Cohen, R. (1989). "Bush Details 7-Point Program for 'Educational Excellence.' " *Newark Star-Ledger*, April 6, pp. 1, 23.

Coleman, J. S. (1981). "Quality and Equality in American Education: Public and Catholic Schools." *Phi Delta Kappan*, **63**, 169–164.

Coleman, J. S., Hoffer, T., and Kilgore, S. (1981). *Public and Private Schools*. Washington, D.C.: National Center for Education Statistics.

deLone, R. H. (1979). *Small Futures: Children, Inequality, and the Limits of Liberal Reform*. New York: Harcourt Brace Jovanovich.

Dowell v. Board of Education of Oklahoma City (1988). 606 F. Supp. 1548.

Eagleton Institute of Politics (1988). *Choice in Public Education*. New Brunswick, N.J.: Eagleton Institute.

Esposito, F. (1988). *Public School Choice: National Trends and Initiatives*. Trenton, N.J.: New Jersey State Department of Education.

Evans v. Buchanan (1977). 416 F. Supp. 328.

Foderaro, L. W. (1988). "In Yonkers, a Measured Integration of Schools." *The New York Times*, September 25, pp. 1, 42.

Friedman, M., and Friedman, R. (1980). *Free to Choose*. New York: Harcourt Brace Jovanovich.

Gallup, A. M. (1986). "The 18th Annual Gallop Poll of the Public's Attitudes Toward the Public Schools." *The Gallup Report*, **252**, 11–26.

Gilder, G. (1981). *Wealth and Poverty*. New York: Bantam.

Glasser, I. (1978). "Prisoners of Benevolence: Power vs. Liberty in the Welfare State." In *Doing Good: The Limits of Benevolence*, edited by W. Gaylin et al. New York: Pantheon.

Goertz, M., et al. (1982). *Plain Talk About School Finance*. Washington, D.C.: National Institute of Education.

Goldberger, A., and Cain, G. (1982). "The Causal Analysis of Cognitive Outcomes in the Coleman, Hoffer, and Kilgore Report." *Sociology of Education*, **55**, 103–122.

Grant Foundation Commission on Work, Family and Citizenship (1988). *The Forgotten Half: Pathways to Success for America's Youth and Young Families*. Final Report. Washington, D.C.: Grant Commission.

Green v. County School Board (1968). 391 U.S. 430.

Harrington, M. (1973). *Socialism*. New York: Bantam.

Jencks, C., et al. (1970). *Education Vouchers*. Cambridge, Mass.: Center for the Study of Public Policy.

Jordan, K. F., and McKeown, M. P. (1980). "Equity in Financing Public Elementary and Secondary Schools." In *School Finance Policies and Practices*, edited by J. W. Guthrie. Cambridge, Mass.: Ballinger.

Keniston, K., and The Carnegie Council on Children (1977). *All Our Children: The American Family Under Pressure*. New York: Harcourt Brace Jovanovich.

Keyes v. Denver School District (1973). 413 U.S. 189.

Kluger, R. (1976). *Simple Justice*. New York: Knopf.

Kristol, I. (1978). *Two Cheers for Capitalism*. New York: Basic Books.

Lefelt, S. (1988). *Abbott v. Burke*. Initial Decision. Trenton, N.J.: State of New Jersey Office of Administrative Law.

Levine, D. U., and Havighurst, R. J. (1989). *Society and Education*. Boston: Allyn and Bacon.

Mathis, N. (1989). "Education Not a Fundamental Right, Appeals Court Says in Decision Upholding Texas State-Aid System." *Education Week*, **8**, 15 (January 11).

McCloud, L. (1980). *The Effect of Racial Conflict in School Desegregation on the Academic Achievement and the Attitudes of Black Pupils in the Englewood Public Schools*. Doctoral dissertation, Rutgers University.

Mead, L. M. (1988). "The New Welfare Debate." *Commentary*, **85**, 44–52.

Milliken v. Bradley (1974). 418 U.S. 717.

Moran, B. (1987). *Inside a Gifted/Talented Magnet: An Analysis of the Enrollment and Curricular Patterns by Race and Gender in the Hillside School in Montclair, New Jersey*. Doctoral dissertation, Rutgers University, New Brunswick, N.J.

Murray, C. (1984). *Losing Ground: American Social Policy, 1950–1980*. New York: Basic Books.

National Governors Association (1986). *Time for Results: The Governors 1991 Report on Education*. Washington, D.C.: National Governors Association.

Paterson, J. T. (1986). *America's Struggle Against Poverty: 1900–1985*. Cambridge, Mass.: Harvard University Press.

Reischauer, R. D., and Hartman, R. W. (1973). *Reforming School Finance*. Washington, D.C.: The Brookings Institution.

Riddick v. School Board of Norfolk (1983). 784 F.2d 521.

Robinson v. Cahill (1972). Docket L-18704, Superior Court of New Jersey, Hudson County.

Robinson v. Cahill (1973). 62 N.J. 473, 303 A.2d 273.

Rutter, M., et al. (1979). *Fifteen Thousand Hours: Secondary Schools and Their Effects on Children.* Cambridge, Mass.: Harvard University Press.

St. John, N. (1975). *School Desegregation: Outcomes for Children.* New York: Wiley.

San Antonio Independent School District v. Rodriguez (1973). 411 U.S. 1.

Serrano v. Priest (1971). 96 Cal. Rptr. 601, 437 P.2d 1241.

Simon, W. E. (1978). *A Time for Truth.* New York: McGraw-Hill.

Smith, A. [1776] (1976). *The Wealth of Nations.* Edited by Edwin Cannan. Chicago: University of Chicago Press.

Snider, W. (1988). "In Chicago, Implications of Reform Bill Please the Grassroots, Dismay Others." *Education Week,* **8,** 6 (December 14).

Spring, J. (1988). *"Conflict of Interests: The Politics of American Education."* New York: Longman.

Swann v. Charlotte-Mecklenburg Board of Education (1971). 402 U.S. 1.

Thomas v. Stewart (1981). No. 8275 (Ga. Super., Polk County).

Thurow, L. C. (1980). *The Zero-Sum Society: Distribution and the Possibilities for Economic Change.* New York: Basic Books.

Tocqueville, A. de. [1835] (1968). "Memoir on Pauperism." In *Tocqueville and Beaumont on Social Reform,* edited by S. Drescher. New York: Harper Torchbooks.

Weinraub, B. (1989). "Bush Wooing Educators, Urges Choice in Schools." *The New York Times,* January 11, p. B28.

Wilkinson, J. H. (1979). *From Brown to Bakke: The Supreme Court and School Integration, 1954–1978.* New York: Oxford University Press.

Wilson, W. J. (1987). *The Truly Disadvantaged: The Inner City, the Underclass, and Public Policy.* Chicago: University of Chicago Press.

VOUCHERS OR
COMMON SCHOOLS

POSITION 1
For Choice

Some time ago, during the first administration of President Nixon, a proposal emerged from the U.S. Office of Economic Opportunity that provoked a heated debate. The initial excitement passed after a few years when the proposal did not bear much fruit in terms of implementation. However, the debate continued on a back burner of public policy discussion. In recent times, during the second administration of President Reagan, the flame has been turned up by proposals from the U.S. Department of Education. The Nixon and Reagan proposals are called by either of two names: "family choice" or "vouchers." "Family choice" is the longer name but it captures the spirit better, so it is the term that will be used in this argument. The family choice idea merits consideration for three reasons: (1) it will not go away; (2) it fills many people, including officials at the highest levels of government, with great hope for the future of American education; and (3) it is an idea of such intrinsic promise that it cries out for a fair test.

Family choice means that the family chooses the school its children will attend. The family can make this choice from all the schools within a reasonable commuting distance. That would include literally scores of schools in the more populous areas of the United States. But even if there are only five schools in the less populous areas, that would be five times more choice than families have now.

To pay for the school of its choice, the family will be given a check (or voucher) by the government (most likely the state government, since education is primarily a state responsibility). The government will get the money for these checks from the taxes it collects. In other words, schools will still be tax-supported, but a family will be able to get its hands on its share of the tax money and use that to buy the kind of education it *really* wants. All families will get the same amount of money per child depending on the needs of the child. For example, the amount of the checks (or vouchers) for handicapped children will be more than for children without handicaps because it costs more to educate the handicapped. For all children in the same educational category, the amount of the checks will be the same.

BREAKING THE EDUCATIONAL MONOPOLY

Obviously, none of this would make any sense if the family could choose only from among schools that were all the same. That is why the idea doesn't make much sense in today's school market, where the vast preponderance of schools are interchangeable clones of each other. "If we first implement choice, true choice among schools, we unleash the values of competition in the education marketplace" (National Governors Association, 1986, p. 6). What the idea is intended to do, therefore, is to replace that amorphous mass of jelly that passes for education in America with some really solid alternatives from which families can select.

The neighborhood school will no longer be forced upon families once they have the money to buy their way out. The captive clientele of today's schools will be set free. Family choice in education is a liberating act of the twentieth century. And just as eighteenth-century indentured servants who had worked off their period of servitude could remain with their owner or strike out on their own, families can stick with the neighborhood school or go off to some school that has deliberately fashioned itself to be attractive and interesting. Indeed, the neighborhood school will probably refashion itself in an effort to keep families from fleeing.

The possibilities for attractive and interesting schools are everything that you and your friends can imagine, plus much more that may not even occur to you. For example, one of the public schools in the East Harlem section of New York City is a maritime academy, with the East River serving as a natural laboratory. Cleveland has an aviation high school whose curriculum includes flying lessons. Or a school could be truly "user friendly" by taking the experiences of the kids in the neighborhood as the building blocks of the curriculum (Raywid, Tesconi, and Warren, 1984, p. 24). This richness of choice will be especially true if families can select from among not just the public schools of an area but also the private and parochial schools. This variety of schools already has some diversity to offer, but the choices will be multiplied many times as *all* schools scurry to attract parents with vouchers. Without vouchers, a school will have no income and will have to shut down. With declining patronage, a school will have decreasing income and will have to lay off staff. These dismal prospects will cause schools to work harder than they ever have to attract customers and keep them satisfied. Up to now, a public school has not had to work hard at all because it has had a virtual monopoly grip on the education in its neighborhood.

THE RIGHTS OF PARENTS

In the United States, parents have extensive and legally sanctioned control over their children. The theory which justifies the legal authority of parents is that parents are the people who are most likely to understand the needs of their children, and are also the ones most concerned about their welfare. "In its unique opportunity to listen and to know and in its special personal concern for the child, the family is his most promising champion" (Coons and Sugarman, 1978, p. 53).

The rights of parents over their children are not unlimited, and should not be. There are needs of children which parents simply are not competent to meet and for which they have to rely on expert help. Medical care is one example. Education is another. Parents may lack pedagogical skills and have to turn to professional educators for assistance. However, professional educators have a transitory relationship with children and never acquire the intimate knowledge and concern which parents have. Moreover, they do not have to live with the consequences of a miseducated and unhappy child. Therefore, parents should always be the senior partner of the educational team for their child. And they should certainly have the most to say about the primary educational decision: the school the child will attend.

Or not attend. Parents' rights in the education of their children have been recognized by courts as including the right to educate children at home. Parents need only demonstrate their competence to deliver the basic education expected by the state. Home schooling is not widespread yet, but if parents could cash in the "choice" voucher themselves instead of signing it over to some school, it would become financially feasible for more parents to do what they've always wanted—create family schools.

ESCAPING SECULAR HUMANISM

In addition to having the right to choose something good for their children, parents have a right to protect their children against things that are bad. One of the things that most worries parents is having their children come under "evil influences." Parents forbid their children to play with certain other children because they fear that their children will be led astray.

For many parents, especially among those who are devoutly religious, the public school itself is an evil influence. It is evil because it is so nonreligious. In its attempt to avoid indoctrinating children into any religion, the public school shuns all but the most neutral presentation of religion, treating religious faiths as purely historical phenomena. It presents all religions as being equally good and equally arbitrary manifestations of people's search for meaning. This obviously suggests to students that their family's religion is just one among equals and no more divinely inspired than any of the others, and maybe not at all.

Parents believe that the noncommittal approach of the public schools weakens their children's religious commitment. It turns children from spiritual sources of certain truth and guidance to merely human ones that are uncertain and relative. Naturally, parents whose own lives are made meaningful and whose own behavior is guided by religion dread having their children weaned away from religion by the nonreligion of the public schools. Some parents go so far as to say that because the public school's approach has consequences for their religion, it is, in fact, a form of religion itself. They call this form "secular humanism," meaning a religion that elevates human beings to the highest moral realm. And that means that their children are in a school where a competing and hostile religion is being taught.

Choice is the way to protect the right of these parents to protect their children's salvation as they see fit. It is a violation of religious freedom to require parents to send their children to an institution that undermines the parents' religious values.

THE BENEFITS FOR STUDENTS

One of the recurring and most common complaints about American education is that it leaves students bored out of their skulls. You can judge for yourself how much this complaint echoes your own experience. The complaint has been around a long time, but school officials have never had to do anything about it because there was no choice for children or their parents. Kids had to go to school, they had to go to the school some authority said, and they could literally go to jail if they did not go to that school. Well, they may have to go to school for their and society's benefit, but they should at least be able to go to a school they like.

The literature of professional education contains some truths that remain remarkably absent from the *practice* of education. One of these truths is that different children have different needs and interests. That's so obvious as to be a truism. Another truth is that children learn more when they are motivated than when they are longing desperately for the bell to ring. That too is a truism. Family choice means that finally, at long last, these two fundamental truths of education will actually be *applied*.

The truths are being applied already, but for only a few students. Those are the ones whose families can afford to send them to a school beyond the control of the local authorities. Family choice will give all of us a right that now exists in reality only for the well-to-do. It is true that the poor can scrimp and save and scrape by to send their children to parochial schools, but parochial schools for the poor are not markedly better, and from the student's point of view may be much worse, than the local public schools. Why should only the rich be allowed to have effective control over their children's education?

If poor families can pick schools outside their neighborhoods, then minority families will be able to integrate their children into majority schools. As things stand now, American schools are notoriously and thoroughly segregated. If someone wants to find a school that is populated overwhelmingly by minority students, it is very easy to do. It is just as easy to find an almost lily-white school. A tragedy of our times is that these schools can be found in such close proximity to each other. They are on opposite sides of an arbitrary and artificial line known as the school district boundary. Family choice on a nondiscriminatory basis offers real promise of getting past this disgraceful condition.

Racial and social-class integration of schools, to the extent that it has been tried in the United States, has had a rocky history. There are many cases in which it seems to have done more harm than good, and to have been a huge waste of time, energy, money, patience, and kids' lives. Those have all been cases of legally forced integration. With family choice, the integration will come about naturally, that is, voluntarily. The students in a given school will not have race or social class in common, but they will have common interests and needs. Those commonalities are more important to children than the superficial characteristics of race and class about which adults get hung up. Family choice is a way to honor the good sense of children to everyone's advantage. The Hervey School in Medford, Massachusetts, did just that by offering such interesting programs that it attracted a multiracial student body (Bastian et al., 1985, p. 76). It is even possible to have a "choice" school whose theme is integration. "Educational alternatives can be based on a newer conception of integration—multicultural education, which establishes cultural diversity as its founding principle" (Fantini, 1973, p. 229).

THE BENEFITS FOR TEACHERS

Family choice does not sit well with teacher unions because it is thought to pose a threat to the job security of their members. Every family that pulls out of a school puts the teacher's job closer to extinction. If families are not allowed to pull out, the teacher can bask in the assurance of guaranteed employment. That is the negative attitude toward family choice, and it paints teachers as wanting nothing more than to be civil service lifers. It is a demeaning portrait of teachers, and it ignores the positive aspects of family choice for them.

Family choice frees teachers to design schools as they wish. The deadening uniformity and ritualism of schools can be as enervating to teachers as to students. Teachers know that they would like to do something to make school exciting for themselves and their students, but they have no chance to do it because they are locked into the bureaucratic monolith. The "something" may be little more than a series of interest-arousing community explorations which don't fit into the standard organization of the school day. What the teachers would like to do cannot be done because it does not fit into the Procrustean bed of the "system." David Kearns, chairman and chief executive officer of the Xerox Corporation, says that America's public school system has to be broken up just as business corporations had to be in recent years, and for the same reason: they have become bureaucratic dinosaurs which impede the productivity of their employees. Choice is the way to disassemble them (Kearns and Doyle, 1988). All teachers can do now is struggle around the periphery of the dinosaur until they become exhausted, and then content themselves with going through the motions until retirement—or get out of teaching altogether. Family choice will give the bolder and more creative teachers an opportunity to break loose and start their own schools. A school could be created on the basis of a shared enthusiasm for a particular approach to education. It could be formed out of friendships among teachers, with the particular educational approach being hashed out collegially, and revised the same way (Raywid, 1987). If the school is small, the teachers will still be able to maintain their standard of living while saving the cost of a lot of administrative overhead. A sufficiently small school could be operated out of a home or storefront, so both capital and custodial costs would be kept to a minimum.

Teachers of a more timid nature could redesign the school in which they've been working, perhaps dividing it into mini-schools. The school administrators who might be rendered superfluous by this action need not be fired. They could take on more strictly educational duties, and they should welcome this prospect if they are truly committed to working with children.

Family choice, then, will have the effect of *empowering* teachers. Not only will they remain in direct contact with students, there will no longer be a bureaucratic Maginot line between them and the parents, or the school policies. Schooling will become a cooperative venture among the three essential parties to it: students, teachers, and parents. This does not mean that all of the new schools will be better than any of the present schools. It means that students, teachers, and parents will be able to have the kind of school in which they feel the most comfortable and confident.

These prospects could in themselves solve the problem of a teacher shortage. People who do not deign to teach in the present system will be excited enough by the chance to be true educational professionals that they will make career switches. The Friedmans report that people have told them that "I have always wanted to teach [or run a school] but I couldn't stand the educational bureaucracy, red tape, and general ossification of the public schools" (Friedman and Friedman, 1980, p. 169).

RESPECTING DIFFERENCES

Teaching children to respect differences among people is supposed to be a goal of today's public schools. However, the schools betray this goal in two major ways. First, they are segregated along racial and social-class lines. The message which is sent to students by this situation is that some people are more worthy of avoidance than respect. Second, the public schools are like giant food blenders, where differences are ground into mush. It's all right for the teachers to talk about tolerance, but the kids don't get much chance to assert anything about themselves that could require toleration.

Religion, politics, aesthetic sensibilities, and expressive styles are all carefully constrained in the public school of today. No one is allowed to get "too far out of line" or be "too radical." Everyone walks on eggshells. Genuine self-expression is like a time bomb that has to be defused. Eccentricity is a scandal, and in today's frantically vanilla schools it does not take much to be eccentric. The norms in urban poor schools may be different than those in suburban affluent schools, but they are just as limiting and oppressive. The frantically chocolate leaves no more breathing room than the frantically vanilla.

Family choice means freedom for the misfits in today's schools. That they are misfits reflects not on them but on the intellectual and social rigidity of the schools. These "oddballs" are as likely to be supernormal as subnormal. Their only crime is in falling outside a field of tolerance that is not very wide. The only choice they have now is for an education that is either painful or inauthentic. If they display their true selves, they suffer rejection and ridicule from their peers and constant badgering by the school authorities. If they dissemble to get by, they feel false and dishonest, which can cause them to reject themselves. Family choice can widen the field of tolerance *across* schools, so that the misfits, some of whom are misfitted unto suicide, begin to belong. It may not increase the tolerance within a school, and could even reduce it, but at least children would know that society respected them enough to find places for them all.

BUILDING IN SAFEGUARDS

Family choice is vulnerable to abuse. Hucksterism is the abuse that usually leaps to people's minds first. Schools-for-profit are permitted—indeed, encouraged—by family choice. Some of the profiteers are going to be hucksters willing to do some pretty unscrupulous things to attract and bilk families. False advertising, misrepresentation, inflated claims, hidden charges, and bait-and-switch are some of the practices which have to be prevented. As with other businesses, the best way to prevent these white-collar crimes is to have a monitoring mechanism that can detect them, and then some swift and severe penalties. Dishonest educational practices are among the worst kinds of consumer fraud because the victims are children and the harm can be long-lasting. A well-staffed agency should be able to keep the abuses to a minimum and to catch them quickly.

Another potential abuse of the family choice system is discriminatory admissions practices. A school might want to make itself attractive to both families and teachers by excluding certain kinds of students. These could be black students, low-achieving students, handicapped students, or students from a minority religious group. It might be permissible to exclude students who perform poorly on a test that is related to the purpose of the school, or students who are so profoundly handicapped that the school is simply not equipped to help them. There will be other schools that specialize in such problem students, so the needs of these students can be met in a variety of other ways. However, exclusion on the bases of race and religion and other illegitimate criteria are abuses which the fair practices agency should be charged to prevent.

A third form of abuse would be failure to provide the minimally adequate education expected for all normal children regardless of the school they and their families choose. A school may attract students because it is warm and friendly and fun, but then not assist them in acquiring the academic skills needed for gainful employment and useful citizenship. Society has a right to establish minimum achievement standards and to test to see that students are reaching them. Many states already have statewide standards and tests, so it is simply a matter of maintaining them under the family choice system.

A fourth safeguard that should be built into the system is the cost of transportation. Students should be transported at public expense to any school within the region covered by the family choice system. Otherwise, the choices a family has will be circumscribed by the cost of transportation. For poor families, this cost can be prohibitive, so they will have no real choice apart from the school(s) in the neighborhood. It is not likely that suburban students would be attracted to an urban school if that school is nearly crammed to capacity with kids who are trapped in the neighborhood. Without a transportation allowance, then, the family choice system will offer a lot less choice and may bring about very little racial and social-class integration.

Once a choice system is under way, other dangers may appear and other safeguards will then have to be devised, but human ingenuity should be able to cope with these problems. It is possible to protect everyone's legitimate interest while expanding everyone's freedom. The result will be education characterized by harmonious pluralism. "The ability to get the kind of education one wants for oneself or one's children serves both as a reward for those with a pedagogical interest and as a means of defusing fights between interests over who should have the ability to impose universal requirements on the system" (Kerchner, 1988, p. 390).

POSITION 2
For Common Schools

DEFINING THE TERMS

"Family" and "choice" are powerful words in the American lexicon. They carry a lot of emotional baggage. Both the Democratic and Republican national parties invoke the word "family" as though it were a sacred mantra. And choice is something we instinctively associate with democracy as opposed to tyranny, which is characterized by the denial of choice. So when the words are combined into the term "family choice," the unwitting listener or reader is disposed to agree with the proposal itself.

It's a good debate tactic to give your side of the argument an appealing label. If the debate were just an intellectual exercise, no harm would be done by this, and one side would rack up a few points in the category of "best label." However, the issue under discussion here is one that has momentous implications for us all. The two sides to the debate are not nearly as important as the great in-between, the American public. For the American public to judge the debate fairly and make a well-informed decision about the future direction of American education, it is imperative that it not be blinded by debaters' tricks. Therefore, we will not use the loaded term "family choice," which plays into our opponents' hands, nor will we employ a loaded term of our own. Instead, we will use a term that is so neutral that when people hear it they say "Huh?" The word "voucher" has practically no value connotations at all, except perhaps to accountants, and it is a word that does not even exist in the working vocabulary of most people. The use of this word will not cloud the debate but will allow people to judge the debate on its substantive merits. Moreover, while vouchers are but one form of choice, they are the logical endpoint to which the truncated forms lead. It is for this reason that people suspect the more limited forms of choice of being stalking-horses for vouchers.

PRESERVING DIVERSITY

There are many practical problems to a voucher system, and they will be addressed in later sections. The overriding problem, however, is a philosophical one. The American public school now functions as a crucible of democracy. This is especially true of the comprehensive high school, where students from a good-sized geographic area and a wide range of interests and abilities are brought together.

In today's comprehensive high school there is choice—not a choice of school, but a choice of curriculum track within the school. Thus, students of different interests and abilities have programs that are tailored to them. They also have an easy choice of switching from one program to another since all the programs are in a single school. So there is both choice and ease of choice for the individual, and on top of that there is the benefit of heterogeneity for the individual and for society. Students from different tracks in the high school get to mingle with each other and engage in common activities. The *extra*curricular activities of the school are open to all regardless of curriculum track. But even some of the academic courses mix together students from different tracks. For schools that have tracks but not ability grouping within the tracks, the commingling is even greater.

The net result of this arrangement is that different kinds of people get practice at living together. The practice may, on occasion, be unsettling, even painful. However, it cannot be forestalled forever, and school is a semiprotected environment in which to gain the experience of democratic living. It is a relatively safe place for learning how to get along with others. In the comprehensive high school, "others" does not just mean others like oneself; it also means others with whom one does not have much in common. Students who develop the ability to interact smoothly with a variety of other people are likely to be successful and happy as adults. They will know when to compromise and what behaviors are offensive to what sorts of people. They will also understand the value of reciprocity in relationships. These abilities can only be developed where there is a variety of other people, that is, the comprehensive high school.

The voucher system, by whatever euphemism and in whatever form, will replace the crucible that is the comprehensive high school with a spice rack on which differences are physically isolated and separately contained. That may be snug and comfortable for the students in each little container, but it is poor preparation for the real world. For American students, it is poor preparation for citizenship in a democracy. Learning how to socialize with people who share your interests and abilities is relatively easy, but hardly enough. There are all those other kinds of people out there and you cannot hide from them forever if you wish to have a rich and full life. The voucher system will have the effect of crippling students socially and breeding a divisive defensiveness among groups who have never gotten to know each other.

CHOOSING WHEN READY

Thus far the focus of this discussion has been on the high school and why the voucher system is both unnecessary and undesirable at that level of education. It may seem that the voucher system is justified at the elementary school level because students (and families) now have virtually no choice there at all. There is the single neighborhood school with its single curriculum for everyone. Moreover, that single curriculum is supposed to have a stranglehold on elementary education in America. It *is* our elementary education. Voucher advocates imply that this situation was developed conspiratorially by people who are indifferent to the needs of children. The American elementary school system is a gulag archipelago, they suggest—nothing more than a national system of prisons for children.

This characterization is a gross slander of elementary school educators and an insult to the intelligence of the American people. The elementary schools of America are, in reality, the places where the *common* needs of children are met. The schools are similar precisely because children's needs are common. *All* children who are going to survive and thrive in our society need to know the academic basics of reading, writing, and arithmetic. These are generative skills; they are used as tools for further learning. The fact that all schools teach these skills, along with social studies and science needed by future voters and workers, and art and music for life enrichment, simply reflects the good sense of the American people. Computer literacy is being added to the list because its importance has become obvious, and elementary schools are flexible and prudent enough to accommodate such a significant cultural adaptation. Do we really want to give families a choice of whether their children should have to learn things that are of transparent benefit to them and the rest of society?

Children's needs and the corresponding academic subjects are the same from school to school, and to some extent from grade to grade, which enables children to transfer between schools without disruption of their academic progress. This portability has to be an important consideration for a people as mobile as Americans. It does not mean, however, that all children are expected to learn the basic academic skills in exactly the same way. Different schools have different teaching styles and materials, and this is true for students of different abilities within the same school. The styles and the materials are matters best left to the judgment of trained professionals. Without in any way denigrating the intelligence of parents and children, the indisputable fact is that they have not been trained to make the professional judgments of educators. Moreover, parents may wish to send their children to school outside the neighborhood just because it has become fashionable to do so, much as some college students wish to go to an out-of-state college. If the cost of transportation is only a dollar each way, that could amount to $400 a year per student, or literally millions of dollars for the transportation system that would not be available for the education system.

Voucher advocates argue that the differences in styles and materials to be found in today's elementary schools aren't different enough. Not even the differences that a school district creates when it makes each school a magnet site with its own unique theme are enough to satisfy the voucherites. They insist on a veritable multitude of choices, in the naive belief that children and parents are capable of wading through this wild abundance and making an intelligent selection. Elementary school children are too young to have this responsibility imposed on them, and most parents lack the time and expertise to make distinctions among a host of closely competing alternatives. The voucher proponents subscribe to the silly notion that there can't be too much of a good thing. Choice is a good thing, but too much of it can be as paralyzing as too much cough medicine for a cold. If more choice is desired by the public, it should be brought about gradually and cautiously within an already proven system.

INEQUALITY OF CHOICE

Should a voucher system succeed in bringing about a wide variety of schools, choosing is going to be damnably difficult for even the most intelligent and assiduous parents. Ploughing through the promotional material and independent assessments of the many schools could entail an enormous amount of reading. Interpreting this material could require technical expertise not possessed by the ordinary parent. Visiting schools that look good on paper to check out the reality is a task many parents don't have time for. Other parents lack the self-confidence to embark on such a bold venture.

What this brief consideration makes obvious is that not all parents are equal when it comes to choosing. The most educationally disadvantaged students are likely to have parents whose own poor education does not equip them to make wise choices for their children. Recent news disclosures have shocked us with the revelation that many parents brutalize their children and are not to be trusted with their children's welfare in any way. Thus, the already educated and concerned parents will be able to take advantage of a voucher system in ways that won't even occur to the ignorant or the indifferent.

Making the choosing situation equal will require considerable money for the production of reliable and cognitively accessible information packets, in more than one language, and for a goodly number of qualified counselors. This money may have to be subtracted from the value of the vouchers, leaving less for the actual education of children. Mario Fantini's blithe suggestion that those who lack the ability to choose well can simply continue doing so on a trial-and-error basis until they get it right (Fantini, 1973, pp. 74–75) ignores the huge educational and psychological cost for youngsters who flounder from school to school year after year.

The reproduction of low social status across generations is something that poor parents engage in unwittingly. And in a voucher system, "parents will be able to send their children to schools that [may] reinforce in the most restrictive fashion the family's political, ideological, and religious views. That is, school will be treated as a strict extension of the home" (Levin, 1980, p. 251). The upshot will be that working-class parents will pick schools that stress discipline, basic skills, and following orders, while middle-class parents pick schools that foster independence and higher-order thinking skills. Working-class kids will learn how to be low-wage workers; middle-class kids will be readied for high-salaried professions. The working-class students will be limited by their parents' constrained conception of success.

Since minorities are represented disproportionately among the poor, social-class tracking by school will mean racially segregated schools. It is instructive to recall that the south used "schools of choice" as a way to guarantee the continuation of a dual-school system, and it worked. Now that we know how fiercely northern communities have resisted desegregation, "it is fatuous to believe that the white community will permit a voucher system to operate so as to remove the barriers that they have laboriously erected to protect themselves and their children from what they consider to be the undesirable behavior patterns of the disadvantaged" (Ginzberg, 1972, p. 106). Whites will fight to make sure that "choice" is intradistrict only, leaving them safe to choose from among schools that will remain predictably white. New Jersey trumpets its "choice" initiative, but it is an intradistrict plan only, meaning no threat to Newark's suburbs.

The same result is possible with interdistrict choice if schools are allowed to choose students after the students have indicated their choice of schools. Schools could establish admission criteria that would predetermine the composition of the student body, not just in terms of academic ability but also socioeconomically and racially. An example of how this might work is the New York City school system, where there are four tiers of high schools: academic schools, theme schools, vocational schools, and neighborhood schools. The top-tier schools cream off the most able and manageable students, leaving the most needy and therefore least desirable students to the neighborhood schools (Bastian et al., 1985, p. 75). The choice for the disadvantaged is to stay put.

THE INTERESTS OF SOCIETY

It is interesting to note how the voucher proposal is pitched to the self-interest of different groups. Parents are told of the latitude it will give them in deciding where their children go to school. Students are regaled with visions of candy-store education where they will be able to go on shopping sprees. Teachers are led to believe that, finally, they will have total job control. Very little emphasis is placed on the *responsibilities* these groups will acquire: time-consuming, anxiety-provoking, selfishness-inducing responsibilities.

Worse yet, no attention is paid to the interests of the whole, the common good. We as a society have interests that transcend the self-interests of individuals, and which cannot be left to the whims of individuals. The more legitimate such interests society has, the less freedom each individual or group can be allowed. The public interest requires that we be constrained in the exercise of our selfish interests.

What are society's interests in education? First, that all children acquire the communication skills and the knowledge of government necessary for full and active citizenship. When these have been spelled out in detail by the state authorities charged with doing so, a good part of the K–12 curriculum has been specified. This becomes more and more the case as democracy demands greater and greater sophistication of its members. Society's second major interest is in preparing young people for effective functioning in the world of work. This involves the development not only of marketable skills but also of work habits and attitudes. This should eliminate from any "choice" equation schools whose principal attraction for students is low expectations. In addition to having high expectations of its schools, the state has an obligation to monitor the schools to ensure a satisfactory level of fulfillment.

The state's third interest is a negative one. The state has a definite interest in keeping every school it pays for free of religious and ideological indoctrination. Public schools—and all voucher schools would be publicly funded—are not places for brainwashing students into the agenda of any interest group. As the U.S. Supreme Court said in the *Epperson* case, involving the teaching of Darwinian theory in Arkansas:

> Judicial interposition in the operation of the public school systems of the Nation raises problems requiring care and restraint. Our courts, however, have not failed to apply the First Amendment's mandate in our educational system where essential to safeguard the fundamental values of freedom of speech and inquiry and of belief. By and large, public education in our Nation is committed to the control of state and local authorities. Courts do not and cannot intervene in the resolution of conflicts which arise in the daily operation of school systems and which do not directly and sharply implicate basic constitutional values. On the other hand, "The vigilant protection of constitutional values is nowhere more vital than in the community of the American Schools." (*Epperson v. State of Arkansas,* 1969)

Preserving freedom of speech and inquiry and of belief will mean that a lot of people find themselves ineligible for voucher money with which to impose their personal convictions on youngsters. If not, we are going to see public subsidization of socially divisive and miseducative institutions, such as white supremacist and black nationalist schools.

KEEPING TEACHERS SANE

Teacher unions get a bum rap for being opposed to vouchers. The unions are accused of having the attitude of job protection above all and let the public be damned. If the voucher system is adopted, the public *will* be damned just as surely as there will be a dramatic drop in the number of teachers.

No one wants to work in a frightfully insecure environment. Everyone wishes to have some stability and predictability in employment. To ask teachers to subject themselves to *no-guarantee* jobs for the rest of their working lives is to expect of them a sacrifice which no other workers would willingly make. Each summer teachers would have to wait for word that their schools had attracted enough students for them to return to work in September. Their anxiety would then end only briefly, since student transfers during the year (another choice in the voucher radical choice scheme) could put them back out on the street. It might be possible for a teacher in a low-draw school to transfer to a high-draw school, but this could require that the teacher abandon a teaching philosophy in which he or she believed sincerely. The teacher's effectiveness would have to be seriously impaired by such coerced insincerity. Certainly his or her job satisfaction would be diminished.

Over time, the constant tensions inherent in a voucher system are bound to have an insidious effect on even the most dedicated teachers. They will know that their livelihoods are at stake in every interaction with their pupils. Dissatisfied pupils (and parents) will have the choice of pulling out even if their dissatisfaction is in no way justified. There will be lots of shopping around for a good deal, not a good education. Grade inflation, already at a scandalous level in American education, will render teacher judgments meaningless. Teachers will be in the untenable position of being the direct employees of the very people they are expected to evaluate. *Caveat vendor* should not be the watchword of education.

This is not a call for the continuation of the tenure system for teachers. It is much more modest, and therefore should be much less controversial, than that. It is only a call for some continuity and independence in the professional lives of teachers so that they can do their jobs honestly. Vouchers will drive teachers into other careers, and the first teachers to go are likely to be those who value honesty the most.

CONTROLLING TEMPTATION

This brings us to another consideration of honesty or, rather, dishonesty. Voucher schools will be public schools insofar as they are to be funded publicly and open to the public. However, a salient feature of public schools historically is that they have also been nonprofit. Budgets are subject to public approval, including the budget items for employee salaries, and there are no stockholders who get dividends or capital gains. In short, the opportunities for public school officials to make a profit from their positions are severely limited, and in many cases can be exercised only through legal or ethical misconduct. Even then, the amount to be gained may be so small no one would take the risk of being detected and punished.

The voucher system will put public education in the for-profit category. People who run the schools will be allowed to earn as much as they can wring from the public. The thickness of their wallets will no longer be limited to the amount of their previous salaries. Public education will be transformed into just another capitalist venture. "Supply-side competition introduces strong incentives for providers to present superficial or inaccurate information on effectiveness, to package information to promote their product, and to protect as proprietary certain types of information that would be useful in making client choice" (Elmore, 1986, p. 34). If the recruiting brochures used by colleges have only a coincidental relationship to the actual colleges they are supposed to portray, imagine all the misleading fluff that will go into the promotional material of voucher schools.

A corrupt practices control board for the voucher system will have its hands full. Its first order of business will be to figure out what constitutes a corrupt practice in this strange new form of business. No doubt it will encounter, among other abuses, those that have been so rife among proprietary schools: inflated placement claims for graduates; inflated projected earnings for graduates; elastic definitions of success, such that someone who becomes a file clerk in a public defender's office is credited with a career in law enforcement. The prohibited practices will necessarily be defined in general terms, so there will be large gray areas where all kinds of shady practices can take place. The number of independent public schools will increase geometrically, and just conducting paper audits of each one of them could consume all the time of a well-staffed control board. On-site inspections would take place maybe once every five years. The off-years would be the stealing time.

What makes these prospects all the more horrendous is that a group of families who are especially presumed to benefit from a voucher system—the poor—are most likely to be the victims of its abuses. The poor will be sold a bill of goods by sleazy operators who prey on their ignorance. The poor may even be sold a bill of ideological and racial goods so that they end up rallying to the defense of the people who stole their money and their children's futures.

If the profits to be made from voucher schools are large enough, members of the control board may find themselves looking the other way in order to get their piece of the action. In other words, all the sickening travesties of corporate America and its regulatory bodies will be visited upon public education. For centuries now, the young have been shielded from that danger by a public school system that controlled corruption by controlling temptation. We shouldn't throw teachers and students to the wolves of the profit system.

FOR DISCUSSION

1 Randomly select any two public schools with the same grade levels and get information on their curricula, scheduling of class periods, average class size, and instructional methods. Compare the two schools for significant differences and similarities. Does it really matter which of the two schools a student attends?

2 If there are different kinds of schools (with different goals, teaching styles, governance structures, and organizational arrangements), should there be different kinds of teacher training programs in the colleges in order to prepare people to fit well into a particular kind of school?

3 Will a wide variety of school types force college admissions officers to rely much more heavily on standardized test results (for example, the Scholastic Aptitude Test), since they will have no clear sense of all the kinds of schools from which applicants are coming?

4 Following is a table that shows different ways by which choice can be built into a school system. There are four different ways of *financing* a choice system. There are also four ways of *selecting the students and teachers* who will be assigned to a school. And last, there are four ways of *deciding on the curriculum*. Which components do you think would make for the best choice system?

ILLUSTRATIVE CHOICE OPTIONS

School organization			
Local centralization	**School-site decentralization**	**Cooperative contracting**	**Regulated market**
Finance			
Payment to districts; centralized budgeting	Lump-sum payment to schools; decentralized budgeting	Contracting with consumer or producer cooperatives	Payment to clients
Attendance and staffing			
Central assignment with centrally administered exceptions	Centrally administered matching	School-level selection; minimum regulation	School-level selection; minimum regulation
Content			
Central rulemaking; decentralized implementation	School-level planning; decentralized rulemaking and implementation	Examination-driven	Consumer-driven

Adapted from R. F. Elmore, *Choice in Public Education,* East Lansing, Mich.: Center for Policy Research in Education, 1986, p. 20.

REFERENCES

Bastian, A., et al. (1985). *Choosing Equality: The Case for Democratic Schooling*. New York: New World Foundation.

Coons, J. E., and Sugarman, S. D. (1978). *Education by Choice: The Case for Family Control*. Berkeley: University of California Press.

Elmore, R. F. (1986). *Choice in Public Education*. Madison, Wis.: Center for Policy Research in Education.

Epperson v. State of Arkansas (1969). 393 U.S. 97.

Fantini, M. D. (1973). *Public Schools of Choice*. New York: Simon & Schuster.

Friedman, M., and Friedman, R. (1980). *Free to Choose*. New York: Harcourt Brace Jovanovich.

Ginzberg, E. (1972). "The Economics of the Voucher System." In *Educational Vouchers: Concepts and Controversies*, edited by G. LaNoue. New York: Teachers College Press.

Kearns, D. T., and Doyle, D. P. (1988). *Winning the Brain Race: A Bold Plan to Make Our Schools Competitive*. San Francisco: Institute for Contemporary Studies.

Kerchner, C. T. (1988). "Bureaucratic Entrepreneurship: The Implications of Choice for School Administration." *Educational Administration Quarterly*, **24**(4), 381–392.

Levin, H. (1980). "Educational Vouchers and Social Policy." In *School Finance Policies and Practice: The 1980's, A Decade of Conflict*, edited by J. Guthrie. Cambridge, Mass.: Ballinger.

National Governors Association. (1986). *Time for Results: The Governors 1991 Report on Education*. Washington, D.C.: National Governors Association.

Raywid, M. A. (1987). "The Dynamics of Success and Public Schools of Choice." *Equity and Choice*, **4**(1), 27–31.

Raywid, M. A., Tesconi, C. A., and Warren, D. R. (1984). *Pride and Promise: Schools of Excellence for All the People*. Washington, D.C.: American Educational Studies Association.

CHAPTER 3

PRIVATE SCHOOLS OR PUBLIC DEMOCRACY

POSITION 1
For Private Schools

MEETING THE CONSTITUTIONAL TEST

The U.S. Constitution has been interpreted by the U.S. Supreme Court as permitting, and even justifying, the existence of private schools. The very first amendment to the Constitution guarantees freedom of assembly and freedom of religion. Private schools get legal protection from the freedom of assembly clause, and parochial schools are protected by both clauses. In addition, the Tenth Amendment says that education is a power implicitly reserved to the states and not to the national government. Since education is a state power, it is noteworthy that none of the fifty states has ever prohibited the existence of private or parochial schools.

The U.S. Supreme Court ruled over sixty years ago that private and parochial schools are constitutional (*Pierce v. Hill Military Academy, Pierce v. Society of Sisters*, 1925). There have been numerous cases since then, all having to do with how much public support could be given to private and parochial schools and in what forms, but none challenging the fundamental right of these schools to exist.

Altogether, then, the legal shield around private schools is pretty much invincible.

PREVENTING A PUBLIC SCHOOL MONOPOLY

Saying that private schools are legal is like saying that tatoos are legal. It does not explain why they *should* be legal. Some things are legal simply because they do no harm, at least not to anyone but the individual who chooses freely to engage in them. Other things are both legal and socially *beneficial*. Private schools are in the second category; they serve the public interest.

Probably the most important way in which private schools serve us all, whether we are patrons of them or not, is by keeping the public schools from having a monopoly over education. If all education were public education, the public would have no choice but to take the only product being offered.

Imagine that Chrysler became the official auto manufacturer of the United States, with General Motors and Ford being forced to close and no imports allowed. You might still have some choice of cars, but it would be from a very limited selection, and in your price range it could mean choosing between a Horizon and its clone, an Omni. Some choice!

Competition does for schools what it does for cars. It makes them better at the same time that it makes them cheaper because the producer is under pressure to please the purchaser. An unhappy customer can do more than gripe; he or she can go elsewhere. If enough customers go elsewhere, the producer goes broke.

Producers of public education, if you will, do not go broke because compulsory attendance laws and school zoning ordinances guarantee them a steady flow of customers. As a result, the customers are at their mercy rather than their being at the service of the customers. The public education producers can therefore do a poor job with impunity. "In modern times, the diligence of public school teachers is more or less corrupted by the circumstances, which render them more or less independent of their success and reputation in their particular professions" (Smith [1776] 1976, pp. ii.300–301). This statement continues to be relevant more than 200 years after it was written.

Today the public schools already have too much of a monopoly. If a family cannot afford private schools, and if their religious convictions rule out parochial schools, the family has no choice but the public school in their neighborhood. The children will be assigned to classes in that school, and if a class turns out to be a very painful experience for a child the process of getting reassigned can be painful, too. One reassignment is about the most a school will tolerate. For an elementary school child, this can mean being stuck for a full year with a teacher who is truly an ogre in the child's eyes. Parents who are able and willing to make the financial sacrifice to send their child to a private school to protect that child's well-being have a legal and moral right to do so.

BEING CHILD-CENTERED

Private schools *have* to do a good job of education because they cost money. Public schools cost money, too, of course, but this money is raised from all the taxpayers, whether they use the schools or not, so the burden on an individual family is lightened by the contributions of other people, including people who themselves use private schools. Private schools therefore operate at a disadvantage with the public schools from the outset. They have neither a captive audience of students nor a guaranteed cash flow, and their patrons are expected to pay private school tuition on top of public school taxes. As a consequence of their handicapped position, private schools are like the Avis car rental agency up against the Hertz agency. They can stay in business only by trying harder than the public schools.

One of the ways that private schools try harder is by providing specialized environments to satisfy special needs of students. A private school may be a military academy, where a student's need for discipline and regimentation in an atmosphere of rugged physicality can be met. Or it may be in a serene, sylvan setting, with small classes and lots of personal attention for the student of delicate sensitivity. Or it may be in the middle of an urban ghetto and designed to rescue minority children from the ravages of uncaring public schools, as is the St. Thomas Community School in Harlem (Taylor, 1981). The possibilities are limited only by the needs of children and the imaginations of educators.

The reason these possibilities can be realized in private schools is that private schools are not part of large bureaucracies in which possibilities are delimited by a fetish for prescriptiveness, uniformity and standardization (Chubb, 1988; Wise, 1979). Private schools tend to be small, independent enterprises organized so loosely that they have the flexibility to be responsive to student needs. Public schools, on the other hand, expect—indeed, insist—that students have the flexibility to adapt to *their* needs. Private schools step to the beat of the students; public schools require that students march to their tune.

FOSTERING INTELLECTUAL DIVERSITY

It is not just the different kinds of school *climate* that make private schools a treasured resource of America. Private schools add ingredients to the intellectual stew of American education that make it much more nutritional and flavorful. Academically elite private schools like St. John's in Maryland ensure that the great books of western civilization will be read and understood by at least a small proportion of American youth. These classics, with all their potential for humanizing us and deepening our perspectives (Bloom, 1987), are fast becoming unknown to public school students, who are pampered along on the intellectual pablum of easy literature anthologies and history survey texts.

The intellectual diversity provided by private schools can mean *ideological* diversity as well. An African-American school in a ghetto community obviously does not present to its students the world view that permeates the public schools, including public schools in the ghetto. Harsh reality may be exaggerated by the African-American school, but it is not glossed over. And the children in these schools acquire a racial pride and a self-confidence that enable them to stand tall in a racist society and not be beaten down by it.

At the other end of the private school spectrum, in social class as well as ethnic terms, is the prep school for children of affluent white Anglo-Saxon Protestant families. Here the ideology is one of a natural aristocracy of privilege and civic leadership for the American gentry. This ideology is the opposite of the doctrinaire egalitarianism that is the religion of the public schools. The hold it still has in a few private schools in America is a last bulwark against stultifying groupthink. It and the prep schools in which it is propagated should be cherished for that reason alone. We glorify Soviet dissenters from communist ideology and wonder why the Soviet authorities get so uptight about them. We even wonder why the American authorities become so unglued by dissenters from capitalist ideology. And yet the notion of a natural aristocracy of talent and breeding is one that pretty much unnerves the rest of us, and one which we don't mind having banned from the "free" marketplace of ideas. Maybe we're not so different from the Soviet authorities, after all.

THE INADEQUACY OF EDUCATION VOUCHERS

It is currently being argued that diversity can be expanded among the public schools by giving parents a choice of the school their children will attend. Magnet schools and open enrollment plans are supposed to provide choice and thereby foster diversity. Vouchers which parents can use to pay for the education of their children at any school are another device to bring about choice and diversity. These schemes are all inadequate for matching the amount of diversity that is now provided by private schools, and the voucher scheme could actually reduce this diversity.

Public schools are severely constrained in the degree of diversity they can provide by the fact that they are publicly controlled. That means they are controlled by politicians who seek a consensus kind of education. The public schools have to avoid offending people because they are parts of large-scale enterprises requiring widespread public acceptance. "The particular samenesses which characterize public education are chosen less often for their perceived educational advantage to the child than for other reasons—particularly for their unobtrusive harmony with majoritarian social and political standards" (Coons and Sugarman, 1978, p. 43). The parameters within which the public schools operate are simply tighter than for private schools.

This is true not just within public school districts but throughout entire states, and increasingly so. States have always had legal authority over the public schools, but in past years they were content to delegate most of it to local school districts and to have only a few statewide mandates. Not so of late. "The most striking feature of state/local relations in the last 10 years has been the continued growth in state control over education" (Kirst, 1988, p. 75). The person who said this should know, since he was president of the California State Board of Education. As states have assumed more financial responsibility for the public schools, they have insisted on more accountability from them. That has meant many more state-imposed curriculum requirements and state testing programs. Public schools are being homogenized, not diversified, by the states.

Vouchers will therefore give people somewhat more choice, but within a system where the total choice is being shrunk by the state. If private schools are allowed to accept public vouchers, and if they do so as a way of staying solvent, they will come more directly under state control, and suffer a host of infringements on their curricular freedom.

GIVING THE PUBLIC SCHOOLS SOMETHING TO AIM FOR

Private schools and public schools are different, to be sure; otherwise, there would be no demand for private schools. But as the French say, *Vive la différence*. We can revert to the example of car manufacturing to illustrate why the difference is beneficial to both sets of schools, and thus to all of us.

Recently the Ford Motor Company came up with a new aerodynamically styled car, the Taurus (or Sable, as it is called in the Mercury division of Ford). The car won rave reviews and has earned millions of dollars for Ford. Its positive effect on Ford was a negative effect on General Motors and Chrysler, which suffered losses in their share of the market. However, a good idea is a good idea, and it cannot be patented in all its particulars. So, General Motors and Chrysler, having gotten a good sense from Ford of what the car-buying public wanted, have been trying ever since to go Ford one better. Even Ford has been imitating itself by restyling its other cars to more closely resemble the Taurus.

The point is that progress consists of building on good ideas. If you wish to think of this as stealing good ideas, so be it. But the public gets what it wants, which is the essence of economic democracy. Private schools promote *educational* democracy, not just by giving people a choice, but by generating alternatives that are so popular the public schools adapt them (or just plain *adopt* them) and make them available to children generally.

THE LIGHTHOUSE EFFECT

In their looser settings, private schools can be more experimental than public schools. It is almost as though they serve as the research labs for the public schools. The term commonly used in educational circles is "lighthouse," with good private schools acting as lighthouses to show the way for the lumbering supertankers that are the public schools. Private schools perform this useful service to the public schools free of charge.

Recently James Coleman, a famous American sociologist, along with some of his colleagues, completed a study which showed that private schools get better results than public schools in terms of students' academic achievement. This, Coleman argued, is true even when the private schools are working with the same kinds of kids as the public schools with whom they are being compared. Coleman speculated that the reason for the private schools' better results is that they have a more cohesive culture, are more demanding, and have more parental support than do the public schools (Coleman, Hoffer, and Kilgore, 1981; Hoffer, Greeley, and Coleman, 1987). Chubb and Moe (1986) have illustrated how these conditions are facilitated by the autonomy and independence of private schools. Critics have responded that it is unfair to compare public and private schools at all, given the much different set of circumstances in which the public schools have to operate. The critics have also pointed out a slew of methodological problems with the Coleman study (Haertel, James, and Levin, 1987). However, private schools may be demonstrating to the public schools that it is time to stop complaining about the surrounding circumstances and work directly on them in order to provide more effective education. If you can't get good results in the present circumstances, change the circumstances to make them more like the ones in which private schools operate.

SECURING A RIGHT FOR US ALL

It is true that private schools exist only for those who can afford them or who can get the relatively rare scholarship. Even parochial schools in inner cities have tuition charges that are beyond the means of many families. However, there are many rights which Americans enjoy but which cannot be exercised by everyone at every moment. To deny a right to others because you cannot take advantage of it right now is to deny that right to yourself in more propitious circumstances. Rights are not just immediate opportunities; they are hopes for the future. Many students in private schools today are the children of parents who themselves were consigned by circumstance to public school educations. That these parents can now offer their children something better than they had is the American dream come true.

One form of private education that exists even for poor families is home schooling. If a family can demonstrate its ability to educate its children adequately in the basics demanded by the public schools the children would otherwise have to attend, then the family can get permission to educate its children at home. Once the public school basics have been met, the family is free to educate its children as it thinks best. Home schooling offers some real relief from the tyranny of the majority in public schools. It is a protection not only for eccentrics but for anyone who would spare his or her child the public school indoctrination of the times.

ADVANTAGES TO THE POOR

It might seem strange to suggest that private schools help the poor who cannot afford to use them. But in addition to the role they play in inspiring the poor to work harder, private schools help in more direct ways.

Many private schools have scholarships for poor but promising students. These scholarships are paid for from the tuition of the affluent students and special bequests from their families and alumni. A splendid example of this is All Children's House in Manhattan, a nursery school where parents who can afford it pay $7,200 in tuition so that children from welfare hotels can also attend the school (Lee, 1989). The private schools that are also boarding schools can fairly be said to rescue poor youth from streets of crime.

Private schools that remain within the city (and large cities have many exclusive private schools) keep affluent families from fleeing to the suburbs. These families maintain their expensive city homes and pay heavy property taxes which are used to support the public schools (Glazer, 1983, p. 95). "There can be no doubt that the availability of nonpublic schools has been a major factor that has kept many middle- and upper-income families from leaving central cities" (Reischauer and Hartman, 1973, p. 118).

The best private schools graduate exceptionally well educated young people who go on to leadership positions in industry and government. The education which has enabled them to assume these leadership roles has equipped them for making positive contributions to American life. They increase the gross national product and the revenue available to the government for social programs; they design the programs; they create jobs so that others have gainful employment and self-respect.

The value of private schools to all of us has been acknowledged in the numerous court decisions permitting public support of private schools. This aid is used to pay for myriad items: money for textbooks, transportation, special education teachers, diagnostic services, nutrition programs, and health services, to name only a few. It is clear that the American public is willing to support the work of the private schools.

KEEPING AMERICA FREE

It may seem overweening and transparently self-serving for private schools to claim that they keep America free. But stop and think about it. The public schools have for some time now been subjected to increasing central control by the state. Many people wish to see further *federal* control, and elsewhere in this book you can read about the movement to create a national cultural literacy program for all schools. As public education becomes more centrally controlled, the prospects for totalitarian brainwashing increase. This brainwashing would hardly be of the vulgar, brute form we associate with dictatorships, but precisely because it would be so much more subtle, it would be more insidious. It could be a means by which the political party in power shrewdly manipulates attitudes to keep itself from being voted out of office. Textbooks might be required to emphasize the political and cultural values of the incumbent political party. Teachers might come to understand that their chances for tenure and promotion were contingent on how well they echoed the party line. Students would realize that they were being graded on the same basis.

Increasingly, these conditions exist among the public schools. However, with the remnants of local control, the mindset of School District A can still be balanced by that of District B. As the public schools become further centralized, the only balancing force will be the private schools. Thus, trends already well under way make private schools more indispensable to America than they have ever been.

POSITION 2
Against Private Schools

UNDOING THE UNNECESSARY

Private schools would be defensible if they were necessary. They're not, and the argument that they give us something we can't get any other way is a smokescreen. No matter how often this argument is repeated and how thick the smoke gets, it takes only one good gust of common sense to clear the air.

The private school argument really consists of fashioning a false image of the public schools. Public schools are portrayed as rigid and of deadening sameness across America. They are supposed to be the big gray blob of American education, with the private schools providing the only color and twinkle. Public schools were never this unvariegated, and in recent years especially they have burst forth in a profusion of forms.

Public schools have been under government pressure to integrate their student bodies racially, which also means socioeconomically. One of the most successful approaches the public schools have devised for accomplishing this is the "magnet" or "theme" school. Instead of public school students all having to choose the same kind of mass model school, which is no choice at all, they are being given more and more models from which to select. Indeed, the magnet school approach has been so successful that it is being used in school districts that are under no pressure to integrate.

A magnet school might have as its theme marine studies. This is the actual theme of a magnet school (the Maritime School) in the Spanish Harlem section of New York City (Fliegel, 1989, p. 101). The East River serves as a natural laboratory for the students, and it is a place where they play all the time anyway. This and other magnet schools in East Harlem are so popular that parents outside the district have their children bussed to school in East Harlem (Esposito, 1988, p. 74). Performing arts is a popular theme for a magnet school, and one which has been made famous by the movie and TV series *Fame*. More traditional themes are college prep and vocational studies. The themes that are used to attract students are potentially limitless, and local people can create the schools that reflect the needs and interests of their community and its kids. The kids can be ones who are in trouble. California has eighteen Partnership Academies for potential dropouts. In addition to their teachers in school, these kids study with people in industry in preparation for taking above-entry-level jobs in industry (Esposito, 1988, p. 36).

When magnet schools in all their variety are added to the different curriculum tracks that public high schools have had for years, the diversity within the public school sector of American education is truly impressive, and growing. These many different curricular emphases also mean many different social climates among and within the public schools. Enriching the mix even more is the fact that some public schools are virtually private schools due to the affluence and exclusiveness of the communities in which they are located. Certainly no one would ever confuse New Trier High School in Winnetka, Illinois, with Central High School in Newark, New Jersey!

As all of this suggests, the good that private schools do can be and is being done in the public schools. If it is not being done to the extent that private school advocates would like, that is merely a matter of expanding further on something already well under way. Parochial schools would take exception to this statement by noting that the public schools can never be places of religious indoctrination. However true that may be, it does not follow that religious indoctrination must take place in an *academic* school. Parents who desire to have their children indoctrinated into some religion can arrange to have this done in other ways than in a parochial school. There can be Sunday schools or after-school religious instruction or Bible camps, for example. But math, science, English, social studies, foreign languages, vocational subjects, and so on can all be learned just as well, if not better, in a public school. They are not parochial subjects.

In this last respect, it should be noted that there are many religious groups which oppose public aid for parochial schools. Baptist, Disciples of Christ, Jewish, Methodist, and Unitarian groups have all opposed such aid on the basis that it violates the constitutional separation between church and state (Hollings, 1981, p. 89; Reischauer and Hartman, 1973, p. 113). For "state" one can read "secular." The secular subjects can be taught in secular, i.e., state, institutions. There is no reason at all why math or science, for example, should be taught in a religious setting. They are nonsectarian subjects, and if taught otherwise they cease to be math or science and become theology.

UNIFYING US AS A PEOPLE

Despite their increasing diversity, the public schools remain a unifying force for America. Indeed, the diversity itself is a unifying force because it draws together students of different backgrounds into the same school. Curricular diversity across schools has meant diverse student populations within schools. Instead of students on one side of town having only their neighborhood school to attend, they can now choose to go across town to a school that really interests them and where they'll meet kids from all sides of town. If America is a melting pot where people of different ethnic and economic origins are brought together, the public school is the place where the fire burns brightest.

The reason the public school is uniquely suited to this democratizing role is that it is *free*. The poor can afford the public schools. Moreover, they are compelled to attend them under state compulsory attendance laws. It is only the public schools, then, that *guarantee* the inclusion of the poor, giving them the benefit of socializing with the nonpoor. The benefit is not to the poor alone, since they have lessons to offer those with whom they socialize. The single most important lesson to be learned by all in the public schools is tolerance. It is a lesson that is learned most lastingly through daily interaction with people of different backgrounds. Only public schools are designed to impart this lesson through direct experience, which is to say with genuinely felt meaning.

Tolerance is a necessary virtue for democracy, but it is a minimal one. To their great and sole credit, the public schools do more than foster tolerance; they engender an appreciation for our common purpose as a people. Tolerance of difference is fine and essential, but awareness of mutuality elevates democracy above its tensions to a plane of harmony. In private schools, only book reading and teacher talk can attempt to convey the message of mutuality. Alas, this message is subverted by the very nature of the private school: *private*, not mutual.

The appreciation of common purpose that the public schools engender does not mean unanimity on ways of achieving that purpose. On the latter point one can expect that there will be robust exchanges of ideas, given the heterogeneity of public schools. The homogeneous environments of the private schools make it difficult to stimulate such debate except in very artificial ways. Public school education thus prepares students better for the hurly-burly of public controversy that they will encounter as adults. The public schools are "common" schools.

> The term "common school" has a proud history and . . . intent which is still valid. We are more than individuals. Each of us is a member of many publics. Sooner or later, we must learn how to communicate with those publics as we face intimate personal problems and urgent social concerns. Self-contained educational systems, whether they are religious, economic, racial, geographical, forfeit the necessary function of the "common" school. (Kniker, quoted in Levine and Havighurst, 1989, p. 490)

Public school students come to know firsthand more than different points of view on an issue; they witness the authentic passions with which those points of view are held.

EQUALIZING OPPORTUNITY

The patrons of private schools have motivations which they may be loath to admit even to themselves. They may tell you that they find the college prep program of study, the discipline, the warmth, the extracurricular activities, the tough competitiveness, the beauty of the campus, or the striking blue blazers with crests to be the reason for having their children attend private schools. And they may be telling a partial truth. But there is another truth that they often fail to mention. They use the private schools as a way of buying for their children advantages which are denied to other children, and which give their children a head start over other children in life's race. The advantage may be small classes, where their children get lots of personal attention to keep them from falling behind and dropping out. It may be very expensive extracurricular activities, such as horsemanship and yachting. Or it may be enriched (and extravagant) academic programs, such as excursions to Europe and Asia.

In many cases, however, the advantage that is deliberately sought and bought is that of "contacts." Parents purchase their children a place in the "right" school so that they will be placed with the "right" peers. The "right" peers, of course, are those who have parents with wealth and power, and who will be able to do great favors for their friends throughout life. What the parents are buying, then, is not just an in to the private school but also an in to the higher social strata of society. What separates those who attend exclusive private schools from those who do not is not talent or intelligence, but parents with money who wish to position their children for more of the same.

This buying of privilege is a form of robbery. It robs other children of equal opportunity. The costlier the crime for the perpetrator, the greater the amount of privilege being bought and, conversely, the amount of opportunity being denied. Tuition and fees at prep schools nationwide now average more than $10,000 a year. At the Peddie School in New Jersey, tuition is $8100, or $12,900 if the student boards (van Tassel, 1988). That's not out of line with other elite private schools, and it's as much as many parents save for years for *college* education. It's certainly a large outlay of money, and it makes one doubt that the only return expected on that kind of investment is smaller class size or more personal attention. Getting their children into the right circles is probably uppermost in the minds of parents who pay such large sums. Children whose parents cannot afford this are denied access to those circles and, however well they may do in their large impersonal public schools, they will never have the advantage of already being connected intimately to power when they start out on their careers.

A classic tome from which the well-to-do draw support for this unequal situation is Friedrich Hayek's *The Road to Serfdom*. The book is an extended argument for free enterprise and the inequalities it generates across generations. Thus, the following:

> Although under competition the probability that a man who starts poor will reach great wealth is much smaller than is true for the man who has inherited property, it is not only possible for the former, but the competitive system is the only one where it depends solely on him and not on the favors of the mighty. (1944, p. 102)

If the book is a classic, this quote from it is a classic non sequitur. In the first part of the quote, the author acknowledges the powerful role of property inheritance in determining one's station in life, but in the second part he says that one's station depends "solely on him and not on the favors of the mighty." Clearly, if one attends an elite private school it is because of the mighty—parents who are mighty rich.

PUBLIC AID FOR PRIVATE SCHOOLS

It is the height of presumption for people who can afford to send their children to private schools to ask for help from people who cannot. That is precisely what is sought when private school parents demand public assistance in the form of vouchers or tuition tax credits for sending their children to private schools. It is akin to demanding public aid toward the purchase of a Mercedes Benz, knowing that the cost to the government will have to be borne by the poor slobs who ride the subway.

The wealthy are ordinarily opposed to proposals for redistributing the wealth in America on a more equal basis. Vouchers and tuition tax credits are examples of their willingness to have the wealth redistributed on a less equal basis. Tuition tax credits would do this even more than vouchers, since only people who can afford to pay tuition in the first place would get the credit. The most likely beneficiaries would be whites with high incomes (Catterall, 1983, p. 149).

The most recent Gallup poll on this subject shows that 27 percent of the respondents approve of tax money being spent on private schools, whereas 40 percent approve of this for parochial schools (Gallup, 1986). The public appears to have some appreciation for the fact that parochial schools generally serve families who are less well off than those who use private schools that are not religiously based. The public is willing to adjust public aid on the basis of need, even where there is a constitutional question of church-state separation. Obviously, 73 percent of the public do not recognize private schools as being in need of public charity, and 60 percent feel that way about parochial schools. Their response is justified by the facts.

> . . . nonpublic school enrollments are drawn from higher-income groups than public school enrollments, and white families are more likely than some minority groups to send their children to nonpublic schools. Thus, if the current balance of enrollments remained the same after public support for private schools was increased, the increased support would probably benefit a whiter, wealthier group of families than the public schools serve. (Muller, 1983, pp. 53–54)

ELIMINATING REFUGES FOR THE RICH

As long as there are private schools, the rich will be able to avoid public problems. One of the most persisting public problems is the state of the public schools. The rich, with their disproportionate share of America's wealth and power, are better situated than other people to help in solving the problems of public education. Whether they will do so is largely a matter of whether they, through their children, experience public education themselves. They cannot be expected to have a sense of urgency about public education if it is something that happens only to other people's children. Indeed, they might even take some secret satisfaction in the fact that their own children's competitive edge gets extended by each decline in the public schools.

> Why should we be concerned about erosion of support for the public schools? Why should it bother us if there appears to be a trend toward a sharp division of society, in which the children of the affluent attend private schools, and the public school system exists for the poor and black? . . . The answer to these questions lies in the recognition—the realization that public education has been the leavening agent by

which our multi-ethnic, multi-racial society has been able to rise and become a whole loaf.

It is *because* we had public schools, which most children attended, that we were able to assimilate so rapidly the great influx of immigrants. . . .

It is largely *because* we had public schools, in which children from the most diverse of backgrounds learned to live and work together at an early age, that we have been able to maintain social harmony in such a heterogeneous conglomerate of people. (Federal Judge Thomas Wiseman, quoted in Pride and Woodard, 1985, p. 251)

The children of the rich, regardless of the schools they attend, will grow up able to exercise undue influence in civic affairs as part of their patrimony. If they attend public schools they will acquire a deeper sensitivity to the dilemmas in which public schools are perennially ensnared. They should also contract some empathy for less fortunate classmates, and some understanding of the role that social conditions play in the fate of those classmates.

Noblesse oblige is the French way of saying the obligations of nobility. The "nobility" of the United States are the rich, and if they arrogate unto themselves special responsibility for the condition of society, then they certainly have a responsibility not to duck the less pleasant aspects of that condition. If they can hide out and shelter themselves from the vicissitudes that befall the rest of us, their aspiration will not be to improve society for *all* of us but rather to perpetuate conditions that favor them at our expense. Private schools are sanctuaries for the rich.

REOPENING THE CONSTITUTIONAL ISSUE

Private schools are so socially deleterious that it is time to rethink their constitutionality. The last time the U.S. Supreme Court addressed the issue directly was in 1925, a long time ago. Much has happened since, and the Court has issued several decisions around which a legal case against private schools can be built.

For example, in 1925 education was not considered to be a fundamental right of Americans. However, in 1954 the Court wrote:

Today, education is perhaps the most important function of state and local governments. Compulsory school attendance laws and the great expenditures for education both demonstrate our recognition of the importance of education to our democratic society. It is required in the performance of our most basic public responsibilities, even service in the armed forces. It is the very foundation of good citizenship. Today it is a principal instrument in awakening the child to cultural values, in preparing him for later professional training, and in helping him to adjust normally to his environment. In these days, it is doubtful that any child may reasonably be expected to succeed in life if he is denied the opportunity of an education. (*Brown v. Board of Education of Topeka,* 1954)

The Court has also grown more suspicious of wealth as a basis for allotting or withholding rights. "We should say now, and in no uncertain terms, that a man's mere property status, without more, cannot be used by a state to test, qualify, or limit his rights as a citizen of the United States. 'Indigence' in itself is neither a source of rights nor a basis for denying them'' (*Edwards v. California*, 1941).

Moreover, the Court requires that where a practice is constitutionally suspect the defendant has to demonstrate that society has a ''compelling interest'' in continuing the practice. The continuation of private schools is not something in which the public, most of whom don't and never did attend private schools, has a compelling interest. The benefits which private schools are alleged to confer on society are more than offset by these schools' inherent unfairness.

Lastly, the Court has said that under the Fourteenth Amendment to the Constitution, education for the many cannot be drastically inferior to education for the few. ''The opportunity of an education . . . where the state has undertaken to provide it, is a right which must be made available to all on equal terms'' (*Brown v. Board of Education of Topeka*, 1954). By allowing private schools, states have effectively created the condition which the Court says is unconstitutional.

The current Supreme Court is too conservative to act on these arguments (and its own precedents) and make America a more just nation. Its own members are products of private schools and colleges. But there are tides in the affairs of the Court, and there is sure to be an egalitarian tide in the future that will wash away the inequality of America's dual school system.

FOR DISCUSSION

1 Senator Moynihan (D., N.Y.) has proposed that since the federal government now provides financial aid to needy students who attend private (including parochial) colleges, and since this is constitutionally acceptable, there is no good reason for denying this help to elementary and secondary students. How convincing is Moynihan's logic?

2 In the *Nyquist* case (413 U.S. 756 [1973]), the U.S. Supreme Court ruled that tax exemptions for parents who send their children to parochial schools were unconstitutional because they amounted to state support of religion. However, in the *Walz* case (397 U.S. 664 [1970]), the Court said that religious organizations were themselves entitled to tax exemptions. Can you reconcile this seeming contradiction in the Court's reasoning? If not, which ruling makes more sense to you?

3 Comparing public and private schools in terms of their effectiveness is said to be like comparing apples and onions: there are crucial differences which make a fair comparison impossible. What are the most crucial differences you can think of, and is there any way to make a fair comparison even with these differences?

4 Following is a list of modern industrial societies with the percent of their students who attend private schools. How do you explain the fact that the percent for most of these countries is so much higher than in the United States?

| | Percent private | |
	Primary	Secondary
Australia	10	26
Belgium:		
Flemish	63	72
French	32	48
England and Wales	5	8
France	15	21
Germany	2	9
Ireland	98	91
Italy	8	7
Japan	1	15
Netherlands	69	72
New Zealand	10	12
Sweden	1	2
USA	18	10

Adapted from E. James, "The Public/Private Division of Responsibility for Education: An International Comparison," in *Comparing Public and Private Schools*, vol. 1, edited by T. James and H. Levin, New York: Falmer, 1988, p. 96.

REFERENCES

Bloom, A. (1987). *The Closing of the American Mind: How Higher Education Has Failed Democracy and Impoverished the Souls of Today's Students*. New York: Simon & Schuster.

Brown v. Board of Education of Topeka, Kansas (1954). 347 U.S. 483.

Catterall, J. S. (1983). "Tuition Tax Credits: Issues of Equity." In *Public Dollars for Private Schools: The Case for Tuition Tax Credits*, edited by T. James and H. M. Levin. Philadelphia: Temple University Press.

Chubb, J. E. (1988). "To Revive Schools, Dump Bureaucrats." *The New York Times*, December 9, p. A–35.

Chubb, J. E., and Moe, T. M. (1986). *Politics, Markets and the Organization of Schools*. Washington, D.C.: The Brookings Institution.

Coleman, J. S., Hoffer, T., and Kilgore, S. (1981). *Public Private Schools*. Washington, D.C.: National Center for Education Statistics.

Coons, J. E., and Sugarman, S. D. (1978). *Education by Choice: The Case of Family Control*. Berkeley: University of California Press.

Edwards v. California (1941). 314 U.S. 160.

Esposito, F. (1988). *Public School Choice: National Trends and Initiatives*. Trenton, N.J.: New Jersey State Department of Education.

Fliegel, S. (1989). "Parental Choice in East Harlem Schools." In *Public Schools by Choice*, edited by J. Nathan. St. Paul, Minn.: The Institute for Learning and Teaching.

Gallup, A. M. (1986). "The 18th Annual Gallup Poll of the Public's Attitudes Toward the Public Schools." *The Gallup Report* **252**, 11–26.

Glazer, N. (1983). "The Future Under Tax Credits." In *Public Dollars for Private Schools: The Case for Tuition Tax Credits*, edited by T. James and H. M. Levin. Philadelphia: Temple University Press.

Haertel, E. H., James, T., and Levin, H. M., eds. (1987). *Comparing Public and Private Schools*, vol. 2: *School Achievement*. New York: Falmer.

Hayek, F. A. (1944). *The Road to Serfdom*. Chicago: University of Chicago Press.

Hoffer, T., Greeley, A. M., and Coleman, J. S. (1987). "Catholic High School Effects on Achievement Growth." In *Comparing Public and Private Schools*, vol. 2: *School Achievement*, edited by E. H. Haertel, T. James, and H. M. Levin. New York: Falmer.

Hollings, E. F. (1981). "The Case Against Tuition Tax Credits." In *Private Schools and the Public Good: Policy Alternatives for the Eighties*, edited by E. M. Gaffney. Notre Dame, Ind.: University of Notre Dame Press.

Kirst, M. W. (1988). "Who Should Control Our Schools?" *Issues '88*. Special edition of *NEA Today*, January, pp. 74–79.

Lee, F. R. (1989). "Poor and Rich Children Join in Novel Day-Care Center." *The New York Times*, January 23, pp. B1, B4.

Levine, D. U., and Havighurst, R. J. (1989). *Society and Education*. Boston: Allyn and Bacon.

Muller, C. B. (1983). "The Social and Political Consequences of Increased Public Support for Private Schools." In *Public Dollars for Private Schools: The Case for Tuition Tax Credits*, edited by T. James and H. M. Levin. Philadelphia: Temple University Press.

Pierce v. Hill Military Academy, Pierce v. Society of Sisters (1925). 268 U.S. 510.

Pride, C. A., and Woodard, D. (1985). *The Burden of Busing*. Knoxville, Tenn.: University of Tennessee Press.

Reischauer, R. D., and Hartman, R. W. (1973). *Reforming School Finance*. Washington, D.C.: The Brookings Institution.

Smith, A. [1776] (1976). *The Wealth of Nations*. Edited by Edwin Cannan. Chicago: University of Chicago Press.

Taylor, B. (1981). "The St. Thomas Community School: A Harlem Success Story." In *Private Schools and the Public Good: Policy Alternatives for the Eighties*, edited by E. M. Gaffney. Notre Dame, Ind.: University of Notre Dame Press.

van Tassel, P. (1988). "Keeping the Peddie School's Aims Alive." *The New York Times*, December 11, p. NJ-3.

Wise, A. E. (1979). *Legislated Learning: The Bureaucratization of the American Classroom*. Berkeley: University of California Press.

CHAPTER 4

EQUITY OR DISPARITY IN SCHOOL FINANCE

POSITION 1
For Equity in School Finance

GAUGING THE GAP

The American system of free public education is touted as being the great equalizer of opportunity. It exists for all children regardless of their parents' station in life. In virtually every state, the child and the parents have no choice but to take advantage of this educational opportunity, since school attendance is required by law up to a certain age, usually 16. Moreover, the guarantee of a public school education is good for several years beyond the school-leaving age. Because the opportunity is compulsory and because the guarantee extends over so many years, the United States can justly pride itself on giving all its children an education, even those who are residents only and not citizens.

This educational birthright for America's youth is a prize worth many different dollar amounts, however. For the child in an affluent suburb, it can be worth about $9,000 a year, the amount actually spent on his or her education in the local public school. For a child in a large city or a rural area, the prize can be worth only half that amount, or $4,500. The $4,500 difference multiplied over the twelve years of school comes to $54,000 more education for the suburban child than for his urban or rural counterpart, not counting inflation or interest. All American youth are guaranteed an educational opportunity, but there is no guarantee that the opportunity will be equal for all, and in reality it is quite unequal. No wonder that James Conant, a former president of Harvard University, was moved to write that "the contrast in money available to schools in a wealthy suburb and schools in a large city jolts one's notion of the meaning of equality of opportunity'' (Conant, 1961, pp. 2–3). What appalled Conant almost thirty years ago is appalling still.

The inequality is even more pronounced than the above numbers indicate. The child in the plush suburb is likely to come to school already advantaged educationally to a much greater degree than the urban or rural child. The suburban child may have traveled abroad with his or her parents even before entering first grade, and foreign travel may be part of every summer vacation. The child may have been "prepped" for first grade by attendance at an expensive nursery school. Books, including a variety of costly and up-to-date reference works, may abound in the child's house. The child's parents are likely to be proficient readers. Educational toys will probably be plentiful. A personal computer is becoming a standard possession of children in suburbia. Summer camps which feature specialized educational programs are an annual rite of many suburban kids. The very conversations that a suburban child has with his or her well-educated parents are intellectually enriching. Add to all this the robust good health that proper nutrition and medical attention can assure. "There is no mystery about it: the child who is familiar with books, ideas, conversation—the ways and means of the intellectual life—before he begins consciously to think, has a marked advantage. He is at home in the House of Intellect just as the stableboy is at home among horses or the child of actors on the stage" (Barzun, 1959, p. 142).

Contrast this bountiful life with the austere life of an inner-city child. The contrast reveals starkly an accumulation of privations for the inner-city child. No foreign travel and perhaps not even intra-city travel. There are adolescents who have grown up in Brooklyn, for example, who have never been to Manhattan. Funding for Head Start programs has been drastically reduced in recent years, so only a small proportion of children eligible for this poor person's nursery school actually get it. No books other than comic books, and a few magazines of the trashier sort left lying around by adults. A personal computer is as removed from possibility as a private spaceship. Maybe a charity summer camp like one sponsored by the Fresh Air Fund or the St. Vincent dePaul Society. Conversations with adults whose use of English puts the child at a *disadvantage* in school. Few conversations with adults at all, and these of a very abrupt nature, because the only permanent adult in the home is a badly harried mother trying to hold her life together. A "home" that may be a room in a welfare hotel (Kozol, 1988). The television set as constant companion and purveyor of distorted reality and false hopes. A diet of junk food or no food, and the perfunctory medical care that one gets in a municipal hospital emergency room when something really serious happens. Serious injuries which never get reported or treated because they are the result of child abuse, including sexual abuse.

Thus, the poor require more than the rich when they get to school because they have so much less at home. They come to school undereducated in the things that schools consider important, so they need *compensatory* education to be brought to the same starting line as the rich. What happens, instead, is that the disadvantage which the poor bring to school is aggravated by the underfunding of their formal education, whereas the advantage of the rich gets augmented by the generous funding for their schooling. In short, the American system of education uses public money to favor the already favored. It is the great *disequalizer* of opportunity.

UNDERSTANDING THE CAUSE

Before getting specific about the educational advantages that taxpayer money can buy in schools, it would be well to explain why such glaring inequality exists between the schools of the rich and poor. The answer, in two words, is *local control.* To the extent that rich communities pay for their own schools and poor communities pay for theirs, there will be inequality. The rich can afford to pay more, so they have better schools. State governments try to smooth over the gaps by giving more state money to the poor schools than to the rich ones. But except for the state of Hawaii, where all public school funding is by the state government, the gap between rich and poor schools is never closed completely. In many states it is a yawning chasm.

You should be able to get from the education officials in your state a break-down of how much is spent per pupil in each of the school districts in the state, including the one where you went to school. For example, in 1984 New York City spent an average of $3,639 per pupil. This was less than the amount spent in *any* of the school districts immediately to the north in suburban Westchester County, where the county average was $5,338, and where many districts spent more than $6,000 per pupil (New York State Education Department, 1984, pp. 167, 175, 177). In 1987 in New Jersey, the city of Camden spent $3,098 per pupil; Newark spent $3,789; and Jersey City spent $3,834. The average for the entire state was $4,189, and twenty-three suburban districts were spending more than $6,000, not including the high-cost vocational schools (New Jersey Education Association, 1988, pp. 10–24). "We must also take note of the fact that children from rich families stay in school longer than children from poor families. When we take this into account, we estimate that America spends about twice as much on the children of the rich as the children of the poor" (Jencks et al., 1972, p. 27). Information such as this for your state may cause you to realize that you yourself have already been denied an equal educational opportunity compared to other young people in the state. Of course, the information could reveal that the inequality was in your favor compared to most of your state peers.

Local control is what explains the inequality in American education. It does not, however, explain the continuing American allegiance to educational inequality. That explanation is to be found in the unequal power arrangements between rich and poor.

We must recognize the ways in which powerful groups are able to arrange better opportunities for their children, despite the rhetoric of standard and therefore equal education. Families with the economic and political power to give their children an advantage are unlikely to relinquish that advantage willingly. Most people with influence over public education have at least some measure of such an advantage and are surrounded by associates who share it as well. They are likely to share a perspective that makes the maintenance of separate schools with superior human and material resources for the white middle class seem natural and necessary. Their vested interests are served by muting the recognition of differences in the opportunities offered by schools accessible to children of different races and social classes. (Metz, 1988, p. 60)

The rich have reason to rig the system in their favor. "Significant changes toward a more equal educational system . . . would be associated with equally significant changes in the statistical relationship between education and the distribution of economic rewards. . . . unequal schooling perpetuates a structure of economic inequality which originates outside the school system" (Bowles and Gintis, 1976, p. 248).

SPECIFYING WHAT THE GAP MEANS

There are people who say that money cannot buy a good education. Let's see what it is that money can buy. You get some idea of this even before entering a school building. The exterior of the building tells you whether the building is new, attractively designed, and in good repair, or old, fortresslike, and ramshackle. Many old city school buildings are not only ugly; they are in such disrepair as to be safety hazards. "Many schools have rundown physical facilities that are, in some cases, safety and health hazards. . . . If this sample of schools is any indication, the physical plants of many of the nation's urban schools need substantial rehabilitation and modernization" (Ford Foundation, 1984, p. 68). However, it costs so much to renovate old buildings or replace them with new buildings that they are made to do year after year. Inside, a building may be bright with window and fluorescent light and cheery with decorative touches and comfortable with carpeting and the latest in school furniture. Or it may be gothic and gloomy. City (and rural) school buildings, because they are on average so much older than suburban schools, are much more likely to fall into the latter category. One of the elementary schools in the city of Camden occupies a three-story building, but it has only one boys' and one girls' lavatory, both on the first floor. The building is so crowded that two of the classes have to be held in the cafeteria of another school (Lefelt, 1988, p. 32).

More important than the buildings are the educational materials they house. Poor schools have small libraries with few recent additions to the book collection, only a few magazine subscriptions, and very little audiovisual equipment and software. The A-V equipment may be so old and unreliable that teachers have given up on it to spare themselves the awkward delays in trying to adjust or just restart the darn stuff. The libraries themselves serve mostly as study halls. They don't even have comfortable chairs. The libraries of suburban schools are much more richly endowed, and some are absolutely alluring in their architectural splendor and creature comforts, not to mention the wide array of multimedia material.

The auditorium of a poor school may be little more than a cavern with chairs and a stage. For the rich school, it is a professional theater, with all the technical paraphernalia needed for live stage productions. These lavish productions not only instill school spirit among the student body, they also inspire parental pride and support.

The suburban school is much more likely to have a swimming pool and a fully equipped gym, with perhaps a weight room, as well as a basketball court with spectator stands. The spacious grounds on which the school is located allow for regulation-size athletic fields, which are well maintained by professional groundskeepers.

The vocational shops and home economics rooms in a suburban school have all the latest gadgetry, whereas their counterparts in the urban school consist of stuff that has been used by generations of students, with new equipment acquired in the most incremental fashion, so that only a small amount of the equipment is ever really new. Poor vocational education prepares kids for jobs that no longer exist.

The science labs of urban schools can be laughable. Some test tubes, a few Bunsen burners, a couple of microscopes, some old jars of chemicals, and a washbasin comprise the total inventory. Students do not have a variety of materials with which to learn, and the materials they do have are present in such limited quantities that they have to wait their turn to share them. Suburban schools, by contrast, are likely to approach a state-of-the-art lab station for each student in the class.

Computers—the communication tool of our common tomorrow—are much more prevalent in the rich schools of today than the poor ones. In some fortunate schools, each child is assigned his or her own computer, much as a textbook is assigned at the beginning of a course. Those are the schools where the kids also have a computer in their bedroom at home.

In English and social studies classes, the texts used in some poor schools have been through thirty years of page turning, according to the president of the New York City teachers' union (Weiss, 1988, p. 60). The texts are beat-up and out-of-date, and not all the pages are there to be turned. Supplementary reading consists of a desultory book collection approaching antiquity on a bookshelf in the back of the room. The pages of those old fossils remain intact because no one ever turns them. Rich schools have spiffy new texts that catch your eye even if they don't hold your attention. There is a cornucopia of new paperback books for supplementary reading. Of course, the students in these schools have no trouble creating their own paperback libraries at home.

Saddest of all is that even the teachers in rich schools tend to be better than those in poor schools. At least they are better educated, having gone to superior colleges and universities, and long enough to get advanced degrees. That is why they got job offers from the rich schools. The offers were eagerly sought because teaching in these schools means working with students who are relatively docile and pliable, and who, by and large, come prepared to learn regardless of the teacher's communication skills. Teaching in these schools also means more money. Rich schools have higher salary ranges than poor schools, just another of the things they can afford to buy. When teacher salaries are computed by the number of students a teacher has, teachers in poor schools fare even worse because poor schools control costs by having large classes.

EQUALIZING EDUCATIONAL OPPORTUNITY

Those who say that money cannot buy a good education live in good neighborhoods with good schools on which a lot of money is spent. Some of these people do not deign to use the good public school in their neighborhood; they send their child to a private school in an effort to buy what they say cannot be bought. If they are correct that money cannot buy a good education, then it would seem that the poor have as much right to be disappointed by this fact as the rich (Coons, Clune, and Sugarman, 1971, p. 30). Some of the rich who patronize private schools are candid enough to admit publicly the relationship between money and quality education. The chairman of the board of trustees of the Peddie School says that "as one would expect, the more assets the better the education. . . . Funds are necessary to employ able teachers, to provide reasonable facilities and to provide a reasonable student-faculty ratio. If you achieve this, you can have a very fine education" (vanTassel, 1988, p. NJ3).

Educational opportunity can be equalized simply and straightforwardly by equalizing the money spent among pupils. It is necessary to do this within as well as between school districts because single districts often spend more on schools in the better neighborhoods (Sexton, 1961). The parents in the better neighborhoods may be more demanding, so that they succeed in getting for their children materials, programs, and even teachers not available to schools in the poorer parts of town. Such disparities can develop almost imperceptibly, so it is important for the district to be on the watch for them.

This does not mean that districts cannot spend different amounts for students in different educational categories, for example, handicapped versus non-impaired students, high school versus elementary school students. These differences result from real differences in the costs of educating different kinds of students. They are not the same as spending different amounts on students who are in the *same* educational category.

Equalizing educational opportunity *across* school districts is a responsibility of the state. Under our constitutional system, education is legally a prerogative of state government, so states already have the authority to intervene in local school operations. What better justification for intervention could they have than to redress elemental fairness? The unfairness is so egregious that it forces the question of why states have allowed it to exist for so long. As already indicated, the answer is a political one: the people who profit from the unfairness are the rich, and the rich have more political power than the poor. If the rich are going to continue exercising their power at the expense of the poor, then they should at least have the decency to stop pretending that there is justice and fairness and equality in American education. If the children of the poor are going to be treated shabbily by the state simply because of the plight of their parents—a plight for which the children will suffer enough as it is—then the state is an oppressor of its people in the same way that a Latin American oligarchy is.

It is desirable to equalize educational opportunity not just among schools and districts within a state but also among the fifty states of the union. There are wide variations in the amount of dollars spent per pupil from state to state, even taking into account cost-of-living differences. So even if there were full equalization within states, the poor states would still be spending less than the wealthier ones. When John Fischer was president of Columbia University Teachers College, he said, "If we really mean it when we say that every American child—rather than every Californian or every Arkansan—is entitled to equal educational opportunity, we must be prepared to use federal means to bring about such equality" (quoted in Herbers, 1972, p. E3). Only the federal government has the capacity to deal with inequality on this level, but the Constitution gives it no clear warrant for doing so, and the political clout of the rich can be as intimidating to members of Congress as to members of a state legislature. Perhaps the most that can be expected from our national leaders is that they be more restrained in their rhetoric about the greatness of the American educational system. There is as much reason to be ashamed of that system as to be proud of it.

THE BENEFIT TO SOCIETY

John Donne's poetic insight that "no man is an island entire of itself" is truer in today's interdependent world than when he wrote it. Its application to American education at the end of the twentieth century has been captured by Lester Thurow: "I am willing to pay for, indeed insist upon, the education of my neighbor's children not because I am generous but because I cannot afford to live with them uneducated" (Thurow, 1985, p. 187).

As Thurow correctly understands, educating the children of the poor is in the interest of us all. It saves corporations the cost of searching excessively for minimally qualified employees or of minimally educating those who come unqualified. It gives people legal opportunities so they desist from taking illegal ones, with the corresponding cost in human and property loss.

Educating the poor necessarily entails some additional costs to compensate for the disadvantage they bring to school. For example, urban communities have unusually high percentages of students whose native language is not English, and these students are from literally scores of different language groups.

There is debate about how best to make these students proficient in English, but general agreement that it requires extra resources regardless of the approach used. Urban districts also have security costs just to keep the schools safe enough for children to venture into them. Guards have to be paid, and their walkie-talkies cost about $1,000 each. Suburban schools are spared these costs.

Philanthropies and corporate leaders have recognized the need and have some appreciation of the cost for effective education of the poor and minorities. The Ford Foundation, after completing a national study of city high schools, came up with a list of twenty "lessons" it had learned. At least twelve of these lessons involve more money, and four of them specifically mention the need for more funds (Ford Foundation, 1984, pp. 66–68). The Carnegie Foundation for the Advancement of Teaching has issued a more recent report on urban schools, and it concludes with a call for a national urban schools program. All eight of the points in this program are high-cost ones (The Carnegie Foundation, 1988, pp. 37–38). The Institute for Educational Leadership examined the working conditions of teachers in thirty-one schools spread among five large cities. Its conclusion was that "urban teachers . . . labor under conditions that would not be tolerated in other professional settings. This is true of teaching in general, but the compounding of problems in urban schools creates extremely difficult and demoralizing environments for those who have chosen to teach" (Corcoran, Walker, and White, 1988, p. xiii). This study, too, emphasizes the lack of resources available to urban teachers. Imagine the following generalization being applied to suburban teachers: "Urban teachers often do not have even the basic resources needed for teaching. There are serious shortages of everything from toilet paper to textbooks; teachers have limited access to modern office technologies, including copiers, let alone computers" (Corcoran, Walker, and White, 1988, p. xiii). The Committee for Economic Development, composed of chief executive officers of American corporations, in true business fashion presents a list of "cost-effective programs" and "investment strategies" for helping the educationally disadvantaged. All of these recommendations cost money, and more than is now being spent (Committee for Economic Development, 1987).

To be blunt, urban schools need more money. Moreover, they need more money per pupil than suburban schools just to have an equally good chance at effective education. Presently, they are struggling to make do with less money. This condition is not in our interest as an interdependent society, and the socially deleterious consequences are available for all to see. The money spent on poor schools can be an especially good social investment since formal education has a greater impact on poor students than on their better-off peers, as was demonstrated over twenty years ago in the largest study of education ever undertaken (Coleman et al., 1966). But perhaps the best reason for doing something now is to make us a more honest society. It will reduce not only the opportunity gap between rich and poor, but also the gap between our lofty rhetoric and the grim reality (Bell, 1976, p. 263).

POSITION 2
For Freedom in School Finance

GAUGING THE GAIN

There is, to be sure, a strong undercurrent of capitalism in American education. But instead of fretting over this fact and becoming defensive about it, people should assess the benefits which it brings.

In education, as in the free enterprise system generally, inequality is both inevitable and desirable. The prospect of getting to the top and the possibility of falling to the bottom are what motivate us as individuals to do our best. That is just basic human nature. And when all of us are working hard to get to the top or avoid falling to the bottom, the whole ship of state is buoyed up. America is made stronger and we as a people are enriched materially.

Government-guaranteed equality denies people their drive. What's the point of striving if you can't advance beyond the level of the person who sits around doing nothing? Even communist countries like China and the Soviet Union have come to appreciate the motivating force of capitalist inequality. Inequality is not only a great goad to human effort, it is a very just way of distributing the blessings of liberty. You get what you earn or, as the Bible says, you reap what you sow. To earn something is to *deserve* it. Capitalist inequality is intended to ensure that everyone is rewarded appropriately in the fair competition of the free marketplace. We are all well aware that this system does not work perfectly, but what Churchill (1947) said about democracy as a political system can be said about capitalism as an economic system: "No one pretends that democracy is perfect or all-wise. Indeed, it has been said that democracy is the worst form of government except all those other forms that have been tried from time to time." And despite its imperfections, the free enterprise system has created a wealth of opportunities for upward mobility. Millions of successful people have come from humble beginnings, so that the top ranks of government, the arts, the professions, and business are filled with people whose origins were no more auspicious than those of Ronald Reagan or Leontyne Price or Jonas Salk or Famous Amos.

Education is a right of all Americans, to be sure, and it is guaranteed to all Americans because it is essential to our progress as a nation and our fulfillment as individuals. However, the guarantee is only for a minimally adequate education. There is no unanimity as to how high the guaranteed amount of education should be. There is a general consensus that public education should be free through high school, but no agreement on what a student should have learned by graduation. The higher the expectation, the more it will cost taxpayers to bring every student to that level. Frankly, it does not seem that the level need be very high to satisfy the needs of society.

> Our definition of a basic education is considerably . . . restricted. It consists of those things necessary for minimal effective functioning in a democracy. This includes the ability to read, write, and do basic arithmetic, and knowledge of our democratic

government. These goals are relatively clear-cut, and accomplishment is more easily measured than in other curricula. Most people would agree that they form the core of education, while few would agree on other curricular objectives. It should be possible to complete this basic education by the end of the eighth grade. (Garms, Guthrie, and Pierce, 1978, pp. 241–242)

There is no guarantee that everyone will graduate from high school, let alone go to medical school and become a doctor or to law school and become a lawyer. Education beyond the minimum guarantee is something that has to be earned just like any other valued commodity. Moreover, society creates social dynamite by educating people beyond its capacity to absorb them into careers that are congruent with their education. People who are overeducated for the jobs they hold are discontented workers, which makes them ripe for revolutionary appeals. Hayek finds this condition to have been a cause of Hitler's success. "The resentment of the lower middle class, from which fascism and National Socialism recruited so large a proportion of their supporters, was intensified by the fact that their education and training had in many instances made them aspire to directing positions and that they regarded themselves as entitled to be members of the directing class" (Hayek, 1944, p. 117).

The commodities children value are sometimes earned directly by the children. A child can use the money from his paper route to buy a bicycle. Another child can study hard and earn herself a scholarship to a private school. But mostly it is parents who earn the commodities for their children. They buy the bike and pay the private school tuition. The most common way parents buy their children an education beyond the state's minimum guarantee is to buy a home in a community that has good schools.

Good schools are one of the most cherished blessings of liberty, and parents struggle very hard to earn a good education for their children by living near good schools. A great, if not the greatest, motivator for parents is being able to provide a good education for their children. One parent has written movingly of his decision to relocate his family to a small town so that his children would have good schools. He realized that in abandoning the city he violated some of his own convictions, but concluded that "*no one is willing to sacrifice their children on the altar of their social principles*" [author's emphasis] (Nocero, 1989, p. 30). Real estate agents are well aware of this, which is why they use the quality of the local schools as a major selling point to prospective home buyers. To deny parents the right to influence the quality of their children's education in this way is worse than denying them a basic right as citizens in a free society; it is to deny them a *natural* right as parents. And it is to deny society the benefit of the parents' highly motivated labor.

EQUALIZING HOW?

Egalitarians espouse noble sentiments that we all endorse to some extent. However, they avoid discussing those troublesome specifics that gravely weaken their case. When they exhort us to equalize per pupil spending throughout an entire state, they fail to tell us in which direction and how far this should be done. These are hardly minor details! Suppose this is the situation in your state:

Top spending districts $10,000 per pupil
Average spending districts $ 7,000 per pupil
Bottom spending districts $ 4,000 per pupil

Should the state allocate money to equalize everyone up to the top of $10,000 per pupil? That's going to cost the state and its taxpayers, including poor folks who pay taxes, an awful lot of money. It may be more than the taxpayers are willing to provide, and they'll make their reluctance known at the ballot box in good democratic fashion. Besides, it will mean to the family already living in the $10,000 district that it has to pay additional taxes for the benefit of someone else's children. It is already paying stiff taxes to guarantee its own children a good education, and those children will not benefit at all from the additional taxes it pays to help poor school districts. In fact, their education will become relatively devalued.

Maybe the state should equalize everyone *down* to the level of the $4,000 districts. That would require putting a ceiling on how much the affluent districts could spend on their children and forbidding them to spend any more. The poor districts would not get any more money; they would just have the spiteful satisfaction of knowing that everyone else was as bad off as they. (Many conservative commentators—Hayek, 1944, p. 139, for example; also Kristol, 1978, p. 220—have remarked on the symptoms of envy and greed among egalitarians.) The $10,000 and even the $7,000 districts would have to make major adjustments. Their budgets would be slashed by 60 percent and 42 percent, respectively. These are enormous reductions, and even if they were phased in gradually, the ultimate result would be a huge decline in the quality of education. People will not sit still and let something that disastrous happen to their children. If they cannot stop it from becoming law, they will surely find ways to get around the law. They would probably arrange all kinds of ways of making "voluntary" contributions to their schools to make up for the loss in official revenue. There would be bake sales galore.

The middle ground is a compromise that avoids all of one approach while including a bit of both. The affluent districts could be equalized down to the $7,000 level while the poor districts were equalized up to it. However, the affluent districts might not be much more willing to suffer a 30 percent reduction in their budgets than a 60 percent one, even though 30 percent is twice as easy to make up in bake sales. To avoid the problem of affronting the affluent, they could simply be left alone at their $10,000 level. However, egalitarians would no doubt declare this to be a cop-out, and people in the average districts would feel that the poor had been thrown into the same pot with them while the rich escaped the soup altogether.

It is not up to people who value educational liberty to work out a politically viable means of vitiating that liberty. It is up to the egalitarians. Even if they can come up with a scheme that the citizens will support, it will prove to be a failure in the long run because it will contradict human nature and the values which have made America great. Those values were upheld by the U.S. Supreme Court when it refused to strike down the Texas system of local financing of schools and found that system to be "rational" (*San Antonio Independent School District v. Rodriguez,* 1973).

POURING MONEY DOWN RATHOLES

All but one of the schemes discussed above have something in common: they would all inject a large infusion of cash into poor school districts. This would be on top of the huge amounts of financial aid already given to those districts over the past twenty years. Unfortunately, the recipient districts have a dismal record for spending money unwisely and even illegally. The poor performance of their students is as much due to mismanaged money as to insufficient money. For example, there is money that never gets spent on the pupils for whom it is targeted. "Entitlement funds have frequently been treated as discretionary monies, and have been diverted from their original purposes" (Bastian et al., 1985, p. 30). Urban districts have taken state compensatory education money intended for remedial programs and used it to pay regular classroom teachers to continue doing what they had been doing all along. They justified this diversion of funds by pointing to the money they were saving their taxpayers. The result was that suburban districts, with few remedial pupils, were spending roughly $150 in additional services for each of their neediest children, whereas one urban district was spending only $7 extra on each of its many needy youngsters (Carlson and Rubin, 1979).

Even when the money is spent for the targeted population, coordination is inadequate to ensure that the expenditure approved by some assistant superintendent results in a teaching tool that actually becomes known to and used by the teachers. Fancy instructional hardware gathers dust in the storerooms of poor school districts. Moreover, there are simply too many assistant superintendents and other administrators, all busying themselves with things that never percolate down to the classroom. When the late Richard Green became chancellor of the New York City schools he announced that he intended to clean out the board of education headquarters and send a whole bunch of people out to the schools where they might finally be able to do some good for kids.

Besides allowing people to spin their wheels for no apparent educational purpose, poor school districts, and urban districts in particular, are pestholes of corruption. The poor citizens who live in these districts lack the expertise to detect the corruption and the political skills to attack it. They are at the mercy of slick operators with education certificates who rip off them and their children, and who are likely to live in suburbs where their own children are getting a decent education. These parasites on the poor have lots of taxpayer money to spend, and much of it they keep for themselves in the form of kickbacks. The company from which the most money can be extorted is the one with which they do business, whether it benefits the students or not. They manage to give their friends and relatives no-show jobs on the district payroll, and then they take a share of the unearned paycheck. They treat themselves to lavish perks such as expensive dinners when they're in town, and luxurious travel accommodations when they're out of town, ostensibly on school business.

Recently New York City witnessed the spectacle of an elementary school principal being arrested on the street near his school for making a drug purchase. He turned out to have a record of absenteeism from his job. A detailed report beginning on the front page of *The New York Times* opened with the sentence: "Members of a community school board in Brooklyn formed an interlocking power base to secure jobs and promotions for relatives and friends and advance a major private development project, according to school employees, parents and personnel records" (Lewis and Blumenthal, 1989, p. 1). Lest it be thought that this is the behavior of minorities, it should be noted that all the members of the board are white. In another recent report, on the business practices of the Jersey City school district, a nationally known accounting firm listed a host of irregularities in the awarding of contracts, the maintenance of payrolls, and the operation of the personnel office (Peat Marwick Main & Co., 1988). In Newark, a member of the board of education admitted that he offered to secure school principalships for people who were willing to pay him (Sullivan, 1989).

Until such time as honest and effective people take control of poor school districts, it would be foolish for the taxpayers of a state to be sending care packages to crooks and incompetents in the form of extra revenue. As Henry Levin put it after studying the impact of expenditure increases on school effectiveness, "spending increases will have a much greater effect on the economic status and employment of educational professionals than they will on the educational proficiencies of children" (Levin, 1976, p. 194).

THROWING DOLLARS IN THE DARK

We know how we do not want to spend school money: on waste and corruption. But we are not sure how we do want to spend it. Educational research and past experience do not tell us clearly what works.

> Research currently available in this arena is deficient in both focus and rigor; findings often are nonconfirmatory or contradictory. For example, teaching experience and advanced degrees are major determinants of teachers' salaries, but these variables are not clearly related to improvements in school outputs. . . . Education has not been able to provide cost/benefit data as readily as have some other public services, and the citizenry appears less sanguine about the efficacy of public schools than was true in the past. (McCarthy and Deignan, 1982, p. 102)

> Detailed research spanning two decades and observing performance in many different educational settings provides strong and consistent evidence that expenditures are not systematically related to student achievement. (Hanushek, 1989, p. 49)

Other researchers are forced into a more agnostic approach when reviewing the evidence. As James Guthrie puts it:

> Everybody's arguing for more school decision making, and the school finance people and the economists say they don't know how to advise them on the appropriate spending of resources. What the field needs is to better understand how money is spent inside a school, what are we buying, and what is it we ought to buy, and what leads to more learning. (Quoted in Colvin, 1989, p. 13)

Some of the things that seem to work in poor schools peter out in effectiveness after a while. It is as though what really works is novelty. But even then, some novelties do not work as well as others, or at all. Some of the things that are said to work either are beyond the control of schools or do not cost money. Good families and stable neighborhoods are said to work, and this makes intuitive sense, but these conditions are largely the responsibility of other government agencies and private charities. Parental participation in school affairs is said to work, but suburban schools are able to get this without paying for it. Principals who take an interest in the quality of classroom instruction are said to be more effective, but this does not cost more money, only a reordering of the principal's priorities. Aligning the curriculum with the tests by which student achievement will be assessed should not cost much money, and it is so commonsensical that it should have been done long ago. Keeping students on task and not distracted by silly administrative interruptions is something else that does not cost money and is patently desirable.

Given all this uncertainty about the things that cost money and the much greater certainty about the things that don't, spending more money on poor schools is like throwing dollars in the dark and hoping they land somewhere they can do some good. The uncertainty is certainly not restricted to poor schools; rich schools spend money on lots of things that have no demonstrated effect on the schools' goals. An Olympic-size swimming pool is certainly nice to have, but it is hardly essential. Luxuriantly carpeted and paneled offices create an elegant ambiance, but their relationship to staff or student productivity is elusive. The same is true for beautifully manicured grounds surrounding the school building. The difference is that rich schools spend (or waste) their own money; poor schools are asking for money from people who don't use these schools and don't live anywhere near them. Poor schools cannot expect people to invest in them before they establish a record for getting results with their own money.

It is not at all impossible that poor school districts already have enough money to do the job. They may have only half as much per pupil as rich districts, and their students may have a multitude of educational handicaps, but by emphasizing a few really important goals they could concentrate their staffs' energy toward accomplishing those goals. If the vast majority of the students are deficient in the basic skills of reading, writing, and arithmetic, the poor districts should focus their time and money on those areas. Full-fledged art and music programs may be luxuries that poor districts cannot afford and that detract from the kids' real needs.

Dedicated urban educators can get results without waiting for more largesse from the state treasury. Jaime Escalante, a math teacher in California, gets such startling results that his story has been made into the movie *Stand and Deliver*. Joe Clark, a New Jersey high school principal, has been lionized in a *Time* magazine cover story and in the movie *Lean on Me*. Whatever one thinks of these individuals' tactics, the fact is that they had latitude for action that did not cost money, and they acted.

The simple fact that a rich district spends twice as much money per pupil as a poor district could mean that the rich district is wasting half its money on frills that its students don't need. However, it could also mean that the students are so educationally advanced that they require expensive programs and materials in order to continue their intellectual development. When a school has a sizable number of students who are able to handle expensive laboratory equipment and to learn from doing so, buying that equipment is a legitimate educational expense. But to buy that equipment for students who are incapable of comprehending it is to pay for a foolish equality. Educationally backward students don't need sophisticated equipment, and they are not likely to have much respect for equipment that they find frustratingly difficult. The propensity of students from poor communities for destructive behavior often leads to schools with expensive, unused, and *damaged* equipment. Equal education for rich and poor students does not mean the same education; it means equally appropriate education. Rich students tend to do better in school than poor students, so it is a good social investment to spend more on them. These students *earn* the additional expenditure by dint of their hard work and native ability.

MAKING STUDENTS RESPONSIBLE

Society gives students a free start in life but not a guaranteed finish. Students are the adults of the future, and one of the things they must learn in school in order to assume their adult roles is responsibility. They must learn and act on the conviction that they are the major determiners of their fate.

A society that insists on excusing the transgressions of students does a tremendous disservice to young people. It gives them the notion that others are always to blame for their behavior. In the case of poor students, it is society itself that is supposed to be at fault. These children are pitied to the point of being denied all free will. That attitude, however charitably it is grounded, is insulting and damaging to poor children. It will have the effect of maintaining them in their poverty and dependency. The lesson these children must learn is that society simply cannot afford to give everyone an unending free ride. After a certain distance, some payment has to be made by the riders. The ability and willingness to make such payments are traits of responsible, self-sufficient individuals. Students in poor schools may not be able to make cash payments toward their education, but they can certainly make payments of effort. If they do, they will find their own children attending suburban schools, just as so many earlier generations of the poor worked their way out of poverty.

FOR DISCUSSION

1 Have each member of the class find out the current per pupil expenditure for his or her home school district, and then do in-class comparisons. Or get the official expenditure numbers from the state education department (in some states this is called the department of public instruction) and then make in-class comparisons of several school districts. How tolerable are the spending disparities across school districts?

2 The Committee for Economic Development* lists the following as major reasons why children do poorly in school. Try to devise cost-free or inexpensive means of dealing with these conditions to determine whether it is really necessary to spend more money on schools where the conditions are endemic.

They may come to school poorly prepared for classroom learning or not yet ready developmentally for formal education.
Their parents may be indifferent to their educational needs.
They may be children of teenagers who are ill equipped for parenting.
They may have undiagnosed learning disabilities, emotional problems, or physical handicaps.
They may have language problems or come from non-English-speaking homes.
They may experience ethnic or racial prejudice.
They may have access only to schools of substandard quality.

3 It is often said that he who pays the piper picks the tune. If states start giving more money to poor school districts, they will try to exercise more control over these districts to make sure the money is spent well. Make a list of the areas over which states should be exercising direct, prescriptive, uniform control. Then make a list of the areas which should be left to the judgment of local officials, no matter how much money the state is contributing. Areas that appear on your lists might include the hiring and evaluation of personnel, the determination of curriculum content and teaching materials, the testing of student achievement, the requirements for a high school diploma, the length of the school year, the safety standards for buildings. Do your lists indicate that you prefer a centralized statewide school system or a localized system?

4 Following is a list from the U.S. House of Representatives of programs for children that are actually supposed to save the taxpayers money in the long run. These programs are targeted primarily to poor children. Review the list as though you were the U.S. Director of the Office of Management and Budget, charged by the President with finding programs to eliminate or cut back in order to reduce the federal budget deficit. You also have a third choice, of recommending that some programs be expanded, but your third choice won't be heeded by the President unless you've made some hard first and second choices.

*Committee for Economic Development, *Children in Need: Investment Strategies for the Educationally Disadvantaged,* New York: CED, 1987, p. 8.

COST-EFFECTIVE PROGRAMS FOR CHILDREN

Benefits for children	Cost benefit	Participation
WIC: special supplemental food program for women, infants and children		
Reduction in infant mortality and births of low birthweight infants.	$1 investment in prenatal component of WIC has saved as much as $3 in short-term hospital costs.	3.1 million participants—about ⅓ of those potentially eligible—received WIC services in Spring 1985.
Prenatal care		
Reduction in prematurity, low birthweight births, and infant morbidity.	$1 investment can save $3.38 in cost of care for low birthweight infants.	23.9% of live births in 1982 were to mothers who did not begin prenatal care in the first trimester of pregnancy. The rate for white births was 20.7%, for black births 38.5%.
Medicaid		
Decreased neonatal and infant morbidity and fewer abnormalities among children receiving Early Periodic Screening, Diagnosis, and Treatment (EPSDT) Services.	$1 spent on comprehensive prenatal care added to services for Medicaid recipents has saved $2 in infant's first year; lower health care costs for children receiving EPSDT services.	In FY 1983, an estimated 9.5 million dependent children under 21 were served by Medicaid, including 2.2 million screened under EPSDT. In calendar year 1983, there were 14.3 million related children in families below the poverty line.
Childhood immunization		
Dramatic declines in incidence of rubella, mumps, measles, polio, diphtheria, tetanus, and pertussis.	$1 spent on Childhood Immunization program saves $10 in later medical costs.	An estimated 3.4–3.8 million children were immunized with vaccine purchased under the Childhood Immunization program in FY 1983. In 1983, the total percent of children, ages 1–4, immunized against the major childhood diseases ranged from 74.4 for mumps to 86.0 for diphtheria-tetanus-pertussis. For those 5–14, percent immunized ranged from 86.2 for mumps to 92.9 for DTP.
Preschool education		
Increased school success, employability and self esteem; reduced dependence on public assistance.	$1 investment in quality preschool education returns $4.75 because of lower costs of special education, public assistance, and crime.	In 1983, there were 10.2 million children ages 3–5. 5.4 million of them were enrolled in public and non-public pre-primary programs. 442,000 children—fewer than 1 out of every 5 eligible—now participate in Head Start.

COST-EFFECTIVE PROGRAMS FOR CHILDREN (Continued)

Benefits for children	Cost benefit	Participation
Compensatory education		
Achievement gains and maintenance of gains in reading and mathematics.	Investment of $500 for year of compensatory education can save $3,000 cost of repeating grade.	In 1982–1983, 4.7 million children—an estimated 50% of those in need—received Chapter I services under the LEA Basic Grant Program.
Education for all handicapped children		
Increased number of students receiving services and more available services.	Early educational intervention has saved school districts $1,560 per disabled pupil.	During 1983–1984, 34,094,108 children ages 3–21 were served under the State Grant program. The prevalence of handicaps in the population under age 21 is estimated to be 11.4% (9.5–10 million children).
Youth employment and training		
Gains in employability, wages, and success while in school and afterwards.	Job Corps returned $7,400 per participant, compared to $5,000 in program costs (in 1977 dollars). FY 1982 service year costs for Youth Employment Training Program (YETP) were $4,700; participants had annualized earnings gains of $1,810.	Between October 1983 and July 1984, 83,426 youths were enrolled in Job Corps, and about 240,000 in Job Training Partnership Act (JTPA) Title IIA; 753,000 youths participated in summer youth program in 1984. The annualized numbers of unemployed persons 16–21 years old in 1984 was 2,278,000.

Source: Report of the Select Committee on Children, Youth, and Families, U.S. House of Representatives, Washington, D.C., August 14, 1985.

REFERENCES

Barzun, J. (1959). *The House of Intellect*. New York: Harper and Row.

Bastian, A., et al. (1985). *Choosing Equality: The Case for Democratic Schooling*. New York: New World Foundation.

Bell, D. (1976). *The Cultural Contradictions of Capitalism*. New York: Basic Books.

Bowles, S., and Gintis, H. (1976). *Schooling in Capitalist America: Educational Reform and the Contradictions of Economic Life*. New York: Basic Books.

Carlson, K., and Rubin, L. (1979). *Analysis of the Development and Implementation of Local and Statewide Standards in Basic Skills in the State of New Jersey: A Final Report*. Washington, D.C.: National Institute of Education.

Carnegie Foundation for the Advancement of Teaching (1988). *An Imperiled Generation: Saving Urban Schools*. Princeton: Princeton University Press.

Churchill, W. (1947). Address to House of Commons, November 11.

Coleman, J. S., et al. (1966). *Equality of Educational Opportunity*. Washington, D.C.: Government Printing Office.

Colvin, R. L. (1989). "School Finance: Equity Concerns in an Age of Reforms." *Educational Researcher*, **18**(1), pp. 11–15.

Committee for Economic Development (1987). *Children in Need: Investment Strategies for the Educationally Disadvantaged.* New York: The Research and Policy Committee of the Committee for Economic Development.

Conant, J. B. (1961). *Slums and Suburbs.* New York: McGraw-Hill.

Coons, J. E., Clune, W. H. III, and Sugarman, S. D. (1971). *Private Wealth and Public Education.* Cambridge, Mass.: Harvard University Press.

Corcoran, T. B., Walker, L. J., and White, J. L. (1988). *Working in Urban Schools.* Washington, D.C.: Institute for Educational Leadership.

Ford Foundation. (1984). *City High Schools: A Recognition of Progress.* New York: Ford Foundation.

Garms, W. I., Guthrie, J. W., and Pierce, L. C. (1978). *School Finance: The Economics and Politics of Public Education.* Englewood Cliffs, N.J.: Prentice-Hall.

Hanushek, E. A. (1989). "The Impact of Differential Expenditures on School Performance." *Educational Researcher,* **18**(4), pp. 45–51, 62.

Hayek, F. A. (1944). *The Road to Serfdom.* Chicago: University of Chicago Press.

Herbers, J. (1972). "School Financing: A New Way to Foot the Bill." *The New York Times,* March 12, p. E-3.

Jencks, C., et al. (1972). *Inequality: A Reassessment of the Effect of Family and Schooling in America.* New York: Basic Books.

Kozol, J. (1988). *Rachel and Her Children: Homeless Families in America.* New York: Crown.

Kristol, I. (1978). *Two Cheers for Capitalism.* New York: Basic Books.

Lefelt, S. (1988). *Abbott v. Burke.* Initial Decision. Trenton, N.J.: State of New Jersey Office of Administrative Law.

Levin, H. M. (1976). "Effects of Expenditure Increases on Educational Resource Allocation and Effectiveness." In *The Limits of Educational Reform,* edited by M. Carnoy and H. M. Levin. New York: McKay.

Lewis, N. A., and Blumenthal, R. (1989). "Power Base vs. Schools in Brooklyn District." *The New York Times,* February 10, pp. 1, B4.

McCarthy, M. M., and Deignan, P. T. (1982). *What Legally Constitutes an Adequate Public Education?* Bloomington, Ind.: Phi Delta Kappa.

Metz, M. H. (1988). "In Education, Magnets Attract Controversy." *Issues '88.* Special edition of *NEA Today,* January, pp. 54–60.

New Jersey Education Association. (1988). *Basic Statistical Data of New Jersey School Districts.* Trenton, N.J.: New Jersey Education Association.

New York State Education Department. (1984). *Annual Educational Summary, 1983–1984.* Albany, N.Y.: New York State Education Department.

Nocero, J. (1989). "The Case Against Joe Nocero." *The Washington Monthly,* February, pp. 22–31.

Peat Marwick Main & Co. (1988). *Executive Summary of Jersey City Schools Investigation.* Trenton, N.J.: New Jersey Department of Education.

San Antonio Independent School District v. Rodriguez (1973). 411 U.S. 1.

Sexton, P. C. (1961). *Education and Income: Inequalities in Our Public Schools.* New York: Viking.

Sullivan, J. F. (1989). "School Official Admits Guilt in Bribery Case." *The New York Times,* January 24, p. B3.

Thurow, L. C. (1985). *The Zero-Sum Solution.* New York: Simon & Schuster.

vanTassel, P. (1988). "Keeping the Peddie School's Aims Alive." *The New York Times,* December 11, p. NJ3.

Weiss, P. (1988). "The Education of Chancellor Green." *The New York Times Magazine,* December 4, pp. 42–44, 60–62, 81, 92–94, 109.

CHAPTER 5

FORCED OR VOLUNTARY SCHOOL INTEGRATION

POSITION 1
For Legal Integration

ASSESSING THE DAMAGE OF SEGREGATION

The major and most often quoted reason which the Supreme Court gave in 1954 for its decision outlawing racial segregation in American schools was that such segregation did psychological damage to black students. The damage may be so severe that it can never be undone, said the Court. In the exact words of the Court, "To separate them [blacks] from others of similar age and qualifications solely because of their race generates a feeling of inferiority as to their status in the community that may affect their hearts and minds in a way unlikely ever to be undone" (*Brown v. Board of Education of Topeka,* 1954). Legally, the Court could only look at "legal" segregation, that is, segregation which was being imposed by law. The Court ruled that segregation by law was, in fact, illegal: it violated the highest law in the land, the U.S. Constitution.

The Court ruling against "legal" segregation has caused profound changes over the past thirty-five years. The civil rights movement was given tremendous momentum by the ruling; schools throughout the nation were desegregated; blacks acquired many opportunities for better education, employment, and housing. Some blacks were even given preferential treatment over whites in securing these benefits. The progress of blacks during the thirty-five-year period may be symbolized most dramatically by the presidential campaigns of Jesse Jackson.

And yet after all the tumult and all the genuine progress of the past thirty-five years, where does the United States stand today? It is still a racially

segregated society. Several American cities now have majority black populations, including Atlanta, Birmingham, Detroit, the District of Columbia, and
New Orleans (National Urban League, 1987, p. 182). In many areas of the
country, the segregation is more extensive than it was thirty-five years ago.
Indeed, it is so extreme in the urban areas of the north that social scientists
have new names for people trapped in the ghettoes: "the underclass" and "the
truly disadvantaged." The underclass and the truly disadvantaged are worse
than poor, they are without hope. They can see no legitimate way out of their
poverty, either for themselves or for their children. The attempted way out for
many of them is the illegitimate route of crime, which so often leads only to
prison, or death.

The plight of these people is passed from generation to generation because
they are isolated in the ghetto without role models. When there was total racial
segregation, successful blacks had their homes in the ghetto and could serve
as guides and role models for black children. Successful blacks have since been
able to escape to suburban residences, leaving the black children who are still
in the central cities with nothing but models of defeat. William Julius Wilson,
in examining the cities of New York, Chicago, Los Angeles, Philadelphia, and
Detroit, made these findings:

> Although the total population in these five largest cities decreased by 9 percent
> between 1970 and 1980, the poverty population increased by 22 percent. Furthermore,
> the population living in poverty areas grew by 40 percent overall, by 69 percent in
> high-poverty areas (i.e., areas with a poverty rate of at least 30 percent), and by a
> staggering 161 percent in extreme poverty areas (i.e., areas with a poverty rate of
> at least 40 percent). It should be emphasized that these incredible changes took place
> within just a 10-year period. . . . the significant increase in the poverty concentration
> in these overwhelmingly black communities is related to the large out-migration of
> nonpoor blacks." (Wilson, 1987, pp. 46, 50)

The result of this massive and sudden dislocation for people left behind is that:

> . . . people experience a social isolation that excludes them from the job network
> system that permeates other neighborhoods and that is so important in learning about
> or being recommended for jobs. . . . in such neighborhoods the chances are over-
> whelming that children will seldom interact on a sustained basis with people who
> are employed or with families that have a steady breadwinner. . . . the relationship
> between schooling and postschool employment takes on a different meaning. . . . In
> such neighborhoods, therefore, teachers become frustrated and do not teach and
> children do not learn. (Wilson, 1987, p. 57)

The schools of the underclass are a national disgrace. They catch the con-
tagion of hopelessness from the ghettoes in which they are located. As a result,
they add to the despair and hostility which the students bring in off the streets.
The U.S. Department of Education reports the following differences between
black and white students in elementary and secondary schools in America.
While the numbers include students in integrated schools, it is simply the fact
that relatively few black or white students attend such schools.

	Black, %	White, %
Enrollment	16	70
Suspensions	30	59
Corporal punishment	31	60
Educable mentally retarded	35	58
Trainable mentally retarded	27	60
Seriously emotionally disturbed	27	65
Learning disabled	17	71
Gifted and talented	8	81

Source: National Coalition of Advocates for Students, 1988.

Black students are 16 percent of the total school enrollment nationwide, and white students are 70 percent. However, blacks are much more than 16 percent of the students in the problem categories, and they are only 8 percent in the nonproblem category of gifted and talented. Thus, black students are not being served well by the schools they attend, and most of them attend segregated schools.

The acuteness of the problems of urban schools led the National Governors Association to adopt the position that states should be prepared to take over their urban school districts that are locked in a cycle of failure (NGA, 1986). One state, New Jersey, has announced its intention to take over the second largest school system in the state, Jersey City, on the grounds that the residents of Jersey City have demonstrated repeatedly that they are unable to give an adequate education to their own children. The state plans to replace both the Jersey City board of education and the chief administrators with its own appointees. In the Chelsea school district in Massachusetts, the local authorities asked Boston University to take over management of the schools because they feel powerless to overcome the impact of poverty on their schools.

Obviously, the plight of the American underclass has reached crisis proportions. The newsmagazines have taken to doing cover stories on them; *The New York Times* carries periodic front-page reports; and the television networks run prime-time specials. This means that the problem has risen to the top of the national political agenda. When the answers are being formulated, it is the U.S. Supreme Court of thirty-five years ago that should have the first word.

FOCUSING ON EFFECTS, NOT INTENTIONS

Remember, the Supreme Court spoke of the possibly permanent damage done to youngsters by racial segregation. The Court's answer at that time was to outlaw various forms of "legal" segregation. If the segregation was not being imposed by some law somewhere, if it just happened to come about because of private choices that individuals made, then it was all right. But that did not mean the psychological harm caused by this second kind of segregation was any less.

Moreover, it can be impossible to tell whether segregation is due to official action or just to a series of innocent acts. For example, the United States is now largely divided into cities and suburbs. Blacks tend to be clustered in the cities and whites in the suburbs. When the suburbs were being established by state incorporation laws after World War II, it might have been an *intention* of the lawmakers to create racially segregated communities. They must certainly have known that racial segregation would result from their action. Indeed, the federal courts, including the Supreme Court, found this to have been the case in several metropolitan areas of the north (for example, *Keyes v. School District No. 1*, 1973; *Evans v. Buchanan*, 1976). If segregation was brought about *deliberately* in other metropolitan areas of the north—and this seems probable given the prejudices of the period during which the suburbs were being developed—none of those responsible would admit it today. Thus, all we can know with certainty is the *effect* that the state incorporation laws had: white suburbs and black cities, white schools and black schools. "Requiring proof of intentional segregation before calling for any remedy is . . . not the most sensible [policy]. The injury that children suffer from racial separation has nothing to do with its cause" (Kirp, 1982, p. 285).

The answer to America's apartheid, then, is to integrate America. The constitutionality of the segregation we now have may be debatable, but the harm it is doing is not. There are some obvious strategies that we can (and must) use to bring about an integrated society.

INTEGRATING THE SCHOOLS

First and cheapest is to redraw school district boundaries. One of the reasons why the south has had more success with school desegregation than the north is that southern school districts are countywide. The districts are spread out over large enough areas to include a good mix of students from both races, although busing may be necessary to get children from their respective neighborhoods to a common school. When a state has large, racially mixed school districts, the ease of fleeing to a lily-white district is reduced. So is the desire to do so, since the integration is spread out enough to allay white panic.

The north has many racially segregated and economically inefficient little school districts that could be consolidated profitably into large integrated districts. Getting students of the different races into the same school may require some busing, but not as much as opponents claim. Black (and Hispanic) students who live on the periphery of the city may already be closer to the nearest suburban school than they are to the city school they are now forced to attend. The reverse is true for some suburban students whose homes are near the city line.

Interdistrict integration is the only kind that is feasible now that city schools have become so predominantly black and suburban schools so exclusively white. "Desegregation in a society where whites have run to the suburbs to establish a 'white noose' around decaying, predominantly minority central cities requires metropolitan desegregation" (Mahard and Crain, 1983, p. 124). There is also evidence that integration in a limited area engenders more resistance than does large-scale integration (Hochschild, 1984, pp. 54–70, 147). This may be due to the fact that large-scale integration has effects that are popular with whites as well as blacks. "A range of desirable goals for an effective school desegregation program—such as furthering genuine integration, cost and transportational efficiency, equity, and parental choice—can all be more effectively advanced within a metropolitan context" (Pettigrew, 1981, p. 163).

Even if there were better racial proportions within the cities, it is fairer to integrate over a larger geographical area. When the working-class Irish and blacks had their schools in Boston integrated under court order, the noted Harvard psychiatrist Robert Coles had the following reaction:

> The busing is a scandal. I do not think that busing should be imposed like this on working-class people exclusively. It should cross these lines and people in the suburbs should share it. . . . [Working-class whites and blacks] are both competing for a very limited piece of the pie, the limits of which are being set by the larger limits of class which allow them damn little, if anything. (Quoted in Lukas, 1985, p. 506)

THE BENEFITS FOR STUDENTS

People typically want to know what the educational rewards will be for such large-scale reorganization and the added time and cost of busing. The people who ask this question typically think of educational benefits in terms of such things as math and reading and SAT scores. They do not seem to be aware of the learning that children can realize through associating with children from other backgrounds. This can contribute to children's success in later life, and it is absolutely indispensable for getting beyond the poison of America's racial past and present. This kind of attitudinal change may not be as easy to measure as gains in academic achievement, but it is no less important for the future of America.

We know that schools can be integrated successfully. Traditional academic achievement need not be sacrificed in order for children to reap the benefits of a multiracial, multicultural environment. "White children almost never experience declines in performance on standardized achievement tests as a result of desegregation. Minorities benefit academically from desegregation much more often than they experience negative effects" (Hawley, 1981, p. 151).

We are also sophisticated enough to know that the *process itself* of creating an integrated school can be a valuable learning experience. Integration has to happen not just in the school but in its classrooms. Classroom integration permits cooperative learning tasks where black and white students can work together toward common goals. This usually has a positive effect on the racial attitudes of both groups (Conard, 1988; Schofield and Sagar, 1983, pp. 78–85). Adults are somewhat sheepishly aware that young people are more adaptable in these matters than we are. But what we should understand most keenly of all is the necessity of preparing the next generation to handle the vicissitudes of a multiracial world better than we have. It is a world in which Anglo-Americans are becoming a smaller and smaller proportion (or percentage), both worldwide and within the United States itself.

A large integrated school district can afford the best of both worlds. Because it is large, it can purchase school supplies and equipment in large quantities at discount prices. It can afford to offer special programs, such as four years of Russian or Chinese, because it has enough students to make these programs economical. On the other hand, a large district does not have to be a bureaucratic nightmare. It can be broken down into fairly independent units, with perhaps each school having considerable self-governance. There can even be schools-within-schools to give students a greater sense of belonging. Thus, a large district makes racial (and cultural) integration possible; it makes a richer education program possible; and it does not preclude the existence of decentralized control.

INTEGRATING THE NEIGHBORHOODS

School integration can accomplish only so much. Its benefits for all groups end each day when the students are bused back to their segregated neighborhoods. Not only do the black and Hispanic students return to segregated neighborhoods, they are likely to return to poor neighborhoods as well. Many of these neighborhoods are so impoverished that they are crime- and drug-ridden. Students who live in such environments are discouraged from doing well in school. It is difficult for them to concentrate on homework assignments because of the turmoil around them. They are told by the hoodlum element in the neighborhood that it is not cool to be a good student, or to attend school at all. They are under constant threat of physical harm because the neighborhood is so impacted with desolation and hopelessness that violence is rampant. And it is not only the neighborhood that is inundated with these conditions. Very often, and tragically, the conditions have seeped into the home as well.

The abolition of ghettoes is the only way to fully liberate the youngsters who live in them to lead successful and lawful lives. Abolishing ghettoes will require that the people now trapped in them be given the means to escape. They need housing allowances, since their meager incomes do not permit them to buy or rent decent housing now. They also require *available* housing outside the ghetto. Fortress suburbia has to be opened up to make room for our fellow citizens. The fair housing law passed by Congress makes this goal explicit. It stipulates that all federal agencies "shall administer their programs and activities relating to housing and urban development in a manner affirmatively to further the purposes of this title [housing integration]" (as quoted in Orfield, 1978, p. 436).

Suburban communities have erected numerous barricades against the poor. The barricades are called "zoning laws." One zoning law says that no house can be built on a lot smaller than two acres in size. The cost of the lot alone drives up the price of the house beyond the reach of poor people. Another zoning law says that no house can be occupied by anyone but the immediate nuclear family. This requires that grandparents be abandoned to live elsewhere, and it assumes that separate housing can be afforded for the grandparents or other relatives who are not in the immediate family. Another zoning law says that no house can be smaller than so many thousand square feet: the larger the house, the greater the cost. Still another law forbids apartment housing and mobile homes, often the only kind of housing the poor can afford.

These laws are defended with the argument that they keep the community "nice." Nice means rich and, mostly, white. It is as though being poor means you are not entitled to live in a nice neighborhood. This is true even if you are a full-time worker performing a vital job but at a poverty wage, defined by the federal government in 1987 as an annual income of less than $11,200 for a family of four (Rosewater, 1989, p. 9).

These artificial barriers can be broken down, as the state of New Jersey has shown. The New Jersey Supreme Court has ordered the state's suburban communities to change their zoning laws to permit the construction of housing for people with low and moderate incomes. Builders have agreed to put up low- and moderate-income housing, even though they will not make much of a profit from it, because they are also allowed to put up expensive and profitable housing. Unfortunately, even the low-income housing is too expensive for many families, which is why housing allowances are needed. To accomplish this on a national level requires greatly expanded government intervention in the housing market, with much more government control of what the housing industry is allowed to do, and many more incentives to get them to do the right things (Downs, 1973; U.S. Commission on Civil Rights, 1974).

It is ironic that rich folks want to keep the poor folks out, and yet rich folks are themselves now invading the neighborhoods of the poor. They are engaged in a process called "gentrification," whereby they purchase city dwellings, evict the poor or hire thugs to terrorize them out, expensively refurbish the dwellings, and then sell or rent them to other rich folks. The reason rich people want to live in cities like New York is that it puts them close to where they work and to the cultural center of the region. Alas, the poor who get pushed out to make room for the rich cannot afford to go to the suburbs. Many of them have wound up in welfare hotels or in abandoned buildings without heat or running water. Others are living on the streets as part of America's growing population of homeless people.

MAKING THE ONLY CHOICE

It might seem just too costly to integrate the schools and communities of the United States. The busing costs for school integration could be low enough for the taxpayers to take on this burden. However, the cost of housing allowances for residential integration could demand too much sacrifice from the taxpayers. Given the federal budget deficit, housing allowances could also be what President Reagan referred to as "budget busters." Taxpayers might well resent having to use part of their own hard-earned income to subsidize the housing of people they consider unworthy. This resentment could be exploited by politicians to get elected on the promise of "rolling back all these government handouts."

To a large extent, that, in fact, is what happened at the end of the 1970s. There was a political backlash against the poor by the middle and upper classes. It became popular to think that the problems of poverty could be dealt with *cheaply*. In some circles it was even thought that increased misery was the most effective way to snap the poor out of their poverty. In addition, there was the genetic argument. It was said that the poor were poor because they were "naturally" dumb and shiftless. They had been born that way just as though they had been born with an incurable disease. Nature *meant* them to be poor, and they were too brutish even to mind a whole lot.

This kind of thinking is an indulgence the United States can no longer afford. It is selfish thinking, and the best answer to it is selfish thinking of a more realistic sort. It is unrealistic to think that the problems of the poor do not affect the rest of us.

We may not want to incur the costs of school reorganization and busing, but those can still be cheaper than property and insurance losses due to urban crime, and productivity losses due to high rates of joblessness. We may not want to bear the costs of integrated housing, but they can still be cheaper than the costs of building prisons for criminals whose breeding ground is the ghetto. We may wish we could forgo the initial tensions, suspicions, and hostility of intergroup association, but these are still easier to cope with than the riots and physical assaults—as well as the constant threat of them—that result from intergroup alienation. We may want our children to acquire a large competitive edge in the occupational marketplace against the children of the poor, but with the American workforce declining numerically and with the structure of future work so difficult to predict, it might well be in our mutual interest to have *everyone's* talents fully developed. We might desire to treat our minority citizens as though they were citizens of a Third World country, but we can hardly expect to defeat communism in the Third World if we do. Even now, the Soviets get plenty of propaganda mileage by showing films of America's ghettoes.

We can choose to ignore the problems of segregation in our society and hope that they will vanish in time. We can do as we've been doing for so long: treat the problems with Band-Aids and lip service. Or we can determine that the problems must be eliminated now. The latter choice is the one most clearly in our self-interest, and the interest of our consciences. Moreover, public opinion is swaying in this direction. In 1971, 43 percent of the public thought that integration improved education for black children, and 23 percent thought that it also helped white children. In 1988, 55 percent thought that it helped blacks and 35 percent believed that white children benefited, too. Over the seventeen-year period, the percentages went up by 12 points regarding both black children and white children. Additionally, in 1973, 30 percent of the public thought that more should be done to integrate the schools; in 1988 the figure was 37 percent

(Gallup and Elam, 1988, p. 39). This was at the end of the Reagan era, after a long federal retreat from integration as a goal for America. If the public's mood could change in the opposite direction during that time, the prospects for the future are indeed good.

POSITION 2
Against Legal Integration

KEEPING GOVERNMENT OFF OUR BACKS

Let's not mince words. "Legal" integration is simply a euphemism for *forced* integration. Integration forced on us by law is as objectionable as segregation forced on us by law. "Legal" integration is as contrary to the freedom guaranteed to Americans in the U.S. Constitution as "legal" segregation was.

One can be an integrationist without being rabidly so. The rabid integrationist is willing to invoke all the forces of government to bring about a goal that is *not* guaranteed in the Constitution. A racially integrated society was not even envisioned by our slave-owning Founding Fathers, let alone guaranteed (Higginbotham, 1978). However desirable a racially integrated society may be, it is not the role of government to force such a society on free individuals, black or white. If an integrated society is to emerge in the United States, it must be through the *uncoerced* interaction of individuals.

Federal Judge John Parker, "a moderate jurist who had issued several racially progressive rulings" (Wilkinson, 1979, p. 81), interpreted the *Brown* decision in the only reasonable way:

> . . . a state may not deny to any person on account of race the right to attend any school that it maintains . . . but if the schools which it maintains are open to children of all races, no violation of the Constitution is involved even though the children of different races voluntarily attend different schools, as they attend different churches. Nothing in the Constitution or in the [*Brown*] decision of the Supreme Court takes away from the people the freedom to choose the schools they attend. The Constitution, in other words, does not require integration. It does not forbid such discrimination as occurs as the result of voluntary action. It merely forbids the use of governmental power to enforce segregation. (*Briggs v. Elliott*, 1955)

The freedoms the Constitution guarantees us are largely freedoms *from* government. The Founding Fathers had fought a war to rid themselves of the restraints of a repressive British government. They wanted a government that would itself be restrained from interfering in the affairs of its citizens. As Thomas Jefferson said, "That government governs best which governs least."

Tyranny can creep up on us in small steps, so government must be prevented from taking any steps that are not absolutely essential for the common good. Even when a proposed government action appears benevolent, the question must be raised whether the result of that action will be worth the loss of individual freedom that will inevitably occur.

For example, in 1974 the U.S. Congress grew dismayed at the sheer number of deaths due to automobile accidents. The Congress then passed a law requiring all newly manufactured cars to contain an alarm system that would continue sounding until a car's occupants had fastened their seat belts. For people who hated to buckle up, the sound might drive them crazy as they drove, but better nuts than dead was Congress's reasoning. Others reasoned differently: that however benign its intention, Congress was protecting a large number of people against their will and had thereby forfeited too much basic human freedom for too little added automobile safety. The law was soon rescinded, at the urging of both liberals and conservatives. (The high cost of automobile insurance may have caused people to be more forbearing with state laws requiring the use of seat belts.)

The next time you are tempted to support government interference into the private lives of your fellow citizens for their own good—perhaps in the form of a government ban on all tobacco smoking—pause to consider some of the many ways the government could compel you to do things that might be in your best interest. The government could control most of your waking hours in the sincere belief that it was making you a better person. Each time government is allowed to control you at all, it acquires an argument for controlling you further.

GIVING GOVERNMENT MANAGEABLE TASKS

Nothing breeds disrespect for government so much as its failures. We have become used to hearing such expressions as "government mess" and "real government foul-up." The messes and the foul-ups very often occur because the government arrogantly decides to take on an enormous task beyond its capability. Even if it does so reluctantly in response to public pressure, the result may be the same. The job may be so complicated that it cannot be done well by any human agency. If it cannot be done well, whoever undertakes it is foredoomed to failure.

Sometimes the government invites predictable disasters which then make it such an object of ridicule that people start breaking the law out of contempt for the government's bungling. A good example of this is the widespread practice of tax cheating, which many people rationalize on the basis that the government's tax collection system is conceded even by officials of the Internal Revenue Service to be unnecessarily confusing and unfair. At other times the law so tramples on a cherished right that breaking the law becomes an honorable pastime. Prohibition violated people's assumed right to drink alcohol, and they defied it with zest. In instances like these, the government is reduced to ignoring or repealing its own laws to avoid the mischief which will result from further enforcement.

The right of association is a cherished American right, and one that is actually addressed in the freedom of assembly clause of the First Amendment of the Bill of Rights. The government has already curtailed this right by forcing people who engage in most forms of commerce to do so on a nondiscriminatory basis. This government action is designed to prevent a harm: the denial of opportunity to minorities. For the government to go the next step and insist that people integrate (associate) with groups they dislike is to provoke wholesale defiance of the law. "Most groups (racial and ethnic) prefer to live among their own kind. While this may look and have the same effects as prejudice, it really is different. For one thing, it may affect blacks in the same way as whites. For another, the housing decision is not one based on prejudice against a specific group" (Glazer, 1981, p. 138). Moreover, people who live in the suburbs consider their residence a reward for achievement. They will not tolerate government intrusion into that hard-earned sanctuary. If a person's home is his or her castle, the neighborhood around it is the moat. And to maintain the dollar value of the castle, it is necessary to maintain the quality of the moat.

The task of enforcing compulsory integration would be monumental even if it were tolerated. Many, many more government officials would have to be hired for this task alone. They would have to keep track of racial proportions community by community to ensure that the "correct" balances were being achieved. They would, of course, first have to decide what the "correct" balance should be for each community and school. As the proportions got out of the proper balance, adjustments would continually have to be forced on people of both races to restore the right racial mix. School attendance patterns would be redrawn regularly—perhaps every year—to keep the numbers to the satisfaction of some bureaucrat. Housing allowances for families and construction permits for builders would be subject to constant government manipulation. Altogether, it would be a task of tremendous social engineering which government has already proven itself unable to handle, and which would cause everyone endless exasperation. It might succeed in uniting blacks and whites, but only in their disgust with the government. A good example of how the best-laid plans of government can go awry in large-scale social planning is to be found in Daniel Patrick Moynihan's aptly titled book, *Maximum Feasible Misunderstanding* (1969). This details consequences of the War on Poverty program that *no one* intended.

How difficult the task of metropolitan school integration would be was suggested by a series of questions the U.S. Supreme Court raised when it rejected the attempt to integrate the Detroit metropolitan region:

> Entirely apart from the logistical and other serious problems attending large-scale transportation of students, the consolidation would give rise to an array of other problems in financing and operating this new school system. Some of the more obvious questions would be: What would be the status of authority of the present popularly elected school boards? Would the children of Detroit be within the jurisdiction and operating control of a school board elected by parents and residents of other districts? What board or boards would levy taxes for school operations in these 54 districts constituting the consolidated metropolitan area? What provision could be made for assuring substantial equality in tax levies among the 54 districts, if this were deemed requisite? What provisions would be made for financing? Would the

validity of long-term bonds be jeopardized unless approved by all of the component districts as well as the State? What body would determine that portion of the curricula now left to the discretion of local school boards? Who would establish attendance zones, purchase school equipment, locate and construct new schools, and indeed attend to all the myriad day-to-day decisions that are necessary to school operations affecting potentially more than three-quarters of a million pupils? (*Bradley v. Milliken*, 1974)

It is important to bear in mind that the compulsory integrationists do not limit their benevolence to blacks. They are more altruistic than that. They also seek to integrate into the American mainstream Hispanics and the poor in general. The grander the goals of the integrationists, the greater the government action needed to achieve them. So all the difficulties we have been discussing are going to be made even worse. Moreover, the huge expansion of the public, or government, sector of society called for by the integrationists' ambitious agenda will necessarily reduce the size of the private, or productive, sector. In other words, the *revenue-producing* sector of society will be reduced in favor of the *revenue-consuming* sector. This will obviously have negative consequences for the health of the U.S. economy, but just how negative will depend on how zealously the compulsory integrationists pursue their dreams.

We can get some sense of the risk by looking at the parlous state of the Soviet economy. The Soviets have a centrally planned society with a massive government bureaucracy, and their budget deficit is estimated to be as high as 20 percent of their national income (Shelton, 1989). Our deficit has been kept below 6 percent, which explains why the Soviets are seeking to do business with us and to be more like us. We should not be adopting practices that they are trying to abandon.

CHALLENGING THE INTEGRATIONIST ASSUMPTIONS

All the aggravation and pervasive government control of our lives might be worth bearing if the results could be predicted with some certainty to be beneficial. However, we cannot know beforehand whether the results will be beneficial at all, let alone how much. The compulsory integrationists act as though their *assumptions* about the benefits are already proven facts accepted by all. In making their assumptions, the integrationists may be guilty of nothing more than excessive optimism about human nature. But even so, to base social policy on their Pollyanna attitudes is to take a big and dangerous gamble.

One of the most obvious assumptions of the integrationists is that different groups will grow to respect each other if they are forced to live and work in close contact. The danger is that they might, in fact, grow to dislike each other so much that instead of having a productive relationship, they will spend all of their time in bitter enmity. It is true that some cases of forced integration have turned out reasonably well. Unfortunately, these cases are more than counterbalanced by cases in which physical violence was a recurring event, and even now, years later, there is mutual antagonism and tension between the groups. A series of studies on the interactions that occur between blacks and whites in integrated schools in both the south and the north resulted in the following conclusions:

> The racial cleavage reported time and again in these studies suggests that while the student populations may have been desegregated, they were not integrated. . . . For most participants, school desegregation spelled trouble, and to keep it at arm's length was thought to be success enough. . . . Violence was thought to be just below the surface of daily behavior. . . . the racial attribute of being "white" carried high status, while that of being a member of a racial minority carried low status. Given that so many members of the minority groups were also economically poor meant that status characteristics were reinforced with class characteristics. (Rist, 1979, pp. 8–10)

What worked in the happy cases of integration may be unique to the contexts in which those cases unfolded, and since we cannot be sure what *that* was, we cannot know whether or how to apply it to all other cases. But we do know that there are many unhappy cases. There is just too much at stake for us to rely on government by guess and wishful thinking in the matter of integration. As a California newspaper said in opposition to the forced integration of the Berkeley schools, "The board of education is destroying a city to test a theory" (quoted in Kirp, 1982, p. 161).

A second assumption of the compulsory integrationists is that the down-trodden will respond to kindness with gratitude. "Just give 'em a chance and they'll come around," is their thinking. However, it's possible that the down-trodden will perceive kindness as a weakness to be exploited. During the high-tide years of the War on Poverty in the late 1960s and early '70s, the poor and minorities spent a good deal of time not in reforming themselves but in ripping off the system that was trying to help them (Lemann, 1988–1989). If the abuses are not as great today, it's because the benefits have been cut back so that there are fewer opportunities for abuse than there once were. The integrationists may have naive notions about human nature or, at least, notions which cannot be generalized to *every* human being. At any rate, it is possible that some people's personalities are so warped, by either genetic predisposition or life experience or both, that kindness is a medicine that will no longer work. The bleeding-heart integrationists refuse to acknowledge that such a grim situation is even possible.

THE AFFRONT TO BLACKS

A third assumption of compulsory integrationists is so offensive that it demands discussion in a section by itself. This is the belief that blacks long for the chance to live and work among whites. This assumption brings the integrationists close to being racists. Behind it is the further assumption that blacks *should* want to live and work with whites. The reverse assumption is not made: that whites should want to live and work with blacks. Thus, the compulsory integrationist position is insulting and condescending to blacks because it fails to represent their real feelings. The last Gallup Poll to sample people's opinions toward busing to integrate the schools showed that fully 31 percent of blacks were opposed to busing (Gallup, 1981). The fact that 78 percent of whites were also opposed to busing can be interpreted to mean that both races want good schools for their children, period. They do not crave the chance to mingle with each other.

It is true that much of the school desegregation litigation has been initiated by black organizations, most especially the National Association for the Advancement of Colored People. However, it is false to infer from this that it was integration per se that blacks wanted.

> . . . blacks and Mexican-Americans who supported desegregation did so primarily because they believed that desegregation would enable their children to receive the same kind of education as white children. The underlying black assumption . . . is that chances are greater that their children will receive equal or quality education if they attend the same classes with white children. Many parents said that in a desegregated school, classroom minority and white children would be exposed to the same curriculum materials and other resources and would most likely be treated alike by teachers and other school personnel . . . *the perspective on the desegregation situation given by these parents is not the same as that held by social scientists* [emphasis added]. (Ogbu, 1986, p. 40)

Thus, what blacks want is not integration but equal educational opportunity. This is what Kenneth Clark, the black psychologist whose evidence was so influential in the Supreme Court's *Brown* decision, meant when he argued for equal schools regardless of integration (Clark, 1965).

John Ogbu notes that blacks are often disappointed by desegregated schools. They find that the schools become segregated inside, with the black students being shunted disproportionately into special classes for problem students (Ogbu, 1986, p. 41). After all the agony to get the Boston schools integrated so children would have a better chance, what was the result? "Far and away the gravest failures in the Boston story concern the continuation of generally poor instruction. The number of students denied promotions is still significant, and it reveals a sorry state of affairs. Academic achievement has been improved in a few schools but such is not the case in most" (Dentler and Scott, 1981, p. 233).

For integration to be palatable to whites, their children have to constitute a large majority of the integrated school. When their children get below 75 percent of the student body, the "tipping point" is said to have been reached, after which the whites start pulling out. Therefore, the usual integration pattern is for black youngsters to go from segregated schools where they are a majority to integrated schools where they are a distinct minority. Metropolitan integration is intended to keep blacks in this minority status so whites will not be unduly alarmed. The predictable result for black children—for any children— when they are put into a strange and hostile environment is that their self-esteem drops. "Many researchers have found that black children tend to indicate a higher degree of self-esteem than white children, but that desegregation often has a discouraging effect . . . desegregation tends to threaten the self-esteem of minority children'' (St. John, 1981, p. 91).

> The desegregated experience, then, is one of enhanced awareness of the broader society's negative attitudes towards one's race. . . . In segregated settings, the self-esteem of black children from separated or never-married families is just as high as that of children from intact families; but in the desegregated setting it is substantially lower. In addition, in desegregated settings black children are more likely to be poorer than those around them than in the segregated settings. In several important respects, social comparisons tend to be more unfavorable in desegregated than in segregated settings. (Rosenberg, 1986, pp. 186–187)

What black parent should be expected to subject her child to the psychological torment attendant on integrated education? Some might find this a reasonable price for a child to pay in exchange for improved academic performance. Unfortunately, the evidence for the effect of integration on black academic achievement is not at all clear. The data are ''mixed and ambiguous'' (Granovetter, 1986, p. 99). ''The very best studies available demonstrate no significant and consistent effects of desegregation on Black achievement'' (Armor, 1984, p. 58). Is this indeterminacy worth the price in self-esteem?

SPARING THE INNOCENT

The United States has a horrible history of racism, a fact beyond dispute. In recent decades, however, remarkable progress has been made in removing the overt manifestations of racism. This progress has affected attitudes as well, so that racism no longer lurks in the American mind as it once did. The laws that forbade racist behavior among the older generations of Americans have gradually caused those generations to purge themselves of racist attitudes, which are now looked back upon with shame. The younger generations, with a very few well-publicized exceptions such as Howard Beach, have never been guilty of racist behavior, and they have learned from schools and the media that racist attitudes are discreditable.

And yet it is the younger generations from whom the compulsory integrationists expect the greatest sacrifice in their bold experiment. It is young married couples and their children who are being asked to redeem the United States from its legacy of racism. School integration will involve them directly; all the trauma will be visited upon them as though they personally had to make restitution for the crimes of others. Worse, it will be visited upon them by people who arrange to avoid it for themselves, as Nathan Glazer has noted.

> The leading advocates of transportation for integration—journalists, political figures, and judges—send their children to private schools which escape the consequences of these legal decisions. This does raise a moral question. The judges who impose such decisions, the lawyers who argue . . . for them would not themselves send their children to the schools to which, by their actions, others poorer or less mobile than they are must send their children. Those not subject to a certain condition are insisting

that others submit themselves to it, which offends the basic rule of morality in both the Jewish and Christian traditions. (Quoted in Wilkinson, 1979, p. 210)

If we could be sure that the school integration experiments would go smoothly, it would be reasonable to subject innocent children to the inconveniences involved in them for the long-term good of society. The resistance is not to an integrated society per se, or to the use of children in bringing about that goal. The resistance, the absolute refusal, stems from fear of gratuitous harm to the innocent of both races.

This harm can take several real forms, as past experiments with integration have shown. First, gentle and well-bred children will be forced into close and constant association with children of violent tendencies. How the violent children got that way is beside the point; they threaten and will occasionally inflict physical harm on children who have done nothing to provoke it. The possibilities of this physical harm do not stop short of murder. Second, the threat of physical harm will be used to extort money from frightened children. Some schoolchildren have gone without lunch for long periods of time because their lunch money was being extorted and they were too terrified to tell even their parents. Third, the availability of drugs in or near the school is likely to increase, as are the pressures to engage in drug abuse. This risk is made all the more intolerable as newer drugs are formulated which the body itself is less able to tolerate. Fourth, the school's academic mission will become more diffuse as students of different ability have to be accommodated. As the school's focus becomes blurred, energy and resources will be spread more thinly than when they were concentrated on single-purpose efforts. Everyone will lose. Fifth, a less homogeneous (less segregrated, if you will) school community will cause a loss of school spirit. Neither students nor parents will be able to identify with the school as they did when it more fully reflected their own values and aspirations.

The list of the harms that can and do result from school integration experiments indicates that blacks as well as whites run the risk of a worse educational experience. For blacks who are transported from a predominantly black school near home to an overwhelmingly white school miles away, the sense of being an unwelcome outsider can be most dispiriting. Just as there are innocent white children who ought not to be victimized by the integrationists' grand schemes, there are innocent black children whose most valuable possession is their sense of self-worth. Putting that in jeopardy is a most serious matter, and something that should not be done in our present state of social policy forecasting.

Finally, the fundamental difference between the compulsory integrationists and those who oppose them is not the goal they want to achieve. We should all wish for an integrated society. The difference lies in each group's sense of the possible, and in the opposing group's conviction that good intentions are not enough. It would be wonderful to have a better society but, given the fragility of human relationships, it would be quite easy to create a worse one.

It is fitting that the final word be given to William Bradford Reynolds, the

U.S. Assistant Attorney General for Civil Rights during the Reagan administration, who fought so hard, against so much slander, to restore morality and common sense to American education:

> We have learned something from this unfortunate social experiment, which has led needlessly to the sacrificing of quality education on the altar of racial balance. It is a lesson that should not soon be forgotten, with respect to school desegregation or civil rights generally. We must always be aware of the danger to an individual's civil rights that lurks in group-oriented policies grounded on racial preferences, racial-balancing, and proportionality. If we ever succumb to this threat, the great civil rights movement will have tragically, and unnecessarily, exhausted all credibility. Once the noble ideal of equal opportunity is compromised, it is not easily retrieved, and all Americans suffer. (Reynolds, 1986, p. 13)

FOR DISCUSSION

1 If, as William Julius Wilson demonstrates, black children in the inner city are isolated from good role models as well as from good job contacts, how can this isolation be broken?

2 Louise Day Hicks, the chairperson of the Boston School Committee, justified her resistance to the court's desegregation order in the following terms:

> Why is there resistance in South Boston? Simply stated, it is because it is against your children's interest to send them to schools in crime-infested Roxbury. . . . There are at least one hundred black people walking around in the black community who have killed white people during the past two years. . . . Any well-informed white suburban woman does not pass through that community alone even by automobile. Repairmen, utilities workers, taxi drivers, doctors, firemen, all have refused at one time or another to do what Judge Garrity demands of our children on a daily basis. (Quoted in J. A. Lukas, *Common Ground,* New York: Knopf, 1985, p. 412.)

If you were Judge Garrity, how would you have answered Mrs. Hicks?

3 How would you explain the following facts for the city of Washington, D.C.?

> Black children five to fourteen years old outnumber white children more than ten to one. The ratio is more than eight to one among those aged fifteen to nineteen. After children finish school, the ratio shifts. Almost one-third of the residents aged twenty to twenty-four are white. But then the ratio shifts back: in the thirty-five to thirty-nine-year-old group, there are about four blacks for every white. For people over 50 the ratio shifts again in the other direction. (From G. Orfield, *Why Must We Bus?,* Washington, D.C.: The Brookings Institution, 1978, p. 95.)

4 Following is a list* of all the things that can be taken into account when studying

---

* From W. D. Hawley, C. H. Rossell, and R. L. Crain, "Directions for Future Research," in *The Consequences of School Desegregation,* edited by Rossell and Hawley, Philadelphia: Temple University Press, 1983, pp. 177–178.

the effectiveness of school desegregation. How confident does this list make you that the existing studies have been done well and that future studies will be easy to do?

Key Variables in the Study of Desegregation Processes and Outcomes

1   Who has been desegregated with whom?
   a   Racial/ethnic mix
   b   Social class of each group
   c   Degree of tracking between and within schools
2   What was the process by which desegregation initially occurred?
   a   How desegregation came about (court-ordered, board-ordered, mandatory, voluntary, and so on)
   b   Duration of desegregation
   c   Amount and duration of conflict
   d   Amount of community preparation
   e   Amount and type of in-school work with students on racial issues
3   What are the characteristics of the schools and classrooms being studied? (Although the list of school characteristics that might be studied is long, the list of factors that have been linked to student outcomes is much shorter.)
   a   Content and duration of teacher inservice program
   b   Staff attitudes related to race
   c   Racial and ethnic composition of staff
   d   Type of instruction
   e   Time on task for particular topics
   f   Nature of reward systems
   g   Opportunities for interracial interaction
   h   Extent and type of extracurricular activities
   i   Extent and type of remedial programs or special programs
   j   School suspensions and discipline policy
   k   Experience of staff in desegregated settings
   l   School size and staff-student ratio
   m   The leadership role and style of principal
   n   Parental involvement
4   What are the individual characteristics of the students being studied?
   a   Sex
   b   Race
   c   Age
   d   Age of first desegregated experience
   e   Years in desegregated school
   f   Capacity for academic achievement
   g   Interracial contact outside of school
5   When the learning of individuals is part of the research, what is the student's family background?
   a   Learning resources available to the student
   b   Educational background of parents
   c   Level of support for achievement (or other student objectives)
6   What are the characteristics of the community in which school desegregation is taking place?

      a Racially relevant history (including the history of the region)
      b Level of information about schools
      c Racial composition
      d Role of community leaders
      e Degree of SES heterogeneity
      f Economic vitality
  7 What are the consequences for students?
      a Achievement
      b Racial attitudes
      c Racial behavior
      d Sense of self-confidence, attribution of personal causation
      e Student victimization
  8 What are the consequences for alumni?
      a College attendance, field chosen, completion
      b Job-hunting process
      c Racial contacts
      d Housing choices
      e Political participation
  9 What are the consequences for the school system?
      a New innovations
      b Changes in administration
      c Parent participation and pressure on schools
      d School board election outcomes
      e Tax and bond referenda outcomes
10 What are the consequences for the community?
      a Racial controversy over school issues
      b Racial initiatives in nonschool areas
      c Desegregation in housing
      d Impact of racial issues in nonschool elections
11 What characteristics of the school and the school system affect the implementation of desegregation plans and strategies?
      a School system population size
      b School system geographic scope
      c Proportion minority
      d Fiscal capacity
      e Housing patterns, etc.

REFERENCES

Armor, D. (1984). *The Evidence on Desegregation and Black Achievement.* Washington, D.C.: National Institute of Education.
Bradley v. Milliken (1974). 418 U.S. 717.
Briggs v. Elliott (1955). 132 F. Supp. 776.
Brown v. Board of Education of Topeka (1954). 347 U.S. 483.
Clark, K. (1965). *Dark Ghetto: Dilemmas of Social Power.* New York: Harper and Row.
Conard, B. D. (1988). "Cooperative Learning and Prejudice Reduction." *Social Education* **52**(4), 283–286.

Dentler, R. A., and Scott, M. B. (1981). *Schools on Trial: An Inside Account of the Boston Desegregation Case*. Cambridge, Mass.: Abt Books.

Downs, A. (1973). *Opening Up the Suburbs: An Urban Strategy for America*. New Haven: Yale University Press.

Evans v. Buchanan (1977). 416 F. Supp. 328.

The Gallup Report (1981). **185,** 29.

Gallup, A. M., and Elam, S. M. (1988). "The 20th Annual Gallup Poll of the Public's Attitudes Toward the Public Schools." *Phi Delta Kappan* **70**(1), 33–46.

Glazer, N. (1981). "Race and the Suburbs." In *Race and Schooling in the City,* edited by A. Yarmolinsky, L. Liebman, and C. S. Schelling. Cambridge, Mass.: Harvard University Press.

Granovetter, M. (1986). "The Micro-Structure of School Desegregation." In *School Desegregation Research: New Directions in Situational Analysis,* edited by J. Prager, D. Longshore, and M. Seeman. New York: Plenum Press.

Hawley, W. D. (1981). "Increasing the Effectiveness of School Desegregation: Lessons From the Research." In *Race and Schooling in the City,* edited by A. Yarmolinsky, L. Liebman, and C. S. Schelling. Cambridge, Mass.: Harvard University Press.

Higginbotham, A. L., Jr. (1978). *In the Matter of Color, Race and the American Legal Process: The Colonial Period*. New York: Oxford University Press.

Hochschild, J. L. (1984). *The New American Dilemma: Liberal Democracy and School Desegregation*. New Haven: Yale University Press.

Keyes v. Denver School District No. 1 (1973). 413 U.S. 189.

Kirp, D. L. (1982). *Just Schools: The Idea of Racial Equality in American Education*. Berkeley: University of California Press.

Lemann, N. (1988–1989). "The Unfinished War." *The Atlantic Monthly,* December 1988, pp. 37–56; January 1989, pp. 53–68.

Lukas, J. A. (1985). *Common Ground: A Turbulent Decade in the Lives of Three American Families*. New York: Knopf.

Mahard, R. E., and Crain, R. L. (1983). "Research on Minority Achievement in Desegregated Schools." In *The Consequences of School Desegregation,* edited by C. H. Rossell and W. D. Hawley. Philadelphia: Temple University Press.

Moynihan, D. P. (1969). *Maximum Feasible Misunderstanding: Community Action in the War on Poverty*. New York: Free Press.

National Coalition of Advocates for Students (1988). *A Special Analysis of 1986 Elementary and Secondary School Civil Rights Survey Data*. Boston: NCAS.

National Urban League (1987). *The State of Black America 1987*. New York: National Urban League.

Ogbu, J. U. (1986). "Structural Constraints in School Desegregation." In *School Desegregation Research: New Directions in Situational Analysis,* edited by J. Prager, D. Longshore, and M. Seeman. New York: Plenum Press.

Orfield, G. (1978). *Why Must We Bus? Segregated Schools and National Policy*. Washington, D.C.: The Brookings Institution.

Pettigrew, T. F. (1981). "The Case for Metropolitan Approaches to Public-School Desegregation." In *Race and Schooling in the City,* edited by A. Yarmolinsky, L. Liebman, and C. S. Schelling. Cambridge, Mass.: Harvard University Press.

Reynolds, W. B. (1986). "Education Alternatives to Transportation Failures: The Desegregation Response to a Resegregation Dilemma." *Metropolitan Education* **1,** 3–14.

Rist, R. C. (1979). "Introduction." In *Desegregated Schools: Appraisals of an American Experiment*, edited by R. C. Rist. New York: Academic Press.

Rosenberg, R. (1986). "Self-Esteem Research: A Phenomenological Corrective." In *School Desegregation Research: New Directions in Situational Analysis*, edited by J. Prager, D. Longshore, and M. Seeman. New York: Plenum Press.

Rosewater, A. (1989). "Child and Family Trends: Beyond the Numbers." In *Caring for America's Children*, edited by F. Macchiarola and A. Gartner. New York: The Academy of Political Science.

St. John, N. H. (1981). "The Effects of School Desegregation on Children: A New Look at the Research Evidence." In *Race and Schooling in the City*, edited by A. Yarmolinsky, L. Liebman, and C. S. Schelling. Cambridge, Mass.: Harvard University Press.

Schofield, J. W., and Sagar, H. A. (1983). "Desegregation, School Practices, and Student Race Relations." In *The Consequences of School Desegregation*, edited by C. H. Rossell and W. D. Hawley. Philadelphia: Temple University Press.

Shelton, J. (1989). *The Coming Soviet Crash: Gorbachev's Desperate Search for Credit in the Western Financial Market*. New York: Free Press.

U.S. Commission on Civil Rights (1974). *Equal Opportunity in Suburbia*. Washington, D.C.: Government Printing Office.

Wilkinson, J. H. (1979). *From Brown to Bakke: The Supreme Court and School Integration, 1954–1978*. New York: Oxford University Press.

Wilson, W. J. (1987). *The Truly Disadvantaged: The Inner City, the Underclass, and Public Policy*. Chicago: University of Chicago Press.

PART TWO

WHAT SHOULD BE TAUGHT?

The theme of this section is the fundamental struggle over knowledge: what knowledge is most valuable, who gets to decide, who is to have access to it, and how it is to be transmitted. Whoever gets to define what is most worth knowing also gets to define "literacy," since that term implies the possession of socially approved knowledge. This struggle to control what is accepted as knowledge and literacy is inevitably a struggle for power. To control people's minds is to control their expectations, their behavior, and their allegiance.

In ancient times, when magic and witchcraft had social credibility, sorcerers had great power and status. Their pronouncements were often translated into law and policy; knowledge of their secret rites was reserved for a select few. Later, when witchery came to be viewed as evil knowledge, sorcerers were punished. In modern society, where scientific knowledge is more prized, sorcerers are seen as interesting eccentrics. The major difference among these situations is the way in which we have changed our definition of knowledge. Note that the definition of knowledge incorporates the concept of literacy. A literate person in a time of belief in witchery is one who shares the language and values of that knowledge form. In an age of computers, a literate person may be defined as one who shares the language and values of computer knowledge. Thus the term "literate" may be thought of as a verbal badge given to those who possess knowledge considered socially valuable. Schools provide literacy credentials in the form of diplomas, degrees and various types of professional certificates.

LITERACY AND THE SCHOOL CURRICULUM

Schools have become the major means of access to socially approved knowledge, and literacy, defined in differing ways, has become the goal of schooling. This isn't as simple as it seems. Do we want to define literacy as elementary ability to read, write, and calculate, or do we give it a broader meaning that includes cultural understandings, self-exploration, technical skills, and critical social activism? These forms of "literacy" require different types of schooling. And these approaches to schooling draw from different, and often conflicting, ideologies that find expression in both the visible and the hidden curriculum of schools.

An expanded vision of literacy is offered by Judith Langer in a recent volume:

> Issues of literacy are critical to society—to its innermost workings at economic, political, and social levels. Literacy involves how people think, and learn, and change—and how society changes as a function of the changes in its people. . . .
>
> Literacy is seen "not as a set of independent skills associated with reading and writing, but as the application of particular skills for specific purposes in specific contexts." This view marks an end to the simple dichotomy between literate and illiterate citizens in favor of a literacy profile, based on a variety of contexts and uses of literacy. (Langer, 1987, pp. 1, 2)

Because of difficulties in constructing a single, widely accepted definition of literacy, recent discussions have tied it to specific contexts and uses. Thus, types of literacy include functional, technical, cultural, economic, visual, political, scientific, computer, and critical literacy. Different forms of literacy are supported by different special interests.

"Functional literacy" is not much more precise than plain "literacy," but suggests criteria that are related to the uses to which skills and knowledge may be put. It denotes the knowledge needed to function in the society, but that is subject to many interpretations. "Technical literacy," which may include the ability to read and to follow instructions on how to assemble toys or set up telephone answering machines, can also involve such abilities as deciphering prescriptions and operating equipment. Business would like more people with technical literacy for workers and purchasers. "Cultural literacy" often refers to knowing information in the humanities and arts, such as historical data, books considered important as literary masterpieces, and material from various forms of the arts. College professors and college graduates often push this form of literacy.

"Economic literacy" refers to the ability to understand employment, personal finance, consumer affairs, and principles of supply, demand, and scarcity. Consumer advocates, economists, and economics teachers think this would include the ability to find the best consumer interest rates, to apply for jobs, and to balance a checkbook. "Political literacy" includes knowing enough about the political system to be a participating member of the democracy. "Visual literacy" refers to the ability to understand and be critical of such media as TV, movies, photography, painting, and advertising. "Scientific literacy'' includes knowledge of basic scientific principles and a minimal under-standing of the impact of science on life. Teachers of civics, the arts, and science, respectively, would like these as literacy requirements.

"Computer literacy," a current favorite, means the ability to understand and use computers. This can include elementary computer knowledge of such things as the names of major computer components, and use of a program to play games or do limited word processing. It can also include the ability to use a variety of programs, to do complicated mathematical tasks, and to draft and revise computer programs. Computer companies and major businesses fancy this form. "Critical literacy" refers to the knowledge needed to be liberated from oppressive societies or social forces. Education to enlighten people about their human rights or to emancipate them from repression under dictatorial regimes requires literacy, even when some school efforts may be in opposition to government or business interests (Freire, 1970; Freire and Berthoff, 1987).

The most common forms of literacy pertain to socially approved bodies of knowledge that are part of the school's visible curriculum, those mandated and expected courses of study that are obvious and formal. The specific courses and emphasis within the curriculum depend upon prevailing visions of the good individual and the good society. In our age, as in every other, there are disparate views on what kinds of individuals and society are most desirable.

Some educators want to assist individuals to be free, independent, and crit-ical, while others advocate behavior modification to control deviation and to ensure social conformity. Some want each person to learn specific, standard information, while others recommend unlimited variety and creativity. Some demand that schools instill prescribed moral values and beliefs, while others demand release from moralisms and prescriptions. Some school people desire respect for authority and others prefer challenges to authority. Some would use precollegiate schooling to supply the occupational needs of society by giving specific preparation for students to become workers, managers, engineers, and doctors, while others would promote broad schooling with no vocational ori-entation. Underlying each of these competing views is a concept of the good individual and the good society. The visible curriculum is the mix of courses and sequences that schools offer to produce the desired person.

PRACTICAL, THEORETICAL, AND MORAL SCHOOLING

Disputes over how school should develop the good individual and the good society have filled western literature since its beginnings. Aristotle considered the state the fulfillment of our social drives and saw education as a state activity to provide social unity. He said, "Education is therefore THE means of making it [the society] a community and giving it unity. . . . education should be con-ducted by the state" (*The Politics*, 1962, pp. 55, 333). In his introduction to and discussion of Chapter 2, Book 8 of *The Politics*, Aristotle also recognized the continuing curriculum issue of whether schools should teach practical knowledge, moral character, or esoteric ideas:

[There is an] absence of any clear view about the proper subjects of instruction: the conflicting claims of utility, moral discipline, and the advancement of knowledge. . . . At present opinion is divided about the subjects of education. All do not take the same view about what should be learned by the young, either with a view to plain goodness or with a view to the best life possible; nor is opinion clear whether education should be directed mainly to the understanding, or mainly to moral character. (1962, pp. 333–334)

Modern curriculum debate continues to focus on the relative emphasis that should be given to practical, theoretical, and moral schooling. What knowledge will best fulfill the needs of individuals and society for (1) developing the skills for doing the practical work of the society; (2) pursuing advanced, theoretical knowledge in areas such as mathematics, literature, logic, and the arts; and (3) providing a set of moral guidelines and ethical values for judging right from wrong?

Disputes over emphasis and kinds of knowledge to be presented in schools continue. Contemporary comprehensive public schools offer some useful applied educational programs, such as reading, writing, driver's education, woodworking, home economics, computer operation, physical education, and vocational education. They also offer study of theoretical and more esoteric "higher knowledge" material in English, math, social studies, the arts, and science. And schools provide various forms of moral education, including the study of selected historical material and literature which convey ideas of the good person and the good society, and learning from school rules and teachers to be respectful, patriotic, loyal, and honest. The mix of these forms of education varies as different reforms become popular and as local communities make changes. Dress codes for students were abolished in the 1960s and arose again in the 1980s; flag salutes diminished in schools and are now returning; sex education was limited before the AIDS epidemic.

The report of the National Commission on Excellence in Education, the lightning rod of the 1980s reform movement, proposes a high school graduation requirement of four years of English, three of mathematics, three of science, and a semester of computer science (National Commission on Excellence in Education, 1983). Significantly, vocational education, one of the most prominent features in the school reforms of the 1930s and 1940s, is ignored in this 1983 report; physical education, part of major school reforms between 1910 and 1920, is also dismissed in the national reform of the 1980s. The arts are given only passing reference in the National Commission Report, but the proposed emphasis on computer science is actually a practical course, not unlike business education proposals of the 1920s and 1930s. The whole report is oriented to restoring America's competitive edge in international business and in national defense. These are very practical purposes, and suggest that the required core of courses should be bent toward knowledge that is useful in business.

High School (Boyer, 1983), a very influential book on 1980s reforms from the Carnegie Foundation for the Advancement of Teaching, describes the four essential functions of a high school as helping students:

Develop critical thinking and effective communicating
Learn about themselves, the human heritage, and the interdependent world
Prepare for work and further education
Fulfill social and civic obligations

These functions incorporate practical, moral, and higher knowledge. Boyer's curriculum proposal includes required courses in writing, speech, literature, arts, foreign language, American and world history, civics, science, technology, health, and a seminar on work and a senior-level independent applied project. This is an effort to cover as many of the bases as possible to cope with an "interdependent, interconnected, complex world." It includes some of each of the practical, moral, and esoteric knowledge that Aristotle had posed as disputable in education.

The formal curriculum in American schools is largely determined by external forces. It has evolved from a rather narrow interest in teaching religious ideals to multiple, and often conflicting, interests in providing broad knowledge, skills, and values in nearly every aspect of social life. The ancient Middle Ages curriculum of "seven liberal arts" including rhetoric, grammar, logic, arithmetic, astronomy, geometry, and music has been replaced by a list of American school subjects too long to include here.

The "liberal arts" of the Middle Ages were for an elite group in the society who had the privilege of schooling and leisure time to pursue it. It included the ideas of literacy in language (rhetoric and grammar), philosophy (logic), arts (music), science (astronomy), and math (geometry). The standard American curriculum of today offers an array of language and literature, social studies, science, math, arts, vocations, and specialty topics such as computers, in courses from kindergarten through twelfth grade for all students. And the formal school curriculum is certainly not all that students are expected to learn in school.

THE HIDDEN CURRICULUM

In addition to the visible school curriculum, which is composed of the various courses that are prescribed and offered to students, there is also a hidden curriculum consisting of those unexpressed and usually unexamined ideas, values, and behaviors that are conveyed to students through informal means. These are the subtle, often unintended, things that are learned by students (and teachers, too) as they go about their lives in school. They represent underlying ideologies, root ideas about human values and social relations.

At the simplest level, the hidden curriculum can be exemplified by three brief examples. Students are told by teachers to be independent and to express their own ideas, but the student who exhibits independence and expresses ideas the teacher doesn't like is often chastised or punished. What is learned? Students are taught in health classes that smoking is dangerous, but they see teachers, including the coach, smoking. What is learned? Students are taught in history courses that justice and equality are guaranteed by the U.S. Constitution and Bill of Rights, yet they recognize that compliant and properly dressed students who are liked by teachers get special privileges and better grades. What is learned? The hidden curriculum is a vast, relatively uncharted domain that is often much more effective in terms of what students actually learn in school than the official formal curriculum.

Beneath the surface hypocrisies of teachers saying one thing and doing another lies a deeper conflict of competing ideologies. The hidden curriculum is in conflict with the stated purposes of the visible curriculum. A stated purpose of schools is to protect diversity; however, the hidden curriculum expects conformity. The stated curriculum advocates critical thinking; the hidden curriculum supports docility. The visible curriculum professes equal opportunity; the hidden curriculum actually separates students by social-class background and channels them into social-class differences.

Recent critical literature examines the hidden curriculum and its ideological bases.* From this critical view of schooling, the "great debates" about school that are extensively covered in the media and the mainstream educational literature are merely narrowly constructed trivial differences between liberals and conservatives that do not raise ideological concerns about the control of knowledge and its social consequences. Mainstream arguments about whether the curriculum should stress the basics, provide vocational courses, allow electives, or emphasize American values do not raise significant educational questions. Critical examination in depth leads to more fundamental disputes involving who controls the school curriculum and what the consequences are of that control. Critical education studies expose ideologies and interests that lie behind the superficial debates.

CURRICULUM CONTROL

Control of knowledge, as seen through school curriculums, is a product of both prevailing social goals and prevailing social structures. During most of America's formative years, religion was the basis for the school curriculum. Although there were differences among the colonies, it was expected that all young children would be taught religious precepts at home or at Dame or Writing schools. The purpose, of course, was to thwart the efforts of "that ould deluder, satan," who sought to keep men from knowledge of the scriptures. After learning to read and write, however, most girls were not permitted further education and returned home to learn the arts of homemaking, while boys from more affluent homes continued schooling at Latin Grammar Schools. Blacks and Native Americans, however, were virtually excluded from the schools.

---

* See such works as Anyon, 1979, 1980; Apple, 1977; Cherryholmes, 1978; Giroux, 1988; Giroux and Purpel, 1977; Popkewitz, 1977; Young, 1970.

Historically, the struggle for control of knowledge has paralleled social-class differences. Practical knowledge was presumed to be needed by the workers, higher knowledge by the privileged class, and moral knowledge by both, but with some disparity in the kind of morals needed. Craft apprenticeships to learn practical knowledge were for the masses. Formal schooling to learn critical thinking and to study philosophy, science, and the arts was for the aristocratic class. In terms of moral instruction, the masses were to gain the moral character to obey, to respect authority, to work hard and be frugal, and to suffer with little complaint. Members of the privileged class were supposed to gain the moral character to rule wisely, justly, and with understanding.

One of the central purposes of schooling is to prepare the leaders of the society. Schooling, however, is controlled by those of the powerful class, and is responsive to their interests in what is taught.* Within an elitist society, the essential curricular question is: What should members of the ruling class know? In more democratic societies, such as the United States, Canada, the U.S.S.R., Europe, China, and Japan, where there is an effort to educate the masses, curricular questions often revolve around what all members of the society should be expected to know. Even in democratic societies, however, special attention is given to additional curricular needs of those identified as potential leaders. This can be seen in the higher academic tracks and honors programs that characterize many modern high schools in the United States. The correlation between social expectations, social class structure, and what is taught is obvious and deserves ongoing examination.

H. I. Marrou, for example, notes that in ancient Arabia the "upper class is composed of an aristocracy of warriors, and education is therefore of a military kind . . . training character and building up physical vigour rather than developing the intelligence." Marrou found similar conditions in old oriental, Indian, and western educational systems (Marrou, 1956, pp. xiv, xv).

R. H. Tawney (1964), observing that "educational policy is always social policy," criticized the elite "public boarding-school" tradition of the wealthy in England, and advocated improvements in the developing system of free schools for the working classes. He saw how the very nature of the elite system was a part of the hidden curriculum, teaching the sons of the wealthy, "not in words or of set purpose, but by the mere facts of their environment, that they are members . . . of a privileged group, whose function it will be, on however humble a scale, to direct and command, and to which leadership, influence, and the other prizes of life properly belong" (p. 83).

Social class is not the only major factor lying behind curricular decisions. Race, gender, national origin, and religion have been identified as other conditions that influence what knowledge is given to which people in society. The concept of privilege, and the education that privilege brings, has included racism

---

* There is an extensive body of literature on this topic. See the reference list for works by Anyon, Apple, Bernstein, Bourdieu, Carnoy, Bowles and Gintis, Freire, Giroux, Oakes, and Young.

and sexism in American and other national histories. Educational discrimination against nonwhites, women, Jews and Catholics, Indians and Eskimos, and others is a sorry tradition in a democratic society.

A quarter-century ago Kenneth Clark put the case clearly:

> The public schools in America's urban ghettos also reflect the oppressive damage of racial exclusion. . . . Segregation and inferior education reinforce each other. . . . Children themselves are not fooled by the various euphemisms educators use to disguise educational snobbery. From the earliest grades a child knows when he has been assigned to a level that is considered less than adequate. . . . ''The clash of cultures in the classroom'' is essentially a class war, a socio-economic and racial warfare being waged on the battleground of our schools, with middle-class and middle-class-aspiring teachers provided with a powerful arsenal of half-truths, prejudices, and rationalizations, arrayed against the hopelessly outclassed workingclass youngsters. (1965, pp. 111–117)

Similar descriptions of educational discrimination based on factors of religion, nationality, and gender are common in critical literature (Hofstadter, 1944; Clark, 1965; Katz, 1971; Feldman, 1974; Spring, 1976; Apple, 1977; Sadker and Sadker, 1982; Walker and Barton, 1983; Grimshaw, 1986). As Rosemary Deem comments, ''women have had to struggle hard against dominant patriarchal power relations, which try to confine women to the private sphere of the home and family, away from the public sphere or production and political power'' (1983, p. 107). Schooling, in which different knowledge and skills are given to students who differ only in race, gender, class, religion, or nationality, contributes to a continuation of inequality of treatment and to stereotypes.

The chapters of Part Two examine some of the curriculum disputes that have emerged as part of the current reform movement in education. These disputes are clearly tied to the question of what knowledge is most valuable in our society, a question that, in turn, is tied to our differing visions of what constitutes the good individual and the good society.

SOCIAL EXPECTATIONS: FUNDAMENTALS OR CHILDREN

Chapter 6 poses the question: What should be taught—subject matter decided by adults to have basic value or material of direct student interest? Should what is to be learned be determined externally or internally? If we expect individual students to develop independent critical judgment and to actively participate in improving our democratic society, we should expect schooling which leads to that outcome. If we value a society where only a few people have power, and where most people are expected to be docile and to accept conformity to social norms, we should expect schooling which leads to that outcome.

Of course, the choice is not as simple as those two hypothetical statements suggest. There are complex and changing relationships between the kinds of individuals we desire, the society we want to develop, and the schooling we provide. These relationships often lead to conflicting signals for schools, and these conflicts become embedded in the school curriculum. We want students to become self-sufficient individuals, but not too self-sufficient too early, so we allow them little latitude in deciding what to study until college. We want a society which is democratic and which inspires voluntary loyalty, but we don't trust this to occur by open inquiry, so we insist that courses stress nationalistic patriotism.

The functions of schools can be fit under two interrelated categories: individual-making and society-making. Individual-making functions include those schooling activities which assist with self-development and fulfillment. Society-making refers to schooling that intends to instill social values and socially valuable knowledge and behavior. Individual-making and society-making represent overall goals of schooling. These goals are translated into what is taught in schools.

Some people really enjoy mathematics, even word problems. For some, learning about the Platt Amendment or reading Shakespeare is very enlightening. There are also those who like to cut up white mice in biology, to saw wood in woodshop, or to do calisthenics in gym. Some are completely baffled or utterly bored by textbooks and teachers. Different strokes, as they say. But aren't there some things that everyone should know, whether they enjoy it or not? Is there a set of skills that all should master? Should we require that anyone who graduates from high school be literate? Who should decide the criteria for literacy? What does it take to be educated as we enter the final decade of the twentieth century?

LITERACY: NATIONAL MANDATE OR LOCAL OPTION

The essays in Chapter 7 focus on whether or not a national curriculum should be established. A national curriculum is one way to establish national standards for literacy, but it has the obvious problem of standardizing knowledge to the detriment of local interests. The formal school curriculum is one of the most visible parts of a school, and it indicates the relative value the school puts on various forms of knowledge. Actually, it isn't each individual school that determines the relative value of portions of the curriculum; there are a number of factors which influence what is taught and which contribute to a voluntary, but relatively standard curriculum in the schools of the United States.

The various states mandate certain courses that their legislatures believe are necessary for all students, such as English and American history, and many states encourage other courses, such as drug and alcohol education, by providing special funding or political pressure. Accrediting agencies in each region examine schools periodically; the curriculum is one area that undergoes review for conformity. A school which does not provide a standard curriculum or its equivalent is threatened with loss of accreditation. Publishers, aiming at a national market, produce teaching materials that fit a national curriculum. A school which deviates from that pattern will have trouble finding texts. And, school district curriculum coordinators and department heads attend national conferences and read common journals which stress standard curricular structures. So the outlines of a general national curriculum exist based on common practices, even though each state may vary.

A national curriculum threatens not only local interests, but also the diverse ideas about knowledge that will not be expressed if all students in all schools are taught the same things. A national curriculum would be subject to heavy governmental influence and censorship in order to avoid regional controversies. It is difficult enough to develop sound knowledge through the school curriculum when state legislatures pass laws requiring certain views to be presented and certain others to be excluded from schools. The prospect of a national curriculum makes this task appear even more grotesque. Pressure from special interest groups, major corporate interests, patriotic and religious organizations, and others who want to impose their views upon the young could lead to extreme politicization of schools.

Who should define literacy for the nation? Should we prescribe a national curriculum for all students, or should local communities be able to define the nature of literacy and the schooling needed to develop it?

TRADITION VERSUS LIBERATION

A central issue in the struggle for control of knowledge can be stated thus: Is traditional knowledge wisdom or oppression? The essays in Chapter 8 illustrate two opposing views on what should be taught, traditional values or liberating knowledge. One of the many characteristics of literacy is that it includes a set of ideological values and beliefs.

Religious values were the dominant strand in school curriculum in early America. In New England, where secondary schools started, wealthy boys were taught Latin, Greek, Catechism, and Bible to prepare them to go to college, where many were to prepare for the ministry. The religious motive continues to influence schooling, primarily in parochial schools but also as a basis for many of the values taught in public education today.

Prior to the Revolutionary War, religion was waning as the primary social glue. Political interests and early nationalistic leanings were emerging. The schools changed to meet changes in frontier life, city development, and more secular and sectional economic interests. After the American Revolution, and into the nineteenth century, nationalism replaced religion as an educational force. Literacy became important, not for religious salvation, but for the preservation of liberty and participation in a new democracy. The typical New England school curriculum around 1860 included:

At the eight- or nine-year elementary level. Spelling, writing, reading, accentuation, numbers, geography (usually emphasizing U.S.), penmanship, declamation, algebra, geometry, general history, U.S. history

At the three-year high school level. Latin, geometry, bookkeeping, surveying, advanced algebra, state history and government, U.S. history, ancient history, natural philosophy (chemistry, botany)

In larger city schools. Greek, rhetoric and logic, French, astronomy, geology, intellectual and mental science, and political economy

Since most students completed only elementary-level school, instruction in the subjects noted above was considered appropriate for citizenship with basic literacy in English, knowledge about the United States, and needed skills for initial employment.

For high school the curriculum offered a program of "classical" study for those going to college, and an "English" program for those not. In addition, some practical courses were available.

The political-nationalistic tradition remains very strong in American schools, with a renewed emphasis each time social values appear threatened. During the period of overt racism in America, and as a reaction to the abolition of slavery, literacy tests became one of the devices used to restrict voting rights in some areas. Since slaves were prohibited by law in some states from being educated, these tests were intended to keep former slaves and the poor from voting. They were also used to limit participation by immigrants. An Imperial Wizard of the Ku Klux Klan is quoted in a history text by David Tyack as saying, "Ominous statistics proclaim the persistent development of a parasitic mass within our domain. . . . We have taken unto ourselves a Trojan horse crowded with ignorance, illiteracy, and envy" (Tyack, 1967, p. 233).

The "Red Scare" of the 1920s, McCarthyism in the 1950s, and recent anticommunist political rhetoric exemplify reactions to perceived threats to American values. The effect on curriculum each time has been to strengthen nationalistic study of history, government, literature, and economics. Currently, anxiety about international competition in technology and trade is translated into increased curricular emphasis on math, science, technological subjects such as computers, and foreign languages. These curricular changes represent changes in social values and traditions that were based on a presumption that the United States was a world leader in technology and trade.

Opposite to the traditional definition of literacy used as a tool to separate and control the masses is the idea of literacy for liberation, Paulo Freire's "revolutionary" concept (Freire and Berthoff, 1987). It upends the use of literacy as a weapon for the dominant class, and enables literacy to become a political tool through which the oppressed can overcome the oppressors. Freire, born in one of the most impoverished areas of Brazil, came to know the plight of the poor. He vowed to dedicate his life to the struggle against misery and suffering, and his work led him to formulate the concept of "culture of silence" of the disadvantaged. Freire understood that social domination and paternalism of elites created ignorance and political apathy.

Freire realized the power of knowledge and recognized that education was one of the means used by the dominant class to perpetuate the culture of silence among the victims. He developed a method of instruction to teach literacy to adults to liberate them from their situation. As a professor of education in Brazil, he experimented with this program to erase illiteracy and his ideas became widely used in literacy campaigns by private groups in Brazil. He was considered such a threat to the government that he was jailed after a military coup in 1964, and was later forced to leave his native country, going to Chile to work with UNESCO, to the United States, and to the World Council of Churches in Geneva as Head of the Educational Division.

The program advocated by Freire involves the development of critical consciousness. It includes using means of communication which expose oppression, and in which the teacher and student are "co-intentional"—that is, they equally share in dialogues about social reality and develop a critical understanding which can liberate them from the culture of silence. This is a rejection of the traditional education that Freire calls:

> . . . banking, . . . an act of depositing, in which the students are the depositories and the teacher is the depositor. Instead of communicating, the teacher issues communiques and makes deposits which the students patiently receive, memorize, and repeat. . . . In the banking concept of education, knowledge is a gift bestowed by those who consider themselves knowledgeable upon those whom they consider to know nothing. Projecting an absolute ignorance onto others, a characteristic of the ideology of oppression, negates education and knowledge as processes of inquiry. (Freire, 1970, p. 58)

Henry Giroux, a leading theorist in critical educational studies and interpreter of Freire's work, argues that we need a redefinition of literacy to focus on its critical dimensions. Mass culture includes ideas and values that guide common views of what is good and bad in society. Because television and other electronic media are under the control of dominant economic interests, offering only immediate images and unthoughtful information, mass culture is influenced. This creates a "technocratic" illiteracy, and is a threat to self-perception, to critical thought, and to democracy. Giroux states:

> Instead of formulating literacy in terms of the mastery of techniques, we must broaden its meaning to include the ability to read critically, both inside and outside one's experiences, and with conceptual power. This means that literacy would enable people to decode critically their personal and social worlds and thereby further their ability to challenge the myths and beliefs that structure their perceptions and experiences. (1988a, p. 84)

Should schooling emphasize traditional values or liberation? What are other options?

TECHNOLOGY VERSUS HUMANISM

A current example of a shift in the concept of literacy, and of its relation to a set of traditional social values, is represented in Chapter 9 by two essays which diverge on the proper status of technological knowledge in schools. One major social factor influencing the school curriculum is the traditional American interest in practical innovations within the ethos of capitalism. Benjamin Franklin serves as a stereotype of the American captivated by invention and utility. Carnegie, Rockefeller, Gould, Getty, Trump, and others illustrate the American belief in entrepeneurship and the values of "free enterprise." The idea of rugged individualism that permeated our early national literature represents a combination of survival by wits and invention and a determination to succeed at any cost.

The idealization of technology and capitalism in American society creates a need for adequately prepared engineers, technicians, assembly workers, maintenance and secretarial personnel, salespersons, and managers, as well as eager and moderately knowledgeable consumers of new products. The schools are pressured and enticed by business interests to prepare people with skills and attitudes that enhance technological development and capitalism, just as schools were earlier used to inculcate religious and nationalistic loyalty. Schools are expected to train people in necessary skills for employment, and in attitudes that will help them succeed in the workplace: television and videotape equipment are widely available in most schools; personal computers are provided free or at very low cost by computer companies to stimulate mass computer education and eager consumers; news media carry stories of the need for technical literacy.

In curricular terms, this technological-capitalistic combination, following the industrial revolution, assisted in the demise of the classical curriculum, and in the rise of applied subjects and science. Latin, Greek, ancient history, philosophy, and many of the arts are not considered useful knowledge, whereas vocational subjects, commercial courses, physical and biological sciences, and economics are considered useful. More recent examples of the shift toward technological-capitalistic study in school are the stress on computer literacy for all students, courses on reading and writing for employment purposes, required courses in "free enterprise" in some states, and the development in colleges of entrepeneurial programs and management science.

In addition to the more obvious examples of the influence of technology and capitalism on school subjects, industrialization and rapidly expanding technology create social problems that also influence the school curriculum. Urbanization and suburbanization follow employment opportunities and social-class patterns, and this creates social and individual difficulties that schools are often expected to ameliorate. Violence, crime, alcohol and drug abuse, broken families, suicide, unemployment, prejudice, dislocation, alienation, financial chaos, and many other social ills illustrate these kinds of issues. As another example, scientific and technological improvements in medicine and nutritional knowledge have been obviously beneficial, but have also created social and individual problems in areas like care for the aging, costs of health care and social security, providing death with dignity, sexual freedom and abortion, and drug abuse.

The stress associated with late-twentieth-century life in a technological and capitalistic society is the subject of books, lectures, and a new industry of human resource development. The school curriculum has changed since 1990 to provide courses in sociology, psychology, urban problems, financial planning, family studies, drug education, sex education, computer studies and death and dying. These are the school responses.

BUSINESS AND EDUCATION

Chapter 10 examines the issue of whether or not business and industrial views should dominate the struggle for control of ideas expressed in schools.

The movement toward common schools in America has included support from some business and some labor leaders. Preparation for employment is now considered one of the basic purposes for schools. Vocational education evolved as one of the major school responses to dual problems of the needs of business and the dropout rate of nonacademic students. A concern of many parents is that their children should learn skills which make them employable. In families of academically talented students there is pressure to study material that has "payoff" in economic terms—that will help get the student into the right law or medical school to ensure the proper job placement.

Even the organization and operation of schools is the product of business organization and ideas. School board members are often elected because they promise to bring "more businesslike efficiency" to the schools. Businesspeople are often members of blue-ribbon boards and committees which are asked to review the operations of schools. School administrators are required by state licensing laws and university degree requirements to study management material taken from the literature of business schools and translated into school management practices. The standard textbooks on school administration advocate business management techniques.

Businesses provide considerable financial and other support for schools. School districts are very pleased to have "ratables," taxable businesses which pay for schools but which produce no students. Businesses also give large sums of money to local schools for various programs, teaching materials, and sponsorship of school events.

At the college and university level, business provides major funding for many research and teaching projects. Grants from businesses to education total many millions of dollars per year. Businessmen are often the strongest advocates of schools, offering speakers, part-time employment for students, educational material, and a myriad other subsidies.

While these business relations with schools may sound worthwhile, they pose some obvious and subtle threats to education. The influence of business on what is taught is enormous. The visible and hidden curriculums are subject to business manipulation. And business is not without blemish itself; it is scarcely an ideal model for social values and ethics. Should corporate interests dominate the definition of proper knowledge and literacy? Should the schools ignore business interests? Chapter 10 contains two of the many divergent views of what the business-school relation should be.

REFERENCES

Anyon, J. (1979). "Ideology and U.S. History Textbooks." *Harvard Educational Review.* **7,** 49–60.

—— (1980). "Social Class and the Hidden Curriculum of Work." *Journal of Education,* **162,** 67–92.

Apple, M. (1977). *Ideology and Curriculum.* London: Routledge.

—— (1982). *Education and Power.* London: Routledge.

Aristotle. (1962). *The Politics of Aristotle.* Translated by E. Barker. Oxford: Oxford University Press.

Bernstein, B. (1977). *Class, Codes, and Control.* Vol. 3. London: Routledge.

Bourdieu, P., and Passeron, J. (1977). *Reproduction in Education, Society, and Culture.* London: Sage Publications.

Bowles, S., and Gintis, H. (1976). *Schooling in Capitalist America.* New York: Basic Books.

Boyer, E. L. (1983). *High School.* New York: Harper and Row.

Butts, R. F. (1955). *A Cultural History of Western Education.* New York: McGraw-Hill.

Carnoy, M. (1975). *Schooling in a Corporate Society: The Political Economy of Education in the Democratic State.* 2d ed. New York: McKay.

Carnoy, M., and Levin, H. (1985). *Schooling and Work in America.* Stanford: Stanford University Press.

Cherryholmes, C. (1978). "Curriculum Design as a Political Act." *Curriculum Inquiry,* **10,** 115–141.

Clark, K. (1965). *Dark Ghetto.* New York: Harper and Row.

Deem, R. (1983). "Gender, Patriarchy and Class in the Popular Education of Women." In *Gender, Class and Education,* edited by S. Walker and L. Barton. Sussex, England: Falmer.

Feldman, S. (1974). *The Rights of Women.* Rochelle Park, N.J.: Hayden.

Freire, P. (1970). *Pedagogy of the Oppressed.* Translated by Myra B. Ramos. New York: Herder and Herder.

Freire, P., and Berthoff, D. (1987). *Literacy: Reading and the World.* Granby, Mass.: Bergin & Garvey.

Giroux, H. (1981). *Ideology, Culture, and the Process of Schooling.* Philadelphia: Temple University Press.

Giroux, H., and Purpel, D. (1983). *The Hidden Curriculum and Moral Education.* Berkeley: McCutchan.

Giroux, H. (1988a). *The Teacher as Intellectual: Toward a Critical Pedagogy of Learning.* Granby, Mass.: Bergin & Garvey.

Grimshaw, J. (1986). *Philosophy and Feminist Thinking.* Minneapolis: University of Minnesota Press.

Hofstadter, R. (1944). *Social Darwinism in American Thought.* Philadelphia: University of Pennsylvania Press.

Katz, M. B. (1971). *Class, Bureaucracy, and Schools.* New York: Praeger.

Langer, J. A., ed. (1987). *Language, Literacy and Culture: Issues of Society and Schooling.* Norwood, N.J.: Ablex.

Marrou, H. (1956) [1982]. *A History of Education in Antiquity.* Translated by George Lamb. Madison, Wis.: University of Wisconsin Press.

National Commission on Excellence in Education (1983). *A Nation at Risk*. Washington, D.C.: U.S. Department of Education.

Nelson, J., Carlson, K., and Linton, T. (1972). *Radical Ideas and the Schools*. New York: Holt.

Oakes, J. (1985). *Keeping Track: How the Schools Structure Inequality*. New Haven: Yale University Press.

Popkewitz, T. (1977). "The Latent Values of the Discipline-Centered Curriculum." *Theory and Research in Social Education*, **13**, 189–206.

Sadker, P., and Sadker, D. M. (1982). *Sex Equity Handbook for Schools*. New York: Longmans.

Soltow, L., and Stevens, E. (1981). *The Rise of Literacy and the Common School in the United States*. Chicago: University of Chicago Press.

Spring, J. (1976). *The Sorting Machine*. New York: McKay.

Tawney, R. H. (1964). *The Radical Tradition*. London: George Allen & Unwin.

Tyack, D. (1967). *Turning Points in American Educational History*. Waltham, Mass.: Blaisdell.

UNESCO (1957). *World Illiteracy at Mid-Century: A Statistical Study*. Paris: UNESCO.

———— (1976). *The Experimental World Literacy Programme: A Critical Assessment*. Paris: UNESCO.

Walker, S., and Barton, L. (1983). *Gender, Class and Education*. Sussex, England: Falmer.

Watts, A. (1960). *The Spirit of the Zen*. New York: Grove Press.

Young, M. F. D., ed. (1970). *Knowledge and Control*. London: Collier-Macmillan.

CHAPTER 6

FUNDAMENTALS OR CHILDREN

POSITION 1
For Fundamentals

It is very clear that schools have taken on far too many tasks, have failed in the most significant ones, and have been put in the position of replacing parents, church, and society. The *Wall Street Journal* in 1989 carried a story entitled "System Failure," which pointed out that "schools are decrepit and getting worse" (Lopez, 1989). Not long ago, the president of Xerox Corporation charged that American schools had put the society "at a terrible competitive disadvantage" by producing workers with a "50 percent defect rate." He argued that one-fourth of the students dropped out and another fourth were "barely able to read their own diplomas" (*The New York Times,* 1987).

Gilbert Sewall, education editor for *Newsweek,* visited about thirty schools in eight states and reviewed all the current writings about American schools. In an important book summarizing his findings, he wrote:

> For youngsters of all backgrounds and capabilities, academic outcomes are low and, at least until very recently, have been shrinking. Why? To begin with, few pupils at the secondary level are required to take courses in the basic subjects—language, math, history, science—in order to qualify for a high school diploma. . . . Even more disturbing, curricular revisions have steadily diluted course content. New syllabuses in basic subjects have appeared, purged of tedious or difficult units. Vacuous electives have proliferated, allowing some students to sidestep challenging courses altogether. . . . Endless courses in family life, personal adjustment, consumer skills, and business have crowded out more rigorous subjects, notably in science and foreign language. (1983, pp. 6, 7)

Sewall concludes his book with strong support for the teaching of fundamental disciplines and for the setting of high expectations for and clear standards of student performance. He argues that the schools have taken on "new
and distracting duties to care for every unfortunate and antisocial child, increasingly acting as flunkies and surrogates for self-absorbed, overburdened,
or negligent parents" (Ibid., p. 177). The schools should return to their primary
purpose, allow other social institutions to conduct their proper social welfare
functions, and recognize that the best route to vocational education is through
solid preparation in fundamental knowledge.

In a well-reasoned book, published more than a quarter-century ago, historian Arthur Bestor called attention to this educational issue:

> The disciplined mind is what education at every level should strive to produce. . . .
> The idea that the school must undertake to meet every need that some other agency
> is failing to meet, regardless of the suitability of the classroom to the task, is a
> preposterous delusion that in the end can wreck the educational system without in
> any way contributing to the salvation of society. . . . The school promises too much
> on the one hand, and too little on the other, when it begins to think so loosely about
> its functions. (1953, pp. 59, 75–76)

Bestor further proposed the identification of the fundamentals needed in
schools: "Educational reform must begin with the courageous assertion that
all the various subjects and disciplines in the curriculum are NOT of equal
value. Some disciplines are fundamental. . . ." It is those fundamental studies,
the basic disciplines of science, math, language, and history, that should be
returned to primacy in the schools. Bestor directed his attack on the progressive
educationists who claimed not to "teach history," but to "teach children."
Pointing out the inanity of this claim, he said that children must be taught
something, and that he argued strongly for subject matter content. Bestor
supports public education, but not education about nothing or about everything
with no intellectual focus.

The basic purpose of schools is to teach young people fundamental skills
and their cultural heritage. Fundamental skills are necessary for anyone to
survive in contemporary society; the cultural heritage has been developed over
time, and has served the society well. Yet, even in this basic task of schools,
there is failure.

LACK OF SCHOOL SUCCESS IN FUNDAMENTALS

In the Report of the National Commission on Excellence in Education (1983),
A Nation at Risk, thirty-seven different study findings were presented to sup-
port the statement that there was "a rising tide of mediocrity" in the schools.
These findings included the facts that:

Average academic achievement test scores were lower than in 1957, when
Sputnik was launched.

SAT test scores were in continual decline from 1963 to 1980.

National test scores in science had steadily declined from 1969 to 1977.

Remedial math courses in public colleges had increased by almost 75 percent by 1980.

In comparison with students in other industrialized nations on nineteen academic achievement tests, American students were never first or second, and were last seven times.

The amount of homework had decreased.

Textbooks had been written at lower levels to accommodate declining student reading abilities.

About one-half of the new teachers of math, science, and English were not qualified to teach these subjects.

School grades had risen, on average, as student achievement had fallen.

This is a depressing and distressing list of failures in the school curriculum in those areas of fundamental knowledge. The nation is at risk if we do not reverse these failures. There simply is not enough time or resources for schools to deal with every possible topic. Our society must decide which subjects are important and then focus our schools on teaching them well. That means we have to decide what to jettison and what to improve. This decision requires a consideration of the pressure on schools to do everything, but nothing well.

THE DUMPING-GROUND SCHOOL

Instead of teaching students necessary skills and knowledge, schools of today are seen as places to learn how to drive a car, be a parent, avoid drugs and alcohol, gain self-respect, get along with others, adjust to society, get a job, have safe sex, appreciate the arts, behave in public, learn secular morality and values, and do whatever is the next fad of the educationists.

Even in these more frivolous tasks the schools have not been successful; meanwhile energies have been diverted from the basic purpose of education. Many people may want schools to take over all responsibilities for children, but they don't recognize the threat that represents to our free society. School would replace family and church. Schools operated or supervised by the government have limited capacity to know what's best, and financing those behemoth operations strains the tax budget.

Unfortunately, the school curriculum has become a dumping ground for every special interest group's pet idea. There is a problem with crime; we think it will be solved by having the schools teach about crime. Teenage sex and pregnancy show up on the front page of the papers; a new course is proposed for the schools. There is a threat of war somewhere in the world, and we find calls for ''peace education'' in schools. A very few students commit suicide, and there is an effort to develop new antisuicide classes encouraging ''improved self-concept.'' Some students fail, and the schools respond by taking up curricular time with courses on study habits and test-taking. The AIDS epidemic leads to special courses. We even presume to resolve the threat of nuclear war by teaching a class against it.

Some of these topics are important social issues, but our schools have limited time and other, more significant, purposes. Moreover, these are topics which are heavily value-laden, and our children should not be subjected to a teacher's interpretation of them. Furthermore, it is folly to believe that students who have difficulty reading and calculating, or who lack basic knowledge and experience, can adequately deal with such topics as crime and nuclear war. Even if we agreed that schools were appropriate places to solve the society's problems, has that happened?

LACK OF SCHOOL SUCCESS IN PERIPHERALS

The school has not been successful in teaching fundamentals, and it has also not been successful in the pursuit of solutions for all of society's ills.

In the list of excessive responsibilities taken on by schools provided earlier, there is only one that has been performed moderately well, and that only at great cost. Driver's education may help slightly in gaining lower insurance premiums for drivers under 25, but that has been accomplished by sacrificing valuable and limited school time, using expensive teachers in very inefficient settings with a small number of students, eliminating one of those areas where parents can pass on maturity and skill to their children, and saddling school budgets with unnecessary costs for automobiles and equipment.

Consider other items in the list. Is school the best, or even a good, place for children to try to learn parenting, self-respect, drug avoidance, safe sex, and morality? Daily newspaper stories show that parenting, self-respect, and morality have declined in American society, even as the schools "teach" them. It is also clear that drug use has not abated despite school efforts. Unsafe and immoral sex of a variety of types seems to be at epidemic levels regardless of sex education programs. The backbone of American society, the family, is eroded because these educative activities are given over to schools. The historic and appropriate functions of families include providing security and nurturing. The nurturing function is essentially educative—providing guidance and values for the young.

Contemporary family life, in the half of the population where parents still live together, appears to consist of a place to sleep and eat, to watch television, and to wave good-bye as the parents go to work or the child goes to school. How can children gain respect for their parents and other relatives when the basic family responsibilities are given over to a government institution, where they are homogenized? And those families where nurturing is taken seriously run the risk of having a different set of values taught in school. Obviously, this is also a problem for religions. Secular schools often subvert and ridicule basic religious values, symbols, and practices.

ADJUSTMENT AND CONFORMITY

Other items on the list above are adjustment to society, getting along with others, getting a job, behaving in public, and appreciating the arts. These items smack of Big Brother. One of America's claims to world leadership is our diversity. Who is to decide what adjustment, behaviors, and arts are to be honored? Do we want monolithic schooling that requires each student to adjust to whatever the school determines to be the good of society?

Life adjustment education, brought in by the "progressives" just following World War II, assumed that educators knew what society needed and would determine how students would adjust. It was a form of social engineering that failed. The emphasis was on vocational courses to prepare people for work, not to provide intellectual or cultural enrichment. It was based on the false premise that over half of America's students could not benefit from learning traditional subjects, and were destined to working-class existence. This movement opposed academic study, and promoted trivial activities like social dancing, playing party games, selecting movies, and relieving the tensions of young people by meditation. This period of silliness in curriculum has passed, but there are remnants still in the schools.

STRESS THE FUNDAMENTALS

A school curriculum built on current fads and the latest social issue has no lasting value, and cannot hope to prepare young people for productive lives in American society. Similarly, a curriculum designed simply to make students feel better about themselves does not develop maturity; rather, it is only likely to exaggerate personal problems and dependency on others. Meanwhile, these curriculum types rob the students of important time and teacher energy which should be devoted to real education. There are many truly important things that students should be learning in school, things that are consistent with the basic purposes of education. Compulsory education is predicated on the assumption that children do in fact learn those things in school. If they don't, why require all children to go to school?

NECESSARY SKILLS

There is no solid argument against the necessity of teaching the traditional skills of reading, writing, and arithmetic. Disputes arise in such matters as how they should be taught, for how long, and how to measure their mastery, but even the hard-core "happy children" advocates agree that children need to be able to communicate in language and numbers.

That would seem sufficient to guarantee strong emphasis on these skills in schools. But there are serious problems. A large number of students are not obtaining these skills, and will suffer as they try to make their way in our society. Our society will suffer also, since these otherwise productive workers will not have the capability to survive in employment. And there are many other students who manage to pick up some fundamental skills, but not enough to be competitive. These are destined to hold marginal roles in society, and to be recipients of social welfare programs.

One reason why the schools fail in even this most commonly agreed upon part of the curriculum is that insufficient time is spent teaching these skills to assure that children master them. There are too many distractions in school, including the dumping-ground problems identified before. Another reason for the failure is that the basic skills are taught in isolation from the disciplines of knowledge that students will study as they go through school. Instead of literature or history, children learn to read from texts specially designed to avoid ideas and to present only insipid stories using "a limited vocabulary." A third reason, tied to the last one, is that schools do not motivate students because of low expectations, and as a result students become bored and shut out education. Students in earlier periods could read complicated material that stretched their minds. The McGuffey *Readers* contained difficult ideas and language. Texts that are "dumbed down" to meet a minimal standard are demeaning to students and stultify their development.

BEYOND THE FUNDAMENTAL SKILLS

Not only do we need to reemphasize the fundamental skills in elementary schools, we need to insist upon rigorous evaluation of those skills before we allow students to continue in school. Requiring students to master the skills early will enable them to fully use those skills in further study of important knowledge. We do a disservice to students who have not mastered the skills, as well as to those who have, if we merely pass them on to higher grades.

The knowledge humanity has acquired over a long period of time, and with great effort, is stored in the major disciplines which have been traditionally taught in schools. This is the intellectual and cultural heritage that all new generations must learn in order to preserve and extend the culture. The development of disciplines has assisted in establishing categories of knowledge and methods of study that make access to the cultural heritage easier and more systematic. Learning is difficult work, and should be, but study of the basic disciplines provides logical avenues that help in understanding.

The disciplines represent differing ways that humans have organized wisdom, and they offer the means to intellectual power. Among these basic disciplines are:

Math, because we live in a world where quantity and numerical relationships are important

Language, because accumulated knowledge is set down in various languages

Sciences, because they provide understanding of our environment and its workings

History, because an understanding of current life requires study of the past

Of course, there are other disciplines that one can study in becoming an educated person, but these are the basic ones that deserve focus in schools. They are the liberal arts disciplines, whose purpose is to liberate people from ignorance.

Although the liberal arts have changed over the course of time, they still represent the storehouse of knowledge that an educated person requires. Our modern society requires citizens who are prepared in math, language, science, and history in order to take on the responsibilities of democratic self-governance.

A thorough understanding of mathematical and scientific principles is necessary for life in a technological world. A thorough understanding of the humanities, represented by literature and history, is necessary to comprehend the human condition and to communicate effectively. This combination is the essence of education. To organize school studies otherwise is to stunt the educative process and to condemn our children to ignorance.

SUMMARY

This program of school studies takes time and concentration. One cannot master fundamentals and our cultural heritage on a part-time basis, while devoting considerable time to such things as "getting along with others," "improving self-respect," and "learning how to learn." The focus on current fads and personal problems trivializes the heritage, and consumes precious school time. Furthermore, it is clear that schools have not solved social problems and, as a result of the time taken up with them, are not very successful in just doing what they should be doing.

The most valuable education for individual students and for society is to build basic skills, and emphasize the liberal arts disciplines.

POSITION 2
For Children

The artificiality of school is obvious. Schools are separated from society, from the lives of children, from families, and from reality. We ring bells to signal when one is supposed to start learning. We drill children to memorize terms that have no meaning for them. We substitute tidiness and punctuality for thought. We preach platitudes about a life that is not recognizable in children's existence. We require students to learn categories of information that do not relate to their experience. We test them on trivial details, and falsely presume that their scores represent what they know about the world. And we pretend that this is preparation for life. School takes children who are living a real life and substitutes artificial content, claiming that it is education.

School becomes something to be dreaded, a regimen of rules, boredom, inert ideas, and stuffiness. We all start with immense curiosity about the world, and most start eager to go to school. That curiosity is stifled and that eagerness is dulled as we progress through school. Isn't that an incredibly ironic situation? The institution intended to stimulate learning about the world is instead the institution that presents the most obstacles to such learning.

The academically successful student in school is not usually the most curious or creative, but the one best able to follow the teacher's directions and to take tests on what the books say. The schools reward conformity and obedience, not diversity and independence. Schooling becomes training, not education. Students become passive receptacles for accumulations of adult ideas. And student learning is defined by adult-constructed measures. The student is a bystander in schooling. Sizer's (1984) study of high school students showed them to be compliant, docile, and lacking initiative. He attributed this disaster to the heavy school emphasis on getting right answers and on too little emphasis on being inquisitive. Goodlad (1983), after examining data from observations in over 1,000 classrooms, documented the high degree of passivity among students, and the lack of time or concern given to student interests and opinions.

The most neglected part of the school reform movement of the 1980s was the student. The focus of virtually every report, governmental statement, and legislation proposed was the school curriculum, the school organization, or the school officials. The general concern was to make some organizational or op-erational change in the structure of the institution; no interest was shown in students and their lives in school. More tests, higher standards set by adults outside the school, longer school days and years, more homework, more stress on teachers and administrators, and less enjoyment in education were the major achievements of the 1980s. Students were ignored once again while they were forced to suffer the results of inconsistent and confusing impositions.

In a particularly clear-headed review of the 1980s reform movement, English teacher Susan Ohanian (1985) summarized the point:

> We must be ever wary of wasting some youngster's life just because of a dubious notion that a rigorous, regimented curriculum will help restore to the U.S. a better balance of trade. . . . At best, the recommendations of the commissions and task forces on school reform are hallucinatory; at worst, they are soul-destroying. Let us teachers not succumb to the temptation of asking what we can do for General Motors; let us continue to ask only what we can do for the children. (p. 321)

WRONG FIRST QUESTION

The essential concern in education should not be what is taught, but what is learned. We have, for too long, posed the wrong question in considering the school curriculum. Certainly we need to consider what is, or should be, taught, but that is a secondary issue. The primary focus should be on what is, or should be learned. We can't properly address what we want to have taught in schools without first determining the nature of learning and the learners. The beginning of curriculum artificiality in schools is the presumption that we can ignore the needs and interests of children in favor of a set of traditional pronouncements.

The pronouncement that children must learn to read, write, and do arithmetic is satisfying to members of an older generation who believe that all must suffer what they suffered. Communication and mathematics skills are important, but they are important because of their value to individual children in their experience, not simply because previous generations had to learn them. The pronouncement that everyone has to learn the same information in the same way is satisfying to those who accept standardization. Information is essential, but why must everyone know the same things? The pronouncement that only that knowledge which is considered important by certain adults can be important to children is satisfying to those certain adults. It is not adult satisfaction but human experience that determines what knowledge is of value.

And the pronouncement that school should be a place of serious devotion to discipline and high standards is satisfying to those who would restrict freedom and control others. Discipline and high standards are nothing more than means for social conformity and restriction. Individual creativity, human development, and rational social purposes should be the goals of schools, not externally required discipline and standards. This is not a new school problem, but it has recurred in the current age of educational repression.

Half a century ago John Dewey's remarkably cogent book, *Experience and Education,* differentiated between traditional and progressive education on the basis of a historical opposition in educational theory "between the idea that education is development from within and that it is formation from without . . ." (1938, p. 17). He notes that traditional education consists of information and skills that "have been worked out in the past," that standards and rules of conduct are prescribed by adults, and that the school operates as though it were separate from the lives of children and the rest of society. This requires schooling where the subject matter and the rules of conduct are imposed on children, and the attitude of pupils must "be one of docility, receptivity, and obedience" (Ibid., p. 18).

Progressive education, Dewey says, arose out of discontent with this traditional imposition of learning on the child from above and outside. Its principles are the opposites of traditional education's principles:

> To imposition from above is opposed expression and cultivation of individuality; to external discipline is opposed free activity; to learning from texts and teachers, learning through experience; to acquisition of isolated skills and techniques by drill, is opposed acquisition of them as a means of attaining ends which make direct vital appeal; to preparation for a more or less remote future is opposed making the most of opportunities of present life; to static aims and materials is opposed acquaintance with a changing world. (Ibid., p. 20)

Unfortunately, the schools have never taken progressive education seriously. A number of cosmetic changes in schools have made them appear more humane, but they have not shed their basic misplaced authoritarian and traditional aim of imposing selected information and morals on children. Schools continue to teach as though education were not life, but preparation for some later event. They ignore individual children in favor of standardization in curriculum and test scores.

The premise for education must be the child's development, not the adult's categories of knowledge, values, and proper behavior. When we focus on what is to be taught, we are inclined to forget about the student and produce lists of things we were taught. We introduce the teacher as authority, rather than wise guide. And we structure the schools to systematically destroy the creative interests of children by forcing all to learn the same material. A focus on what is to be learned permits consideration of the learner. Of course, it possible to avoid that consideration by assuming that what is learned is what is taught, but that only continues the artificiality of the school. What is learned is what has meaning for the student, no matter what is taught and what is on the examination. It is this focus on the learner that makes what is learned the primary question.

NATURAL AND UNNATURAL LEARNING

There is a substantial battle in the long history of educational thought between those who think that people learn naturally from within and those who believe that external force must be brought to assure learning. This battle is illustrated currently by the difference of opinion between those who want freedom in school for students to pursue their natural inclinations to learn, and those who want to impose a set of conditions and ideas on the minds and actions of students. It can also be illustrated by a quote from Nat Henthoff:

> One afternoon as we were walking down the street, Paul Goodman turned to me and said, "Do you realize that if the ability to walk depended on kids being taught walking as a subject in school, a large number of citizens would be ambulatory only if they crawled." (1977, p. 53)

The first position, freedom, does not mean license for students to do whatever they please. One of the false criticisms of progressive education, and of John Dewey's work, is that the child determines everything. That is simply a misreading or a calculated attempt to discredit the position. Dewey insisted that the most mature person in the classroom, the teacher, must ultimately have responsibility for what is taught, but that the teacher's decision is predicated upon the needs and interests of the child. And, it is the child, or learner, who actually determines what is learned. Thus, the child-centered, or learner-centered, curriculum is a curriculum designed first with the child's development in mind. The teacher must, in this curriculum, remain sensitive to the learner. License to do whatever one pleases, whether teacher or learner, is inconsistent with this view.

The learner-centered curriculum is in opposition to the subject- or discipline-centered curriculum, where the decision on what is taught starts with consideration of how the discipline is organized. The traditional discipline-centered curriculum represents the imposition of information, categories, and ideas without regard to the learner. In those terms it is an unnatural and external structuring of what is learned. The learner-centered curriculum rests upon the conviction that students want to learn. The authoritarian nature of traditional approaches to schooling destroys that natural curiosity.

DEFECTS IN THE TRADITIONAL STRUCTURE OF SCHOOLING

As suggested, the discipline-centered school has several defects. It imposes an externally determined body of information on children, it ignores natural learning interests and stifles curiosity and creativity, and it requires schools to be places of authoritarianism. This last point, the authoritarianism of schools, deserves further discussion. If one starts with the premise that children are curious, imaginative, and eager to learn, then what happens to make schools restrictive and stultifying places for many students? There are many reasons, but they center on the fact that schools have traditionally been expected to homogenize individual children according to a standard that many thinking adults would reject. What adult lives are organized the way schools are?

The old-fashioned view has it that school should be a cheerless place where the young are trained to become adults by learning what adults think they should know and behaving the way adults think they should behave. Schools are expected to pass on to younger generations skills and information that are based on the past; they are expected to train students to behave according to a set of rules and standards; and they are to do it as efficiently as possible to save tax money and time.

Thus, schools are organized to distill the adult world for children, to impose a set of ideas and morals on them, and to process them much as though they were in a food-packing or auto-assembly plant. Students are classified by grade and test scores to make teaching more efficient, and subjected to severe time schedules, teacher or book presentation of information, required courses, standard textbooks, and excessive testing to assure that all are trained the same way.

As a result, traditional schools are static institutions that stress conformity and adult concepts that have limited meaning in the lives of students. Yet students are dynamic, growing, and concerned about their own individuality. The resilience of youth permits most of them to survive such a stifling environment. Good teachers recognize this paradox between traditional schooling and the needs of youth, and try to find ways to match mandated material and student interests. But it is a struggle. Good teachers also mediate the conformity requirements of school with efforts to recognize individual differences among students. And they attempt to enlarge students' horizons by building on their experiences. But these efforts by good teachers are undermined by such influences as the traditional structure of schooling, standardized tests, and pressure from advocates of the past.

In traditional schools, we reward those who do as we tell them to do whether it involves thinking or not. The main purpose of much schooling is to have students get "right answers," not to engage them in critical thinking. The thinking student might challenge why the school operates as it does, why the material lacks interest, why there is so much conformity, and why the answers are "right." Schools are not usually designed to respond to these kinds of challenges, and teachers and administrators often resort to fear, ridicule, repression, and isolation to dampen them. Students learn quickly that it does not pay to raise serious questions, and they withdraw into the safety of conformity.

Schools present artificial barriers to learning and stimulate fear and repression. The typical student response to school is one of the following: drop out, slip through, fail, find satisfaction in extracurricular activities, learn teacher-pleasing behavior and do well, ignore the school bureaucracy and suffer resulting penalties, or wait for something more interesting. None of these responses represents the best forms of intellectual development. Do we think we are excellent when large numbers of students drop out, fail, or turn off their curiosity?

STUDENT AND TEACHER EXPERIENCES

The primary way that people learn, as opposed to being taught, is through experience. It is an active process, not a static one. When we are involved in some physical activity, such as organizing a group project, building a model village, playing a game, or measuring a room, we are learning. We make errors, seek advice, modify actions, and gain understanding in a real situation. Most teachers will admit, for example, that they learned the most about the subject when they had to teach it, not when they were sitting in a college class. We learn more about cars by trying to fix them than by being told how to fix them.

Not all experiential learning involves physical activity or actual situations. Such vicarious experiences as reading a book or listening to a speaker can provide specially pertinent learning. And, of course, it is impossible, and not even desirable, for students to physically experience all situations for learning to take place. Active engagement, mental or physical, is what produces learning.

Curiosity, interest, or the need to resolve a problem makes the book reading or listening a learning situation where active engagement can take place. Simply being told that something is important, or that something must be learned for a test, does not necessarily stimulate active engagement. Perfunctory reading of a book or listening to a teacher may appear on the surface to be learning, but the active mind of the student may be off on a different track. The teacher teaches, and assigns readings; the student appears to be listening and reading; but what is learned? The student has learned to cope with dry and uninteresting material in a school of boring routine and hourly tasks. That is not the experience the good teacher desires, and many teachers are themselves tired of the dullness and boredom. Certainly, it is not the experience the students desire. But it is typical of schooling in far too many places.

It is also clear that all experiences are not equally beneficial as learning situations; some are actually detrimental. Experiencing the good taste of excessive fats and salts may lead to poor habits in nutrition. The experience of smoking cigarettes may lead to health problems. Only one experience of jumping out of a window may stop learning entirely. It is not simply experience that matters, but the quality and developmental nature of that experience. The teacher's role, then, becomes one of seeking and providing experiences for students that stimulate and extend their interest and enrich their learning. How well a teacher fulfills this role depends, of course, upon the wisdom and knowledge of the teacher, and his or her sensitivity to the students.

THE SUBJECTS LEARNED

The learner-centered school curriculum might appear to have no content, to be so loose and free that nothing intellectual is accomplished. Actually, the opposite is true. In the tightly organized and past-oriented traditional school curriculum the meticulously structured content is largely without meaning in the lives of students, and memorizing material for a test is scarcely an intellectual activity. A properly developed learner-centered curriculum, on the other hand, engages students intellectually in examining topics they can comprehend and utilize in their own development. Lacking in the learner-centered curriculum are what Alfred North Whitehead so eloquently derided in his classic *The Aims of Education* as: "'inert ideas'—that is to say, ideas that are merely received into the mind without being utilised, or tested, or thrown into fresh combinations" (1929, p. 13). He goes on to note that education is "overladen with inert ideas." And he states that "education with inert ideas is not only useless: it is, above all things, harmful" (Ibid.).

The traditional school is filled with inert ideas, bits and pieces of information that fit no pattern and have no vitality for most students. Consider the standard school regimen. Students pass from English class, with a mixed lesson on spelling, vocabulary, and story reading; to history, where they hear about America's victory in some past war; to science, where they watch the teacher mix chemicals; to math, where they put answers on the chalkboard; to art, where they draw; and on to gym, where they do calisthenics and study the rules of a game. One period of inert ideas is followed by another period of different, and apparently unrelated, inert ideas. Each teacher acts as though his or her ideas are awfully important, and will be on the test, and the student goes through the expected motions. Schools are like giant jigsaw puzzles, except that the box cover with the completed puzzle is missing.

The material taught in school is a series of disconnected and lifeless bits of information that have little meaning to students. The student learns that English is separate from history, which is separate from economics and science and math, and the arts and physical education. And the student learns that school is separate from life, and certainly from social and individual problems. How can a student understand and try to resolve a personal or a social problem using traditional school subjects? Are shyness, feelings of failure, apprehension, death in the family, and acne the kinds of problems that traditional subjects can address? Does the student who sees problems of poverty, alcoholism, war, and human rights view them as resolvable by using the bits and pieces learned in math or science or history or English as taught in the schools? It is reasonable for students to suffer school, and look forward to life outside of school. That is an inversion of what school should be, and what knowledge should provide.

Subjects taught in this manner are not intellectual; they do not stimulate thinking and the consideration of diverse ideas. Intellectual vitality arises out of life, not out of the unrelated segments of knowledge we throw at students. We need to abolish this disconnectedness and restore the vitality of learning. That does not mean to destroy the information gained from scholarly study of the subject; it means we need to help students understand the connections that make knowledge valuble and how to utilize that knowledge in solving problems.

KNOWLEDGE AND PROBLEMS

We need to focus on knowledge that is important for students to use in dealing with human problems. These problems include those of individual students as well as global issues. We must identify individual and social problems and find the knowledge that can assist in understanding and addressing them. That is certainly different from the approach which starts with the old-fashioned categories of subjects and presumes that they need to be learned regardless of their value to the learner. Real human problems do not occur simply as literature or history or chemistry problems. Teachers in the traditional curriculum resort to contrived "problems" in their subjects in an attempt to motivate student interest. Standard math story problems are notoriously unreal; American history usually presents problems that the student sees as already resolved and unrelated to current life. Why not start with a problem the students can easily identify, and then find knowledge—regardless of the subject field it comes from—that is useful in tackling it? This approach recognizes knowledge as interrelated and useful, not compartmentalized and ornamental.

The traditional adult manner of organizing knowledge into apparently discrete categories, such as English and American literature, physics, political science, drawing, biology, algebra, European and American history, botany, geometry, economics, psychology, chemistry, and drama, may work well for those whose careers are devoted to advanced study in these areas. (Interestingly, some of the most advanced thinkers in each of these fields recognize the connections among subjects and use theories which draw fields together rather than divide them.) These distinct categories may not be as useful for students in elementary and secondary schools, where there is a greater need to see that knowledge is seamless and valuable in examining the immediate problems facing us.

The identification of problems to study should be a mutual process, with students and teacher jointly engaged. There are some pervasive human problems revolving around such values as justice, equality, freedom, democracy, and human rights. And there are myriad individual problems which are related to the same values. Examples include student rights and responsibilities, fair treatment in school situations, freedom to explore ideas, victimization as a minor, and problems in defining a personal code of ethics. These problems require knowledge from such fields as math, science, history, economics, psychology, literature, the arts, and politics. They also require skills in reading, writing, calculating, organizing, categorizing, and critical thinking. As students mature they gain interests in different problems, types of knowledge, and levels of skills.

Students come in a variety of personalities, colors, backgrounds, and interests. We need a curriculum which recognizes this variety as an opportunity, and the students as a dynamic resource. The static traditional curriculum pushes them into molds and stamps them with a list of subjects studied. The learner-centered curriculum enhances student curiosity and energy, and utilizes knowledge in addressing human problems.

FOR DISCUSSION

1 Fundamentals and children are not necessarily opposites. Frills, or ornamental knowledge, may be a clearer opposite of fundamentals. By one definition, frills would be such subjects as art and music. By another, frills are such things as athletics, cake decorating, landscaping, games, movies, and television. A third definition of frills would include such topics as the classics, advanced science and math, and esoteric foreign languages. Frills could also be astrology, alchemy, and myths and legends. What case can be made that frills are more important than fundamentals?

2 An opposite to children could be adults. If the roles were reversed to allow children to determine what adults should know, what would be the likely curriculum?

3 If you were to construct a school curriculum to assure society that graduates can function successfully and to assure individual students that their rights and interests will be given credible expression, how would that curriculum differ from the one now in schools?

4 Listed below are examples of subjects considered fundamental at different times and places, and often prescribed for the elite classes in society.

Prehistoric. Practical survival skills, folkways
Sumer, Babylonia, Hebrews. Religion, writing, reading
Sparta. Military training, physical stamina
Athens. Letters, music, gymnastics, philosophy, science, math (separation of practical from liberal education)
Roman and Middle Ages. Seven liberal arts—trivium: grammar, rhetoric, logic; quadrivium: arithmetic, geometry, astronomy, music
Renaissance and Reformation. Added sciences, renewed interest in western classics (humanities)

Early America. Religion, reading, writing, calculation, Latin, Greek, ancient history

America in Enlightenment period. English, modern foreign languages, national history, social economy, physical and biological science, math, accounting, commerce and manufacturing, agriculture, gardening, mechanics

Twentieth-century America.

Fill in the space for twentieth-century America with subjects now taught in the schools, and expected of students. Which list seems most suitable for classifying as "fundamentals"? Where is the student's idea of fundamentals? What are likely to be considered fundamentals in the twenty-first century? Will student interests fare better then?

REFERENCES

Bestor, A. (1953). *Educational Wastelands*. Urbana, Ill.: University of Illinois Press.

Dewey, J. (1938). *Experience and Education*. New York: Macmillan.

Goodlad, J. (1983). *A Place Called School*. New York: McGraw-Hill.

Henthoff, N. (1977). *Does Anybody Give a Damn?* New York: Knopf.

Lopez, J. A. (1989). "System Failure: Businesses Say Schools Are Producing Graduates Unqualified to Hold Jobs." *Wall Street Journal*, March 31, R12, 14.

National Commission on Excellence in Education (1983). *A Nation at Risk*. Washington, D.C.: U.S. Department of Education.

The New York Times (1987). "Schools Let Down U.S., Xerox Chairman Says." October 27, p. 28.

Ohanian, S. (1985). "Huffing and Puffing and Blowing the Schools Excellent." *Phi Delta Kappan,* **66**, 316–321.

Sewall, G. T. (1983). *Necessary Lessons: Decline and Renewal in American Schools*. New York: Free Press.

Sizer, T. (1984). *Horace's Compromise: The Dilemma of the American High School*. Boston: Houghton Mifflin.

Whitehead. A. N. (1929). *The Aims of Education*. New York: Macmillan.

CHAPTER 7

NATIONAL OR LOCAL CURRICULUM FOR LITERACY

POSITION 1
For a National Curriculum

A national curriculum will give the public some assurance that students are learning *something*. Naturally, this means that there will have to be national tests to measure how well students are mastering the national curriculum. As things stand now, students are not judged by how many nationally significant things they have learned but instead by how many things they have learned that the particular teachers in their particular schools think are important. Not all teachers can be trusted to make sound judgments about what is genuinely important. Some teachers emphasize trivial things that happen to interest them personally, and even then they don't expect their students to learn very much of the trivia. Teachers are professionals, to be sure, but they are no more infallible than other professionals. The American public is entitled to hold teachers to some nationally uniform standards, and to check on how well the teachers are meeting these standards.

There are whole schools that emphasize trivial things—the notorious Mickey Mouse courses like basket weaving. There are other schools where students get what appears to be a straightforward academic curriculum, but where the course content is so watered down that very little material is covered. Students graduate from these schools with impressive transcript entries but little knowledge. The public is entitled to more accountability than that, and the only way they can get it is to have a national curriculum with which all schools must comply and against which all students are assessed. The public agrees, as indicated by the Twentieth Annual Gallup Poll. The results show that a whopping 81 percent of those polled think there should be national tests by which students can be compared across communities (Gallup and Elam, 1988, p. 41).

PROMOTING ECONOMIC COMPETITIVENESS

As a nation whose economic competitiveness with the rest of the world depends on how well educated our people are, we simply cannot afford to be slack any longer. It is important that we be economically competitive so that we can provide all of our citizens with a decent standard of living.

To be truly competitive, we need people with highly useful technical expertise, but these people must also be educated broadly enough to understand the appropriate uses of their skills. They need an understanding of the society on whose behalf they labor. Human robots need not apply. Mortimer Adler, the renowned philosopher and founder of the Great Books program, puts it in the following terms:

> There is no question that our technologically advanced industrial society needs specialists of all sorts. There is no question that the advancement of knowledge in all fields of science and scholarship, and in all the learned professions, needs intense specialization. But for the sake of preserving and enhancing our cultural traditions, as well as for the health of science and scholarship, we need specialists who are also generalists—generally cultivated human beings, not just good plumbers. We need truly educated human beings who can perform their special tasks better precisely because they have general cultivation as well as intensely specialized training. (Adler, 1988, p. 43)

While Adler thinks this can be accomplished through a prescribed set of required courses, E. D. Hirsch correctly recognizes that required courses do not guarantee the teaching of specific content. The content has to be specified so that children across America will learn things in common. Hirsch and his colleagues have made a major contribution to this effort by creating *The Dictionary of Cultural Literacy* (Hirsch et al., 1988).

EASING GEOGRAPHIC MOBILITY

A national curriculum is especially important for a geographically mobile society like the United States. It may be personally satisfying to learn about the history of your own town, West Overshoe, or your own ethnic group, Transylvanians, and there will still be time to do that. But young people have to be prepared to move out into the larger world because they probably will. Before they die, they are likely to live in several towns and in more than one state. They need a broad perspective, one that they share with the people they will encounter along their way. This broad perspective, this common frame of reference, this similar knowledge base will vastly facilitate social and business communication. It will hold us together as a people, serving as the cultural cement of our society. It will reduce for all of us the culture shock and the period of adjustment in moving from one locale to another.

Without a common culture, the United States can become dangerously pluralistic. The danger in so much diversity is that groups have so little in common that they become strange to one another. The strangeness breeds suspicion which, in turn, leads to hostility, and the hostility can degenerate into a descending spiral of intergroup violence. We do not have to look to the Middle East for examples of this phenomenon. We need look no farther than the Howard Beaches of America.

BUILDING NATIONAL COHESION

It is not enough simply to smooth interpersonal encounters. No nation can long survive if its people lack a sense of nationhood. The history of the nation is a vehicle by which to instill this sense of unity. The stirring examples of our nation's leaders, the enormous obstacles overcome in times of national peril, the daily struggles of plain people, the evolution of social institutions—a knowledge of all these awakens us to our common heritage and our shared destiny. "Indeed, we put our sense of nationhood at risk by failing to familiarize our young people with the story of how the society in which we live came to be. Knowledge of the ideas that have molded us and the ideals that have mattered to us function as a kind of civic glue" (Cheney, 1987, p. 7). President Reagan spoke to this concern in his farewell address when he commented that patriotism, which he defined as an informed love of country, can be promoted by having students learn of America's great triumphs, such as General Doolittle's bombing raid over Tokyo in World War II.

Another way to bring a people together in national unity is through their literary past. The great works of prose and poetry—the canon of American literature—unite us with a shared delight. These literary treasures give us rich insights into ourselves, making it impossible to escape a recognition of the humanity we have in common with our fellow citizens. "Something of value is lost when there is no coherent literature curriculum. . . . Such a curriculum, beginning in the early grades, helps young people understand how the culture came to be what it is, how it was shaped, which writers defined it and thereby changed the way we see ourselves" (Ravitch and Finn, 1987, p. 10).

IMPROVING READING ABILITY

One of the reasons why so many adults cannot, and will not, read even the local newspaper is that it contains too many terms with which they are unfamiliar. They don't have the time or patience to look up the meaning of these terms in dictionaries, encyclopedias, and atlases.

The recently rediscovered insight that literacy is more than a skill is based upon knowledge that all of us unconsciously have about language. We know instinctively that to understand what somebody is saying, we must understand more than the surface meaning of words; we have to understand the context as well. The need for background information applies all the more to reading and writing. To grasp the words on a page we have to know a lot of information that isn't set down on the page. (Hirsch, 1987, p. 3)

If students have been educated thoroughly in the general culture of their country, this information will be stored in their heads and they can draw on it as needed. A passing newspaper reference to the First Amendment or the Korean War, as examples, will not create confusion and uncertainty. Such references will not cause the daily newspaper to take on the remote quality of a technical journal. Rather, the references will be readily grasped and put into context by readers who know the history of their country. Without this information, readers will become discouraged from reading, which will cause them to fall farther and farther behind in their understanding of things. The job of schools, then, is to give children the start-up information they need to get going on their lifelong intellectual development.

ENLIGHTENING THE ELECTORATE

If Americans are not able to *keep* informed because they have never been informed, then there is not much hope for democracy. People will turn off altogether to public affairs because they don't have the background to understand them. Or worse, they will vote without knowing the issues well enough even to realize what is in their own interest. Politicians will be able to manipulate the people with slick slogans. Lies will be as credible as truths. More and more ruthless demagogues will get into power until eventually a despot inveigles the ignorant masses into letting him or her take control. "True enfranchisement depends upon knowledge, knowledge upon literacy, and literacy upon cultural literacy. To be truly literate, citizens must be able to grasp the meaning of any piece of writing addressed to the general reader" (Hirsch, 1987, p. 12).

Recent presidential campaigns may have driven this point home to you. With as many as seven candidates in a single debate during the primaries, and all of them trying to score points with high-sounding rhetoric and claims to expertise, the viewer needed a lot of background knowledge not to be completely flummoxed. Persons lacking this knowledge probably gave up trying to understand what the election was all about, and voted for no good reason or did not bother to vote at all.

The issues on which the electorate is expected to pass judgment are indeed becoming more complex. The technical detail is more numerous and difficult to comprehend, and the consequences of any course of action are less predictable than when the world was a simpler place. Thus, it is imperative that voters be able to fathom the issues in some depth if democratic decision-making is not to become as random as a lottery drawing.

UPLIFTING THE POOR

Americans will be better off when all citizens are well informed. The ones who will reap the greatest benefits, however, are those who are presently the least well informed. The poor, especially the poor minorities who are now so ignorant of mainstream culture, will be given the vocabulary needed to converse on equal terms with the higher social classes. There will no longer be a communication block to their upward mobility. The feeling of being outsiders who are resented and ridiculed will be reduced because a major reason for the resentment and ridicule will have been removed. Cultural literacy will give *power* to the poor so they will be able to compete in the job market and the political arena on a more equal footing. The black Harvard historian and sociologist Orlando Patterson expressed this view when he said:

> The people who run society at the macro-level must be literate in this culture. For this reason, it is dangerous to overemphasize the problems of basic literacy or the relevancy of literacy to specific tasks, and more constructive to emphasize that blacks will be condemned in perpetuity to oversimplified, low-level tasks and will never gain their rightful place in controlling the levers of power unless they also acquire literacy in this wider cultural sense. (Quoted in Hirsch, 1987, pp. 10–11)

Minority cultures certainly add to the richness of the United States, so there is no secret plot to drown these cultures in the mainstream. In fact, the intention is to make minorities themselves truly bicultural. They will retain their original cultures but without any longer being *trapped* in them. Furthermore, they will not be patronized by having celebrated that about their cultures which is simply meretricious, on the misguided notion that minority cultures deserve equal treatment with the mainstream culture in the curriculum. If there is no Tolstoy of the Zulus, there should be no attempt to inflate some hack to that status. Better that minorities be given the tools with which to "cross over" into the dominant culture as they choose. If there is an evil plot, it is on the part of those who pretend to honor minorities by keeping them "pure" (and poor) in their lack of literacy and mainstream culture.

ESCAPING INDOCTRINATION

A national curriculum will surely mean a loss of local control over the curriculum, and this alarms many people. However, the national curriculum will not only get children beyond the parochial and often trivial knowledge they are taught at the local level. It will also give them a broader *value* perspective. Instead of being indoctrinated only in the values of the fundamentalist Christian or Jewish or liberal or conservative community where they happen to live, they will be exposed to the positions of all these groups. Their own values will be challenged and strengthened by this exposure. It is also possible that the exposure will cause students to rethink and modify some of their values. This possibility is what alarms the elders in a community. They worry that the children will be corrupted by outside influences.

These fears are understandable, but the reaction is not. The reaction is to impose an ostrichlike education, with everyone's head stuck in the ground. That kind of education is designed to keep kids ignorant; it is not an education at all. It tells young people that the only way we can get them to believe what *we* tell them is not to let them hear anything else. Truth, however, arises in competition with other "truths," not in silence. Besides, with all the mass communications systems in the United States, it is futile to try keeping children in a soundproof darkroom. Every new sight or sound that breaks through will have a special allure for them because they will recognize it as something they're not supposed to see or hear.

The national curriculum will therefore help save children from the narrow-mindedness of their communities. The elders in a community might still refuse to have certain topics taught to the youngsters, but this enforced ignorance will be reflected in the youngster's national test scores. The elders will soon realize that their attempts to preserve an unknowing innocence are being made at the expense of the youngsters' educational and occupational mobility. That realization should at least cause the elders to reconsider the values they had been able to take for granted for so long.

A MODEST PROPOSAL

Finally, it should be noted that nothing really radical is being proposed here. This is not a suggestion that American schools be overhauled completely. Indeed, this is the most modest of proposals because it will cause so little change. A national curriculum already exists for American schools.

Imagine that you were to be kidnapped and blindfolded and then parachuted out of a plane someplace over the United States. Wherever you landed, the institution that would seem the least strange would be the local public school. The students might talk in strange accents and wear odd-looking clothes, but the things they were being taught would be pretty much the same as what you were taught when you were at that school level.

There is a national curriculum because there are national textbooks and national college entrance exams and national conferences that teachers attend, and a national culture. All that the present proposal would do would be to make more systematized and deliberate that which is now occurring somewhat randomly and coincidentally. The reason for making it more systematic and deliberate is to plug the knowledge gaps from which so many students now suffer. The reason, in other words, is to *guarantee* that all students will be taught the crucial components of our cultural heritage.

POSITION 2
Against a National Curriculum

MAINTAINING LOCAL INTEREST

Granted that there already is a haphazard national curriculum, it would be a disaster to solidify this further through national mandates and testing. There is nothing more certain to depress local interest in schools than to take away local control of what goes on in schools. In recent years, local control has been severely eroded by all kinds of state requirements and monitoring. Specific courses are required; state achievement tests are given in these courses, as well as in basic skill areas like math and reading; and all of this keeps getting added to rather than subtracted from.

To carry the logic of these accountability schemes to the national level is to repudiate the wisdom of the Founding Fathers. Education is a power reserved to the states, according to the U.S. Constitution. Even within states, there is wisdom in letting local school districts maintain the limited amount of curricular control they still have left. First of all, the *informal* national curriculum that we already have ensures that no local district will get too far out of line. Second, the recent spate of state incursions into the curriculum created fairly rigid prescriptions that local districts must follow. What local districts need, then, is not more direction from above but continued discretion over those few areas of the curriculum that they can still tailor to their particular needs.

It is not enough to let local people do their thing in the time that remains to them after the central government has done its thing. The educational program fashioned by the local people must be treated as seriously as that of the central government. Otherwise, the message that will be sent is that the local education program is merely a frill, and teachers should concentrate their time and energy on satisfying the national and state bureaucrats. This message effectively repudiates the legitimacy of determining curricula locally. Greater control of curricula at the national level may be part of the conservatives' agenda for American schools, but it contradicts another part: parental choice of schools. If all the schools are bent on teaching one version of cultural literacy, there won't be much for parents to choose from (Henig, 1988).

DECIDING WHAT IS IMPORTANT

If students lack the cultural literacy that people like Hirsch, Finn, and Ravitch think is important, it may be that the students have yet to be convinced of its importance. The only other possibility is that it is not being taught to the students, which means that teachers are not themselves persuaded of its importance. But this does not mean that students learn nothing in school, or that teachers teach nothing. All it means is that they are not learning or teaching what someone else has decided is important.

Let's take an example from Hirsch's book. One of the terms that Hirsch thinks should be in the vocabulary of a literate person is "Occam's razor." Now that's a wonderful philosophical term going all the way back to the fourteenth century. As you probably already know, it means that the assumptions used to explain something should not be multiplied beyond what is necessary. If the explanation you are given for a stock market crash does not make sense unless you first assume the existence of ten prior conditions, and if an alternative explanation requires only five such assumptions, the alternative is more likely to be true because it entails fewer assumptions which must also be true. Students would certainly not be *harmed* by learning the term, Occam's razor. But here's another philosophical term of even more ancient vintage: Anselm's ontological argument. That—as you, a literate person, probably know—is an argument for the existence of God, surely no small matter. It posits that an attribute of perfection is existence; since God, by definition, is that which is all-perfect, God must exist. This term is not on Hirsch's list.

Obviously Hirsch thinks the first term is important and the second one is not. That's his right, but in exercising it he has engaged in arbitrariness. He has tried to impose his personal preference on other people. Thus, the issue is not whether schools should make students culturally literate. Of course they should. The issue is what constitutes cultural literacy. For Hirsch, one of the crucial items is Occam's razor. For someone else of a more theological bent it would be Anselm's argument. (For a teenager, it might be U-2.)

It is worth noting in this regard that Hirsch has a biased view of American culture, as do we all. "One could waste many happy hours looking things up in Hirsch's tome in an effort to characterize the American culture he imagines. He includes William Faulkner but not Zora Neale Hurston, the Beatles but not the Rolling Stones, Bob Hope but not Lenny Bruce, Chappaquiddick but not SDS, the Monroe Doctrine but not the Truman Doctrine, Solidarity but not the Wobblies" (Margaronis, 1989, p. 14). Hirsch's vision of American culture has a marked conservative bias.

AVOIDING THE MERELY ORNAMENTAL

You might wonder why such terms as Occam's razor and Anselm's argument are worth learning at all. It might suddenly have occurred to you that you rarely come upon these terms in your schoolwork or general reading. Even rarer are the occasions on which you yourself employ the terms.

But wait a moment. Now that your memory of these terms has been refreshed, you might find yourself deliberately dropping them in a term paper (no pun intended) or a class discussion. Wouldn't that impress the professor and intimidate your classmates? It should, but only if the point you were trying to make, and into which you slipped these high-falutin' terms, was itself impressive and intimidating. Otherwise, all you have done is dazzle people momentarily with a sheen of culture that has no subsurface. This is called dilettantism, another term that, interestingly, does not appear on Hirsch's list. Your "literacy" is only ornamental. Its utility consists in dazzling people as a way of distracting them from your shallowness. No matter how high you pile the baubles, bangles, and beads of this ornamentation—even if you adorn yourself with *all* the terms in Hirsch's dictionary (Hirsch et al., 1988)—it is by your own good thinking that others will judge you in the long run, and not too long a run at that. You may be culturally literate in Hirsch's terms, but you will be a functional illiterate in the real world unless you can think well. Good thinking consists of locating relevant data and synthesizing them into meaningful wholes toward the solution of problems. Mere terms alone do not enable you to think.

They only enable you to sound like a deep thinker for a while before people get wise to your superficiality. Knowing Hirsch's terms is no better than knowing the answers to Trivial Pursuit.

SHUNNING ELITISM AND IMPERIALISM

It is likely that the average assembly-line worker in a Detroit auto factory would have trouble understanding Hirsch, who is a professor of English at the University of Virginia. The autoworker would lack familiarity with the terms being tossed around by the professor. One solution to this communication problem would be to drill into the autoworker's head the language of the professor. This, in fact, is the kind of solution being offered by Hirsch and others like him. They are saying, in so many words, that people should be taught to understand *them*. If the rest of us are taught the culture of people like Hirsch, human communication will be enhanced.

No doubt it will. But communication would also be enhanced if Hirsch and others were taught the culture of the autoworker. The idea that my culture is better than yours, so you should learn mine but I don't have to bother with yours, is called "cultural imperialism." The autoworker would probably use a shorter term: snobbery. To say that my culture is more important than yours because my group is more powerful than yours is to talk power politics. It is saying that you have to please me because I am one of the people in charge of running things. That's not education; that's domination. Education is about learning to understand *each other*.

Does that mean we have to learn all the terms of the white male professor's culture and all the terms of the autoworker's culture and every other group's culture, including blacks, Hispanics, women, and gays? That is obviously impossible. The most that can reasonably be expected is that these many major cultural groups be dealt with, and respectfully. What the major groups are will depend, to some extent, on each particular community. For example, a Texas coastal community with a large influx of Vietnamese refugees should include the culture of these people in the curriculum. In order to do this, the Texas town needs some control over the curriculum of its own schools. That is why a national curriculum with lots of detail spelled out would be unwisely restrictive. "Students should have thorough exposure to the core of basic skills, but they should also have a curriculum which is relevant to their social environment ... and which recognizes cultural diversity as a resource, not a deficit, in learning" (Bastian et al., 1985, p. 47).

One group whose culture should always be taken seriously in schools, but seldom is, is youth. The youth culture of the United States (and the local community variation on it) is a most appropriate subject of study in school. The fact that this culture is constantly changing does not mean that its current manifestations can be brushed off as frivolous. On the contrary, these manifestations are responded to eagerly by young people, who are, after all, the clients of schools. Schools should let their clients know that their culture is an important matter, and not something to be ignored until it is outgrown. Schools should stop suggesting to students that people become important only after they get out of school.

HAVING A COMMON CULTURE

The concern that local control will produce too much diversity and keep children from learning a common culture necessary for communication and career success is unwarranted. In the United States, the common culture is learned not only in school but also through the mass media. There are only a handful of major television networks, including the cable ones. The number of newspapers in the United States has been dwindling for a long time now, and there are few newsmagazines. Hollywood makes fewer movies than in the past. What all of this amounts to is a centralization and homogenization of culture by the media. This situation fosters a mass culture, even if it is not the high culture that appeals to Hirsch and others.

The mass culture is the primary basis upon which people relate to each other. Its terms are commonly understood. The subcultures which people need to know in depth to get by in the world are the subcultures of their own jobs, religions, ethnic groups, and so on. People learn these subcultures by living in them. It is the height of arrogance to insist that one's subculture be made the common culture. "What standardized cultures [like Hirsch's] are meant to do is distinguish their owners from the barbarians . . . by classifying the knowledge 'we' have and 'they' don't. . . . it marks the difference between those for whom cultural literacy comes 'naturally'—i.e., those who absorb the information and its context from home and social circles—and those who must acquire it, who feel the rift between their lived experience and what is considered important at school'' (Margaronis, 1989, p. 14).

AVOIDING BIG BROTHER

In his classic novel *1984,* George Orwell warns against a society in which total control is exercised by the few over the many. The few who have the total control (totalitarians) are referred to as Big Brother. If all the schools in the United States are going to teach a single notion of cultural literacy, then the United States will need a Big Brother to spell out the details of that notion for the rest of us. Who should it be? Hirsch? You? Us? A committee of really, really smart people? A committee of people from every important subculture? A bunch of congressmen?

Before this question can be answered, a preliminary question has to be answered: Who decides who gets to decide? If someone or some group is going to be America's cultural czar, then the people who get to pick the czar have to be selected very carefully.

As you can see, this all becomes very complicated and fraught with danger.

The risks and effort might be worth it if we really need a national cultural literacy curriculum, but we don't.

TEACHING FOR CRITICAL LITERACY

Instead of giving students a false sense of culture by having them memorize a lot of big words, we should be making them *critically* literate. This notion is expressed by the Brazilian educator Paolo Freire (1987) and his North American colleagues such as Stanley Aronowitz and Henry Giroux (1985). It means helping people to understand and cope with the real world in which they live. People are taught how to think about their lives by being helped to do this intelligently. They are disabused of misconceptions that cannot withstand scrutiny, and they are shown ways of critically scrutinizing cultural phenomena. They learn to take their own culture seriously through the process of analyzing it. But, in turn, they also have to analyze the larger culture for its impact on their lives. This critical literacy is functional literacy of the highest sort. It not only enables people to survive in their culture; it empowers them to change the negative aspects of the culture.

If young people were to analyze American culture critically, they would surely find that the kind of cultural literacy being advocated by Hirsch and others bears faint resemblance to the kind of literacy that pays off with good jobs and high salaries in our society. They would quickly realize, if they don't already, that their elders are much better at preaching than practicing.

> We honor ambition, we reward greed, we celebrate materialism, we worship acquisitiveness, we commercialize art, we cherish success and then we bark at the young about the gentle arts of the spirit . . . Kids just don't care much for hypocrisy, and if they are [culturally] illiterate, their illiteracy is merely ours, imbibed by them with scholarly ardor. They are learning well the lesson we are teaching—namely, that there is nothing in all the classics in their school libraries that will be of the slightest benefit to them in making their way to the top of our competitive society. (Barber, 1987, p. 23)

FOR DISCUSSION

1 In 1859, John Stuart Mill, the English philosopher, issued the following warning in his classic work, *On Liberty:*

> All that has been said of the importance of individuality of character, and diversity in opinions and modes of conduct, involves, as of the same unspeakable importance, diversity of education. A general State education is a mere contrivance for molding people to be exactly like one another; and as the mold in which it casts them is that which pleases the predominant power in the government . . . in proportion as it is efficient and successful, it establishes a despotism over the mind. . . .

How would you relate this quote to the cultural literacy movement?

2   It has often been said that schools are supposed to optimize each child's educational experience by individualizing instruction according to the child's background and abilities. How is this compatible with the goal of uniform cultural literacy for all?

3   At the end of his book, *Cultural Literacy: What Every American Needs to Know*, E. D. Hirsch, Jr., has a sixty-four-page appendix of terms that every American should know. Following are several of these terms, selected at random from one of the pages, also selected randomly. How many of the terms do you know, and what do you make of your relative "knowledge" and "ignorance"?

Irish potato famine	primrose path
pragmatism	probation
precipitate	procrustean bed
premier	Prohibition
pre-Raphaelite	Provokiev, Sergei
Presley, Elvis	proletariat
Pretoria	Prometheus
Pride and Prejudice (title)	Promised Land
prima donna	prorate
primate	prose

4   The "State Teachers and Principals of the Year" for 1988 compiled a list of recommended books for children of preschool to high-school age.

The educators made their selections at the fifth annual "In Honor of Excellence" symposium held in October 1988. The event was sponsored by the Burger King Corporation in cooperation with the Council of Chief State School Officers and the National Association of Secondary School Principals.

Following are the titles on the reading list.* Do you think it would be a good idea to make this a required reading list for all schools in the United States? Are there any ways in which you would modify the list?

Preschool
Dr. Seuss series, Dr. Seuss
Mother Goose Stories
The Little Engine That Could, Watty Piper
Where the Wild Things Are, Maurice Sendak
Make Way for Ducklings, Robert McCloskey

Primary School (K–3)
The Velveteen Rabbit, Margery Williams
Alexander and the Terrible, Horrible, No Good, Very Bad Day, Judith Viorst
Ira Sleeps Over, Bernard Waber
The Tale of Peter Rabbit, Beatrix Potter
Winnie-the-Pooh, A. A. Milne
Charlotte's Web, E. B. White
Where the Wild Things Are, Maurice Sendak

* *Source: Education Week,* October 19, 1988, p. 30.

Elementary School (4–6)
Charlotte's Web, E. B. White
Tales of a Fourth Grade Nothing, Judy Blume
Where the Red Fern Grows, Wilson Rawls
The Laura Ingalls Wilder series, Laura Ingalls Wilder
Little Women, Louisa May Alcott

Junior High School (7–9)
Where the Red Fern Grows, Wilson Rawls
Anne Frank: The Diary of a Young Girl, Anne Frank
The Red Badge of Courage, Stephen Crane
The Call of the Wild, Jack London
Huckleberry Finn, Mark Twain
Treasure Island, Robert Louis Stevenson
The Outsiders, S. E. Hinton

High School (10–12)
The Grapes of Wrath, John Steinbeck
To Kill a Mockingbird, Harper Lee
Huckleberry Finn, Mark Twain
The Scarlet Letter, Nathanial Hawthorne
A Tale of Two Cities, Charles Dickens
Macbeth, William Shakespeare
The Catcher in the Rye, J. D. Salinger

REFERENCES

Adler, M. (1988). "The Paideia Proposal: Rediscovering the Essence of Education." In *Innovations in Education: Reformers and Their Critics*, edited by J. M. Rich. Boston: Allyn and Bacon.

Aronowitz, S., and Giroux, H. A. (1985). *Education Under Siege: The Conservative, Liberal and Radical Debate Over Schooling*. South Hadley, Mass.: Bergin & Garvey.

Barber, B. (1987). "What Do 47-Year-Olds Know?" *The New York Times*, December 26, p. 23.

Bastian, A., et al. (1985). *Choosing Equality: The Case for Democratic Schooling*. New York: The New World Foundation.

Cheney, L. (1987). *American Memory: A Report on the Humanities in the Nation's Public Schools*. Washington, D.C.: National Endowment for the Humanities.

Freire, P., and Macedo, D. (1987). *Literacy: Reading the Word and the World*. South Hadley, Mass.: Bergin & Garvey.

Gallup, A. M., and Elam, S. M. (1988). The 20th Annual Gallup Poll of the Public's Attitudes Toward the Public Schools. *Phi Delta Kappan*, **70**(1), 33–46.

Henig, J. R. (1988). "Which Way, Mr. Bennett?" *The Washington Post National Weekly Edition*, September 12–18, p. 27.

Hirsch, E. D. (1987). *Cultural Literacy: What Every American Needs to Know*. Boston: Houghton Mifflin.

Hirsch, E. D., Kett, J. F., and Trefil, J. (1988). *The Dictionary of Cultural Literacy: What Every American Needs to Know*. Boston: Houghton Mifflin.

Margaronis, M. (1989). "Waiting for the Barbarians: The Ruling Class Defends the Citadel." *Village Voice Literacy Supplement*, January/February, pp. 12–17.

Ravitch, D., and Finn, C. (1987). *What Do Our 17-Year-Olds Know?: A Report on the First National Assessment of History and Literature*. New York: Harper & Row.

CHAPTER 8

TRADITIONAL VALUES OR LIBERATION

POSITION 1
For Traditional Values

We are subject to increasing abuse in contemporary life. There has been a startling increase in child abuse, so prevalent we have twenty-four-hour telephone "hot lines" to report it. Wife abuse is another item reported almost daily in the newspapers. Animal abuse is so common it no longer makes news. And drug abuse has become epidemic.

There are other abuses in the current world. We abuse our ideals, our respect, our heroes, our national honor, and our religious base. Political and business leaders abuse the public trust by cheating and corruption. It is no longer clear to young people why we fought wars to protect our liberties. Some children refuse to recite the Pledge of Allegiance or sing the "Star Spangled Banner." Graffiti covers many of our national monuments and statues of heroes. Children no longer honor their parents and respect elders.

WHY HAS THIS OCCURRED?

What is the reason for this decline in American values? There are many reasons, but foremost is that the schools have foresaken the teaching of solid values. Instead, they have substituted highly relativistic attitudes that undermine parental and religious authority. Children are taught that all values are equal, so whatever they value is fine. We can't hold children responsible for this travesty on common morality because the natural tendency of children is selfishness. Parents have to teach children to share and to have respect for normal social values. Historically, we have relied upon the school to reinforce and extend this basic ethical code taught in families and churches. In those unfortunate circumstances when parents are unable, or unwilling, to teach children right from wrong, the school has usually performed this important function. People who now run schools have forgotten their history, and those who forget will repeat the mistakes of the past.

Now, with high divorce rates and parental neglect of children's moral development, the schools should be expected to accept an even more significant role in imparting American values to children. It is in times of family and social stress that the schools should exert expanded influence to assure the continuation of our heritage. Active membership in religions is now starting to increase as people recognize the insidious vacuum in morality created during the most recent period of permissiveness. But many of our young parents grew up during the 1960s and 1970s, when there was a sharp decline in religious participation and a significant increase in immorality. Without the value base that strong religious and national traditions provide, Americans may be in trouble. Schools should have assumed increased responsibility for training children in traditional values.

Instead, schools have been taken over by secular humanism and its selfish pursuits. Secular humanism, with its relativistic and narcissistic values, has corrupted much of public life and permeated the public schools, producing people who are permissive and who lack a personal core of values. That is certainly one reason for the deterioration of family life and the decline in religious involvement. Since most young people of the World War II generation were indoctrinated with secular humanism in school, even though they may not have recognized its perniciousness, it is easy to understand how family and religious life would suffer as that generation became parents. We now have had at least two generations go through that program, and are reaping the social discontent that it can produce.

Secular humanists view the state as more important than religion, and believe that humans can create and change their own values without reference to a greater being. This means that whatever is the current fad can become the ethical code for the society. If enough people want to do something, they get laws passed to permit it or put pressure on public officials to ignore higher values. The rapid expansion of legalized gambling, easy abortions, alcoholism, drug abuse, and crime are examples of this in practice.

Secular humanism, and the relativistic values it promotes, caters to the basest of human interests. It provides no guidelines for behavior or thought. It is permissiveness at the highest level. Secular humanism is now the dominant view of the public schools.

Jerry Falwell (1980) has described the destruction of American education:

> Until about thirty years ago, the public schools in America were providing . . . support for our boys and girls. Christian education and the precepts of the Bible still permeated the curriculum of the public schools. . . . Our public schools are now per-

meated with humanism. . . . children are taught that there are no absolute rights or wrongs and that the traditional home is only one alternative. (pp. 205, 210)

Senator Strom Thurmond, a strong constitutionalist, wrote a ringing criticism of Supreme Court decisions that "assault the constitution." Among the decisions he protests as leaving the country open to communism, collectivism, and immorality are the Court's actions to prohibit prayer and Bible reading in public schools. He asserts:

> They [parents] ought to have a right to insist that their children are educated in the traditions and values of their own culture. Above all, they have a right to see that their children are not indoctrinated in a secular, Godless point of view which contradicts the values that are taught at home. (1968, p. 28)

HOW SCHOOLS DESTROY VALUES

Children are taught that no values from home or church are valid. Through such teaching practices as "values clarification," children are led to believe that their individual opinions of what is right and wrong are perfectly satisfactory. No moral guidelines are given for conduct or thought. As examples of "values clarification," children are asked by the teacher to identify situations at home where the father or mother has been wrong, and to substitute the child's view of what should have been done. Children are asked personal questions about their family lives and private thoughts. And children are presented with lists of behaviors and asked to rank them according to the child's own opinions of whether they are "good" or "bad" behaviors. The teacher does not present correct responses or try to explain why they are correct. There are no criteria established against which children are to weigh right and wrong. Instead, the teacher encourages each child to determine his or her own set of values.

In class discussions of values, children with strongly presented personal opinions can influence other children, and the teacher is not supposed to intercede for fear of stopping the "clarification" of values. That is how it is possible for a whole class to agree that tying cans on a cat's tail, committing euthanasia on older people, or sitting during the flag salute may be entirely acceptable behavior. Children also learn to report on their parents, and to ridicule those who hold traditional values of discretion and privacy.

Dr. Elmer Towns, in a hard-hitting book, documents the failures of public education and the resulting threat to American society. In a chapter titled, "The Smell of Deterioration," he writes:

> What has "had it" in public schools? Bible-reading and prayers are not legal; they have "had it." The Puritan/Protestant ethic as a style of life has been edged out by the new morality; it has "had it." Dedication to academic pursuits is no longer prized by the majority of educators; it has "had it." Correct behavior, according to respected society norms, is no longer enforced; it has "had it." . . . the question that screams for an answer is, "Has our nation 'had it'?" (1974, p. 23)

CONFUSING VALUES IN THE CURRENT CURRICULUM

The school curriculum and textbooks being used now present a wide array of relativistic values that only serve to confuse children. Secular humanism is not defined as a school subject per se, and there are no courses in it. Instead, it filters into nearly all courses and is often unrecognized, even by the teachers. Because there is no specific curriculum on morals and values, it is easy for teachers and courses to present differing ones, and to lead students to believe that there are no eternal values, only personal ones. If the courses and the teachers do not attest to a common core of morality, students are left rudderless in school. This spawns confusion or self-indulgence at best, and scorn for morality at worst.

The teaching material presented to children is either vapid, without any connection to moral thought and behavior, or confusing because multiple values are treated as having supposedly equal weight. Current reading material in school includes nonsensical stories that lead nowhere, trash that directs attention to the values of the worst elements of society, and adult stories well beyond the moral development of children. In civics and history, the focus is on political power, not virtue. Children are taught how to manipulate others, and how interest groups get things their way. History texts are bland and noncommittal on basic values, and religion is ignored or treated with disdain. Sex education instruction is oriented toward promiscuity and sexual freedom, not toward abstinence and responsibility. Science ignores religious views and substitutes the idea of being value-free; any scientific experiment is OK. And the arts include study of depraved artists and music, rather than uplifting and positive arts. Innocence, instead of being protected and encouraged, is savaged and debased (Rafferty, 1968).

WHAT SHOULD BE TAUGHT

Clearly, the proper role and function of schools in a moral society has to be rediscovered. America was founded on Judeo-Christian ideals. We have survived, and thrived, because of these ideals. They form the basis of our concepts of justice and democracy. Schools were established here to transmit these values to the young as a way of preserving this society.

Early American schooling was deliberately intended to instill a belief in God and support for religious values. Schools had a clear purpose and a solid direction. Children did not get mixed messages on morality and behavior, and they did not get the impression that they could make up and change their values on a whim.

From the *New England Primer* through McGuffey's *Readers,* the content studied in school was consistent with traditional American values. There is much to be learned from the moral stories presented in these old works. Children learned that it was wrong to misbehave at home, in the community, and at school. They learned the consequences of affronting the common morality by reading what happened to those who did. They gained respect for proper authority in the family, the church, society, and school. We need to reject the permissiveness and valuelessness of our current schools and return to an emphasis on moral precepts and proper behavior. That will require considerable effort in rethinking the curriculum and teaching.

TRADITIONAL VALUES AS THE FOCUS

The curriculum should focus on traditional values at all levels. In elementary school, reading material should emphasize ideals. Through stories of great heroes, children should be taught personal integrity, resoluteness, loyalty, and the productivity of hard work. The main theme, brought out by studying the positive aspects of American history and literature, should be that individuals working together with a suitable goal can succeed. Teachers should stress and expect ethical behavior, respect, and considerateness. Various religions should be studied with the purpose of understanding their common values, and the application of these values in life. Providing time in school for children to reinforce their religious beliefs would be appropriate.

Signs and symbols in school should reinforce American values. Pictures, displays, and assemblies on morality can offer students a chance to see how important it is to the school. Inviting speakers into classes, showing films, and taking students to see significant monuments to American values are examples of helpful techniques. Teachers can emphasize good values by giving direct instruction on moral precepts and rewarding children who show good citizenship in the school.

At the secondary level, the emphasis on traditional values should continue with more sophisticated material and concepts. A special course on sex education is not needed if family values are covered well in other courses. A student honor roll, citing acts of particularly good school citizenship, could be as prominently displayed as the athletic trophies that now dominate glass cabinets near the typical principal's office. Libraries are particularly good places to have special sections of books and displays that feature the kinds of thoughts and behaviors we seek.

American and foreign literature that portrays the rewards of moral behavior and the negative consequences of immorality should be featured. Essay contests on subjects that convey a concern for morality should be school-sponsored. American history should express the ideals for which we stand, and our extraordinary historical achievements. Science courses should feature stories of hard work and success in scientific discoveries, as well as stories of how basic values and religious views have guided many scientists in their work.

The arts are a rich place to show values through study of paintings, compositions, sculptures, and other art forms that express the positive aspects of human life under a set of everlasting ideals. Not only can religious music and art be used; there are thousands of examples of nonreligious art and artists who idealize such things as the golden rule and personal virtue. In the vocational subjects there are numerous ways to present good attitudes toward work and family, responsibility, loyalty, decency, and respect. Sports are an especially important place for these same values to be reaffirmed; there are numerous examples of professional and college teams who pray together before matches, and many players who are leading figures in setting high standards of moral conduct.

TEACHERS FOR AMERICAN VALUES

We need teachers who themselves have a strong commitment to traditional values, and who exhibit that commitment in their behaviors and lives. Such teachers are the key to improved teaching of values. Changes in curriculum or teaching materials will have no impact if no moral criteria are set for the teachers who work directly with the young. Obviously, the determination of moral beliefs goes beyond the transcript of college courses, since the subjects studied bear little relationship to moral conduct and belief.

In order to preserve and protect American values in schools, states have a right to require high moral standards from those who obtain state licenses to teach in the public schools. Colleges which prepare teachers should be required to examine the records of students and to deny those with criminal or other socially offensive backgrounds such as alcoholism or gambling. Applicants for teaching credentials should be expected to submit reference letters which attest to their moral character. That is an expectation for lawyers taking state bar exams; why shouldn't it be for those going into teaching? Schools, as a part of the application procedure for teaching positions, should require applicants to prepare essays on their beliefs. Clearly, the period of student teaching and the first few years of full-time teaching provide ample opportunity to screen young teachers in their school and public lives to assure that moral standards are upheld. If these criteria are clearly and publicly stated, fair warning will have been given. Teachers found wanting in their morality would need to find employment in some other occupation. They should not be retained in positions which influence the ideals of young people.

With a strengthened corps of teachers in the schools, there will be a re-building of American values. These teachers will demand better curricula, better teaching materials, and better student behavior. There will be an infectious quality about this rebuilding that will influence parents, government, and the media. The schools have a rich opportunity.

It is possible to restore these American values to the schools, and to our young people. But being possible is not enough. It is crucial that we move quickly to reinvigorate our school leaders with a resolve to do it. There is a crisis of values in society, and it is reflected in schools. Our society is extremely vulnerable. The school must reassume the responsibility for moral teachings that was its original purpose.

POSITION 2
For Liberation

The primary purpose of education is liberation. Freedom from slavery, from dictatorship, and from domination are based on freedom from ignorance. Freedom to think and to act are based on freedom to know. Any society which intends to be free and democratic must recognize the elemental schooling equation: liberation = education. Schools which restrict and contort the minds of the young are in opposition to that principle and democratic civilization is the victim.

Liberation is not, however, a set of teacher techniques, a specific lesson plan, or a textbook series for school adoption. There is no mechanistic or teacher-proof approach to students that will produce liberation. There is no room for such devious and robotlike schooling ideas as behavioral objectives and mastery learning in liberation education. Indeed, liberation is in direct opposition to the conformist mentality that produced such ideas. Liberation is the emancipation of students and teachers from the blinders of class-dominated ignorance, conformity, and thought control. It is dynamic, seeing students and teachers as active participants in opposing oppression and improving democracy.

LIBERATION EDUCATION

Liberation education is complex, because the social forces which it addresses are complex. Its central purpose is to liberate the individual and the society from oppressive ideological domination. That requires a broad distribution of liberating power and a set of values, including justice and equality, that serve as ideals in opposition to oppression. It further requires critical understanding of the many cultural crosscurrents in contemporary society and the mechanisms of manipulation which hide ideological purposes. Liberation education includes the uncovering of the dominant culture(s) to expose its myths and injustices, especially for the disadvantaged. It also includes an expectation that the powerless can, through education, develop power. This requires a recognition that the forms of knowledge and of schooling are not neutral, but are utilized by the dominant culture to continue their power.

Schools must be seen as sites where the manifold conflicts of humankind are examined, in increasing depth, to understand the ideological and cultural bases on which societies operate. The purpose is not merely to recognize those conflicts or the ideologies, but to enable students to engage in actions that will constrain oppression and expand personal power. This is a profound and revolutionary educational concept, and it goes to the heart of what education should be. Schools themselves should be subject to this liberating critique, and to the resulting actions that could make them more truly democratic. This would mean schools which respect students and teachers, which permit participation in decisions, and which offer fairness rather than authoritarianism.

Other social institutions are also necessary subjects of examination and action. It is obvious that "liberation education"—a redundant term—is controversial in contemporary society and in education. Liberated people threaten the traditional docility and passivity that are now imposed by schools.

MAINSTREAM MYSTIFICATION

There is too little in popular educational literature that speaks to liberation, opposition to oppressive forces, and improvement of democracy. The vast majority of mainstream educational writing raises no questions about the context within schools function; most writing seems to accept the conservative purposes and operations of schools and merely intends to "fine-tune" them a bit. Standard educational writing does not see schooling as a problematic issue, subject to critical examination of assumptions, ideologies, and complexities. Instead, teachers and teachers-in-training read articles on teaching techniques and slight modifications in school curriculum. There is nothing critical in these pieces, no liberation of the mind from the strictures of a narrow culture. The dominant concern is to make the school more efficient, more mechanical, more factorylike, more conformist.

Mainstream educational literature rests upon a narrow current of thought in American society that is bounded by standard conservative and liberal ideas. It is not considered good form to read material, pose ideas, or raise criticism from outside of this band of thought. Those who do are labeled radical or "un-American" and are viewed with great suspicion. Their ideas and criticisms are not given public credibility. The effort to improve the way democracy works by subjecting it to critical evaluation is disdained, and neither conservatives nor liberals are pleased to have American democracy critically examined in schools.

Conservatives and liberals do seem to agree, in their writings, that schools in America should be related to democracy. Numerous platitudes about schools preparing citizens for democracy, or being mini-democracies, fill the standard mainstream literature. This literature can be classified as mystification in that it uses high-sounding phrases to cover its ideology of the status quo, a continuation of the power of the already dominant class. It is not active democracy, with its liberation values, that this literature commends. Its real purpose is to keep the masses content as uncritical workers, believing themselves to be free but actually powerless. The function of mainstream writing is to mystify its uncritical readers with a rhetoric of freedom which hides the actual ideological domination.

Schooling terms such as "excellence," "mastery," "humanistic," and "progressive" fill mainstream periodicals. Although these can be useful in discussing education, they are often used as camouflage. "Excellence" and "mastery," from conservatives, are used to mask the interests of dominant classes in justifying their advantages, and the interests of business in the production of skilled and docile workers. "Humanistic" and "progressive," from liberals, hide a soft and comfortable individualism that ignores basic problems and conflicts in society. The combination continues the business ideology that dominates schools and society, and the narcissism that prevents groups from recognizing the defects in that ideology. That is mystification, an effort to mystify the public and keep hidden the real agenda in schools.

That agenda is to maintain what Joel Spring (1976) calls a "Sorting Machine," where the different social classes are given different treatment and sorted into various categories of citizenship; what Raymond Callahan (1962) documents as a business orientation in schools to prepare the masses for efficient work and the elite for management; what Jean Anyon (1980) shows as the actual curriculum of docility and obedience taught to the lower classes; and what Henry Giroux (1988) describes as the hidden curriculum which imposes dominant class values, attitudes, and norms on all students.

John Stuart Mill, in his classic essay *On Liberty,* defines the commonplace education as conformist, stating:

> A general State education is a mere contrivance for moulding people to be exactly like one another; and as the mould in which it casts them is that which pleases the predominant power in the government—whether this be a monarch, a priesthood, an aristocracy, or the majority of the existing generation—in proportion as it is efficient and successful, it establishes a despotism over the mind, leading by natural tendency to one over the body. (1859; reprinted 1956, p. 129)

Mill's comments are still appropriate today. Much is made of the conservative and liberal arguments about schooling, but in fact there is little that separates them. The schools can and do, by slight modification every few years, accommodate each side for a while. There are pendulum swings in a narrow arc from the center, but schools remain pretty much the same, with only cosmetic changes. With conservatives in power, there is more concern about competition, grading, passing tests, and knowing specific bits of information. With liberals, the effort is to make students feel happy, to allow more freedom in the curriculum, and to offer more student activities.

In regard to democracy and schooling, the differences between conservative and liberal views lie in how narrowly democracy is defined, and at what age democracy is to be practiced. The conservative rhetoric calls for a more narrow definition and the forming of good habits and values by students before they can participate. That usually means that the school is a place to learn their narrow definition and learn loyalty to American democracy without practicing it. Liberals write about a somewhat broader definition, and about the schools as places where a form of democracy should actually be practiced.

Neither the conservative nor the liberal mainstream view raises basic questions about the nature of democracy or the means used to achieve it. Neither view is critical of existing class domination of knowledge and schools. Neither sees democracy as problematic, deserving of continuing critical examination in order to be improved. Both views assume a basic consensus on what democracy is, and that the schools are merely an agency for obtaining it. As a result, there is really very little practical difference between conservative and liberal views about schooling in a democracy. There are only shallow differences in what subjects are emphasized and how much limited freedom students are given. Those may sound like important differences, but debates over such matters as how tough grading practices should be, or whether extra time is needed for reading drill, do not address serious and significant issues of democratic life. Ideologically, conservatives and liberals share basic beliefs.

REACTIONARY INDOCTRINATION
AND CULTURAL REPRODUCTION

Only the reactionary fringe, the far right, appear on the surface to desire schools and a society that are basically undemocratic in purpose and operation. At least the far right wing is honest and direct, though simply wrong. These reactionary groups, including religious fundamentalists, are clear that there is a natural hierarchical order to society that must be imposed on children in schools. There is nothing democratic in that premise. They are open advocates of indoctrination and censorship. If you know the TRUTH, why let other ideas be presented? Dissent, of course, should be stifled because it confuses children of all ages. And deviation cannot be tolerated. It is refreshing to see such clarity and determination in the face of general uncertainty in the modern world, but this view has potentially disastrous consequences for any democracy and its schools.

Interestingly, conservative and liberal views also expect indoctrination, but they are loath to tell anyone because it sounds undemocratic. Instead, since they control the schools and the society, they can impose their dominant views by more subtle means. By virtue of state laws put in place by this coalition, school curriculum, textbook selection, school operation, and teacher licensing are controlled. State agencies—such as a state department of education—monitor schools and prescribe limits. The news media, under similar domination by mainstream conservative and liberal forces, persuade the public that the democracy and the schools are working relatively well. There is very little basic criticism of either in the news media; the news mainly reports minor disagreements on tactics and personalities. Ideological disputes are not confronted because there are none between standard conservative and liberal views.

So indoctrination to the mainstream is what schools are expected to do, and the mainstream has the power to actually require this conformity. Another term for this mainstream indoctrination is "cultural reproduction," where the dominant cultural ideology is reproduced by each generation because it is imposed on them. In America, this cultural reproduction takes two forms: (1) a set of positive beliefs that America is a chosen country, with justice and equality for all and the best of economic systems, and (2) a set of negative beliefs that any views which raise troubling questions about American values are automatically anti-American. This twofold reproduction ensures that teachers and students do not engage in serious critical thinking, but merely accept dominant ideologies. Thus, the very nature of democracy, and the means for improving it, are not seen as problematic; instead, they are perceived as naturally existing and beyond the schools' examination.

In school, students read mainstream literature, hear mainstream views from teachers and peers, see mainstream films, hear mainstream speakers, and engage in mainstream extracurricular activities. The school library carries only mainstream periodicals and books. It is virtually impossible to find highly divergent ideas under examination in schools. When students are not in school, they read the mainstream press, watch mainstream TV, and live in families of people who were educated in the same manner in previous generations. Teachers are prepared in colleges where they study mainstream views of their subjects, and mainstream ideas about teaching. It is no wonder that schools are prime locations for cultural reproduction. There are no other sources of ideas. To have mainstream ideas broadly represented in schools is certainly not improper; but to deny critical examination of those ideas, and to limit students to such a narrow band of ideas, is not liberating.

Students often are very surprised to stumble on a radical journal or book that legitimately challenges basic assumptions about capitalism and American politics, and their impact on justice and equality. These students then rightfully question an education which did not permit consideration of opposing values and ideologies. Unfortunately, the vast majority of students never stumble on radical materials, or they automatically and unthoughtfully reject any divergent views because the schools have been effective in sealing off their minds.

MAINSTREAM CONTROL OF KNOWLEDGE

Not only do schools sort and label students, and limit the range of views permitted for examination; the kind of knowledge available to differing groups of students also is class-biased. Michael F. D. Young, a British sociologist, has argued that "those in positions of power will attempt to define what is taken as knowledge, how accessible to different groups knowledge is. . . ." (1971).

Essentially, what occurs in schools is that knowledge which is considered of "high status" is guarded by those in power. It is used to assist the group in power to retain power, and to differentiate it from the masses. High-status knowledge is determined by those who already have power. Although the work of auto mechanics involves complex skills and knowledge, it is not considered high-status work. Law and medicine, also utilizing complex skills and knowledge, are considered high-status and access to them is restricted.

As Michael Apple (1977) notes, there is a relation between economic structure and high-status knowledge. A capitalistic, industrial, technological society values knowledge which most contributes to its continuing development. Math, science, and computer study have demonstrably more financial support than arts and humanities. MBA degrees are more valuable, especially from "prestigious" institutions, than are degrees in humanities fields. Technical subjects, such as math and the sciences, are more easily broken into discrete bits of information, and more easily testable than arts and humanities subjects. This leads to easy stratification of students, often along social-class lines. The idea of school achievement is to compete well in those "hard" technical subjects where differentiation is easiest to measure. The upper-class student, however, is not in the competition, since he or she is protected and not usually in public schools; the upper-middle class provides advantage for its children; the working-class child struggles to overcome disadvantage.

The separation of subjects in the discipline-centered curriculum serves to legitimate the high status of "hard subjects" and the academic preparatory sequence. The organization of knowledge is not examined or understood as class-based or problematic. Instead, information is presented in segments and spurts, with testing on detail and ranking on how well one has accepted the school's definition. We pretend that knowledge is neutral, with the numerous subject categories and titles merely logical structures to assist in understanding. This separates school learning from social problems, reinforces the domination of existing authority on what is identified as important to know, and maintains students as dependent and uncritical thinkers.

WHAT SHOULD BE TAUGHT

Liberation education requires the blending of curriculum content with pedagogy. What is studied cannot be separated from how it is studied. The basis of this approach to schooling is to have students engage in critical study of the society and its institutions, with the dual purpose of liberating themselves from simple cultural reproduction and liberating the society from oppressive manipulation of the masses. Critical study is both method and content. It expects open examination and critique of diverse ideas, and sees the human condition as problematic. That places all human activity as potential curriculum content, and makes all such activity subject to critical scrutiny through a dynamic form of dialectic reasoning.

Obviously, students cannot examine all things at all times. Thus, the selection of topics to be studied at any one time depends on several factors, including whatever has been previously studied and the level of those critiques, which contemporary social issues are significant, the interests and maturity level of students, and the knowledge of the teacher. There is no neatly structured sequence of information that all students must pass through and forget. Knowledge is active and dynamic; it is complex and intertwined. Students should come to understand that, and to examine the nature of knowledge itself. That can lead to liberation.

Among the topics of early and continuing study should be ideologies. Students need to learn how to strip away layers of propaganda and rationalization to examine root ideas. Those ideas may be phrased in language of mystification intended to persuade people. Critical study enables students to see through this surface expression.

Racism and sexism are not considered proper public views in America, yet they often lie behind high-sounding pronouncements and policies. Using test scores from culturally biased tests to segregate those given favored treatment from those excluded can be rationalized in neutral-sounding nonracist and nonsexist terms, but the basic causes and the consequences may well be racist or sexist. Engaging in imperialism is not considered proper behavior in current international relations, but powerful nations do attempt physical or political-economic control of other nations while calling their actions defensive or "freedom-fighting." Ideological study can help students situate events in historic, economic, and political settings that are deeper and more complex than the surface explanations.

THE DYNAMIC DIALECTIC

Liberation education requires teachers and students to engage in a dynamic form of dialectical reasoning to uncover ideological roots. A dialectic involves analyzing ideas by considering opposing ideas and delving deeper into the basis of each to attempt a more reasoned understanding of the issue. There are at least two forms of dialectic reasoning. One, as proposed by Plato, structures and limits the discourse to lead students to one fixed idea of truth. For example, Socrates knew the truth and led students to it by taking their answers to questions and subjecting those answers to further questions until the students came to accept Socrates' view. That is an authoritarian form of dialectic; a democratic dialectic does not require the student to accept the teacher's answer.

The dynamics of democratic dialectic opens topics to examination. It does not proceed by a set of absolutes to a known truth, but operates more like a spiral, digging deeper into rationales. It involves seeing the topic in its total social context, not in segments as studied in the discipline-centered curriculum. And it requires a vision of liberation that allows students to go beneath the surface or obvious parts of the topic to see the basic relationships to the structure of society and dominant interests. The purpose of the dialectic is to cause students to transcend their traditional nonactive and sterile roles, and to accept roles as active and knowledgeable participants in the improvement of civilization. In theory, the dialectic is never-ending, since civilization is in continual need of improvement. In practice in schools, the dialectic is limited by time, energy, interest, and the topics under study.

Liberation education expects that highly divergent ideas will be examined in schools. That in itself is insufficient. These divergent ideas have to be examined in a setting where they can be fully developed and can be perceived as legitimate, rather than strange or quaint. There has to be adequate time and resources available, without censorship and authoritarianism.

For a truly liberated society one cannot expect less of schools than education for liberation. An emancipatory climate in schools will regenerate students and teachers to full use of their intellects and increasing creativity. Those are fitting and proper goals for schools, unachievable under the restricted mainstream forms of schooling now practiced.

FOR DISCUSSION

1   Who should decide which values are taught in schools? What is the justification for your answer?

2   Florida, in the 1950s, passed legislation that required school students to take a course entitled "Americanism vs. Communism." What is a rationale for such a course, and what are some examples of the content that one would expect to be included?

3   Examine textbooks and other teaching material used in a local school to determine the major values being expressed to students. How could these values be categorized? Are students expected to accept the values or to critically examine them?

4   The following is from a textbook on citizenship education for teacher education courses:*

> ... we will explore two concepts that are central to the education of citizens in a democracy. The first concept is SOCIALIZATION—the process of learning the existing customs, traditions, rules, and practices of a society. The second is COUNTERSOCIALIZATION—the process of expanding the individual's ability to be a rational, thoughtful, and independent citizen of a democracy.

Identify some school examples of socialization and countersocialization. What differentiates them? What chance does countersocialization have if socialization is successful? Can we expect teachers to give equal consideration to countersocialization? Whose interests and values are involved in each?

REFERENCES

Anyon, J. (1980). "Social Class and the Hidden Curriculum of Work," *Journal of Education,* **162,** 67–92.

Apple, M. (1977). *Ideology and Curriculum.* London: Routledge.

Callahan, R. (1962). *Education and the Cult of Efficiency.* Chicago: University of Chicago Press.

Falwell, J. (1980). *Listen America!* Garden City, N.Y.: Doubleday.

Giroux, H. (1988). *Teachers as Intellectuals.* Granby, Mass.: Bergin & Garvey.

Mill, J. S. (1859). *On Liberty.* Reprinted 1956. Edited by C. V. Shields. Indianapolis: Bobbs-Merrill.

Rafferty, M. (1968). *Max Rafferty on Education.* New York: Devin-Adair.

Read, L. (1968). *Accent on the Right.* Irvington-on-Hudson, N.Y.: Foundation for Economic Education.

Spring, J. (1976). *The Sorting Machine: National Educational Policy Since 1945.* New York: McKay.

Towns, E. T. (1974). *Have the Public Schools "Had It"?* New York: Nelson.

Thurmond, S. (1968). *The Faith We Have Not Kept.* San Diego: Viewpoint Books.

Young, M. F.D. (1971). *Knowledge and Control.* London: Collier-Macmillan.

---

* S. Engle and A. Ochoa, *Education for Democratic Citizenship.* New York: Teachers College Press, 1988, p. 29.

CHAPTER 9

TECHNOLOGY
OR HUMANISM

POSITION 1
For Technological Competence

The speed with which technology has changed our lives is dazzling. However, the speed with which the schools are preparing students to meet the challenges of the new technological society is snaillike. This is creating a major problem for our future generations, and for our society. Alvin Toffler's *Future Shock* (1970), a book which outlined the social trauma of sudden and unexpected confrontation with change, could have been written entirely about schools and their lack of preparation for a technological age. "Education shock" is what many students experience when they leave traditional schools and enter the work force without technological competence. Technological illiteracy, where members of the society do not understand and cannot cope with technical advances, is an educational problem of immense proportions.

In addition to this form of illiteracy, many schools are unintentionally fostering an irrational fear of technology that Harold Hellman identified as "technophobia" (1976). Technophobia is beyond illiteracy, incorporating the mentality that technology is bad and should be feared. Technophobia may be the result of, but certainly becomes the rationalization for, technical illiteracy. People who avoid contact with such common things as computers, copying machines, videotape recorders, and cars with obvious electronic equipment may be suffering from this fear. Trying to educate such people is extraordinarily difficult. Their exasperation and helplessness when confronted with machine breakdown are not rational, and they are unlikely to seek instruction from manuals or experts. They give up easily, kick the machine, call the repair person, or quietly leave the scene hoping it will all go away. The incident only confirms their fears and suspicions about the evils of technology.

People can feel guilty about illiteracy, and can be persuaded to correct this deficiency; a phobia is much deeper and more difficult to overcome. Schools which do not develop technological literacy in their students may be dooming them to life on the margins of a technological future; worse, illiteracy breeds fears and distrust that threaten education and society.

"Technological literacy" is a term which has many meanings, but there is a core of knowledge, skills, and attitudes which are basic. Knowledge includes the fundamental scientific principles on which technology rests, and a minimal understanding of technical language. Skills include techniques useful in handling and working with the results of technology. And attitudes include an optimistic view that recognizes the value of technology to civilization.

It is nearly impossible to engage in daily activities without contact with some aspect of technology which has developed in just the past thirty years. Recent developments in computers, lasers, robotics, gene splicing, telecommunications, and transportation influence everyday events for millions of people. The schools, however, are nearly the same as they have been for 100 years. There is little that changes schools, and nothing seems to change them quickly. Yet, the rapid speed of technological development is evident in all other parts of society. Some schools have made halting and sporadic efforts to catch up, but most have kept themselves in the Victorian age.

Children who are technologically literate are often self- or family-taught. Many children have some knowledge of the results of advanced technology through computers and television; they have gained some skill in manipulating new technology, and their attitude is one of positive curiosity and eagerness about the latest advances. But these same children may attend schools where the chalkboard is the standard level of communicative technology, where teacher records are kept laboriously by hand, and where the typical teacher's attitude is to fear or to scorn new technology. We are in the ludicrous position of having schools far behind the level of technological knowledge known to children, while those children are in school presumably to learn to live in the next century.

Schools now have computers and TVs, but seldom enough for each student. This equipment is often perceived by teachers and the school as special and separate from standard work in the classroom. The machinery is outdated and sometimes poorly maintained, and the teachers often have limited personal experience with it. Each student has access to school-level technology for only a few minutes each week.

Schools provide very little education about other new technology. Very few schools utilize the most up-to-date technology in daily functions of teaching, learning, and administration. Schools are still horse-and-buggy operations existing in a rocket-launch environment. Although the local supermarket and newspaper have become transformed by new technology, the local schools are almost unaffected. We are rapidly becoming a technologically ignorant society because of the gap between new technical knowledge and schooling. This gap is potentially serious, not only because we are graduating individual students who have limited literacy and considerable fear of technology, but also because the nation is losing its competitive edge in technological advances.

BECOMING A BACKWARD NATION

There is an intense international competition in many areas of modern life. Nations in Europe and Asia have become major manufacturers and exporters of automobiles, electronic equipment, computers, and other high-technology goods. With new technology and a willing and trained work force, these countries have overtaken the United States in manufacturing steel, setting up robotic assembly lines, and producing household appliances. Until very recently, America was the leading nation in the manufacture of high-quality goods and in business innovation. We have a long history of technological advancement including development of electric lights, automobiles, airplanes, phonograph and TV, household appliances, and heavy industrial equipment.

The United States has had the good fortune to be populated by people who had entrepreneurial spirit and scientific intelligence. And we have been fortunate in having a government and an economic system which encourages individuals to find new ideas for consumer goods and services. These new ideas have not only made life easier and more comfortable for American citizens, they have also produced a strong economy with low unemployment and many opportunities for hardworking people to attain high incomes. America now faces greater competition from other nations which have developed considerable skill in maufacturing and in business innovation. This is a threat to our standard of living, and to our ability to remain a world leader in international affairs. We must address this rapidly changing global economy, and its threats to our lives.

Rather than simply attack other countries because they are now doing a better job in technological development, we should look at how we can improve the American approach. Many of our economic rivals in the modern world, like Japan and North Korea, have made dramatic advances by carefully examining how American technology has worked, and then improving on it. We should now make an increased effort to examine our own technology and business enterprises, and to improve on ourselves.

THE SPEED OF TECHNOLOGICAL CHANGE

To illustrate how the pace of scientific and technological change has been increasing, with significant impact on our lives, let us look at some examples in transportation, communication, and calculation (Faure, 1972). From the time of the earliest humans several million years ago until the locomotive and bicycle, walking and using animals were the major means of land transportation. Speed was relatively slow, and distances were covered at great expense of time. The Spanish missions up the coast of what is now California were spaced one day's ride apart, about twenty-five miles. In the industrial revolution by the end of the nineteenth century, the development of the steam and the internal combustion engines gave humans the ability to travel at a speed of just over sixty-five miles an hour. By 1945, jet aircraft were going at speeds ten times that. Today, astronauts travel through space at around 23,000 miles per hour. People in the first part of the last century stayed near their homes; it was a major trip to visit 100 miles away, and cross-country travel could take months. Now, in the last decade of the twentieth century, large numbers of people drive 20,000 miles and fly another 30,000 miles each year; and some have signed up for space travel.

In communication there has been equal technological change. The unassisted human voice, smoke, drums, and other means of communication were limited in distance, volume, and clarity. The telegraph and telephone changed that significantly, but recent developments in laser and electronic transmission have made wire transmission seem primitive. Instant communication with people in other nations, including video and document fax transmissions, is becoming commonplace. Millions of people throughout the world heard and saw astronauts, with delays of only about three seconds, landing on the moon and setting up space stations. Fifty years ago that was only a fantasy dreamed up by comic-book cartoonists.

In earlier times humans used fingers, stones, sticks, and abacuses to calculate and measure. Mechanical adding machines, aided later by the addition of electricity, became the standard in accounting, banking, and retail shops. Some were pretty fast, but none could match the first computers, just five decades ago, in speed or quantity of data handled. These first computers were large, cumbersome, and complicated. Their vacuum tubes generated considerable heat and required extensive maintenance. Now we have new supercomputers with ever-increasing power and decreasing size and maintenance problems. We also have tiny computers with solar power and memory banks for phone numbers, budget calculations, and calendar reminders. Cars have computers small enough to fit in the hand that provide constant and immediate calculations of automobile speed, distance, fuel consumption, gas and air mix, and mechanical problems.

THIS BOOK AS AN EXAMPLE

This book was written on a personal computer, using a word processing program. We punched keys on a typewriterlike keyboard, but the machine automatically translated the punches into mathematically determined symbols that could be "read" by the computer and stored on diskettes. We mailed the diskettes containing magnetized bits of information, not reams of paper with words, across the U.S. and reproduced the material on printers by pressing the right buttons. We could edit the material before it was printed, shifting words, paragraphs, and pages around on a screen.

When we had to discuss something, we picked up the phone and talked about it although we were 1,500 miles apart. On occasion we traveled to meet together, flying about two hours or, in one case, driving for two days. We don't know for certain how this book was printed and distributed, but we assume that it was set up on computers, with other computers keeping track of the number of copies and where they have been sent. And, up to the limits of copyright infringement, material from the book may be instantly reproduced on a photoduplication machine. Technically, it would have been possible, but not economical, to print this book with a special inscription to each person who buys a copy: This book is dedicated to _____. Some advertisers and prize contests use such personalized computer-generated devices; perhaps publishers will move in that direction. Someday books may be available on a circuit that permits students or libraries to simply "call them up" on a TV monitor and print segments as desired. Each step in the process of producing the book required a different set of skills and technical literacy from that required to produce books in earlier times.

This book was not produced by writing with quill pens on parchment by candlelight in rooms smoky from poor-heating fireplaces. We did not wear rough woven clothing, unless it was in style, nor did we eat only local wild fruits and berries we had gathered. We did not stand on the corner and holler to each other. We did not hitch up a cart to a donkey and travel for weeks to meet. The printing process was not done by hand copying, or by hand placing each letter, manual inking, and pressing each page. The distribution system for this book is not by an individual carrying a single copy in a bag, or reading segments aloud on street corners.

SCHOOL AS BASIC TO TECHNOLOGICAL DEVELOPMENT

There is no better way to assess the future development of American science and technology than by examining our educational system. It is in the schools that the future of American enterprise exists. The schools are at the center of any large-scale effort to stimulate scientific achievements, improve technology, and make business more efficient. It is true that we can tinker with our current technology and business structures for short-term improvements, but any long-lasting developments depend upon new generations of scientists, inventors, and business leaders, as well as skilled workers and knowledgeable consumers. If the schools fail to educate these new generations about technology, we are committed to a continuing decline in our nation's leadership in the world.

We need to refocus our education on national needs in science and technology. Education should emphasize science, to stimulate the small proportion of students who will become the new discoverers of knowledge, and to assist the rest in understanding scientific achievements. Education should also emphasize technology, to stimulate those who will take active roles in developing innovations, and to prepare the rest for lives in the modern world.

America's deficiencies in science, math, and technology education are highlighted in recent reports, including one by the National Science Board (1983).

Comparative results on math and science achievement tests show American students to be far behind those of some European countries and Japan. The national importance of correcting these deficiencies is noted: ''Prepared citizens (especially in science, mathematics and technology as well as other basic academic and technical subjects) are required for the operation of the nation's essential industries and services'' (*Educating Americans for the 21st Century*, 1983, p. 65).

SCIENCE, MATHEMATICS, AND TECHNOLOGY

Science is the systematic study of things. Mathematics is one of the languages of science, a tool that offers a clear and understandable means for communicating. Science attempts to classify, to understand, to predict, and to control things. Scientific discoveries are often made in areas where there is no immediate application, but where later developments show the value of scientific work. When science has progressed enough to be able to predict or control, technology takes over. Technology is the application of scientific knowledge to make it useful in society.

There is a gap in time between discoveries in science and their development into applied technology for popular use. This technological gap is made up of a long series of efforts by inventors and others to find ways to use scientific achievements. Thomas Edison's extensive trials to find suitable material for incandescent light are an example. The speed of change in technology is, however, making the gap much shorter. For example, in the eighteenth century it took over 100 years before basic scientific discoveries about light were transformed into the technology for photography. In the nineteenth century the science behind electric motors took sixty-five years to mature into technology; later in that century the science underlying radios required only thirty-five years to be applied. In the twentieth century, the gap between discoveries in atomic theory and the technology of atomic weapons was reduced to six years, and the gap from science to application for transistors was only three years (Ginsberg, 1964).

There is another gap in time, between technological developments and their use in education. This gap seems to remain large. Technology is moving rapidly, but schools do not change quickly. That is the gap that now needs our attention.

Scientific knowledge about rock formations helps us to understand how the earth was formed, but is also applied in developing technology to extract important minerals and raw materials for human use. Scientific knowledge about astronomy helps us understand and predict events in our galaxy; it is also necessary for the development of technology for weather predictions and space exploration. Scientific knowledge in biology and genetics may someday provide the basis for technology to eliminate certain diseases, to improve crops, to save lives of burn patients, and to correct birth defects.

These and myriad other major benefits to humanity come about because of the pursuit of science and the development of technology. Education is crucial to science and to technology. Every advancing society requires scientists, mathematicians, and applied scientists who can translate science into technology. It also requires technologically informed citizens who understand the necessity of providing support for science, and who can reap the benefits from technology in their lives. A technologically illiterate society is bound to superstition, excessive human physical labor, unnecessarily shortened lifespans, discomfort and inconvenience, and decline.

THE THREAT OF TECHNOLOGICAL DISLOCATION

People without technological literacy may pretend to understand. They may avoid contact with new technology by not buying complicated equipment or appliances. They may not protest when errors are made because they don't know it, or they don't want to show their lack of knowledge. But these people are at a serious disadvantage in everyday life. They can be victimized by their lack of technological literacy. And the society is not getting the benefit of their full contribution because they can't communicate in modern technical terms. These people can become dislocated in their own society. They can become marginal citizens, not fully participating in the democracy because of their lack of knowledge or their fear of exposure.

This predicament is similar to the situation that occurred in the period of the industrial revolution in the United States, 1850 to 1900. Changes in technology produced rapid and complicated changes in society. Cities grew dramatically because that's where the new jobs in new industries were. There were public schools, but education was not compulsory in every state, and most people had very limited education. In farm communities and parts of some cities, many children did not go to school at all because the skills then needed did not include book learning. Some of our great-grandparents were barely literate, even though they could be successful in daily work in fields or grain stores.

The new industrial jobs at the beginning of the twentieth century required more complicated reading skills, and more technological knowledge. The compulsory school attendance laws which most states passed during this time were supported by businessmen and workers because they provided for all children to get some basic education which would assist America in developing a strong industrial base. Farming also became much more dependent upon technology, and the federally supported land-grant colleges of "agricultural and mechanical" sciences were established in each state to improve the level of technical knowledge available. The need for a well-educated populace in the United States was widely recognized and that education was understood to include up-to-date technological education. It is clear that we are in another period of rapid and dramatic change in technology and society. We need a revised school program to assure that new generations are capable of continuing the technological advancement of our country.

THE NEED FOR TECHNOLOGICAL LITERACY

Technological advancement depends heavily not only on the achievements of a small number of well-educated scientists, but also upon a general population that has learned basic skills and has a clear understanding of the place of science and technology in modern life. A society cannot continue to develop technology without technological literacy for the vast majority of its people. This literacy is more than the mere ability to read words, write your name, and use simple numbers. It requires an ability to understand some scientific ideas, the application of science in developing technology, and the use of technical language.

A Rip Van Winkle who had slept through the past few decades would have great difficulty reading and understanding a manual for a personal computer. Common computer terms like "floppy disks," "booting," "word processing," "memory," and "file" have technical meanings that require a different reading and speaking knowledge. Some older people who have not maintained their technological literacy are baffled by the dials and directions for new computer-operated parts of cars, or by directions for setting up and operating new stereo equipment. Some people do not understand how new cash registers work at shopping markets, how to use the automated teller machines at their banks, or how to read some computer-generated bills and notices. Our modern-day Rip Van Winkle would, however, immediately recognize the typical school and would see that things in schools had not changed much. Would he suffer from technophobia?

Technological transformation is occurring in virtually all phases of contemporary life. Schools should not be teaching yesterday's skills and knowledge to a generation that needs tomorrow's.

POSITION 2
Against Technological Fads

There is much in the modern world that is commendable. Compared with the turn of the last century, life expectancy is longer and health care is more available; automobiles are more comfortable; and homes are brighter at night. There is also much in the modern world that is worse than before. Health care has become impersonal and factorylike, while elderly people have become burdens to their families, suited only to institutionalization; frustrating traffic jams and significant numbers of deaths and injuries from auto accidents are norms of daily life; and various forms of long-lasting pollution are created in the process of generating electricity to satisfy increasing demands.

Technology can be credited with some improvements for humanity, but it must also be debited with producing serious social and environmental detriments that have not yet been fully exposed. Each improvement from technology requires a trade-off—for each step taken we give something up. Some of the trade-offs are worth making; some are not. Most trade-offs, unfortunately, aren't recognized soon enough for society to make an educated evaluation of their relative value.

Unfortunately, there is a headlong rush to new technology in contemporary America, without full consideration of its potential impacts on our lives and those of our children. We seem to be drawn to the newest and most dazzling gimmick that promises to save us work, pain, time, and thinking. There is a corollary effort to use schools to indoctrinate students with the myth that technology is nearly always beneficial and contains the answers to all human problems. School, instead, should be the place where technology is questioned. Schooling should not produce "true believers"; it should develop critical thinkers. The technology craze threatens this basic premise for education.

America is not the only place where the technology craze has gone amuck. Jacques Ellul (1964), in a particularly informative criticism of the unchecked growth of technology, notes that the whole world is subject to "monolithic" technical manipulation where "man finds that there is 'no exit'; that he cannot pierce the shell of technology to find again the ancient milieu to which he was adapted for hundreds of thousands of years" (p. 428). Ellul reported about three decades ago on technological predictions for the twenty-first century made by serious scientists. These predictions included the development of easily available voyages to the moon and inhabited satellites, the extraction of all necessary minerals from sea water and rocks, and governmental control of population by limiting human reproduction to artificial fertilization using sperm and ova from ideal male and female specimens. In terms of education, Ellul noted:

> The most remarkable predictions concern the transformation of educational methods and the problem of human reproduction. Knowledge will be accumulated in "electronic banks" and transmitted directly to the human nervous system by means of coded electronic messages. There will no longer be any need of reading. . . . everything will be received and registered according to the needs of the moment. There will be no need of attention or effort. What is needed will pass directly from the machine to the brain without going through consciousness. (Ellul, 1964, p. 432)

This prediction is, in many ways, the most chilling of possibilities for technology of the future. It portends a time when human critical judgment is extinguished, when the technocrats and their machines take over our thoughts and our actions. We will be wired to respond as we are told to do. If Ellul's predictions were to come true, this essay would have no opportunity for consideration because it would not be in the interests of government or big business to have people raise questions about technology.

What technology is accomplishing is to make life completely artificial. We are sacrificing everything natural for a manufactured replica, creating a plastic environment entirely dependent upon enormous energy consumption and subject to catastrophic breakdowns or human annihilation (Rifkin, 1983). This facsimile world not only requires an extraordinary commitment of our natural resources, it imposes a dramatic increase in the centralization of power, where a government or a body of scientists or any other technically proficient organization can intrude itself into our daily lives and exert control without warning and without our knowledge.

Aldous Huxley provided a graphic and stark portrayal of a technologically controlled society in *Brave New World* (1932), but he found that not enough people took the threat seriously. In *Brave New World Revisited* (1958) he called for more attention to human freedom and noted the relation of technology to more centralized power:

> We see, then, that modern technology has led to the concentration of economic and political power, and to the development of a society controlled (ruthlessly in the totalitarian states, politely and inconspicuously in the democracies) by Big Business and Big Government. (Huxley, 1958, p. 20)

Huxley argued that democracy cannot flourish where this power is becoming increasingly centralized. The agents of technology are taking over the schools to assure that new generations become true believers without criticism and probing inquiry about human choices on technology. This lack of criticism of technology is a serious threat to schools and democracy.

CONSUMERS FOR TECHNOLOGY

Mass media, through news stories and advertising, create excessive demands and unrealistic expectations for the latest technology. Stories of breakthroughs in medical treatment or new electronic equipment, without complete information on side effects or environmental damage, lead people to believe that technology will overcome disease and satisfy desires. Only later, after serious consequences become obvious, do we become more thoughtful.

The development of X rays is one example. Certainly, it was of benefit to medicine that technology could provide machines to see beneath the skin. The ease of access to use of X rays, however, led to overuse and potential X-ray damage to many individuals. Asbestos, a fine fire retardant, is another example. Technology permitted the easy mining of the mineral, and its abundant use in homes, schools, factories, and stores. Those who worked with asbestos were risking asbestosis but did not know it. The debilitating effects were not felt for many years. Thousands of people were affected, and in millions of buildings asbestos remains a major health hazard. Similarly, formaldehyde and certain plastics used in the manufacture of mobile homes and in household construction and repair material are now viewed as potentially carcinogenic and flammable. DDT and other insecticides were developed in new technology to assist humans in protecting food supplies; we later found that extremely serious damage to the environment resulted from use of this material.

The list of negative impacts of technology is far too long for us to attempt to be inclusive here. The point is not to deny that some benefit has occurred through technology, but to caution against letting our love affair with new technology blind us to its negative consequences. We don't spend enough time and money to explore fully the potential impacts on individuals, society, or the environment. Our rush to train students as consumers of the newest technology also has apparent negative consequences.

THE TECHNOLOGY GENERATION

Social pressures force educators into the position of technology advocates, not educated consumers. Pressure from peers, relatives, and advertising combine with a general competitiveness to be better than others by having the latest thing. Schools succumb to this pressure and technology goes unquestioned. What students learn is that technology is a positive value with a wonderful history of solving the world's problems.

The few resistant teachers who raise environmental and social questions about the march of technology are seen as obstacles to progress and as cranks. The teachers who expect students to read good literature and to discuss ideas thoughtfully, rather than watch videotaped digests of stories and answer questions on a computer monitor, are viewed as academic fuddy-duddies. Those teachers who wonder why the school must provide everyone with a computer to play games, but not provide enough books and magazines in the library, are perceived as Luddites.

The Luddites, a group of English workers about 1810–1820, rebelled against loss of their jobs and craft skills brought about by the intrusion of mechanization and technology. Although the Luddites have been mistreated in many history texts, they may not have been wrong in their efforts. Luddites are portrayed as ignorant louts smashing machines in a blind fury. The Luddites are better described as the unfortunate victims of a technological change that primarily benefited the owners and managers of industry and left the workers unemployed, de-skilled, and with less control over the way they lived and worked (Hammond, 1932; Thomis, 1974; Rybczynski, 1983). Without some contemporary Luddites around, we have created a technology generation sorely lacking in personal independence and ingenuity, social graces, and intellectual stimulation.

How does the technology generation live? Here is a short scene from a day's activity:

A white noise machine blocks out other sounds to help sleep, then our student arises at the sound of music from a quadraphonic stereo clock radio that shifts into a voice softly calling out the time. A programmed timer turns on lights and television, for a thirty-second newscast and six minutes of ads for electronic games. An electric toothbrush, toothpaste from a pressurized dispenser, and a shower under a pulsating showerhead while listening to a waterproof radio are daily routine. With stereo earphones connected to a tape player hung on the belt, a head-nodding greeting is given to parents, and breakfast begins. Coffee comes from a timer-operated machine, toast from an automatic toaster, a speedy microwaved biscuit, and milk from a plastic disposable dispenser in the refrigerator. Next comes a glance at a digital watch, with calculator buttons, and a trip to school in a car with electric doors and windows, electronic speedometer and mileage indicator, and lights to show such things as an unclosed door or low fuel. Air-conditioning makes the car comfortable while parents listen to the six-speaker car stereo and our student hears other music in the earphones. Waving at other earphone-covered students, ours alights near the school door, which opens automatically when anyone approaches. After announcements from somewhere over a loud speaker, and a computer-generated attendance checkoff, the classes begin.

One class consists of sitting at a computer doing workbooklike drills in math. Another is a forty-three-minute videotape of a Shakespeare play. Social studies class has computers and programs for learning the names of states and Presidents. Lunch is a microwaved meal served in plastic containers on a disposable tray. Spanish is in a language lab where earphones connect to tapes. A science class teacher extols the benefits of science and a film shows how lasers work to repair eyes and to make war. Gym seems like work, with exercises and a volleyball game. Art class is a filmstrip set of slide photos of paintings in the Louvre. In between classes earphones are reconnected to ears, and hallways are filled with silent students bouncing to different tapes on different belts. Our student looks forward to an afternoon and evening of TV and stereo, separated by a frozen, then microwaved, dinner, and a bit of time doing homework on the home computer.

The above scenario is certainly not futuristic, but it is one for the upper middle class. If we throw in a self-cleaning and chlorinating swimming pool, hot tub, and sauna we raise the costs, but increase the romantic-sounding quality of this life. Because of extensive advertising, those students who cannot afford these technological gadgets still have intense desires for them. The life described above is comfortable and leisurely; it is uncomplicated because it frees people from critical human thought and interaction. It is also uncomplicated by concern for the personal, social, and environmental costs of expanding reliance on technology.

School should not be a place of leisurely self-centeredness, the kind of narcissistic life described above. School should be pleasurable, but because it excites the students' imaginations, enriches their minds, and extends their vision. It should also serve basic social interests, promoting social values like justice, democracy, and equality. Those values are diminished in a setting where the focus is on personal comfort and convenience, and where there is primary reliance on technology.

WHAT ARE SOME OF THE PERSONAL COSTS?

As just noted, the dependence on technology has the potential to create a narcissistic lifestyle, unconnected to the political, economic, and personal problems of others. Social responsibility is ignored in the quest for self-satisfaction. Much of the new technology used in American society separates people and softens the reality of human suffering. Even TV pictures of the reality of starvation or warfare in countries far away are controlled by simply switching channels, or are watched as though they were curiosities in a travelogue. There is no personal engagement in the matter, as there might have been in an active human discussion of these conditions.

Television and video activities are individual. Watchers sit transfixed in dimly lit rooms, breaking only to snack or answer the phone. TV is intended to package ideas attractively and transmit them, not to involve watchers in analysis or debate. The most popular shows are often ones which require the least mental effort in watching. Even the standard news shows feature short two- to three-minute treatments of important events, less time on those the news office considers less important. There is little continuity and no depth; usually there are no opposing views presented. What is received as the day's news is a homogenized digest of brief glimpses of selected filmable material read by nice-looking announcers who maintain composure regardless of the information. Among other things there is a penchant to feature the violent, the criminal, and the freakish to attract attention and gain a larger share of viewership as measured on technological instruments attached to TV sets in a few homes.

The purpose, thus, is not to educate viewers or examine issues, but to gain more network revenues or to further a career as an anchorperson. We lose our interest in or capacity for examining a line of reasoning longer than the time it would take on TV coverage. We lose the interactive involvement of dispute and opposing viewpoints. We organize our time around TV shows, and lose some of our independence. We lose the ability to differentiate important ideas without help from our favorite newscaster. We lose the curiosity to pursue an argument into background study, library work, and following up on other people's comments. We lose the art and socializing value of conversation.

Computers are another current example of technology which has potential negative consequences for people. Extensive computer activity has the capacity to develop introverted and socially alienated operators. This work is done separately, with operators in cubicles or at individual desks. Except when problems arise in machine or program operation, it is not necessary to have contact with any other humans for hours at a time.

Computer use has also developed new human ailments among operators. These include unusual muscle and eyestrain problems. The eye irritation, fatigue, and headaches caused by video terminals have been demonstrated in medical studies. Crippling hand and wrist pains have also been found among computer operators. And, there is some suspicion that, although the radiation emitted is minimal, the incidence of miscarriages and birth defects may increase for pregnant women who use the machines a great deal. There may also be some longer-term health problems from forms of radiation absorbed during extensive monitor use. Some places are developing laws to require business owners to pay for special medical care for ailments related to computer use.

School computer work, and recreational computer use, are also individual and separate; if there is interaction it is with a machine programmed to respond. There is a sense of unreality and superficiality in this activity. Even war and violence seem distant and controlled by fingerstrokes. As in the film

Dr. Strangelove, we find it quick and painless to start an electronic war with nuclear and laser weapons unleashed on unseen and unheard crowds. There is a feeling that little is happening, except in the displays on the monitor. Wreaking havoc is not fearsome, but fun and frivolous. Disengagement is easy, with the push of a button. The appearance is that no one is really hurt.

School computer work in learning activities has often been simply workbook-type activity, trying to find answers through the machine. This is not real mental engagement; it is more like a drill, with a set of questions and programmed answers. Although there are some educational computer programs which try to actively involve the student in learning more than the design of the game, these are often more complicated to use and take much more time and teacher energy. And, there may be no "right" answers in interactive programs. With the advent of computers in classrooms, and many teachers and students enjoying the game of finding the right path or answer, the main effort is in figuring out the system to get a high score, not in considering alternatives or digging more deeply into a topic. An inclination develops to get the quickest, most efficient right answer, which is hidden in the machine. This translates into a dislike for intellectual work that requires struggle, and where there may be no right answer. We become speed fanatics, but lose the richer texture of human issues that are not mathematically computable. It also becomes easy to believe that we should just let the machines take over, giving instant gratification and demanding little in response.

WHAT ARE SOME OF THE SOCIAL COSTS?

In addition to the costs brought about by technology in personal loss of independence, ingenuity, and intellectual stimulation, there are a variety of social costs. We lose the contributions of many people to the improvement of society when individualism overcomes concern for social responsibilities. The separating quality of much new technology has fragmented people's lives and added to their isolation and alienation. We have become used to the speed of computers, and the quickened pace of TV stories; we have lost the patience and focused attention that thoughtful reflection requires. Further, we have seen a deterioration of social bonds, most seriously the dissolution of the family and home setting for developing social values and attitudes. TV, computers, and headphones have replaced family get-togethers. Violent crime, technologically produced drug abuse, and noninvolvement in community affairs are increasing.

There are other social costs to technology. Consider the workers in technological equipment plants. In the face of continuing advances in technology, workers are always threatened with replacement by robots. And their safety is under constant threat from exposure to chemicals and radiation that carry no obvious warnings. Workers become alienated because of the assembly-line atmosphere of the work. They do not set, nor always understand, the nature of the product or the means for producing it. Certainly, workers are better treated in salary and benefits now than when there were sweatshops and no labor unions. But much of their work, during a shorter workweek, is still dullingly routine and alienating. They are not usually involved in decisions about purposes and management of the work. They come to work, don sterilized garments, perform the same task all day, and go home to watch TV. These workers are trained to perform certain assembly tasks, but are not educated to question ideas or become politically involved. Quality control is by management supervision and requirement, not by craftsmanlike concern and time-taking interest on the part of the worker. These examples represent a cost to society in the workers' loss of pride of effort, contribution to social improvement, and interest in a liberating education.

The environmental costs of technology to society are enormous, and have been largely ignored until very recently. And those who have reaped the munificent rewards for technology have left a burden on the taxpayers for correcting and cleaning up our world. Nonbiodegradable material is piling up in dump sites; waste toxins from technology infect the atmosphere, our water, our land, and our homes; and new experiments in genetic engineering, nuclear development, and laser use threaten us with unknown and potentially annihilating consequences. Massive utilization of natural resources to fuel the technology drive has destroyed or severely damaged much of our earth's fertility and beauty. We have not yet discerned the extent of the environmental costs of our penchant for new technology. We may have already gone too far to recover.

EDUCATION AND TECHNOLOGY

Some predicted that radio would lead to the abolition of teachers and books. Later, TV was expected to replace them. Now it is computers and interactive videodiscs. We should not be seeking the replacement of teachers and books. We should be reinforcing their quality and value by restoring the expectation that teachers will teach, not turn dials and plug in parts.

Technology has a tendency to de-skill teachers by taking away from them all important decisions as to what is taught and how, and substituting a slick package that students can use individually. The teacher's role then becomes that of a technician, a position that can be filled by someone without extensive education, without professional pedagogic talents, without a sense of social responsibility, and without intellectual curiosity. Some producers of education technology even have the sinister idea that we need to "teacher-proof" materials. Why should we call them "teachers"? Technology, without the questioning intervention of human teachers who can think, threatens the concept of liberal education (Apple, 1985).

Classes should not be factorylike locations for students to be plugged into the latest fad. Classes should be provocative, informative, and investigative. It is not enough simply to provide a set of preprogrammed answers to preset questions. Treating students as though they were robots, mechanically preparing them to pass computer-scored state tests of bits of information, is not education.

Schools should educate students about technology. That education, however, should not entail a blind approval of new developments. It should concentrate on preparing students to resist the lure of technology, to become more inquisitive about its possible results, and to become thoughtful and critical consumers of it. Schooling should incorporate much more about the negative aspects of technology, and should offer more support for living a socially responsible and sociable life without demanding instant gratification and quick answers. Schools should not willingly compromise their educational tradition in order to follow the latest fad. Just as war is too important to leave to the generals, technology is too important to leave to the technologists and businesspeople. Schools need to provide the social conscience for technology. They can raise the question of when personal and social costs become too high for the trade-off. Very few other institutions are willing to take on that responsibility. But that is real technological literacy.

FOR DISCUSSION

1   Where does technology begin and end? Is a chalkboard a technological device? Are teacher methods part of technology? How should high technology be defined in schools?

2   If you were on a school board in a community with a reputation for educational quality, how would you approach the issue of technological literacy in the schools? Would your approach be different in a community which has a large high-technology employer?

3   What are the possible consequences of a strong technologically oriented school curriculum? Of a curriculum which ignores new technology?

4   The following is a list of new technologies and some applications:

Lasers and fiber optics. Telecommunications, information processing, entertainment (3-D TV, videodiscs).

Robotics and computer-controlled machines. Replace conventional machines and humans; improve productivity; alter employment.

Computer-integrated manufacturing. Production more flexible; influence worker satisfaction, stress, skills.

Solar energy. Alternative to conventional energy sources. Alter economy, environment.

Biotechnology. Change agriculture and food production, medicine, fuel, waste treatment, ethics.

Micro-electronics. Miniaturization; alter medicine, education, transportation, household life.

High-performance computing. Artificial intelligence. Supercomputers mimic human problem solving; influence medicine, science, legal work, teaching and learning.

What are the likely consequences of each of these new technologies on the schools? What are the consequences for the society and the environment? Should they be encouraged as signs for progress or discouraged as potentially dangerous?

REFERENCES

Apple, M., and Teitlebaum, K. (1985). "Are Teachers Losing Control of Their Jobs?" *Social Education,* **49,** 372–375.

Educating America for the 21st Century (1983). Washington, D.C.: National Science Board Commission on Precollege Education in Mathematics.

Ellul, J. (1964). *The Technological Society.* Translated by John Wilkinson. New York: Knopf.

Faure, E., et al. (1972). *Learning to Be: The World of Education Today and Tomorrow.* Paris: UNESCO.

Ginsberg, E. (1964). *Technology and Social Change.* New York: Columbia University Press.

Hammond, J. L., and Hammond, B. (1932). *The Village Labourer, 1760–1832.* London: Longmans.

Hellman, H. (1976). *Technophobia.* New York: M. Evans Co.

Huxley, A. (1932). *Brave New World.* New York: Harper and Bros.

———— (1958). *Brave New World Revisited.* New York: Harper & Row.

Rifkin, J. (1983). *Algeny: A New World—A New World.* New York: Viking.

Rybczynski, W. (1983). *Taming the Tiger: The Struggle to Control Technology.* New York: Viking.

Thomis, M. (1974). *The Town Labourer and the Industrial Revolution.* London: Batsford.

Toffler, A. (1970). *Future Shock.* New York: Bantam.

CHAPTER 10

BUSINESS VALUES OR SOCIAL JUSTICE

POSITION 1
For Business Involvement

There are some serious problems ahead for America as a result of our schools' failure to give solid skills and workplace values to students. A crisis is developing in American business because significant numbers of employees are economically illiterate or disdainful of the necessary conditions of work. Workers lack competitive spirit, they are tardy and have high absenteeism, and they complain about production needs. The United States is losing its competitive advantage because our work force is undereducated and soft. This crisis is becoming acute now that technology and workers' skills are changing rapidly in other nations. A dramatic shift has already occurred in the production of electronics, automobiles, furniture, and other consumer goods. High-quality goods are now manufactured in Japan, Taiwan, Korea and other places where school and business have become more obvious partners.

We need people who are competent in basic skills, in understanding technical manuals and operations, and in working with mangement in a cooperative effort to strengthen our nation's economy. Far too many schools are producing people who have trouble deciphering simple written forms and directions, understanding low-level technical information, and maintaining interest in work.

As *Newsweek* education editor Gilbert Sewall (1984) describes the situation,

For at least 23 million Americans, the instructions in a laundromat are mystifying; reading a repair manual or filling out a job application accurately is impossible. Bluntly stated, these citizens do not have the survival skills to compete in a highly specialized service economy that values, above all, mental agility and reliability. Consequently, they have little or no stake in the future of democratic capitalism. These functional illiterates are condemned to live on the fringe of the polity as menial laborers, as welfare recipients, as outlaws, as the emotionally tortured and spiritually broken. Doomed to insecure, insolvent, and possibly violent futures, they are what society considers failed people. (pp. 3, 4)

In addition to the general need to upgrade the basic skills and workplace attitudes young people learn in schools, there is a special need to better prepare non-college-bound students for employment. The majority of educational re-form activities in the 1980s were directed at improving the academic quality of schools for those who plan to go to college. The majority of students, however, do not go on to college. They graduate from high school and take jobs immediately, or they drop out before graduation and try to find employment.

The Forgotten Half, a report of a Commission on Work, Family and Citizenship spnosored by the W. T. Grant Foundation, examines this issue of work and non-college-bound youth. Among its findings is that "a larger percentage of them are finding it harder than ever to swim against the economic tide" (Kappan, 1988, p. 410). This commission agrees "with those who say that America needs to 'work smarter' and raise productivity in order to be competitive with other nations" (p. 412). It recommends a number of ways to "bridge the gap from school to work," including intensive training in basic skills, monitored apprenticeships and pre-employment training, improved vocational education, incentives from businesses and mentors for students to do well in school, and better career counseling.

An important recommendation of the commission is to increase alliances between employers and schools. In such alliances business leaders come into schools to teach, talk with students, and assist teachers and guidance counselors in developing programs to improve student skills and attitudes. Such alliances can set up student visits to places of future employment, create work-study programs for students, involve both school and business in producing teaching materials, and gain financial support from business for improving school technology and career guidance. Many businesses participate in "Adopt-a-School" programs which enrich the "adopted" school's ability to prepare students for employment. Others invite teachers to visit, provide teachers summer employment and other opportunities to learn about their operations, and prepare teaching materials which teachers can have free. Business has strong interests in the improvement of education. Industries cannot survive without a well-prepared work force, and they recognize this.

One school-business alliance was formalized by the Boston Compact, signed in 1982, which established a partnership between the Boston schools and the Boston Private Industry Council. Businesses promised jobs to students if the schools got test scores up and dropout rates down. This alliance has provided jobs for over 1,000 school graduates, and reading and math scores have improved (Fiske, 1988, p. B8).

Dale Mann (1987) examined school-business partnerships and concluded that "partnerships between businesses and the schools have made positive contributions to the public schools.... [they] have offered concrete assistance to the schools in a number of ways" (p. 228). These included cash contributions, services, sympathy, and assistance in political and economic coalitions. Mann notes several problems in business alliances with schools, but cites a large number of examples where businesses have been particularly helpful in improving local schools.

The Grant Foundation Commission is also concerned with changes in the kinds of employment available, and with the need for schools to modify their programs to better prepare students for work. There have been some prominent changes in the nature of employment in American society that have major implications for schools. Historically, the shift has been from agricultural to manufacturing jobs; now the shift is from manufacturing to service. In just the last fifty years farmers and farm workers have declined from almost 20 percent of the work force to only 3 percent; since 1950 manufacturing jobs have declined from 32 percent to 27 percent of total employment; and service jobs have increased from 53 percent to 69 percent. Growth in the service sector has been primarily in social and producer services (e.g., health, technology service), rather than in personal (e.g., hairdresser, domestic service) or distributive (e.g., sales, delivery) services. The most prominent change has been in the percentages of kinds of jobs. Bureau of Labor Statistics 1988 data show that white-collar jobs have gone up from about 45 percent of the labor force in 1940 to over 70 percent by the mid-1980s. Blue-collar workers have declined from about 42 percent in 1940 to about 27 percent now (Bureau of Labor Statistics, 1988).

In educational terms, this means a need for more and better schooling. Many agricultural jobs have changed from sheer physical labor, such as hand-plowing, to technical work requiring strong academic skills, such as computerized recordkeeping. White-collar jobs typically demand increased education. In a report on economic trends in America, a group of Oxford scholars commented, "Indeed, it is well documented that over recent decades a person's job and level of income have become influenced more and more by his or her level of education and formal qualifications" (*America in Perspective,* 1986, p. 68). Peter Blau and O. D. Duncan (1967), in a classic study of the relation of education to jobs, reported high correlations between job status and education. Social class and occupational experience were also considered influential in employment status, but education was given greatest emphasis.

In earlier periods in American history, basic literacy could be recommended purely for its inherent value; it had no special relation to the people's work requirements. When most citizens led rural lives as farmers, reading, writing, and calculating were considered nice, but not necessary. Even in those times, there were obvious links between education and employment. An example is a study conducted in 1867 by the Commonwealth of Pennsylvania which showed that income was directly related to literacy; those who could not read averaged $36 per month, those who could read but were otherwise poorly educated averaged $52, and those well educated averaged $90 per month (Soltow and

Stevens, 1981). Modern studies have continued to corroborate this point. Reading and writing, however, are not all that is meant by literacy for business. Lee Soltow and Edward Stevens (1981), examining the history of literacy in the United States, note, "To be literate, as we have seen, did not simply mean to be competent at a specific level of reading mastery. It meant, perhaps more importantly for the employer, exposure to a set of values compatible with a disciplined work force" (pp. 127, 8). There is clear evidence that schools should give more importance to basic skills and workplace values.

All students, college-bound or not, need to be taught more effectively knowledge and attitudes which contribute to our society. The softness of permissive education has led to indolence, narcissism, and a rebelliousness against all forms of authority. There has been the mistaken notion that we can all do as we wish. This, and the equally mistaken ideology of socialism, has caused our society to suffer. Schools need to redirect their energies toward developing students' pride in workmanship, increasing their productivity, and strengthening their patriotism in a nation where competition and free enterprise give the most opportunities for all.

The strength of American society lies in the fortuitous combination of democracy and capitalism. We not only offer freedom and opportunity in politics—the democratic concept—we also offer them in economics. The freedom to engage in enterprise, without obstructive governmental interference, provides opportunities and motivations for all individuals. Free enterprise is a basic condition for entrepreneurs, and entrepreneurs have built and developed this great nation. People and ideas of merit rise to the top. In order for the meritorious to stay at the top, the free marketplace requires continued improvement. That is how this nation moved from a minor colony to a world power. It is also why so many other nations have tried to copy American entrepreneurship. Even the socialist countries are recognizing that individual talents are not developed when there are no rewards, and are moving more toward capitalism.

BUSINESS APPROACHES ARE ALSO GOOD
FOR SCHOOL OPERATION

In addition to the obvious concern for people who are unemployed or underemployed because of their weak education, there is a problem in the operation of schools themselves. Schools are inefficient social institutions. Their organization and operation have not changed during the twentieth century, while industry has made remarkable progress in becoming more efficient and more productive. If a major American industry had been as stultified as the schools, it would have failed long ago. In fact, those businesses which have not improved their efficiency and productivity have failed. Private enterprise cannot survive in stagnation. Yet we have protected our schools from the competition and oversight necessary to show improvement. Schools are sheltered organizations, consuming significant amounts of tax money and having little accountability.

They have been exempted from requirements to show improvements that would be basic to any contemporary business.

Schools have not taken advantage of improved technology and have not been held to standards of increased productivity that would limit the need for costly employees. School budgets are the largest public expense in local communities, and staff salaries constitute about 80 percent of total school expenses. Savings in this area could be used to bring better technology into schools in order to improve student skills or to reduce taxes. The ratio of students to teachers has been virtually stable, about twenty-five to one, in comprehensive school districts for years. In many suburban schools the ratio is less than twenty students to each teacher. There is no evidence that fewer students mean better education. And much of what goes on in a classroom with one teacher could be done more efficiently by larger groups of students and video or computer equipment.

It is important for a teacher to guide the general teaching of students, but it is very expensive, since teacher time equals money, to have each teacher work with a small group of students. Instead, one teacher should present material to a large group of students, while another large group of students should work individually on computers under the general guidance of a teacher or teacher's aide. This would mean very different organization for schools, but that is what is needed. Competition forces business to constantly make organizational changes to strive for higher productivity. It is wasteful not to demand the same of schools.

The proportion of school administrators has actually increased since World War II while the total student population has stabilized. Schools also employ large numbers of other employees to provide services that could be done more economically by contract with private industry. These employees are usually civil servants and keep their jobs regardless of reorganization. Teachers have tenure, lifetime security, and have union contracts which limit their workdays and working years.

School buildings are often large, inefficiently utilized, and costly to build and maintain. In districts where student enrollment has declined, expensive school buildings have been sold, destroyed, or renovated at great public financial loss. And school buildings are used less than half of the year, and one-third of the day. The debt for building these behemoths has been passed on to future generations by bonds.

Many small schools and school districts now requiring separate buildings and school staffs could be reorganized into more effective and less costly regional districts if business concepts were used. The millions of dollars spent on books, equipment, and teaching material by these individual school districts could also be considerably decreased by coordinated effort. Small, expensive schools operate out of pride, not economy.

Meanwhile, businesses have shown that they can train large numbers of employees by using video, computer systems, large lectures, programmed materials, self-study, and other devices that do not consume the level of precious and expensive human resources that the schools use. Further, this training occurs in facilities that are used extensively year-round. These educational activities of businesses are the result of failings of the schools, and business has shown that it can train people better and more economically than schools can.

If the schools could show that their expensive buildings and personnel had been increasingly productive, there would be no problem. In fact, student test scores have been declining, students do not have work values that enhance their employment, and student social behavior is a public disgrace in many parts of the country.

This is not a time for schools to continue the failures of the past. It is a time for them to change, and there are many business-proven techniques which they must use. The structure of business, based upon a competitive marketplace, has withstood the severest tests of war, depression, and relocation. Contemporary business management ideas need to be introduced into education so that the schools can concern themselves with improving efficiency and productivity.

Such a reordering of our schools to give students solid skills and good, positive workplace values is a social, educational, and economic necessity. School operations that more closely approximate good business practice are simply good sense. These are completely compatible and complementary reforms to which schools must attend.

POSITION 2
Against Business Domination

American education has civilizing purposes. Among the most positive of its goals is to enable students to improve the society. In a democracy this means development of expanding social ethics that incorporate a strong concern for others. This educational purpose speaks to the future of American democracy and poses a significant challenge to schools to continually strive for individual and social development. Schools should aim for an increasingly just society. This requires knowledge, critical thinking, cooperative endeavor, and a set of values based on justice.

Unfortunately, these civilizing purposes of American schools have been shortchanged. Students and American society have been deluded by the imposition of business views on education for the past century. The corporate pressure to train the masses to conform to business interests while the elites are provided increased privilege is a deception of the greatest magnitude. It is the most insidious of educational tricks in the new reform movement. Under the guise of "good business management," millions of students are relegated to nonthinking menial schoolwork as preparation for poor jobs, and the schools are expected to make them think they are happy and well educated.

As social critic Christopher Lasch states, there is:

... a new system of industrial recruitment, centered on the school. The modern system of public education, remodeled in accordance with the same principles of scientific management first perfected in industry, has replaced apprenticeship as the principal agency of training people for work. The transmission of skills is increasingly incidental to this training. The school habituates children to bureaucratic discipline and to the demands of group living, grades and sorts them by means of standardized tests, and selects some for professional and managerial careers while consigning the rest to manual labor. ... a willingness to cooperate with the proper authorities offers the best evidence of "adjustment" and the best hope of personal success, while a refusal to cooperate signifies the presence of "emotional problems" requiring more sustained therapeutic attention. (1984, pp. 48, 49)

American schools have been dominated by the values of business and industry since the beginning of the twentieth century, and have ignored their primary purpose of enlightenment for the improvement of social justice. Rather than liberating, schools are indoctrinating institutions. They now serve as providers of docile and hardworking employees on whom business can rely to gain a profit, teaching students an ideology that supports business regardless of ethical considerations and that conditions them to accept unquestioningly the authority of a managerial elite.

Educational reform movements in the United States have often victimized the underclass, on the pretext of making them "fit for work and for democratic citizenship." Schooling subjects them to lessons and conditions requiring the working-class youth to be obedient, punctual, frugal, neat, respectful, and content with their lot in life. There is a duality, a dialectic, here between what is good for business and what is good for society. The work ethic, drawing from Puritan values in the colonies, is of great value to industrialists who desire uncomplaining and diligent workers. This has been acted upon by the schools. Business employment has become the curriculum of the schools to sustain a receptive work force. The carrot of democratic citizenship, however, is mythical, since the economic facts of life are that the elites remain in power while the masses do the work. Education for democratic participation, in the pursuit of justice and equality, is still espoused in the rhetoric of school literature, but is not actualized in the schools.

This disparity in purposes for schooling between preparation for participation as a worker and participation as an equal citizen striving for justice in society is overlooked in much of the reform literature. As the historian Barbara Finkelstein noted:

Nineteenth century reformers looked to public schools to instill restraint in increasingly large numbers of immigrants and native children, while at the same time preparing them for learning and labor in an industrializing society. ... They saw no contradiction in the work of schools as economic sorting machines and enabling political institutions. ... Contemporary calls for reform reflect a retreat from historic visions of public education as an instrument of political democracy, a vehicle of social mobility, a center for the reconstruction of community life. ... Rather the educational visions of contemporary reformers evoke historic specters of public schools as crucibles in which to forge uniform Americans and disciplined industrial laborers. (1984, pp. 276, 277)

Finkelstein also identifies the role of corporate leaders in expanding their influence in public education to assure themselves a work force of competence and compliance. She illustrates this with examples from a business alliance with education at George Washington Carver High School in Atlanta, in which business conducts the daily activities of the school. These include work-study semi-skilled jobs in local businesses, substantial moral pronouncements to promote industrial discipline in students, and public rituals such as celebration of "Free Enterprise Day" and "passports to job opportunity." Such alliances, and other business intrusions into schools, lead to "an effective transfer of control over education policy from public school authorities to industrial councils," and "for the first time in the history of school reform, a deeply materialistic consciousness seems to be overwhelming all other concerns" (Finkelstein, 1984, p. 280).

One need not look much further than the Yuppie generation to recognize the truth of Finkelstein's insight. We have become very good at teaching students to be greedy, selfish, and conniving. Academic students are especially eager to get good grades in order to get into the right college in order to get a good-paying job. They seem uninterested in intellectual development that does not pay off in terms of employment and salaries. They seem uncaring about the homeless, the starving, others of the disadvantaged, and the rest of the world. They are excessively competitive with each other and press for competitive advantage over other groups. Ethical considerations, including the pursuit of justice, seem to pose no obstruction to their efforts. Cheating, buying term papers, using parental influence, taking drugs to temporarily enhance performance, paying someone to take a college admission test, and falsifying résumés are part of the process. Those who aspire to be Yuppies understand that winning is important in order to secure high pay; how one wins is not important.

Interestingly, this is a pattern of beliefs drawn right from big business. Wall Street companies have engaged in securities fraud, insider scandals, and scams of a variety of sorts. Banks appear to have taken advantage of deregulation and loose public control to plunge the country's banking and bank insurance system into serious trouble. Major industries, including Chrysler and Lockheed, have conducted business in a most unbusinesslike manner, leading to virtual bankruptcy, then received taxpayer bailouts that turned principles of "free enterprise" upside down. Big-business "sweetheart" contracts with government, negotiated with current and former officers of government agencies, have fattened profits and increased taxpayer costs exorbitantly. The Pentagon's contracts for extravagant costs for military supplies are an obvious example, as are the scandals surrounding HUD consulting contracts for former government and political party employees who have little knowledge about housing issues. There are many other examples in federal, state, and local government contracts for work and supplies. The big business of professional athletics, until recently and only after public outrage, condoned and supported athletes taking drugs to improve performance. Fraud, misrepresentation, cheating, using or peddling improper influence, falsifying or hiding records, and abusing drugs for business purposes appear to be acceptable ethical standards for many in business. This curriculum is one which many school students have picked up.

The unethical operations of business are manifold, and are reported often enough in the news to suggest that business is not the place to look for views on ethics. Even if one grants that the unethical is not the standard but the exception in business, there remain serious grounds for concern about the business view of social justice and responsibility. The many cases of industrial waste polluting the land, water, and air without industry's accepting responsibility to clean up illustrate the problem. Strong protests by the corporate world have been effective in slowing and stultifying the public regulation of worker health and safety, consumer protection, and improvements in public utilities and services. As Michael Apple (1979) describes it, "Economic and cultural power is being increasingly centralized in massive corporate bodies that are less than responsive to social needs other than profit" (p. 12).

It is not only the Yuppies who are infected by the increased influence of business on schools. Those who are not going to college, and who are less likely to share the American business dream of success, are subjected to second-class treatment in schools and careers. The industrial curriculum is designed to give students employable skills, not knowledge. They are not supposed to think, and the courses are intended to make them believers.

Business leaders criticize the schools because new employees lack basic skills and good work attitudes. The basic skills desired by business do not include critical judgment or persuasion skills that could be useful in reconstituting the moribund union movement or challenging manager dictates. Rather, business basic skills are fundamental reading and computation skills that make one more efficient in carrying out management's policies. A job candidate who demonstrates an intelligent understanding of left-wing ideas and who raises questions about worker safety, environmental hazards caused by industry, and excessive disparities between salaries and benefits received by owners and executives and those received by workers is not likely to be hired. It is the moral curriculum rather than the academic which is of most interest to business. They want workers who believe that what is good for business is good for the nation, and that management knows what is good for business.

Several states now require a course in "free enterprise," not economics. Obviously, this course is not neutral; it is an advocacy course intended to indoctrinate youth. English is taught by using job application forms and answering help wanted ads. General math is turned to preparing for work in stores and making change. History classes teach myths about the virtues of American business leaders, the appropriate power of corporations, and the threat of governmental interference in business. And, as Sheila Harty's (1980) study of business-produced teaching materials showed, students are given biased material which supports business views of environmental, social, and governmental actions. Throughout the schools students are treated as junior workers required to be punctual, have good "work habits," show deference to management, and not engage in critical thought. This hidden curriculum of business has been very successful.

Business has been a major influence on education for a long time, yet still complains about the products of a curriculum dominated by its own ethos. Raymond Callahan, in his historical study of the greatest influences on public education in its most formative period in the early twentieth century, found:

> At the turn of the century America had reason to be proud of the educational progress it had made. The dream of equality of educational opportunity had been partly realized. . . . the basic institutional framework for a noble conception of education had been created. . . . The story of the next quarter century of American education—a story of opportunity lost and of the acceptance by educational administrators of an inappropriate philosophy—[shows that] the most powerful force was industrialism. . . . the business ideology was spread continuously into the bloodstream of American life. . . . It was, therefore, quite natural for Americans, when they thought of reforming the schools, to apply business methods to achieve their ends. (1962, pp. 1, 5)

Callahan considered the business influence tragic for education and for American society because it substituted efficiency for effectiveness and stressed cost control at the expense of high-quality schooling for all. The business dominance in schools stuck, and in the last decade of the twentieth century schools are still controlled by a corporate value system. This explains the factory mentality of schools. It is why teachers are so poorly paid, badly used, and seen as laborers in schools. It is why students are treated like objects being manufactured on an assembly line. It explains the conformity and standardization, the excessive testing, and the organization and financing of schools. It also explains the schools' decreasing concern for social justice and ethics since the business influence became dominant.

Upton Sinclair, who is best known for his devastating criticism of the meat-packing industry for ignoring public health and worker safety (*The Jungle,* 1906), and the resulting federal legislation to regulate food products, also published two books exposing the detrimental effects of business and industry influence on education. *The Goose Step* (1922) detailed how major industrialists determined educational policies and appointments to professorships in the most important universities in America. It is big-business leaders who dominate the governing boards of most colleges and universities, a point made long ago by Thorstein Veblen (1916), who found that business practices and values detracted from academic institutions' primary purpose of liberating students. Sinclair, after spending two years studying the public schools, also described similar heavy-handed control over school policies and practices by business leaders across the United States (*The Goslings,* 1924). He wrote, "The purpose of this book is to show you how the 'invisible government' of Big Business which controls the rest of America has taken over the charge of your children" (p. ix).

There is considerable evidence that things have not gotten better in the almost seventy years since Sinclair wrote about schools and business. What is taught in schools is what business wants. What should be taught is what society needs and justice requires. We need to return to the civilizing purposes of schooling, justice and ethics, and to wrench control over education away from those who see the school as just another agency to support the interests of big business. Certainly, business should be a subject of study in school, but not the whitewash and indoctrination now given. Critical examination of business values and practices, in terms of their impact on social justice and ethical norms, may be of great import. We need to invert the current situation where business controls schools, so that the schools are places where business values and practices are critically evaluated according to standards of responsibility and enlightenment. That would put education in its proper position of monitoring the improvement of society by examining various social institutions, including business. It would certainly improve education, and it might improve business.

FOR DISCUSSION

1   What are "business interests," and how can they be identified in school curriculum and operation?

2   If a local store offers to employ students in a work-study program provided they get some released time from school and have requisite business skills, should the school ignore the offer? What if the offer was from a major corporation and the conditions included having a corporate executive as speaker at school assemblies and a collection of pamphlets put in the library and given to teachers? At what point does business exert too much influence on what is taught?

3   President Eisenhower called public attention to dangers created by the military-industrial complex. Are there parallel dangers in an education-industry complex? What consequences has Eisenhower's warning had? What are the likely consequences of adoption of either of the views expressed in the two essays in this chapter?

4   Review the table on the next page. What accounts for changes in the kinds of employment taken? How does this relate to what should be taught in schools? Should the schools tailor the curriculum according to typical jobs? What kinds of schooling would you propose for each of the occupations listed in the table? Who should control what is taught?

Kinds of employment	Percentage of total jobs held				
	1950	1960	1970	1980	1985
Operatives	19.9	17.6	16.2	14.2	12.0
Crafts	13.8	13.8	13.0	12.9	12.4
Clerical	12.2	14.1	17.0	18.6	18.2
Managers	9.0	8.7	7.9	11.2	14.5
Professional, technical	8.7	10.8	13.9	16.0	15.8
Sales	7.0	7.1	6.9	6.4	6.7
Service, except domestic	7.6	9.0	10.5	12.3	12.5
Farm managers	7.6	3.9	1.7	1.5	1.3
Laborers, nonfarm	6.0	5.1	4.1	4.7	4.7
Farm laborers	4.3	2.3	1.2	1.2	1.0
Domestic service	2.5	2.6	1.4	1.0	.9

Source: Bureau of Labor Statistics (1986), Washington, D.C.: Government Printing Office.

REFERENCES

Apple, M. (1979). *Ideology and Curriculum*. London: Routledge.

Blau, P., and Duncan O. D. (1967). *The American Occupational Structure*. New York: Wiley.

Callahan, R. (1962). *Education and the Cult of Efficiency*. Chicago: University of Chicago Press.

Finkelstein, B. (1984). "Education and the Retreat from Democracy in the United States, 1979–198?" *Teachers College Record, 86,* 276–282.

Fiske, E. (1988). "Lessons." *The New York Times*. December 21, p. B8.

W. T. Grant Foundation (1988). *The Forgotten Half: Non-College-Bound Youth in America* (Interim Report). Washington, D.C.: W. T. Grant Foundation.

Harty, S. (1980). *Huckster in the Classroom*. Washington, D.C.: Center for Responsive Legislation.

Lasch, C. (1984). *The Minimal Self*. New York: Norton.

Mann, D. "Business Involvement and Public School Improvement, Part 2." *Phi Delta Kappan, 69,* 228–232.

Oxford Analytica (1986). *America in Perspective: Major Trends in the United States through the 1990s*. Boston: Houghton Mifflin.

Sewall, G. T. (1984). *Necessary Lessons: Decline and Renewal in American Schools*. New York: Free Press.

Sinclair, U. (1922). *The Goose-Step*. Pasadena, Calif.: Sinclair.

——— (1924). *The Goslings*. Pasadena, Calif.: Sinclair.

Soltow, L., and Stevens, E. (1981). *The Rise of Literacy and the Common School in the United States: A Socioeconomic Analysis to 1870*. Chicago: University of Chicago Press.

Veblen, T. (1918). *The Higher Learning in America*. New York: B. W. Heubsch.

PART THREE

WHAT SHOULD TEACHING BE?

The four chapters of this section have as their general theme the role that teachers should play in matters of school reform and school governance. On one side of the debate are those who argue that unless teachers are given more authority in running schools and directing the curriculum, there is little hope for the future of school reform. Schools are unlikely to become better places for children without the direct, meaningful participation of teachers in all aspects of running the schools. The other side argues that schools are not designed for teachers. To grant teachers greater power would not improve education and would rob parents of their control over the schools attended by their children.

Questions surrounding school governance have implications for the way teachers are educated, their roles in the classroom, and the legitimacy of their claims to academic freedom. School governance is a subject on which reasonable people may disagree, and about which prospective teachers should be well informed. To argue that teachers are the key to public education is to belabor the obvious. Without good teachers, there cannot be good education. Effective teachers are as essential to good schooling as good athletes are to the success of sports teams. The question is one of control: If teachers were given greater power in matters of school governance, would students benefit? Would parents lose?

On one hand, among the oldest traditions of education is the view of teachers as obedient servants of the state. Plato, often cited as the first philosopher of education, paid scant attention to teachers. His concern was the creation of a just society governed by the most able. Education to prepare students for their place in society was under the heavy-handed control of the state. Schooling was compulsory up to the age of 20. The curriculum was scrutinized by censors and was to contain no reference to anything that did not serve public ends. For Plato, the teacher was obliged to follow the curriculum. Any deviation could only be for the worse and was not to be allowed. He wrote:

> In short, then, those who keep watch over our commonwealth must take the greatest care not to overlook the least infraction of the rule against any innovation upon the established system of education either of the body or of the mind. When the poet says that men care most for "the newest air that hovers on the singer's lips," they will be afraid lest he be taken not merely to mean new songs, but to be commending a new style of music. Such innovation is not to be commended, nor should the poet be so understood. The introduction of novel fashions in music is a thing to beware of as endangering the whole fabric of society. (Cornford, 1968, p. 115)

Certainly, few people today would deny teachers the right to be innovative and creative in the classroom. Unlike Plato, most people believe in the possibility of progress and the value of change. However, the control of the curriculum remains, for many, the rightful province of the state or the community and not the teacher. To empower teachers with authority over the curriculum is to disempower taxpayers and their representatives (boards of education).

Consider yourself, for a moment, not as a prospective teacher but as a taxpayer with children in public schools. Would you be comfortable paying hefty tax bills with little or no say in the education of your children? Are you willing to leave decisions about curriculum, textbooks, teaching methodology, and evaluation techniques to teachers who are not accountable to you? Or would you prefer to have these policy matters rest in the hands of school administrators and elected school boards who are responsible to you as a citizen and community resident? Clearly, there is a strong argument to be made for the community control of schools.

On the other hand, it is argued with equal passion that school reform has failed in the past largely because it has ignored the role of teachers. In order for schools to become more satisfying and more educative places for children, they must first become better places for teachers. Teachers must be allowed to assume their rightful place as professionals with genuine authority in the school and the ability to control matters of curriculum, instruction, and policy (Aronowitz and Giroux, 1985). Would you want to work in a school district that refused to listen to you about matters of curriculum and instruction?

Similar to the theme of liberty versus equality that runs through Part Two, competing conceptions of teaching represent poles on a continuum of political thought. The left, or liberal, end of the continuum includes those who tend to be sympathetic toward the rights of workers, teacher empowerment, and the education of teachers as intellectuals. It also includes those with positive views of union involvement in school policy matters as well as those who champion academic freedom for public school teachers. Along the right, or conservative, end of the continuum are those who are more comfortable with the traditional exercise of authority in the schools. They would oppose any attempt to weaken community control of schools by granting greater power to teachers. Those on the right tend to be less sympathetic toward unions, often viewing them as the protectors of incompetent teachers and as unwise meddlers in the management of schools. Conservatives typically share a less than charitable view toward academic freedom for public school teachers, regarding it as an overused shield for spreading poor and even un-American ideas in the classroom.

Of course, we need to be cautious about painting with too broad a brush. Although unions tend to be on the left end of the spectrum, that generalization does not account for the great support former President Reagan enjoyed among union members. Similarly, community control of schools is typically considered to be a plank in a conservative's political platform, but the decentralization of New York City's school system in the 1960s was championed mainly by the left. Our goal is not to label school critics, but to make you more aware of the competing perspectives on education topics. As you consider the issue of what teaching should be, we urge you to consider the arguments of both left and right and to ask yourself where you are now along the spectrum of opinion on each issue.

CHAPTER 11: TEACHER EMPOWERMENT
OR ADMINISTRATIVE LEADERSHIP

> America's school system is in deep trouble. The fact is that if we do not restructure our schools, this nation will be out of business by the year 2000. (D. T. Kearns, chairman and chief executive officer of the Xerox Corporation, quoted in *Education Week,* November 2, 1988, p. 7)

Before deciding what teaching should be in the future, it is first necessary to consider what the working life of teachers is like today. Unlike scientists, engineers, and corporate executives, who conduct their business in private, teachers' work is open, accessible, and familiar. Over 75 percent of the American population has at least twelve years of schooling and experience with as many as fifty teachers. Ironically, despite their job's high profile and familiarity, teachers claim that few people know what it is like to be a teacher in public schools. A New Jersey high school teacher explained that the public does not understand teaching because it is "different," a form of employment whose rewards and pressures make it discontinuous with the work experiences of most adults. He told us:

> We live in a society that values tangible achievements. My brother-in-law is a salesman. He knows at the end of the year how much he's sold and what his worth has been to the company. When he asks me about my job, I think he expects me to answer him in terms of market share and profits and losses. Maybe he thinks that these should be the basis for my salary increments.... Last month I turned two kids on to Shakespeare; I convinced one kid not to quit school; and I got a thankyou letter from [a former student] who's getting A's in college English. In dollars and cents, how much is that worth? I tell my brother-in-law, "Teaching is different." He nods his head, but I don't think he really understands.

Teaching has been described as a "careerless profession," a job in which there is only limited opportunity for promotion or increases in authority and salary (Etzioni, 1969; Lortie, 1968). Upon graduation from college, most people pursue a series of work experiences and job-related career moves that bring additional responsibilities and greater remuneration. A few teachers—mainly those who move from classroom teaching through the principalship to central office administration—follow a similar ascent. However, most teachers do not have access to a promotion path that brings a structured series of increasingly rewarding positions.

Schools, unlike most other large workplaces, are characterized by a flat organizational structure, with most employees occupying a single, undifferentiated job category: classroom teacher. School districts typically do not offer teachers enough routes out of the classroom (for example, as guidance counselors, building principals, curriculum coordinators, department chairs) to give them the career mobility people have in other fields (see Sikes, Measor, and Woods, 1985). The majority of teachers begin and end their careers as classroom teachers, without additional responsibilities or direct influence in running the school. Some sociologists have argued that, because of its structure, teaching is an occupation that has better met the work needs of women than men (Lortie, 1975). Women, the argument goes, can begin teaching, drop out to raise a family, and return to the classroom when their children no longer need them at home.*

In the past, teaching and teachers' work were largely ignored as issues of public concern. If the public was satisfied with the quality of schools and the work of teachers, its satisfaction was expressed inaudibly. When schools appeared to be functioning well, communities rarely considered the problems of a teaching career. As long as student learning appeared to be high and student discipline was relatively unproblematic, few people outside of education concerned themselves with teachers' salary structure, the role teachers should play in schools, or the difficulty of attracting and retaining talented teachers.

By the 1980s, evidence suggested a variety of problems with public schooling. Educational expenditures had never been higher, but scores on standardized achievement tests were at all-time lows. Restive teachers demanded higher salaries, while the popular press was regularly printing stories about increases in school violence, crime, and the numbers of poorly educated students. Studies of schools were critical of everything from student learning to the quality of teacher preparation (Boyer, 1983; Goodlad, 1984; National Commission, 1983; Sizer, 1984). The schools were said to be in crisis and the nation was declared to be at risk because of the poor quality of teaching and learning. Teachers were held up to public scrutiny, and their work was weighed, measured, and

---

*Critics of this analysis note that it fails to account for the fact that women have multiple commitments, which include career and family. Teaching may permit women to pursue multiple obligations, but this does not mean that it satisfies their career needs any better than it does men's (Feimen-Nemser and Floden, 1986).

assessed. Everywhere, researchers found dull, lifeless teaching; an absence of academic focus; bored, unchallenged students; and teachers mired in routine and paperwork. Implicit in this new scrutiny was the assumption that teachers were not doing, or were not able to do, the job expected of them.

School problems were recognized by those on both sides of the desk. Not immune to public criticism nor insensitive to school problems, teachers were found to be increasingly dissatisfied with their work. A poll of classroom teachers conducted by the National Education Association indicated that if they could start over, only 25 percent of the female and 16 percent of the male teachers would again choose teaching as a career. The Carnegie Forum (1986), among others, suggested that a major cause of teacher dissatisfaction was the structure of schools, and it has predicted a diminished pool of high-quality teachers in the future unless schools are reorganized to make teaching more attractive. It has been suggested that there may be something very wrong with the ways in which teachers' work and career paths are organized.

In Chapter 11, two positions are presented on the work and role of teachers. The first calls for teachers to exert influence well beyond the walls of their classrooms as the best means for improving their job satisfaction and performance. It recommends a restructuring of schools to grant teachers decision-making authority in organizing the curriculum, running the schools, and charting the reform agenda. The second position argues that the teacher empowerment suggested in the first essay would be to the detriment of students and the communities. Schools, it argues, need to consider teacher input, but they must be run by professional administrators in order to serve children, their parents, and the needs of the community.

CHAPTER 12: UNIVERSITY- OR FIELD-BASED TEACHER EDUCATION

The perspective society holds toward teachers' work largely determines the investment it is willing to make in their education. If teachers are viewed as those who run the schools and make important curricular decisions, then a great deal of time, money, and intellectual energy must be invested in the preparation of teachers. On the other hand, it would be wasteful to treat prospective teachers to an education that equipped them with the knowledge, skills, and dispositions needed by leaders if all they were expected to do was follow the initiatives of others.

Teachers' education does not have a long history. Until the nineteenth century, schooling was reserved for wealthy white males, an elite who had the leisure to pursue extended study and the financial resources sufficient to excuse them from the necessity of productive work. As with the preparation of other professionals, little formal attention was given to the education of teachers, and no institution or special programs existed for preparing people for the classroom. Pedagogy was not considered a legitimate field of study. Teacher education was based on the liberal arts, a series of courses that promised to free the mind of narrow certainties and uninformed judgments. It was assumed that future teachers, future lawyers, and future businessmen could all be served equally well by reading Cicero, Aristotle, and Quintilian. Professional training was acquired in apprenticeships that were to be entered only after the mind had been formed by a rigorous liberal study. For the poorer classes and women, of course, the beauties and splendors of liberating study were generally unknown; and among the few who controlled knowledge, mass education was considered unnecessary if not outright dangerous.

In the early nineteenth century, the elitist orientation of schooling gave way to general support for mass public education for the working and farming classes, and the nature of public schools and those who worked in them changed forever. The common schools were championed by the better-educated members of the community—typically businessmen, lawyers, and the clergy—who touted education as a potential cure for pauperism, drunkenness, human degradation, avarice, acquisitiveness, fraud, and dishonor (Curti, 1959, pp. 122–123). Common school textbooks contained an undisguised morality. They promoted ''industry, obedience to parents, kindness to the old and animals, temperance, generosity, promptness and the inevitable triumph of the virtuous over the wicked'' (Hofstadter, 1962, p. 39). Character development and vocational training were the key aims of mass public education. Publicly supported education was considered a reasonable investment that could pay dividends in economic self-reliance and moral refinement (Mattingly, 1975).

The motives of the schoolpeople who led the fight for state-supported education are a matter of historiographic debate. Some historians view the founding fathers of education as altruistic champions of the poor who wanted to provide similar schooling for everyone, independent of class. These historians argue that without free, public education, the children of the working classes, rural farmers, and newly arrived immigrants would have been deprived of the skills, civic education, and moral lessons necessary to succeed (Borrowman, 1965; Cremin, 1961; Hofstadter, 1962; Ravitch, 1983).

A less charitable view of the schoolmasters' motives is held by those historians who see the common school movement as being rooted in a desire to control potentially unruly social classes and ethnic groups through a school bureaucracy. These historians argue that common schools were designed to teach a particular brand of morality and to limit access to the benefits of society to those who demonstrated appropriate social behaviors (Katz, 1974; Spring and Gumbert, 1974).

Advocates of public education knew that if schooling was to provide a common set of values and skills to all graduates, more care had to be given to teacher education. Although many of the older colleges in the east had prepared prospective teachers, these schools were considered inappropriate sites for turning out the large numbers of new teachers needed in the common schools. At the time, most colleges were open only to men, and it was assumed that the new schoolteachers would be women. The backers of the common schools were unwilling to pay teachers a salary high enough to attract able and ambitious male college graduates. With few other opportunities open to them, talented women could be forced to work at a rate of pay that was about one-half of a man's salary, and teaching, particularly at the lower levels, quickly became known as women's work. It has been argued that women paid a heavy price for their right to work in schools. As workers, they had to fight the widely held bias against females in a male's world. As teachers, they had to battle the stereotype that their work was not suited for able men (Warren, 1985).

Despite their problems, the common schools proved to be popular and successful. Women teachers were in great demand everywhere, and a new institution was developed to train them for work in the schools. The ''normal school''—its name derived from the French, referring to its function as a school on which others would be modeled—offered a program of study that was purely vocational, in sharp contrast to the liberal arts education of the older colleges. Normal school curricula offered little more content than that which was to be taught in the common school classrooms: reading, writing, arithmetic, vocal music, and the like. Among the wealthy, well-educated members of the community, normal schools were derided as institutions for the lower classes, vocationally limiting and not intellectually challenging. Some leaders of the normal school movement, sensitive to criticism from university graduates, argued for the inclusion of liberal arts training for teachers, but there was no sense of urgency to provide elementary school teachers with a more academic education.

The normal schools produced a large number of the nineteenth century's best teachers. They were succeeded in the twentieth century by state teachers' colleges, many of which expanded their educational mission and became state universities. These two institutions—the old teachers' colleges and the older normal schools—have prepared the majority of the nation's teachers, often under great pressure to do so quickly and cheaply. Although no other institutions were producing better teachers in sufficient numbers to staff public schools, the normal schools and teachers' colleges have suffered widespread criticism—some of it justified, some fanciful—for the problems of public schools and the quality of teachers.

At no time in the history of public education has there been general satisfaction with the ways in which teachers have been trained. Programs for preparing teachers have been roundly criticized by those who went through them as well as those who taught in them, and by the public schools that hired their graduates (Lanier and Little, 1986; Lortie, 1975). Criticism of teacher education programs seems to intensify during periods of increased teacher demand, and the nation is now entering one of those high-demand periods. The baby boomers' babies will be swelling the schools, and although family size is predicted to be smaller, the increased number of new students, coupled with the retirement of many longtime teachers, has led forecasters to predict that the nation will need upwards of 200,000 new teachers a year by the 1990s.

Accompanying the anticipation of a dramatic increase in the demand for new teachers has been a series of reports critical of teacher education and calls for the redesign of the teacher preparation curriculum (Magrath, 1987).* Since the time of the normal schools, every generation has had to answer questions about the preparation of teachers. How should future teachers be trained? Which institutions offer the best site for teacher education? What is the most appropriate course of study for prospective teachers? What is the proper balance between liberal arts training and practical experience in the classroom?

In Chapter 12, two contrasting positions are offered in response to the questions about teacher education. The first position argues for an enhanced version of the current university-based model for the preparation of teachers. It is a position that comports well with a view of university-educated teacher intellectuals trained to assume positions of leadership in the schools. The second position argues that this design has failed us in the past and is likely to do so in the future. Instead, this position calls for a field-based teacher certification plan, conducted in public schools and managed by state departments of education. The second position is likely to be supported by those in favor of a management-directed approach to school governance.

CHAPTER 13:   ACADEMIC FREEDOM OR TEACHER RESPONSIBILITY

If you view teachers as school leaders who deserve a high-quality university education, then you are likely to believe that their right to teach should be protected. If, on the other hand, you prefer to see teachers as practitioners who are free from academic inquiry and administrative responsibility, then you may be less willing to grant them the same degree of academic freedom enjoyed by those who teach in universities.

"Academic freedom," as applied to higher education, is the contemporary American term for the classical ideal of the right to teach and learn (Hofstadter and Metzger, 1955). Socrates, charged with impiety and the corruption of Athenian youth, defended himself by claiming that he and his students had the freedom to pursue truth. All wickedness, he argued, was due to ignorance. The freedom to teach and the freedom to learn would uncover knowledge, eliminate ignorance, and improve the society. His fellow citizens were not persuaded, and Socrates was sentenced to death. In modern times academic freedom has fared better; although regularly battered, it has survived.

Although lacking a crisp, precise definition, "academic freedom," as the term is used in American higher education, typically refers to several related freedoms: (1) the freedom of professors to write, research, and teach in their field of special competence; (2) the freedom of universities to determine policies

---

* Curriculum reviews are common to colleges and universities. Over the past several years, not only teacher education but all of undergraduate education has undergone reconsideration. In response to a series of reports questioning the quality of learning and teaching in the nation's colleges, many postsecondary institutions have undertaken an examination of their undergraduate curricula in the liberal arts as well as in professional schools (see Association of American Colleges, 1985; Bennett, 1984; National Institute of Education, 1984).

and practices unfettered by political restraints or other outside pressures; and (3) the freedom of students to learn.

It is argued that academic freedom ensures the freedom of the mind for both students and scholars, and therefore is essential to the pursuit of truth, the primary mission of higher education (Kirk, 1955; MacIver, 1955). The university should be a marketplace of competing ideas. Students should be exposed to a diversity of views, and the classsroom should be free of restraint and open to the regular and robust exchange of opinions.

The question here is not about academic freedom in universities, but whether or not academic freedom should be extended to those who teach in elementary and secondary schools. The "academy" originally referred to the garden where Plato taught, and academic freedom came to be associated with institutions of higher learning. Public schools are unlike universities, and traditionally public school teachers and students have not automatically been given the same academic protection as their university counterparts. It has been argued that the comparative youthfulness of the students, and the nature of instruction, demand that public school teachers be more accountable to the community for what they teach and how they teach it.

The narrow conception of academic freedom, as a right enjoyed only in higher education, is undergoing challenges from professional associations of teachers and other groups interested in public education* (see Kaplan and Schrecker, 1983). The American Civil Liberties Union, for example, objects to any conception of academic freedom that limits it to university professors. The ACLU claims that academic freedom should be extended to the public schools, the authentic academic community for young people. "If each new generation is to acquire a feeling for civil liberties," the ACLU argues, "it can do so only by having a chance to live in the midst of a community where the principles are continually exemplified" (ACLU, 1968, p. 4).

The courts have, on occasion, been highly supportive of academic freedom for public school teachers. Writing in *Wieman v. Updergraff* (244 U.S. 183) in 1952, Justices Frankfurter and Douglas argued that all teachers, from the primary grades to the university, share a special task in developing good citizens, and all teachers should have the academic freedom necessary to be exemplars of openmindedness and free inquiry. Similarly, other courts have ruled that limiting academic freedom to postsecondary education would discriminate against students who do not attend college.

> To restrict the opportunity for involvement in an open forum for the free exchange of ideas to higher education would not only foster an unacceptable elitism, it would

---

* Many national organizations are concerned with securing academic freedom for teachers in public schools. Students may wish to consult the position on academic freedom taken by the American Association of School Libraries, the American Association of University Professors, the American Bar Association, the American Civil Liberties Union, the American Federation of Teachers, the American Historical Association, the American Library Association, the National Council for the Social Studies, the National Council of Teachers of English, and the National Education Association.

fail to complete the development of those not going to college, contrary to our constitutional commitment to equal opportunity. Effective citizenship in a participatory democracy must not be dependent upon advancement toward college degrees. Consequently, it would be inappropriate to conclude that academic freedom is required only in colleges and universities. [*Cary v. Board of Education*, 427 F. Supp. 945, 953 (D.Colo. 1977), quoted in Rubin and Greenhouse, 1983, p. 116)]

This issue is not likely to be settled by the courts (O'Neill, 1984). Academic freedom and the extent to which it deserves to be extended to public school teachers goes to the core of teaching, and it is properly a matter of educational policy. The issue of academic freedom raises a series of difficult questions that must be addressed by school boards, local communities, and organizations of teachers and teacher educators: Who should be protected by academic freedom? Is it a right that can be extended automatically to all public school teachers? Does academic freedom clash with the community's right to determine what is taught to its children and the manner of instruction? Who decides what is appropriate education for minor children? How do we best prepare our students for their role as citizens? Can higher education continue to claim academic freedom as the special province reserved for university experts (Hook, 1953)? Or do universities ignore restrictions on academic freedom in public schools at their own peril (O'Neill, 1987)?

Chapter 13 presents competing perspectives on the issue of academic freedom for public school teachers and students. The first position encourages a view of academic freedom as a right which is reserved for researchers in universities and which should not be extended to teachers in public schools. Teachers in elementary and secondary schools, it is argued, need no freedom beyond those guaranteed to all citizens by the Constitution. To give them more than those freedoms could jeopardize their role as parental surrogates and political representatives of the society. The second essay is more sympathetic to the empowerment of teachers. It defends academic freedom for public school teachers as a right essential to the search for knowledge and for the freedom of mind necessary for the development of democratic ideals.

CHAPTER 14: TEACHER UNIONS OR SCHOOL MANAGEMENT

> Teacher unions are here to stay. That much is clear. What is not clear is whether they will turn out to be beneficial, harmful or merely irrelevant to the quality of education in American schools. (Finn, 1985, p. 331)

Are teacher unions necessary evils that must be accommodated in wage disputes? Are they potentially evil, with the power to hijack the reform agendas of legislators and school administrators? Or, are unions committed to working in a coalition—along with parents and administrators—that can turn around failing school districts? The answers to these questions help define where you are on the continuum of opinions about school reform. Before discussing the arguments of Chapter 14, let's consider some of the background of teacher unionism.

Teachers have been organized for well over 100 years, but the earliest organizations of teachers were not really unions. The National Education Association (NEA), for example, was established in 1857 to represent the views of "practical" classroom teachers and administrators. Annual conventions of the NEA were not union meetings but exchanges of ideas about teaching that typically avoided discussions of how teachers could influence decisions about their work or wages. The NEA was less concerned with the personal welfare of classroom teachers than it was with advancing the profession of education. In its early years, the NEA was a male-dominated organization *for* teachers that was led by school superintendents, professors of education, and school principals (Wesley, 1957). As one critic of the NEA notes, the role of classroom teachers, especially women teachers, was "limited to listening" (Eaton, 1975, p. 10). Since the 1960s, the NEA has moved more aggressively to represent the views of all classroom teachers, advocating collective negotiations and encouraging its locals to serve as bargaining agents for teachers.

Teacher unionism dates to the early twentieth century, when teachers were organized in Chicago to fight for better working conditions. In 1916, the American Federation of Teachers (AFT) was formed as an affiliate of the American Federation of Labor. Initially, the older NEA and the upstart AFT cooperated. The NEA focused on the professional and practical sides of teaching; the AFT concentrated its efforts on improving the economic aspects of teachers' lives (Engel, 1976). Over the years, local affiliates of the NEA and the AFT have become rivals in an effort to be recognized as teachers' bargaining agents. Since the 1960s, both the AFT and the NEA have recognized the right of local affiliates to use the strike, labor's most potent weapon, as a last-resort measure to gain a satisfactory contract for their members. At the present time, although only 20 percent of workers in private industry belong to labor unions, 90 percent of teachers nationally belong to either the NEA or the AFT.

Today, teacher organizations often bear a greater resemblance to professional associations (for example, the American Bar Association and the American Medical Association) than to labor organizations (for example, the International Ladies Garment Workers Union and the United Automobile Workers), but the leaders of the old AFT identified with unionized workers in other industries. They believed that problems common to all workers could be solved through cooperation and collective action. They wanted teacher organizations to provide economic benefits for their members, and, they argued, teacher unions should also assist labor more generally by improving the education offered to children of the working class. Despite numerous efforts to organize teachers and to revitalize education, including the development of a workers' college and special public schools for workers' children, membership in the AFT declined in the 1920s and remained flat throughout most of the thirties. Teachers were reluctant to join unions, and most school administrators were openly hostile toward them. In the 1920s, fearing worker radicalism and union activity, many school superintendents demanded that teachers sign "yellow dog contracts," agreements that workers would not join a union as a condition of employment.

The National Labor Relations Act (1935) changed the status of unions by recognizing the right of workers in private industry to bargain collectively. "Collective bargaining" refers to the process by which employees, as a group, negotiate in good faith with their employers about wages and the conditions of employment (Lieberman and Moscow, 1966, p. 1). Employees are considered disadvantaged in bargaining with employers if they do so singly, alone against the power and resources of management. Collective bargaining laws recognize the right of workers to join together and elect a bargaining agent (a union) that will negotiate with their employers. The NLRA required employers and unions to "meet at reasonable times and confer in good faith with respect to wages, hours and other terms and conditions of employment."

Questions about its constitutionality clouded the early history of the NLRA. The issue was eventually decided by the Supreme Court, which judged the act to be constitutional in 1937 (*NLRB v. Jones and Laughlin Steel Company*, 301 U.S. 1, 57 S.Ct. 615). This case was a major victory for organized labor, and it represented a great change in the thinking of the courts. Court rulings concerning the right of workers to engage in collective negotiations can be traced to the Philadelphia Cordwainers case (1806). In that case, the workers were found guilty of entering into a conspiracy (a union) to improve their wages. By the mid-nineteenth century, courts no longer believed that those who advocated collective bargaining were involved in criminal conspiracies (see *Commonwealth v. Hunt*, 1842), but unions and collective negotiations were not given full legitimacy until the Supreme Court's 1937 decision.

The NLRA affected only workers in the private sector. Employees of federal, state, or local government are not covered by the NLRA, and this law does not guarantee collective bargaining for public school teachers. Schools are considered to be extensions of the state. School boards are, in a sense, state employers and, as such, they are excluded from federal labor legislation. It has been left up to the states to regulate employment relations in public education. Following the lead of Congress, the majority of state legislatures have taken action to recognize the rights of government workers to organize and negotiate with employers. By the mid-1980s, thirty-three states required school boards to bargain collectively with teachers; eleven states permitted collective bargaining, and only four states had legislation which prohibited it (Johnson, 1988, p. 603).

The organization of teachers in New York City in 1960 is considered the beginning of collective negotiations for public school teachers (Lieberman and Moscow, 1966, p. 35). The United Federation of Teachers, a local affiliate of the AFT, made up of several New York City teacher organizations, asked the Board of Education to recognize the teachers' right to bargain collectively and to conduct an election to determine which organization should represent the teachers. The board was unsure how collective bargaining should be implemented, and it did not move swiftly. The unions accused the board of stalling, and on November 7, 1960, the UFT declared the first strike in the history of New York City education.

It was a brief but effective job action. The next day the teachers were back in the classrooms. The board had agreed to hold an election and not to take reprisals against striking teachers. Union estimates put pickets at about 7,500, and it was claimed that another 15,000 teachers stayed home (Eaton, 1975, p. 165). The strike alerted the nation to the power of teacher unions, and teachers began to recognize the advantages of collective negotiations as well as the power potential of the strike. The events in New York City also sent the two largest unions, the NEA and the AFT, scrambling for members.

The NEA represents about 1.2 million teachers, about twice the number represented by the AFT. These organizations differ on specific issues. In the late 1980s, the NEA opposed standardized tests for teachers and students while the AFT supported them; the NEA supported bilingual education but refused to endorse the "excellence movement." The AFT endorsed the "excellence movement" and opposed bilingual education. A more complete examination of the views of each organization can be found in the journal *The NEA Today* and the AFT's *American Teacher*. Regular columns by the AFT president appear in *The New York Times;* columns by the NEA president appear in *The Washington Post*.

Chapter 14 does not play out the debate between advocates of the NEA and supporters of the AFT, nor does it contain arguments about the morality or appropriateness of strikes by teachers. The issue here is not whether teachers should belong to professional work associations, but whether or not unions are good for the future of education. One position argues that unions are undemocratic organizations that work against the best interests of pupils, parents, and teachers. Collective bargaining, it claims, is not for the public good and will not contribute to school reform. Collective bargaining should be restricted if schools are to serve the children and the community. The second position argues that there has been a positive union effect on education, and collective bargaining and union influence should extend beyond wages and hours to include matters of school policy and personnel. It links the success of future school improvement to the participation of unions in the reform agenda.

REFERENCES

American Association of Colleges (1985). *Integrity in the College Curriculum: A Report to the Academic Community*. Washington, D.C.: Association of American Colleges.

American Civil Liberties Union (1968). *Academic Freedom in the Secondary Schools*. New York: American Civil Liberties Union.

Aronowitz, S., and Giroux, H. A. (1985). *Education under Siege: The Conservative, Liberal, and Radical Debate Over Schooling*. South Hadley, Mass.: Bergin & Garvey.

Bennett, W. J. (1984). *To Reclaim a Legacy: A Report on the Humanities in Higher Education*. Washington, D.C.: National Endowment for the Humanities.

Borrowman, M. L., ed. (1965). *Teacher Education in America: A Documentary History*. New York: Teachers College Press.

Boyer, E. L. (1983). *High School: A Report on Secondary Education in America*. New York: Harper & Row.

Carnegie Forum on Education and the Economy (1986). *A Nation Prepared: Teachers for the 21st Century*. Washington, D.C.: Carnegie Forum.

Cornford, F. M., ed. and trans. (1968). *The Republic of Plato*. New York: Oxford University Press.

Cremin, L. (1961). *The Transformation of the School: Progressivism in American Education, 1876–1957*. New York: Knopf.

Curti, M. E. (1959). *The Social Ideas of American Educators*. Totowa, N.J.: Littlefield, Adams.

Eaton, W. E. (1975). *The American Federation of Teachers, 1916–1961: A History of the Movement*. Carbondale, Ill.: Southern Illinois University Press.

Engel, R. A. (1976). "Teacher Negotiation: History and Comment." In *Education and Collective Bargaining*, edited by E. M. Cresswell and M. J. Murphy. Berkeley: McCutchan.

Etzioni, A., ed. (1969). *The Semi-Professions and Their Organization: Teachers, Nurses, Social Workers*. New York: Free Press.

Feiman-Nemser, S., and Floden, R. E. (1986). "The Cultures of Teaching." In *Handbook of Research on Teaching*. 3d ed., edited by M. C. Wittrock. New York: Macmillan.

Finn, C. A. (1985). "Teacher Unions and School Quality: Potential Allies or Inevitable Foes?" *Phi Delta Kappan*, **66**, 331–338.

Gallup, A. (1984). "The Gallup Poll of Teachers' Attitudes toward the Public Schools." *Phi Delta Kappan*, **66**, 97–107.

Goodlad, J. I. (1984). *A Place Called School: Prospects for the Future*. New York: McGraw-Hill.

Gumbert, E. B., and Spring, J. H. (1974). *The Superschool and the Superstate: American Education in the Twentieth Century, 1918–1970*. New York: Wiley.

Hofstadter, R. (1962). *Anti-intellectualism in American Life*. New York: Random House.

Hofstadter, R., and Metzger, W. P. (1955). *The Development of Academic Freedom in the United States*. New York: Columbia University Press.

Hook, S. 1953. *Heresy, Yes—Conspiracy, No*. New York: John Day.

Jackson, P. W. (1969). *Life in Classrooms*. New York: Holt.

Johnson, S. M. (1988). "Unionism and Collective Bargaining in the Public Schools." In *Handbook of Research on Educational Administration*, edited by N. J. Boyan. New York: Longman.

Kaplan, C., and Schrecker, E. eds. (1983). *Regulating the Intellectuals: Perspectives on Academic Freedom in the 1980s*. New York: Praeger.

Kirk, R. (1955). *Academic Freedom: An Essay in Definition*. Chicago: Henry Regnery.

Lanier, J. E., and Little, J. W. (1986). "Research on Teacher Education." In *Handbook of Research on Teaching*, 3d ed., edited by M. C. Wittrock. New York: Macmillan.

Lieberman, M., and Moscow, M. H. (1966). *Collective Negotiations for Teachers: An Approach to School Administration*. Chicago: Rand McNally.

Lortie, D. (1969). "The Balance of Control and Autonomy in Elementary School Teaching." In *The Semi-Professions and Their Organization*, edited by A. Etzioni. New York: Free Press.

Lortie, D. (1975). *Schoolteacher*. Chicago: University of Chicago Press.

MacIver, R. M. (1955). *Academic Freedom in Our Time*. New York: Columbia University Press.

Magrath, C. P., Egbert, R. L., et al. (1987). *Strengthening Teacher Education: The Challenge to College University Leaders*. San Francisco: Jossey-Bass.

Mattingly, P. (1975). *The Classless Profession: American Schoolmen in the Nineteenth Century*. New York: New York University Press.

National Commission on Excellence in Education. (1983). *A Nation at Risk: The Imperative for Educational Reform*. Washington, D.C.: U.S. Government Printing Office.

National Education Association (1982). *Status of the American Public School Teacher: 1980–1981*. Washington, D.C.: National Education Association.

National Institute of Education (Study Group on the Conditions of Excellence in American Higher Education) (1984). *Involvement in Learning: Realizing the Potential of American Higher Education*. Washington, D.C.: National Institute of Education.

O'Neill, R. M. (1984). "Freedom of Expression: Schools and Teachers in a Democracy." In *The Foundations of Education: Stasis and Change*, edited by F. P. Besag and J. L. Nelson. New York: Random House.

———— (1987). "Higher Education's Responsibility." *Social Education, 51*, 435–437.

Ravitch, D. (1983). *The Troubled Crusade: American Education, 1945–1980*. New York: Basic Books.

Rubin, D., and Greenhouse, S. (1983). *The Rights of Teachers: The Basic ACLU Guide to a Teacher's Constitutional Rights*, Rev. ed. New York: Bantam.

Sikes, P. J., Measor, L., and Woods, P. (1985). *Teachers' Careers: Crises and Continuities*. Philadelphia: Falmer.

Sizer, T. R. (1984). *Horace's Compromise: The Dilemma of the American High School*. Boston: Houghton Mifflin.

Warren, D. (1985). "Learning from Experience: History and Teacher Education." *Educational Researcher, 14*, 5–12.

Wesley, E. B. 1957. *NEA: The First Hundred Years*. New York: Harper and Brothers.

CHAPTER 11

Teacher Empowerment or Administrative Leadership

POSITION 1
For Empowering Teachers

In nineteenth-century fiction, schoolteachers are often portrayed as less than laudable characters of limited social acceptance. Consider Washington Irving's schoolmaster, Ichabod Crane. Described by Irving as "some scarecrow eloped from a field," the gangly teacher enjoyed a modest popularity with some women in the community, who thought him to be more cultured than the local country folks. To the men, however, he was a social outcast and an object of ridicule. Crane's courtship of Katrina Van Tassel ended abruptly when his rival, Brom Bones, masquerading as a headless horseman, frightened Crane and drove him out of town.

Charles Dickens's teacher, Thomas Gradgrind, is a ruthless martinet. Pedantic and callous, he is a thoroughly unsympathetic character.

> "Girl number twenty," said Mr. Gradgrind, squarely pointing with his square forefinger, "I don't know that girl. Who is that girl?"
>
> "Sissy Jupe, sir," explained number twenty, blushing, standing up, and curtsying.
>
> "Sissy is not a name," said Mr. Gradgrind. "Don't call yourself Sissy. Call yourself Cecelia."
>
> "It's father as calls me Sissy, sir," returned the young girl in a trembling voice, and with another curtsy.
>
> "Then he has no business to do it," said Mr. Gradgrind. "Tell him he mustn't. Cecelia Jupe. Let me see. What is your father?"
>
> "He belongs to the horse-riding, if you please, sir . . . "
>
> "Very well, then. He is a veterinary surgeon, a farrier, and horse breaker. Give me your definition of a horse."
>
> (Sissy Jupe thrown into the greatest alarm by this demand.)

"Girl number twenty unable to define a horse!" said Mr. Gradgrind, for the general behoof of all the little pitchers. "Girl number twenty possessed of no facts, in reference to one of the commonest of animals! Some boy's definition of a horse. Bitzer, yours . . . "

"Quadruped. Graminivorous. Forty teeth, namely twenty-four grinders, four eye-teeth, and twelve incisive. Sheds coat in the spring; in marshy countries, sheds hoofs too. Hoofs hard, but requiring to be shod with iron. Age known by marks in mouth . . . "

"Now, girl twenty," said Mr. Gradgrind, "you know what a horse is."

She curtsied again, and would have blushed deeper, if she could have blushed deeper than she had blushed all this time. (Dickens, 1854, pp. 1–4)

Dickens's anger was directed not at classroom teachers but at the grim factory system of nineteenth-century England and the schools that prepared students to work in them. However, Gradgrind is an easy object of ridicule. Indifferent to children's need for approval, insensitive to their imaginative side, and behaving contrary to even the most rudimentary principles of psychology, Gradgrind is hardly a model of good teaching.

"UNMARRIAGEABLE WOMEN AND UNSALEABLE MEN"

To a certain extent, Crane and Gradgrind represent the popular nineteenth-century image of schoolteachers, particularly male teachers. One historian notes that when Brom Bones smashed a pumpkin on Crane's head, "he was passing the symbolic judgment of the American male community on the old-time schoolmaster" (Hofstadter, 1962, pp. 315–316). During the last century it was assumed that most of those who taught school would do so only for a short time. Women typically chose marriage and homemaking after a few years in the classroom. Ambitious men were expected to move from teaching to more lofty, better-paying occupations. Classroom teaching was seldom chosen as lifetime work by the more able, and the treatment of teachers reflected the anticipated short-term job commitment. Teaching was considered as employment for workers who were "passing through," en route to more serious pursuits (Holmes Group, 1986, p. 32).

Teaching was seen as a good short-term job, but it was disparaged as a career choice, and those who chose to stay in the classroom for more than a few years often suffered some social scorn. In 1932, Willard Waller observed that teachers were not treated like other categories of workers. In small towns, for example, he noted that unmarried teachers were expected to live in a teacherage—a special boardinghouse for schoolteachers—apart from single adults who held nonteaching jobs. In barbershops and other male-dominated establishments, the usual exchange of ribald conversation and off-color jokes would be suspended when a teacher entered. A male teacher was not accepted as one of the boys. Waller also noted the popular prejudice against teachers commonly held by the wealthier and better-educated members of the community. "Teaching," he wrote, "is quite generally regarded as a failure belt . . . the refuge of unmarriageable women and unsaleable men" (61).

The nature of the teaching workforce has changed. More women and men look at teaching not just as a job they pursue in their youth, but as a career. Unlike the two years of education held by the normal school graduates of the nineteenth century, those who work in public schools today must complete (in most states) five years of college education. Certification as a beginning teacher now requires a bachelor's degree with a strong general education component, specialized academic coursework, professional study, and practical experience in schools. Many teachers have master's degrees, and more than a few have doctorates.

Ironically, the structure of schools continues to reflect the impersonal employer paternalism of the nineteenth century. Teachers are still treated as though they had neither the skill nor the commitment to make important decisions about education. Teachers are usually told what to do. They rarely are asked to advise administrators on important issues about instruction, curriculum, or personnel, and most school decisions about programs or educational policy are made without teacher participation. Much to their frustration, teachers typically find themselves treated as though they were only slightly more competent than their students: they are considered unworthy to influence the day-to-day policies of the school and are intentionally divorced from the decision-making apparatus of the district.

Teachers learn after only a few years in the classroom that teachers teach and school administrators make decisions about teaching. If teachers want more authority in teaching they are forced to leave the classroom (Palonsky, 1986). Deferring to administrative authority might be less onerous for teachers if administrators had special abilities and talents. However, research indicates that many public school administrators have weak academic skills, poor training, and inadequate notions of the job. Too often, students in educational administration are not drawn from the ranks of the brightest, most capable teachers, but from those for whom the classroom has lost some of its meaning or challenge (Sarason, 1982, p. 142). To make matters worse, the National Commission on Excellence in Educational Administration estimates that of the over 500 institutions offering courses to prepare school administrators, fewer than 200 have the resources and commitment necessary to do the job well (1987, p. 23).

HURTING TEACHERS IN THE NAME OF REFORM

Problems in the structure of teachers' work have been exacerbated by past efforts to reform education. In many states, attempts to improve public education in the period of the mid-1970s to the mid-1980s came in the form of centralized accountability movements. These reform plans, typically stemming from legislative mandates, robbed local school districts of much of their control over the classroom and the curriculum (Carnegie Foundation, 1988). With only token input from teachers, officials of state departments of education determined what should be taught to all children and how student learning was to be assessed. Teachers were told what content was appropriate for their students. The state then administered exams—typically multiple-choice tests—to measure the extent to which student learning had taken place. Teachers in some states were also informed that they would be held accountable for deficiencies in student performance.*

The statewide reform initiatives of the last decade served to diminish the role of teachers in instructional decision-making. They disregarded teachers' skills as curriculum planners, and discounted their knowledge about the students in their classes. Designed to assure taxpayers that money for education was being spent responsibly and efficiently, statewide reforms deprofessionalized teachers by routinizing their jobs (Giroux and McLaren, 1986).

The teachers' loss of the curriculum has been accompanied by an erosion of their freedom to decide the methods of instruction. Textbooks, basal readers, and curriculum packages, typically prepared for a national market, now dictate classroom practice. Classroom instruction has come to be dominated by teacher-proof materials, curriculum kits, and basal readers with step-by-step instructions. These education packages often provide scripted dialogues for teachers and students and an assortment of achievement and diagnostic tests. Teachers are told what objectives their students should attain; they are told how to teach their students; and they are told how to measure the impact of their teaching. As a result, teachers have been taken out of their own teaching, and have been reduced to semiskilled, voiceless workers engaged in the mass production of education (Apple, 1982; Darling-Hammond, 1985).

Top-down administrative structures, state accountability programs, and teacher-proof curricula reflect a view of schooling as mass production of standardized parts rather than an academically nurturing environment for developing individually creative, thoughtful, well-informed students. It should be obvious that teaching is unlike manufacturing and that it does not conform to economic models of production. In teaching, planning cannot be divorced from execution; instructional methods and materials cannot be considered apart from the personalities and interests of students and teachers; and many significant learning outcomes cannot be measured in a multiple-choice format.

Past efforts to reform education did not consider the individual teacher. However, to be effective, teaching must account for the idiosyncracies of each teaching situation. Every teacher must have the authority to make essential curricular decisions about how to teach, how to pace instruction, and how to interact with students. Teachers must also be free to choose the content that is most appropriate for their students and the methods that will best encourage learning. As Linda Darling-Hammond writes, good teaching "requires knowledge of and insight into the minds of students, and relentless imagination in

---

* Some large school districts, including St. Louis, Missouri, have suggested that teachers' salaries should be linked directly to student performance on statewide achievement tests. Teachers claim that this is unreasonable because the tests may not measure accurately the learning that took place in their classrooms.

forging connections that will make understanding the possession of the learner, not just the teacher'' (1987, p. 354). Good teaching is more than the ability to follow instructions. Good teaching requires deep understanding of the ways in which children learn, a sophisticated knowledge of the subjects being taught, and command of a broad repertoire of instructional strategies (Holmes Group, 1986).

EMPOWERING TEACHERS TO REFORM SCHOOLS

Earlier school reforms failed because they did not invite teachers to assume greater authority in the schools. The next agenda for school reform depends on new roles for teachers, in which teachers have responsibilities to improve education as well as opportunities to do so. If schools are to be thoughtful places in which students learn to be informed, creative, productive citizens, the work of teachers needs to be reconsidered and restructured. If students are expected to engage in thoughtful, reasoned decision-making, they must see adults in the classroom whose working lives demand and reward such behavior. Defining teachers as mindless factotums of state education policy, publisher whim, or administrative caprice is self-defeating. It is a cynical assessment of teachers' abilities that offers teachers insufficient control over their work. Few talented people will choose to remain in work situations that fail to recognize their talents and intelligence, and few bright university students will select a career that promises to regard them as powerless employees.

Research evidence suggests that when teachers are given responsibility for school change, it is more likely that these changes will be positive and enduring (Roberts and Cawelti, 1984; Sarason, 1982). It is reasonable to predict that if schools are restructured so that teachers assume greater responsibility for essential school processes—from curriculum to staffing—the education afforded students will be improved. Common sense tells us that people work harder and feel better about their work when they have a personal investment in what they do and a sense of identification with the product of their efforts. Teachers are likely to work toward the improvement of education in direct proportion to their involvement in school processes and decisions. The empowerment of teachers and their assumption of control over teaching and curriculum cannot help but pay dividends in improved education.

POSITION 2
For Increasing Administrative Leadership

EXERCISING AUTHORITY FOR THE GOOD OF STUDENTS

To consider the restructuring of schools and the empowerment of teachers may be intellectually pleasing, but it ignores the demands placed on schools and the authority vested in administrative offices. The management of schools is not a struggle for power; it is the exercise of authority necessary to ensure the most appropriate conditions for learning.

In public education, "power" refers to the ability to produce or resist instructional outcomes. Teachers, for example, have the power to produce intellectual and attitudinal changes in students. Students have the power to resist teachers, to greet instruction with a defiance or an indifference that denies teachers the power to teach effectively. School boards and state departments of education have the power to deliver new programs of instruction, but teachers may disregard these initiatives by private noncompliance. Schools are not run by brute force, but through the authority of administrators to harness the various constituencies in the same direction and move them toward desired ends.

"Authority" in this context means the legally designated exercise of responsibility. In public education, the state has given administrators the authority to run schools and the legal responsibility to bring about effective instruction (Abbott and Caracheo, 1988). It is generally assumed that those given authority will use it properly to produce desired ends. If individual school administrators fail to provide quality education, they should be replaced. If, over time, administrative authority proves to be structurally unsound or unable to promote the conditions necessary for good teaching and student learning, then there should be a transfer in the authority to run schools. However, research suggests no need for change in the authority structure of schools. Administrative authority can be demonstrated to be effective in managing schools. The solution for school problems, now and in the future, is most likely to be realized through the leadership exercised by school principals and superintendents.

Schools are complex institutions that must seek to maximize student achievement. Good management principles demand that in large organizations one person or one small group of people have the authority to direct corporate outcomes. It is part of the culture of American life to view management as accountable for success and failure of the organization. Parents know that this is the pattern found in government and industry, and they expect the same rules to apply to education. In schools, authority and responsibility rest with the administration. When parents have questions about academic achievement, school policy, or curriculum, they call the administrators. Parents assume that some administrators will be in charge, and that those given authority to lead will receive extra compensation and recognition. Parents also assume that those entrusted with leadership will work harder than others in the organization, and that the leaders will suffer the consequences of organizational failure to the same degree that they enjoy the fruits of organizational success.

Good schools could not exist without good teachers, but excellent teachers alone are not sufficient to provide good education. In the same way that a winning baseball team is more than the sum of the athletic skills of the players, a good school is more than the total of the individual abilities of the teachers. The efforts of the baseball team and the school must be organized and directed so that the whole will be at least as good as the sum of its parts. Some person or group of people will always have to manage the operation of schooling, oversee its effectiveness, and chart its course. It is hard to manage and play simultaneously; these activities require complete concentration on separate sets of skills. Just as being a good baseball player does not automatically qualify one to be a good manager, good school leadership requires more than a history of having been a good teacher. Successfully leading children is not a sufficient credential to be the leader of adults. Good schools require specially trained, full-time nonplaying managers.

THREATENING LOCAL CONTROL THROUGH TEACHER POWER

In addition to managing the enterprise, public school administrators must guarantee the public that the schools are run for the best interests of the community. As Milton and Rose Friedman have pointed out, taxpayer support for public schooling in the United States was won on the promise that education would be controlled by the local community. Distrustful of the socialist philosophies that supported state control of education in Europe, American sentiment favored public schooling only if it was to be part of a decentralized education system. The federal Constitution was designed to limit the role of the central government in education, and the various states allowed the local community to control its schools. The schools were designed to be essentially democratic institutions, responsible to parents whose constant vigilance guaranteed the schools' service to community interests (1979, pp. 154–155).

Over time, power to run schools has shifted from the local communities to increasingly more centralized authorities. The city, county, state, and federal governments, combined with militant teachers, have helped strip local communities of most of their original authority to control the education of their children. Effective administrators must protect community control over important aspects of children's education, and must assure parents that the schools are still the servants of the community. Parents and other citizens rightly fear the encroachments of big government and organized labor. They have witnessed the diminution of their authority and the rise of unseen professionals and bureaucrats who control more and more aspects of their lives. Government has become at once more remote and more controlling. One of the last areas over which citizens typically feel a degree of control is the public school system, and it is their right to control their schools. The schools are in their neighborhood, and the schools belong to them. Superintendents and principals must assure the community that education has not become the province of professional educators. Teachers already have a great deal of power. Giving them more power could only come at the expense of parental control over education.

SACRIFICING INDIVIDUAL FREEDOM TO COLLECTIVE POWER

The current structure of education empowers teachers individually. Classroom teachers and school administrators know that a great deal of autonomy is given to each teacher. When teachers close the doors to their classrooms, they have a control over learning outcomes that is unmatched by anyone in the school system, including the superintendent and the board of education. Teachers can control what students learn by the ways in which they pace instruction, group students, and determine levels of difficulty and the criteria for assessment. Teaching is now a very loosely supervised profession, but any change in school structure is likely to cost teachers their freedom as individuals.

Classroom autonomy is one of the key defining characteristics of the teacher's job, and one of the most closely protected. Teachers like the power to teach and control instruction. Much to the frustration of administrators, attempts to break up this autonomy, by introducing team teaching or inserting intermediary levels of supervision, for example, have been met with resistance from teachers. For many teachers, the freedom to teach is among the most attractive aspects of the job. In the past, teachers have purchased this power over their classrooms by relinquishing influence at the school or district level (Corwin and Borman, 1988, p. 217). The current demands for restructuring schools require collective power for teachers to influence schools. Not only do such ideas run counter to the history of schools, they also threaten teacher power in the classroom. If teachers became managers, they would have to relinquish the individual control they now enjoy over their own classrooms.

Cries for restructuring of schools are insensitive to teachers' freedom, and ignore the contributions to schooling made by educational administrators. Educational administration is the art and science of applying specialized academic knowledge to the solution of school problems. It requires the sensitive manipulation of complex variables, including class size, instructional time, physical facilities, the curriculum, and the professional staff (Hoy and Miskel, 1978, p. 27). At its base, school administration requires the experience of a teacher, or at least a deep appreciation of the teacher's art, but in addition it demands an equally strong knowledge of human behavior, management theory, school law, and organizational leadership. Administrators should understand teaching from a teacher's point of view but they must also be able to lead teachers and to bring knowledge from administrative theory and research to bear on schools and the problems of teaching and learning.

APPRECIATING THE LEADERSHIP OF ADMINISTRATORS

The public believes that effective administrators can change schools, and research evidence continues to document the successes of effective school leaders in improving the education of children (Immegart, 1988; Leithwood and Montgomery, 1982; Manassee, 1985). The problem with schools is not that they are headed by principals, and it is not likely that schools would be improved by handing them over to the teachers. In the final analysis, it is the administrators who are responsible for the schools, and they who must exert the leadership and accept the consequences for the outcomes of schooling. Schools need effective leaders who can encourage learning, support and reward good teaching, make the schools satisfying places for students and teachers, and ensure that the community is served and the state's mandates are followed.

Although there is strong evidence to support the effectiveness of good principals, it may not be surprising that the reform potential of administrators has been overlooked and that the leadership aspect of principalship has often been ignored. For too long, the image of the public school administrator was that of the rigid disciplinarian who kept students in line with bluff and bluster, the retired coach who jollied up the board of education with sports talk and assurances that everything was operating smoothly. On the basis of models of management borrowed from industry, public school administration often has emphasized the control of teachers and students rather than educational leadership.

Faced with a set of difficult tasks and marginally prepared teachers, it is little wonder that schools in the nineteenth century were enamored of industrial models of control (Callahan, 1963; Tyack, 1974). Although these models now seem simple-minded or draconian and inappropriate for the achievement of intellectual and humane goals, there were few other models of organization from which school people could choose. Schools were organized from the top down. Teachers were to be managed "scientifically." Their jobs were laid out for them, defined for them, simplified and routinized. In the name of efficiency, teaching was reduced to a series of steps that were managed and monitored by school administrators.

These conceptions of educational administration were abandoned long ago. The image of the poorly prepared principal exists largely in memory. It is a straw man constructed by special interests who would like to seize control of the schools, and who fail to acknowledge the intellectual rigor of contemporary programs in educational administration. Educational management should continue to be vested in a few individuals in every school. The conflicting expectations exerted on schools by the state, the community, teachers, and students demand a specially trained group of managers. Without intelligent leadership from educational administrators, schools would be unlikely to meet any of the goals established for them. Without specially trained, carefully selected administrators to lead educational reform, change would become less likely and educational anarchy would loom as a reality. The future success of public education rests, as it should, in the hands of effective administrators.

FOR DISCUSSION

1 Consider the "1930s Rules for Teachers" listed below. Are any of these rules still appropriate for today's teachers? If you were given the authority to construct a new set of six rules to define the work of teachers, what would they be?

1930s Rules for Teachers

1 I promise to take a vital interest in all phases of Sunday-school work, donating my time, service and money without stint for the uplift of the community.

2 I promise to abstain from all dancing, immodest dressing, and other conduct unbecoming a teacher and a lady.

3 I promise not to go out with any young men except insofar as it may be necessary to stimulate Sunday-school work.

4 I promise not to fall in love, to become engaged, or secretly married. I promise not to encourage or tolerate the least familiarity on the part of my boy pupils.

5 I promise to sleep at least eight hours a night, to eat carefully, and to take every precaution to keep in the best of health and spirits in order that I may better be able to render efficient service to my pupils.

6 I promise to remember that I owe a duty to the townspeople who are paying my wages, that I owe respect to the school board and the superintendent that hired me, and that I shall consider myself at all times the willing servant to the school board and the townspeople and that I shall cooperate with the town, the pupils, and the school.

2 To improve the way in which teaching is organized, some proposals have called for a differentiated staffing model. In every school, there would be hierarchically arranged categories of teachers, each with separate levels of education, authority, and remuneration. Some teachers would supervise other teachers, write the curriculum, and perform much of the work now done by administrators. This staffing model might increase the competition among teachers as they scramble for the good jobs, much in the manner of corporate workers in the private sector. However, it is assumed that the most talented, best educated teachers would be able to earn greater salaries while exerting more direct influence in running the school.

Do you think this would be good for teachers and for the education of children? If this staffing proposal were adopted, would it make the job more or less attractive to you?

3 Which of the arguments for improving education presented in Chapter 11 is more convincing to you? Do you think that schools would likely become better places for students if teachers were given greater decision-making authority? Or is the greater opportunity for school improvement to be found under the current school structure?

4 The Gallup Organization conducts annual polls to gauge the public's attitudes toward the public schools and public school teachers. Consider the following questions and responses:*

* A. M. Gallup and S. M. Elam (1988). "The 20th Annual Gallup Poll of the Public's Attitude toward the Public Schools." *Phi Delta Kappan*, **70**, 33–46.

1 Would you like to have a child of yours take up teaching in the public schools as a career?

National Totals, in percentages

	1988	1983	1981	1980	1972	1969
Yes	58	45	46	48	67	75
No	31	33	43	40	22	15
Don't know	11	22	11	12	11	10

2 Do you think the public schools need to attract more capable students into the teaching profession, or not?

National Totals (1988), in percentages

Yes	89
No	7
Don't know	4

3 Do you favor or oppose an increased pay scale for those teachers who have proved themselves particularly capable?

National Totals (1988), in percentages

Yes	84
No	11
Don't know	5

What do these survey data tell you about the public's attitude toward schools and teachers? Do you think that, at this time, a survey of parents in your hometown or neighborhood would produce similar or dissimilar findings?

REFERENCES

Abbott, M. G., and Caracheo, F. (1988). "Power, Authority, and Bureaucracy." In *Handbook of Research on Educational Administration*, edited by N. J. Boyan. New York: Longman.

Apple, M. W. (1982). *Education and Power*. Boston: Routledge.

Callahan, R. (1962). *Education and the Cult of Efficiency*. Chicago: University of Chicago Press.

Carnegie Foundation for the Advancement of Teaching (1988). *Report Card*. Princeton: Carnegie Foundation.

Corwin, R. G., and Borman, K. M. (1988). "School as Workplace: Structural Constraints on Administration." In *Handbook of Research on Educational Administration*, edited by N. J. Boyan. New York: Longman.

Darling-Hammond, L. (1985). "Valuing Teachers: The Making of a Profession," *Teachers College Record*, **66**, 209–218.

Dickens, C. (1854). *Hard Times, A Novel.* New York: Harper.

Friedman, M., and Friedman, R. (1979). *Free to Choose.* New York: Harcourt Brace Jovanovich.

Giroux, H. A., and McLaren, P. (1986). "Teacher Education and the Politics of Engagement: The Case for Democratic Schooling." *Harvard Educational Review,* **56,** 213–238.

Hofstadter, R. (1962). *Anti-intellectualism in American Life.* New York: Random House.

The Holmes Group. (1986). *Tomorrow's Teachers: A Report of the Holmes Group.* East Lansing, Mich.: The Holmes Group.

Hoy, W. K., and Miskel, C. G. (1978). *Educational Administration: Theory, Research and Practice.* New York: Random House.

Immegart, G. L. (1988). "Leadership and Leadership Behavior." In *Handbook of Research on Educational Administration,* edited by N. J. Boyan. New York: Longman.

Leithwood, K. A., and Montgomery, D. J. (1982). "The Role of the Elementary School Principal in Program Improvement." *Review of Educational Research,* **52,** 309–339.

Manassee, A. L. (1985). "Improving Conditions for Principal Effectiveness: Policy Implications of Research." *Elementary School Journal,* **85,** 439–463.

National Commission on Excellence in Education (1983). *A Nation at Risk: The Imperative for Educational Reform.* Washington, D.C.: U.S. Government Printing Office.

Palonsky, S. B. (1986). *900 Shows a Year: A Look at Teaching from a Teacher's Side of the Desk.* New York: Random House.

Roberts, A. D., and Cawelti, G. (1984). *Redefining General Education in the American High School.* Alexandria, Va.: Association for Supervision and Curriculum Development.

Sarason, S. B. (1982). *The Culture of the School and the Problem of Change,* 2d ed. Boston: Allyn & Bacon.

Tyack, D. B. (1974). *The One Best System.* Cambridge: Harvard University Press.

Waller, W. (1932). *The Sociology of Teaching.* New York: Wiley.

CHAPTER 12

UNIVERSITY- OR FIELD-BASED TEACHER EDUCATION

POSITION 1
For University-Based Teacher Education

The preparation of teachers is among the university's oldest and most distinguished functions. Teacher education is an essential part of the curriculum, and the preparation of teachers should continue to be conducted through university programs. At present, it is academically fashionable to lament the shortcomings of teacher education and to suggest that the preparation of teachers should be wrested away from university control. There is every reason to resist this fashion. In the past, shortcomings have been identified in the education of attorneys, engineers, and physicians. The response was not to pull these programs out of the university, but to examine them and reinvest them with intellectual vigor. Similarly, teacher education programs may need to be reexamined and renewed, but taking these programs away from universities is academically indefensible and unmindful of the long association between universities and the preparation of teachers.

RECOGNIZING THE ART OF TEACHING

The earliest European universities offered degrees that were, to all intents and purposes, certificates to enter guilds and practice particular crafts, including the craft of teaching. The traditional curriculum was quite unlike current programs in teacher education. Pedagogy was not regarded as a legitimate area of study. Field experiences and student teaching were not considered necessary, and the behavioral and social science fields that inform teaching decisions today, such as psychology and sociology, were unknown. Instruction was in the liberal arts, a course of studies developed in the fourteenth and fifteenth centuries that was intended, as one writer notes, "to make men free from the dictates of passion and prejudice, [and] free from the natural limitations of an untutored mind" (Borrowman, 1965, p. 2).

The current array of liberal arts courses retains only a vague suggestion of Renaissance prestige, splendor, and exclusiveness. The subjects that once constituted the liberal arts now form only a minor part of the curriculum at most colleges, and the trivium (grammar, rhetoric, and logic) and quadrivium (arithmetic, geometry, music, and astronomy) have been joined by such newcomers as sociology, anthropology, political science, and economics. Despite changes in the liberal arts curriculum, it remains the core of general education courses common to all students independent of major, and it continues to be the body of knowledge society judges as the mark of a well-educated person.

Prospective teachers should receive an education that is similar in quality and content to the education given to the most talented undergraduates in colleges and universities. Future teachers should have an education that is well grounded in the humanities and the natural sciences, and they should have special knowledge of the behavioral and social sciences.

AN ACADEMIC APPROACH TO PEDAGOGY

Scholarship is an essential first step in the preparation of teachers, but scholarship alone is not sufficient to ensure good teaching. As difficult as it is to master content, public school teaching requires more than the command of complex literature. If all that were required for teaching were the understanding of one's subject matter, then any well-educated person could be an effective teacher. Common experience tells us that this is not true. Not all bright people in command of multitudes of facts and volumes of information are able to be effective in the classroom. Certainly, it takes more than intelligence and academic training to make content interesting, understandable, and enjoyable for students. Good teaching is far more than a smart person taking the knowledge of the university and teaching it to younger students at a lower level or a slower pace. A specialized course of study is needed to encourage well-educated students to develop the skills, knowledge, and practical experiences required of teachers. In addition to courses in content, teacher education programs must include university courses in pedagogy.

An effective teacher education program provides students with sophisticated knowledge about students and schools. Teachers need to know how students learn, how they think, how they respond to different learning strategies and disciplinary techniques. Prospective teachers, during their undergraduate years, should also have direct experiences with public school students to gather data about student behavior, and they need university courses to help them translate these data into teaching strategies and the selection of appropriate content (Shulman, 1987).

This combination of clinical experiences and university coursework is essential teacher knowledge. Classroom teaching is not a set of vocational techniques and how-to-do-it teaching strategies. Teachers must examine the ways in which students interact with the school and the subject matter, and must learn how to integrate these elements into effective curricula. Good teaching requires that teachers understand how students learn new information, how they give meaning to the material they encounter in schools, and how schools work to encourage some students and discourage others. Part of the art of teaching is knowing how to choose from among the variety of teaching strategies to engage students and with the academic content at hand. Good teachers help students do more than memorize and recite. Good teachers show students how to reason; to sort through competing ideas and arrive at sound conclusions; to speak and write effectively; and to decide what knowledge is most worthwhile. Effective teacher education programs require rigorous academic preparation, extensive field experiences in public schools, and directed academic reflection about the nature of the teaching enterprise.

EDUCATING TEACHERS FOR INTELLECTUAL LEADERSHIP

Surrounding the issue of teacher education is the larger question of what prospective teachers are expected to do. Should classroom teachers be trained as technicians who carry out the plans of others and keep children busy and quiet? Should they be prepared to accept commercially designed worksheets and step-by-step instruction manuals? Or, should teachers be trained to design instruction? Should they be prepared only to help students master content, or should they be able to help students select the most appropriate content to master? To put the question more directly, should teacher education programs produce teachers who are followers or teachers who can exercise decision-making authority in education?

Clearly, the university bias is for the latter conception of teacher education. Universities believe that to be effective in the classroom, teachers should be prepared not merely as technicians of instruction, but as the primary actors in public school settings, responsible for designing, implementing, and evaluating all aspects of the curriculum as well as for carrying out instruction. A teacher should know both *how* to do things in the classroom and *why* they are done. This conception of teaching requires that teachers have, in addition to a sound academic background, a command of instruction that enables them to make classroom and school decisions appropriate for students (Britzman, 1986; Giroux and McLaren, 1986; Schor, 1986). A university-based teacher preparation program is the best assurance that teachers will have an education that is sound both academically and pedagogically.

In addition to learning about the highly complex world of public education, teachers need university-based preparation to function as informed, constructive critics of schooling. Teachers should not be educated to regard teaching only as a job description with which they should comply. Each generation of teachers must be educated to ensure that schools evolve democratically, providing appropriate education to new populations of students. Teachers must be given the intellectual skills and the political power necessary to weigh and measure the practice of schooling against the potential of education. As social critics, prospective teachers should have the tools to analyze schools, to examine them at arm's length, to scrutinize their successes and failures, and to chart the course of their future direction. Education students should not be trained to "fit in" as teachers, but, in the best university tradition, should be encouraged to examine the current state of schools and ask hard questions: How well are schools serving society? How can schools be made better? How can schools deliver the best education to all social, ethnic, and racial groups?

ABANDONING THE CYNICAL EDUCATION OF TEACHERS

These are difficult questions. In the formative days of public education, it was cynically assumed that insufficient numbers of high-quality students would ever be attracted to public school teaching. Few people capable of critical thought and intellect were expected to find their way into public schools, and teacher training often reflected the view that most of those preparing to be teachers could not be entrusted with important instructional decisions. The marginal students who would find teaching attractive were not be treated to the academic and pedagogic education necessary for them to function as intellectuals. To accommodate the less able, the job of classroom teacher was simplified, routinized, and stripped of decision-making authority. Prospective teachers were prepared for a job that emphasized mechanics and classroom management strategies. Preparation for teaching was viewed as an apprenticeship program in which the student learned to accept direction and existing practice (Borrowman, 1965; Lortie, 1975).

Today, this view of teaching and teacher training, with teaching considered mainly as a technical occupation controlled by others, is regarded as self-defeating. It discourages bright, creative people from entering the field. Every careful observer of education recognizes that the best way to improve schooling is to encourage the most able students to become teachers. If universities trained teachers as leaders, as active intellectuals responsible for the education of children, teaching would become more attractive to the more able undergraduates.

This ambitious vision of teacher education calls for demanding academic programs. Not only must teachers be trained to assume existing classroom roles, they must also be encouraged to examine the schools and to consider the extent to which they should be changed. This conception of teacher education demands the perspective of universities and the academic freedom necessary to engage in free and open inquiry. Public schools cannot be expected to be their own critics, and they cannot be expected to train teachers who are critical. It is the responsibility of universities to provide schools with well-educated, reflective, and constructively critical teachers.

Learning to be critical, mastering content, learning appropriate pedagogy, and practicing it with public school students will require extended education. It may be necessary for prospective teachers to spend five years (or more) of preparation before taking their first teaching job. While this suggestion draws shudders from those who know how difficult it has been to attract bright young people into teaching with the current four-year required curriculum, unless university-based teacher education programs become more rigorous academically, and until prospective teachers are given extensive training in pedagogy, teaching will continue to suffer.

The preparation of teachers is clearly the responsibility of institutions of higher education (Carnegie Forum on Education and the Economy, 1986; The Holmes Group, 1986; The National Commission on Excellence in Education, 1983). For too long, teaching has been regarded as a vocation, and teacher education too often has been considered to be an apprenticeship program in which students are left to learn on the job, divorced from university knowledge and support (Gordon, 1985). This approach to the preparation of teachers separates those who plan to teach from the academic life of universities and places them in virtual thralldom to the public schools. Instead of learning how to question and how to think, these apprentice teachers learn how to conform; rather than examining competing conceptions of truth, they are taught to accommodate to current practice. The results of such vocationalism have been destructive to teachers and teaching. It has produced too many poorly educated teachers who are unable to assume leadership in matters of public education, and it virtually guarantees that the school's past failures will be taught to new generations of teachers as prevailing orthodoxy.

POSITION 2
For Field-Based Teacher Education

A student in Missouri interviewed after completing third-grade student teaching:

> I really learned everything about teaching during student teaching. I got A's in all of my methods courses, but when I got out there I realized that I didn't know a thing [and] I was scared stiff about discipline! I had a great cooperating teacher. We got along great; I really loved her. If it wasn't for her, I wouldn't have learned anything about teaching. . . . I think if you want to learn to be a teacher you should have *seven* semesters of student teaching and *one* semester of courses. I'm sorry to say it, but I didn't learn that much in my education classes.

TRYING TO MIX THE VOCATIONAL WITH THE ACADEMIC

What's a nice vocational program like teacher education doing in a place like this? Teacher education does not belong in universities. Educating students liberally in the arts and sciences and preparing them to be public school teachers are distinct functions with dissimilar means and ends. The attempt to combine liberal education and professional training in a single undergraduate program has been unsuccessful for so long at so many institutions it is reasonable to conclude that something is wrong with the model. Colleges and universities should get out of the teacher preparation business.

Institutions of higher education are designed for intellectual activities; they are not equipped to provide students with the practical experiences and supervision necessary to become teachers. A college education can enable students to understand culture, history, science, mathematics, and technology, and it can help students develop an appreciation for the fine arts and humanities. Universities and colleges should be limited to doing what they do best: creating and transmitting liberal knowledge. Learning to become a teacher requires a practical program of study that cannot be found in a university.

The problem with university teacher education programs is that they do not work. Courses in pedagogy—education courses—have never measured up to the academic standards of other university courses, nor have they met the challenge of preparing teachers. Ask graduates of teacher education programs to name the courses they found to be the least rewarding intellectually, and then ask them where they learned how to be teachers. Don't be surprised when you hear education courses cited in answer to the first question, and rarely mentioned in response to the second. In a study of teacher education programs which included visits to sixty-three colleges and universities training teachers, James Koerner concluded that those who teach teachers constitute a "sincere, humanitarian, well-intentioned, hardworking, poorly informed, badly educated, and ineffectual group of men and women" (Koerner, 1963, p. 37).

WHY EDUCATION COURSES CAN'T WORK

Although the emphasis of education courses is on developing practical teaching skills (Zeichner and Tabachnick, 1984), practicing public school teachers report that they learned about teaching on the job through trial and error (Lanier and Little, 1986, p. 551). Student teachers typically report that although they have taken over one-third of their undergraduate course work in education courses, they feel unprepared to handle classroom disciplinary problems, present instruction, or evaluate student performance (Duke, 1984). Despite the best efforts of colleges and schools of education, the conclusion is inescapable: Students do not learn how to be teachers by listening to education professors talk about teaching.

The position taken here should not be interpreted as a condemnation of the content of education courses or an indictment of education professors. The professors typically are scholars and researchers in the field who understand teaching and have a lot to tell students. The content of education courses is important, but it is too often meaningless to students who find themselves listening to theories of teaching long before they have had much direct contact with children or experience in real classrooms. Teacher education programs may be presenting the right information to students at the wrong time and in the wrong setting.

Certainly, teachers should be drawn from the ranks of the best-educated university graduates. Prospective secondary school teachers should have an academic major in the field they plan to teach, and future elementary school teachers should complete a course of studies in one of the subjects emphasized in the elementary schools—language arts or mathematics, for example—and minor in one or more of the other subject areas taught in those schools, such as science, social studies, music, or art. Upon graduation, successful university graduates should apply to programs of teacher training conducted in public schools. Although this may sound like a proposal for a graduate program in teacher education or a master of arts program for liberal arts graduates, it is not. The essential difference is that, unlike those other programs, the post-baccalaureate teacher education suggested here is not university-based or even university-affiliated. It is a program of teacher education organized by state departments of education, conducted wholly in selected public schools, and staffed by public school personnel.

Education is a principal function of state governments, and the states bear a direct responsibility for ensuring that there is a steady supply of high quality teachers. Although in the past states have acted only to certify the teacher education programs of colleges and universities, there is nothing to prevent the states' assuming direct control of teacher preparation, and, as several states are now finding, there is a great deal to recommend it. Among the likely benefits of state-operated field-based teacher training is an increased congruence between the state's demand for teachers and the preparation of teachers. For example, it is irresponsible to prepare large numbers of teachers in low-demand fields, such as social studies, industrial arts, and physical education, while ignoring shortages in math and sciences. State-run programs would be better able to match the public school demand for teachers with a reasonable pool of qualified candidates. Students would not find that they had spent four or more years pursuing a career choice for which there was no demand, and public funds would not be squandered in preparing teachers who would not have the opportunity to teach.

Marketplace rationality is not the only advantage of state-run programs in teacher education. State direction assures schools that prospective teachers will have the training the state considers appropriate. It is inefficient for the state to design programs in education and not have direct control over the teachers who will implement them. You are no doubt aware that many colleges of education teach students to be critical of state-mandated programs in planning, discipline, instruction, and assessment. This is unwarranted arrogance on the part of universities, and a disservice to the schools and the people of the state. It is also, no doubt, confusing to prospective teachers, who may find that their university training has been sufficiently discontinuous with public school practice to render it virtually useless.

LEARNING TO TEACH BY TEACHING

The public schools are the most logical site for conducting teacher education programs. The best setting to acquire a complex skill is the place in which that skill is practiced by the most talented artisans. Learning to teach in a public school classroom, under the close supervision of specially selected teachers, would be far more appropriate than studying about teaching at universities. Teaching is a practical field that can only be mastered through experience. Certainly, a limited amount of academic training is appropriate before a prospective teacher has initial contact with children. A few courses in psychology or learning theory might be included in an undergraduate curriculum for preteaching candidates, but the many complex skills needed by teachers can only be developed through varied experiences in the field.

At the present time, universities diminish their ability to educate students by blending courses in the liberal arts with courses in pedagogy. A liberal education demands every semester of an undergraduate's time. There simply is no room in the curriculum for a sound liberal education and professional training. Students should be educated first by universities. Then they should spend a year in public schools learning how to be teachers. As now being done in one state, teacher candidates with liberal arts degrees are prepared for the classroom with as few as eighty hours of professional instruction. Carefully screened and tested for subject matter mastery, prospective teachers can quickly learn the pedagogy initially needed for the classroom. After twenty days of careful, professionally supervised classroom experience in a school district, candidates are ready to begin teaching, and can be placed in classrooms. During the next year, when the inevitable problems of beginning teachers present themselves, the beginning teacher is given an additional 120 hours of professional instruction, along with advice and supervision by experienced classroom teachers and administrators. The advice and supervision are provided when they are needed, and they come from real teachers and administrators who face similar problems in the same school (New Jersey, 1983).

RECOGNIZING THE ART OF TEACHING

Teaching is an art form that universities mistakenly teach as a science. It is a practical art that is unlikely to be learned through academic study. Like other art forms, the art of teaching is developed through repeated practice under the watchful eyes of experienced artists. It is as unlikely that one will become a good teacher by taking education courses as it is that one will become a good musician or painter by listening to others talk about music theory or art history (see Conant, 1963).

If education were a science, prospective teachers could be treated to a wealth of information that would allow them to predict and control with certainty the nature of teaching and the behavior of their students. If education were based on the findings of scientific research, there would be a compilation of lawlike statements that would be universally applicable to the public schools. Unfortunately, the history of education research has produced no science of education. There is little about teaching that can be applied to all students at all times.

Experienced teachers know that what works well with one group of students may not work with another, and that although one activity was effective one time, it may never again be even marginally effective. Like other art forms, teaching skills must be practiced, rehearsed, and tried out before a live audience. The performance should be critiqued, revised, and critiqued again. The development of a teaching style and a sound repertoire of disciplinary techniques requires practice before live audiences, a good director, and helpful critics.

It is deceitful to promise students that they can learn to become teachers through university coursework. Good teachers do not learn to control a class only by mastering theories of behavior modification or reading about school psychology. Teachers learn effective classroom techniques through trial and error with real students under the supervision of highly skilled practitioners. Good teaching requires the full attention and commitment of those who have already graduated from universities. It is not possible to become a good teacher on a part-time basis while attending to an academic education, not to mention the other diversions of undergraduate life. Teacher training should become a field-based enterprise for mature, post-baccalaureate students.

Given the past failings of university-based teacher education and the current demand for teachers, the certification of liberal arts graduates through state-run programs should become a model for the nation. It promises to provide high-quality university graduates with the practical, well-supervised programs they need to master the art of teaching, and it offers the potential for staffing the nation's classrooms with well-educated teachers who did not idle away half of their undergraduate years taking coursework in pedagogy.

FOR DISCUSSION

1 If you were given the opportunity to change the teacher education program in which you are enrolled, what changes would you make?

2 List ten of the most important things you believe a teacher should know or be able to do. For each item on your list, identify the most appropriate place in which to acquire that knowledege or skill. Does your list suggest a university-based program for teacher education, a field-based program, or some balance between the two?

3 What are the advantages and disadvantages to college students of a university-based teacher education program? A field-based program? If you had a choice of enrolling in either one, which would you pursue? Do you think the post-baccalaureate field-based program would have some appeal for university students who are not currently enrolled in a teacher education program? For liberal arts graduates not now in teaching?

4 In 1986, The Holmes Group Report, *Tomorrow's Teachers,* sent shock waves through college and university teacher education programs. Originally composed of deans and other representatives of major research universities, the Holmes Group urged changes in the way in which teachers were prepared and a general reform of the teaching profession. Consider the following excerpts from the Holmes Group Report.* Do you think that these recommendations would lead to better-prepared, more effective classroom teachers?

Teacher Education Curriculum

1 The curriculum for prospective career teachers does not permit a major in education during the baccalaureate years—instead, undergraduates [would] pursue more serious general/liberal study and a standard academic subject normally taught in schools.

2 The curriculum for prospective career teachers requires a master's degree in education and a successful year of well-supervised internship.

3 The curriculum for elementary career teachers would require study in multiple areas of concentration (each equivalent to a minor) in the subject fields for which teachers assume general teaching authority and responsibility.

4 The curriculum for secondary career teachers would include significant graduate study in their major teaching field and area concentrations in all other areas they would teach.

5 The curriculum for all prospective career teachers would include substantial knowledge and skill regarding appropriate policy and practice in teaching students with special needs—advanced graduate study would be required for career professional roles in special education.

REFERENCES

Borrowman, M. L., ed. (1965). *Teacher Education in America: A Documentary History.* New York: Teachers College Press.

Britzman, D. P. (1986). "Cultural Myths in the Making of a Teacher: Biography and Social Structure in Teacher Education." *Harvard Educational Review,* **56,** 442–456.

Carnegie Forum on Education and the Economy (1986). *A Nation Prepared: Teachers for the 21st Century.* Washington, D.C.: Carnegie Forum.

Conant, J. B. (1963). *The Education of American Teachers.* New York: McGraw-Hill.

Duke, D. L. (1984). *Teaching: The Imperiled Profession.* Albany: State University of New York.

Giroux, H. A., and McLaren, P. (1986). "Teacher Education and the Politics of Engagement: The Case for Democratic Schooling." *Harvard Educational Review,* **56,** 213–238.

Gordon, B. (1985). "Teaching Teachers: 'Nation at Risk' and the Issue of Knowledge in Teacher Education." *Urban Review,* **17,** 33–46.

The Holmes Group (1986). *Tomorrow's Teachers: A Report of the Holmes Group.* East Lansing, Mich.: The Holmes Group.

Koerner, J. D. (1963). *The Miseducation of American Teachers.* Boston: Houghton Mifflin.

* pp. 93–95.

Lanier, J. E., and Little, J. W. (1986). "Research on Teacher Education." In *Handbook of Research on Teaching,* 3d ed., edited by M. C. Wittrock. New York: Macmillan.

Lortie, D. (1975). *Schoolteacher.* Chicago: University of Chicago Press.

National Commission on Excellence in Education (1983). *A Nation at Risk: The Imperative for Educational Reform.* Washington, D.C.: U.S. Government Printing Office.

New Jersey State Department of Education (1983). *An Alternative Route to Teacher Selection and Professional Quality Assurance: An Analysis of Initial Certification.* Trenton: New Jersey Department of Education.

Schor, I. (1986). "Equity is Excellence: Transforming Teacher Education and the Learning Process." *Harvard Educational Review,* **56,** 406–425.

Shulman, L. S. (1987). "Knowledge and Teaching: Foundations of the New Reform." *Harvard Educational Review,* **57,** 1–22.

Zeichner, K. M., and Tabachnick, B. R. (1984). *The Development of Teacher Perspectives: Social Strategies and Institutional Control in the Socialization of Beginning Teachers.* Madison: University of Wisconsin Press.

CHAPTER 13

ACADEMIC FREEDOM OR TEACHER RESPONSIBILITY

POSITION 1
For Teacher Responsibility

Teachers are an important resource in society. They have the power to shape the ideas and behaviors of young people. They also serve as agents of the community to assure that the common culture is properly transmitted. The power and agency of teachers impose serious responsibilities on them. Teachers derive their authority from the traditional presumption that they serve in the place of the parent and as agents for the community. This requires them to be very concerned about parental rights and community sensibilities. Instruction which is disruptive or erosive of family and social values has no place in the schools, and should be grounds for teacher reprimand or dismissal. Academic freedom has sometimes been used as a defense for teachers who have been disruptive, but this is a smokescreen to hide subversive and irresponsible teaching. For responsible teachers there is a place for teacher freedom, but academic freedom and teacher freedom are different things. Academic freedom refers to the free search for truth, while teacher freedom refers to choices of materials and methods to use in instruction.

Two important considerations should be borne in mind in any discussion of academic and teacher freedom in the schools. First, academic freedom has been reserved properly and historically to provide limited protection to university-level scholars who are experts in their specialized fields, and is an inappropriate concept to apply to most teachers in schools below college level. Second, teacher freedom in a classroom is not unlimited or unrestrained; it is necessarily related to the tradition of teacher responsibilities.

There is no doubt that within the limits of their responsibility to society, parents, and students, teachers deserve respect and some freedom to determine how to teach. That is teacher freedom, and it can be separated from academic freedom, which is intended to protect the right of experts to present the results of their research. This separation does not denigrate teachers any more than it denigrates lawyers, doctors, and ministers, or other groups of professional people who have no claim to academic freedom in their work. The separation of teacher freedom from academic freedom is required to protect the concept of academic freedom and to maintain the credibility of free speech protections for all citizens.

The American constitutional protections of free speech for all citizens are more than sufficient for teachers; they need no special treatment. Under the Constitution any of us can say what we wish about the government, our employers, or the state of the world, provided we do not state anything which is libelous or imminently dangerous, or obscene. Obviously, we cannot say false things about someone without risking suit for libel, and we cannot do such things as holler "FIRE!" in a crowded theater or "BOMB!" in an airport without risking arrest. We must also accept the consequences for our other statements. It would be absurd for us to expect our employers to continue our jobs if we made public statements which reflected negatively on them. Can you imagine the president of IBM guaranteeing the job of a salesman who wrote customers a letter advocating the purchase of Apple computers, or complaining that his supervisor took two hours for lunch?

In a similar manner, public school teachers should not expect job guarantees when they make negative comments about the schools, the community, or the nation. They should also not expect job protection when they use propaganda in the classroom, or use inaccurate or provocative material to teach children. The public schools are public employers; public school teachers are public employees. Each board of education has a responsibility to provide children with information, skills, and a set of social values and a moral code that strengthen the society. That responsibility cannot be abrogated by teachers.

Further, school is compulsory for children. They are a captive audience, subject to the whims and eccentricities of the teacher. Students range in age from childhood to youth and they are not yet mature. They are much more impressionable than the typical adult and easy prey for a manipulative teacher. Yet, many teachers expect that their jobs will be secure no matter what they say or do in public or in classrooms. They may call this academic freedom, but it is license, not freedom.

ACADEMIC FREEDOM AS A FUNCTION OF ACADEMIC POSITION

Academic freedom is suited to scholars who recognize the academic responsibilities inherent in its exercise. Scholars who have developed expert knowledge in a subject field may conduct research which challenges accepted views in that field. In this way knowledge continues to be refined. Academic freedom provides that such scholars can publish or present their research without fear of losing their positions, but even they have academic freedom only in those areas where they have demonstrated expert-level knowledge. Academic freedom does not extend to everything they do or say. They have no greater freedom than any citizen in areas outside their own expertise. An English professor who joins an activist group blocking traffic in an environmental protest has no claim to academic freedom for these activities. He is not different from any citizen in that his speech is protected by the Constitution, but his faculty job should not be. There is a difference between academic freedom and license, and no academic freedom should exist for those who indoctrinate (Kirk, 1955; Buckley, 1951; Hook, 1953).

In specialized subject areas, where a scholar has demonstrated expertise, he or she may need academic freedom protection to publish or present the results of research which differs from prior research. Some few public school teachers may have developed this expert knowledge and may be conducting research, but that is not true for the vast majority. As philosopher Russell Kirk has eloquently argued, not all subjects are equally deserving of academic freedom:

> The scholar and teacher deserve their high freedom because they are professors of the true arts and sciences—that is, because their disciplines are the fields of knowledge in which there ought always to be controversy and exploration; and their special freedom of expression and speculation is their right only while they still argue and investigate. But if this body of learned men is trampled down by a multitude of technicians, adolescent-sitters. . . , and art-of camp-cookery teachers (whose skills however convenient to us, do not require a special freedom of mind for their conservation and growth) . . . then the whole order of scholars will sink into disrepute and discouragement. (1955, pp. 79, 80)

Unfortunately, for teachers and for scholars, the idea of academic freedom has been abused. Attempts by teacher unions and lawyers to save the jobs of teachers who are incompetent or who espouse antisocial propaganda have clouded the positive meaning of academic freedom. Academic freedom should not be used as a shield for incompetent, antisocial, or un-American teaching. Rather, the idea of teacher freedom related to teacher responsibilities is a much sounder approach to the protection of teachers and to the integrity of the society.

Law professor Stephen Goldstein, in a well-reasoned article on this topic, argues that academic freedom is unsuited to elementary and secondary schools because of the age and immaturity of the students, the teacher's position of authority, the necessarily more highly structured curriculum, and the dominant role of the school in imparting social values (1976). These factors, and others, cannot be dismissed easily. Elementary and secondary school teachers are different from university scholars in their training, their functions, their employment status, and their responsibilities. And the elementary and secondary schools have broad responsibilities to parents, the community, and the state that do not permit giving license to teachers to do what they wish.

RESPONSIBILITY AND POWER IN TEACHING

Teaching is one of the most influential positions in society. In terms of the values and ideas that are carried from generation to generation, teaching is next to parenting in its power. In some respects the teacher exerts more influence on the views and values of children than parents do. Parents have great control over what their children see, hear, and do during the earliest years, but after their children start school parents relinquish increasing amounts of that influence to teachers.

The society places its authority in the teachers for developing sound knowledge and values in children, and for that reason school is compulsory. The child, being weaned from parental influence, looks to teachers for guidance in knowledge and values. This is a heavy and important responsibility, one that needs serious consideration. Teachers bear duties to the parents, to the society, and to the child to provide a suitable education. They also have duties to the profession of teaching. It is that multiple responsibility that teachers and schools must recognize.

All rights and all freedoms are tied to responsibilities. Otherwise there is anarchy, where no social restraint exists. That is not freedom, it is a jungle without rules and without ethics. Civilization demands both freedom and responsibility. Teacher freedom must be tied to the responsibilities of teachers, and teacher rights and freedoms are conditioned on teacher acceptance of those responsibilities. Teacher freedom is supported and limited by the teacher's responsibility to parents, to society, to the child, and to the profession. Let us briefly consider each of these elements.

THE FAMILY IN SOCIETY

The family is the primary element in society. No civilized society can survive where the family unit is dissolved. Attempts to break up families and to take young children for social or communal control have consistently failed, no matter how utopian these programs sound. Prisons and mental institutions are filled with people who are the victims of family disorders. Among the great threats to contemporary American society is the decline of the family. High divorce rates, single or dual working parents with latchkey children, and increasing child abuse are symptoms of that decline. The strength of the society is determined by the strength of the family. This premise is fundamental to consideration of the responsibility of teachers to parents.

If we start with the idea that the good society is constructed from good families, we undersand that good schools are extensions of those families. This is quite a different concept from the all-too-common notion that society is either the faceless government or just a collection of separate individuals. Government, of course, is made up of members of families, and individuals and parts of families. The family is the cement of the society. If the cement is weak, or lacks the right ingredients, the building will collapse. Similarly, the building blocks, social institutions, need to be strong and formed properly. The good society provides social institutions which confirm and sustain the family, even when specific families fail to live up to their responsibilities.

PARENTAL RESPONSIBILITIES AND SOCIAL INSTITUTIONS

This leads to a consideration of the elements of the family, and of the need for social institutions which are responsive to families. Families come in all sizes and shapes. In all of them, however, there are parents and children. In addition to emotionally supportive requirements, parents have biological, moral, ethical, and legal obligations to their children.

Biological obligations include the provision of food, clothing, and shelter. The child's physical development requires these things. Where a particular family cannot provide the minimum biological requirements, a social institution takes over, but no thoughtful person believes that is a better arrangement. It is done to assure that all children, orphans or those in families suffering very hard times, have minimum human care.

Moral obligations of the parents to the child include instruction in determining right from wrong, good from bad. Morality is a set of basic values that guide us. Parents need to provide, by example and persuasion, the moral benchmarks for children to measure their lives. In those situations where parents do not or cannot convey proper moral judgment, social institutions step in to provide protection to the society. But no right-thinking person would argue that prisons and reformatories are the best places to give moral lessons. Families are much more suitable for this purpose.

Ethical obligations, drawing from morality, involve parents' teaching their children a set of socially acceptable behaviors toward other people. This code of conduct includes such behaviors as integrity, honesty, courtesy, and respect. For children from families where ethical standards are not taught well, social institutions have sanctions. These children will not be trusted in business, among peers, or in social discourse. This, again, is not what most people would desire for their children.

Parents have many legal obligations to their children. Laws are often written to coincide with long-term good practice in a society. Much of the law relating to parental responsibilities falls in this category. Parents are expected to take good care of children, and, under the law, parents are given great latitude in providing that care. Parents are presumed to have the child's interests at heart. Only in an unusual circumstance, and with great reluctance, do the courts decide to take a child from his or her parents to place him or her in a foster home or other institution. Parents are even permitted to exercise a level of corporal punishment on their children that is more than any other person would be permitted to inflict upon them, under the legal idea that parents have broad responsibilities. The root principle of parent laws is that parents are responsible for their children's upbringing, morality, and behaviors. Where parents fail, social institutions are brought to bear, but these are not considered the best arrangements.

SCHOOL AS A POSITIVE PARENT SURROGATE

In each of the examples of parental responsibilities noted above, the social institution which picked up the pieces for problem families was established to try to correct or mitigate the defect. Prisons, foster homes, mental institutions, orphanages, family welfare programs, reformatories, and court-mandated separations represent society's attempt to deal with a failure of family responsibility. These institutions try to do a good job of parental surrogacy, but they have great difficulty because they start with the results of a poor situation. Fortunately, these institutions only have to provide for a relatively small proportion of the society.

Schools, however, are a positive social institution. They are specifically intended to continue the development of children, extending the family influence to produce good citizens for the society and good members of future families. Children are not put in schools as punishment, or as a means for correcting family irresponsibility. The schools exist to supplement and expand the good family and the good society.

TEACHER RESPONSIBILITIES TO PARENTS

Thus, schools have a special obligation to be responsive to parents' concerns for their children. It is this reasoning which underlies the legal concept that teachers act in loco parentis. That concept has long social and legal roots, and protects teachers in their handling of student discipline and evaluation procedures. It also requires teachers to remain sensitive to parents' interests in what is taught and done to their children. Parental rights and responsibilities extend far beyond the time parents put their children into kindergarten; children remain parental obligations until adulthood. Parents do not usually take those obligations as merely technical requirements. They have strong emotional commitments to their children that transcend legal and social expectations. Parents want and expect the best possible for their children.

Teachers, standing in the place of parents, take on similar responsibilities for children's development and protection. Although teachers do not have the same biological responsibilities as parents, beyond the provision for a safe and healthy classroom environment, they do have moral, ethical, and legal responsibilities. They also have formal educational responsibilities derived from the parents' concern that their children be taught appropriate knowledge and skills to get along in the society. Teachers discharge these responsibilities well by being responsive to parental concerns about the kind of knowledge and values taught.

Teachers cannot have license to do anything they wish to students, physically or mentally. No one today would argue that teachers should be permitted to physically abuse children, but teachers are expected to exert limited forms of physical control over children to maintain an educational environment. For example, teachers can require students to remain seated, to change seats, to be quiet, to go to the principal's office, or to line up for activities. Teachers are properly prohibited from such abusive activity as striking students without provocation, or torturing students with electric cattle prods. Good teachers would never contemplate such malevolent behavior; it is outside the standards of professional conduct.

Mental abuse of students is equally to be abhorred, but less easy to detect. It leaves scars that are not as obvious as those from physical damage. But it is no less harmful, to the student, the parents, and the society. Mental abuse can consist of vicious verbal personal attacks, indoctrination of antisocial values or behaviors, or manipulation of children's minds against parents or morality. Parents have a right to insist that their children not be subjected to these tactics, but they are often unaware until after the damage has occurred. Good teachers would not contemplate such misuse of their influential role in the lives of children; it would be unprofessional as well as unethical.

Parents have a right to monitor what is taught to their children, to expect the school to be accountable for it, and to protest to authorities about any potential damage to their children.

TEACHER RESPONSIBILITIES TO THE SOCIETY

In addition to the significant interest that parents have in the education of their children, society as a whole has a significant interest in children's education. Society established schools to pass on the cultural heritage, to provide the skills, attitudes, and knowledge necessary for good citizenship, and to prepare children to meet their responsibilities in their families, work, and social activities. Schools are social institutions, financed and regulated to fulfill social purposes.

Society has standards of behavior, values, and attitudes that the school is responsible for conveying to children. These standards have evolved over a long period of time, and represent that society's common culture. The school, and the teachers, are engaged by the society to ensure that social standards, and the ideals that these standards express, are taught in example and in presentation.

Schools do not exist as entities separate from society, able to chart their own courses as though they had no social responsibilities. The schools were not intended to instruct students in antisocial, anti-American, or immoral ideas or behaviors, nor will society allow them to continue to do so.

Teachers are given a position of trust by the society to develop the young into positive, productive, and contributing citizens. Those few teachers who use their position to attempt to destroy social values or create social dissension are violating that trust. Those who sow the seeds of negativism or nihilism or cynicism are also violating that trust. The society has the right to restrict, condemn, or exclude from teaching those whose actions harm society's interests.

TEACHER RESPONSIBILITIES TO CHILDREN

The paramount responsibility of teachers is to their students, the children of parents and the future adult members of society. It is because students are immature and unformed that the influence of teachers must be recognized, and that teacher freedom must be controlled by teacher responsibility. Teachers hold great potential power over the lives of children, and the disparity in authority between teacher and students needs to weigh heavily in teacher decisions on what to teach and how.

In the forming and testing of ideas, attitudes, and behaviors the child looks to the teacher for direction. Children are naturally curious and positive, but they have not fully developed discernment between what is good and bad, proper and improper. Much of what the parents have not been able to teach during infancy and early childhood is entrusted to teachers for the formative period of twelve school years. Teachers have a responsibility to continue the moral and ethical education that comports with good parents and the good society. That is what character education is all about. In addition, teachers need to develop in students the habits of the mind which will help them gain knowledge and appreciation of the language, history, science, and art of their society.

TEACHER RESPONSIBILITIES TO THEIR PROFESSION

The profession of teaching has an extensive and illustrious history. It is based on the idea of service to children and to society. A teacher code of ethics stresses teacher responsibilities as singularly important. Teachers are known for their concern for preserving and conveying the cultural heritage to their students, along with their strong sense of social responsibility. Teachers can ask no less of themselves.

A basic responsibility of the teaching profession is to prepare young people for life in the society. That includes the teaching of social values and knowledge to students, and a level of personal conduct on the part of teachers that exemplifies the ideals of the society. The teaching profession recognizes both the needs of the child and the needs of the society. Teachers have an obligation to their profession not to go beyond its bounds, and to exclude those who would tarnish its reputation.

POSITION 2
For Academic Freedom

Academic freedom is the "liberty of thought" claimed by teachers and students, including the right to "enjoy the freedom to study, to inquire, to speak . . . , to communicate . . . ideas" (*Dictionary of the History of Ideas,* 1973, pp. 9, 10).

The need for strong support of academic freedom for schoolteachers and their students may seem obvious to anyone who supports a free society. One may wonder why this is considered a contemporary issue in education. Who could possibly be against academic freedom? What obstacles exist?

The unfortunate vulnerability of schools, teachers, and students to censorship, political restraint, and restrictions on freedom has a long and sordid history in the United States. Early American schools, under religious domination, imposed moralistic behavior on teachers, firing them for impiety or suspicion of not having sufficient religious zeal. In the nineteenth century, when there were increases in the number of public schools and when many teachers had very limited education themselves, communities required strict conformity to social norms, and teachers could be dismissed for dating, dancing, drinking, visting pool halls, or simply disagreeing with local officials. In the first half of the twentieth century, religious and moralistic restrictions on teachers were replaced by political restraint and censorship (Beale, 1936; Pierce, 1933; Gellerman, 1938). College teachers often fared no better, and suffered considerable indignities at the hands of college officials (Hofstadter and Metzger, 1955; Sinclair, 1922; Veblen, 1957). As the twentieth century draws to a close it is clear that teachers have gained much in professional preparation and stature, but they are not yet free. Certainly, teachers are more free now than when they were indentured servants in colonial times, but significant threats to academic freedom continue to limit education and to impose blinders on students.

The International Herald Tribune on September 17, 1986, carried a headline, "Textbook Censorship Grows in U.S.," and a story that documented this trend. The National Coalition Against Censorship, with affiliation by dozens of professional and scholarly national associations, was formed recently because of the increase in censorship in America. People for the American Way published *Attacks on the Freedom to Learn, 1985–6,* which showed that the number of cases had doubled from 1982 to 1986, and that a much larger proportion of attempts at censorship were successful in getting material removed.

A recent statement in support of academic freedom for pre-college-level teachers by the American Association of University Professors identifies a variety of political restraints imposed on such teachers (AAUP, 1986). *The Intellectual Freedom Newsletter,* a regular publication of The American Library Association, keeps track of the many cases of school and library censorship across the United States. There have always been large numbers of such cases in local communities, but since 1970 the frequency of reported censorship incidents has tripled, and estimates suggest that for each incident formally reported, about fifty censoring activities go unreported (Jenkinson, 1985). Academic freedom remains a significant problem for American teachers. Continuing vigilance is required because of the continuing threats to this freedom.

THE CENSORS AND THE CHILL ON EDUCATION

Topics that arouse the censors and those who want to control teachers vary over time. Socialism and communism dominated in the 1920s and again in the 1960s. They surfaced again in the early years of the Reagan administration. Sexual topics and profanity are constant subjects of the school censors. A more recent, and broader, issue is the charge that "secular humanism" is taught in schools, a charge that teachers and materials are anti-God, immoral, antifamily, and anti-American. Other current topics, sometimes associated with the "secular humanism" issue, that stimulate vocal groups who want to stifle academic freedom include drugs; evolution; values clarification; use of black, feminist, or other minority literature; economics; environmental issues; and social activism.

There is also the chilling effect that publicized censorship and restraint activities have on school boards, administrators, and even many teachers. The mere fear that there might be complaints if a teacher touches on a controversial topic leads to warnings and sinister implications. The chilling effect is apparent in informal statements by administrators directing teachers not to use certain materials, and in the teachers' grapevine, where older teachers suggest that younger teachers should exercise extreme caution on anything remotely controversial. As a result, there is an extraordinary amount of teacher self-censorship that denies to students and to society the full exploration of ideas. Many teachers avoid significant topics, or neutralize and sterilize them to the point of student boredom. Academic freedom for teachers and students is not self-evident in America.

ACADEMIC FREEDOM AND A FREE SOCIETY

Because there has been a general misunderstanding of the central role of schools in a free society, teachers and students have often lived a peripheral existence in America. Teaching has been viewed as "women's work," and its practitioners as not deserving of the public's trust to make wise decisions. States and communities impose restrictions on what can be taught and on the methods of teaching to be used. Teachers and teaching materials are censored by school boards and administrators for dealing with controversial topics. Students are virtually ignored, are treated as nonpersons, or are expected to exhibit blind obedience. These conditions raise questions about American society and the vitality of academic freedom. Academic freedom, the essence of the teaching profession, has been insufficiently developed in the society and in the education of teachers.

The question of academic freedom must be examined in the context of a society which prizes freedom and self-governance, even when those ideals are not always practiced in everyday life. Education serves the ideals of a society. The nature of the academy, at any level, is interlinked with the goals of the society. A restrictive or totalitarian society demands a restrictive or totalitarian education system. A society that professes freedom should demand no less than freedom for its schools.

The defining quality of academic freedom is freedom in the search for truth. This freedom should not be limited to a small elite corps of "experts," but should include students and teachers engaged in the quest for knowledge. The search for knowledge is not limited to the experts, including teachers, but is the purpose for schooling. There is also the risk that when experts control knowledge they will require conformity and not allow challenges or conflicting opinions. We may not like challenges to ideas we find comfortable, but those challenges are the stuff of progress. Without challenges to comfortable super-stitions we would not have had scientific achievements leading to medical and technical progress. Without challenges to the idea of royalty in dictatorial governments we would not have had the idea of democracy.

THE ESSENTIAL RELATIONSHIP OF ACADEMIC FREEDOM TO DEMOCRACY

The one inescapable premise for democracy is that people are capable of governing themselves. That premise assumes that people can make knowledgeable decisions and can select intelligently from among alternative proposals. Thus, education and the free exchange of ideas are necessary conditions for self-governance. To think otherwise is to debase the essence of democracy.

The continuing development of American democracy requires that academic freedom be further extended for schools, students, and teachers. As John Dewey noted over fifty years ago, "Since freedom of mind and freedom of expression are the root of all freedom, to deny freedom in education is a crime against democracy" (1936).

The U.S. Supreme Court demonstrated its commitment to the principle of academic freedom in a 1967 decision finding a state law that mandated a loyalty oath for teachers to be unconstitutional. The Court noted that academic freedom is a "transcendent value" in a statement that concluded:

> Our nation is deeply committed to safeguarding academic freedom which is of tran-scendent value to all of us and not merely to the teachers concerned. That freedom is, therefore, a special concern of the First Amendment, which does not tolerate laws that cast a pall of orthodoxy over the classroom. . . . The classroom is peculiarly the "marketplace of ideas."

The democratic basis of academic freedom is part of its transcendent value. Democracy is overwhelmingly agreed to be the most suitable way to govern American society, and increasing numbers of countries and peoples throughout the world are embracing democracy as an ideal, but the definition of a demo-cratic society is still evolving. Self-governance developed as a set of contrary ideas, actually at odds with the then-prevailing concepts of government, and flowered as a compelling vision of a better social existence for the majority of people.

Similarly, academic freedom has evolved and expanded from a narrow and limited definition to embrace the general framework within which schooling takes place, and the work of teachers engaged in that process. Differences in state laws, and confusing court opinions, have produced a mixed view of what specific actions are legally protected under academic freedom (O'Neil, 1981). There has, however, been an expanding awareness by courts of the need for academic freedom in schools.

Nothing is static. Change is constant in society and in education. Ideas about society and schools arise, are tested, and are expanded and improved or dropped. Democracy and academic freedom are evolving concepts. Outside of basic principles, such as self-governance for democracy and enlightenment for ac-ademic freedom, the practical definitions of these terms are subject to contin-uing development.

Propaganda and public deceit certainly are practiced in all countries, in-cluding democracies, but citizens of a democracy are expected to have the right and the ability to question and examine governmental actions in a manner than can expose those deceits, and then to act upon that knowledge.

Dictatorial regimes do not need, and certainly do not desire, the majority of the population to have an education that provides them the basis for judging from among alternatives and questioning information presented. Totalitarian states maintain their existence by raw power and threat, by censorship and restriction, and by keeping the public ignorant. Democratic governments can attempt the same manuevers, but they run the risk of exposure and replacement. The more totalitarian the government, the more threat, censorship, and denial of freedom in education are exhibited. The more democratic the society, the less threat, censorship, and restricted education are needed. This litmus test of democracy is also a significant measure for academic freedom.

EDUCATIONAL GROUNDS FOR ACADEMIC FREEDOM

Where, if not in schools, will new generations be able to explore and test divergent ideas, new concepts, challenges to superstition and propaganda? Students need to be able to pursue intriguing possibilities, without serious risk of social condemnation or ostracism. For this they need the guidance of free and knowledgeable teachers, and a setting where critical thinking is prized and nurtured. Such an academic environment is in the society's best interests for two fundamental reasons: (1) new ideas from new generations are the basis of social progress, and (2) students who are not permitted to expolore divergent ideas in school can be blinded to society's defects and imperfections, and can be unable to perform the significant critical task of citizens to improve their democracy.

There is no real threat to society in having students examine controversial matters in school. Most of us as young people entertained much more radical ideas in conversations with friends or in thinking about themes presented in films, TV, and other media. In an educational setting opposing ideas can be more fully considered, with opportunity for informed criticism of each view. The real threat to American society is that controversial material will not be examined adequately in schools, and that students will come to distrust schools and the larger society as places for free exchange of ideas. Teachers and students need academic freedom to fulfill their educational mission in a free society.

The primary purpose for education is enlightenment. Although teaching can be conducted easily as simple indoctrination, where the teacher presents material and students memorize it without thought or criticism, that is an incomplete and defective education. Teaching can also be chaotic, with no sense of organization or purpose. That, too, is an incomplete and defective education. Neither of these approaches to teaching leads to enlightenment. In an enlightening education students encounter and challenge increasingly sophisticated and complex ideas. Indoctrination stunts the educational process, shrinking the range of knowledge and constricting critical thinking. Chaotic schools confuse the educational process, mixing important and trivial ideas, and muddling thought. A sound education provides solid grounding in current ideas of knowledge, in challenges to those ideas, and in the process of critical thinking.

Education which provides ideas and challenges, and which stimulates increasingly sophisticated critical thinking, is necessarily controversial. Some of the challenges will not be popular, and critical thinking may raise questions about ideas which are taken for granted in the community. But fear of political reprisal for providing a sound education is an anomalous situation for a good teacher. Teachers need protection from political pressure from any source, whether it be the establishment in power, vocal special interests, or popular trends. Students also need protection from these forces, as well as from incompetent and indoctrinating teachers. Academic freedom for teachers and students is essential to education.

THE CENTER OF THE PROFESSION

Academic freedom is the heart of the profession of teaching. Professions are identified by the nature of their work, their educational requirements for admission, and their commonly held ethics and values. The medical profession is defined in terms of its work in the protection and improvement of health, the specialized education in medical practice, and the commitment to life. Attorneys work in the realm of law, have specialized training in the practice of law, and are dedicated to the value of justice. Teachers devote their efforts to education, have subject knowledge and specialized education in teaching practice, and share a dedication to enlightenment.

Earlier in America, when most teachers were not college-educated and when their main role was to provide minimal literary skills, there were severe limitations on their freedom in many places. Under increasingly rigorous teacher credentialing regulations, and improved professional study and practice, there are now no grounds for excessive restrictions on teacher work.

The nature of teachers' work and their shared dedication to enlightenment require a special freedom, one not required for other occupations, to explore new ideas in the quest for knowledge. This freedom deserves protection beyond that provided to all citizens under the constitutionally protected condition of free speech. Unlike other citizens, teachers have a professional obligation to search for truth and to assist students in that search. It is the practice of this profession, this obligation, which requires special protection from political or other interference. Teachers must not find their jobs at risk for exploring controversial material or considering ideas that are not in the mainstream.

ACADEMIC FREEDOM AND TEACHER COMPETENCY

The provision of academic freedom for teachers is not without limits or conditions. Not every person certified to teach, nor every action of each teacher, warrants the protection of academic freedom. The basic condition for academic freedom is teacher competence. Incompetent teachers should not have the extra protection of academic freedom.

Teacher competence is a mix of knowledge, skill, and judgment. It includes knowledge of the material being taught and of the students in class, professional skill in teaching, and considered professional judgment. It is more than just the accumulation of college credits in a subject and in professional study. It includes a practical demonstration that the teacher can teach in a manner that shows subject and student knowledge, teaching skill, and judgment. As in other professions, measurement of competence is by peers and supervisors, and continues to be refined. In teaching, initial competence is expected at the time of completion of the teaching credential program. That program includes subject and professional study, and practice teaching under supervision. Under the laws of various states, teachers serve several years under school supervision and are granted tenure if they are successful. This long test of actual teaching should be sufficient to establish competence. Incompetent teachers should not get tenure.

TENURE AND ACADEMIC FREEDOM

The main legal protection for academic freedom in schools is the state laws on tenure. Under teacher tenure laws, teachers cannot be fired without cause. A tenured teacher who is threatened with firing must be provided with such due process conditions as a fair hearing and specific allegations of the cause for firing that can be addressed in a court. This is to protect tenured teachers from improper dismissal as a result of personality conflicts or politics. The causes for dismissal are identified in the state law, and often include moral turpitude, professional misconduct, and incompetence. The cause must be clearly demonstrated and documented in order for the dismissal to be upheld. This is reasonable treatment. It should be difficult to dismiss a tenured teacher who has demonstrated competence over a period of years.

Nontenured probationary teachers also deserve the protection of academic freedom because they also are expected to engage in enlightening education. Teachers without tenure, however, do not have the same legal claims as tenured teachers. Tenured teachers serve on "indefinite" contracts, which are not required to be renewed formally each year. Dismissal, or nonrenewal of the one-year contract, of probationary teachers can occur at the end of any given school term, often without any requirement that the cause for dismissal be stated by the school district. That leaves the nontenured teacher very vulnerable. Certainly, if the probationary teacher is not competent as a teacher, dismissal is appropriate. Dismissal for dealing with controversial topics in a competent manner, however, should be prohibited.

There are democratic, educational, and professional grounds for expanding the protection of academic freedom for competent teachers and for students, and there are important social reasons for increasing public support for academic freedom in public education. Tenure laws are important but insufficient. Academic freedom is more than a set of legal statements and court decisions. It should be a fundamental expectation for schools in a free society.

FOR DISCUSSION

1 Should there be any limits to what a teacher can deal with in class? What set of principles should govern the establishment of those limits? Should students be given the same freedoms and limits?

2 The definition of academic freedom may be hazy. Are the definitions of other major social ideas (justice, equality, democracy, authority, power) clearer and more precise? How is a definition of academic freedom related to definitions of these other terms?

3 Which, if any, of the following contents of books should be banned from schools as justified censorship:

Sexism	Explicit sexual material
Racism	Anti-American views
Fascism	Antireligious material
Violence	Inhuman treatment of people
Socialism	Animal, child, or spouse abuse

What are the grounds for justifying censorship of any of the above?

4 The 1987–8 report on censorship of People for the American Way indicated that there was an "energized movement of extremists pressuring public schools on a broad range of fronts."* The report identified 157 incidents of that kind of pressure.

Of the 157 incidents, in forty-two states, reported for the year:

Fifty were in the South.
Forty-six were in the Midwest.
Forty-two were in the West.
Nineteen were in the Northeast.

The most popular topics were:

"Satanism." Most in the West
Sex education. Most in South
Creationism. Most in Midwest

The most frequent target was John Steinbeck's *Of Mice and Men*.

The other most challenged authors were:

Judy Blume
Stephen King
J. D. Salinger

Other challenged books included:

All Quiet on the Western Front
Where the Wild Things Are

There were also challenges to:

Celebration of Halloween
Meeting of Teens for Christ

The focus of attack shifted from secular humanism and globalism to offensive language and satanism and the occult.

Is there a pattern in this one-year survey? What are the likely consequences of such efforts to censor schools? What role do teachers have in knowing about and responding to efforts at censorship? Should the censors be censored?

REFERENCES

American Association of University Professors (AAUP) (1986). *Liberty and Learning in the Schools*. Washington, D.C.: AAUP.
Beale, H. (1936). *Are American Teachers Free?* New York: Scribners.
Buckley, W. F. (1951). *God and Man at Yale*. Chicago: Regnery.
Dewey, J. (1936). "The Social Significance of Academic Freedom," *The Social Frontier*, **2,** 136.

* *Source: Attacks on the Freedom to Learn, 1987–88*. Sixth annual survey. Washington, D.C.: People for the American Way.

Dictionary of the History of Ideas (1973). New York: Scribners.

Gellerman, W. (1938). *The American Legion as Educator*. New York: Teachers College Press.

Goldstein, S. (1976). "The Asserted Right of Teachers to Determine What They Teach," *University of Pennsylvania Law Review*. **124**, 1, 293.

Hofstadter, R., and Metzger, W. (1955). *The Development of Academic Freedom in the United States*. New York: Columbia University Press.

Hook, S. (1953). *Heresy, Yes—Conspiracy, No*. New York: John Day.

Jenkinson, E. B. (1985). "Protecting Holden Caulfield and His Friends from the Censors," *English Journal*, **74**, 26–33.

Keyishian v. Board of Regents (1967). 385 U.S. 589.

Kirk, R. (1955). *Academic Freedom*. Chicago: Regnery.

O'Neil, Robert M. (1981). *Classrooms in the Crossfire*. Bloomington, Ind.: Indiana University Press.

Pierce, B. (1933). *Citizens' Organizations and the Civic Training of Youth*. New York: Scribners.

Sinclair, U. (1922). *The Goose-Step*. Pasadena: Private printing.

——— (1923). *The Goslings*. Pasadena: Private printing.

Veblen, T. (1957). *The Higher Learning in America: Memorandum on the Conduct of Universities by Businessmen*. New York: Sagamore Press.

14

CHAPTER

TEACHER UNIONS OR
SCHOOL MANAGEMENT

POSITION 1
Against Teacher Unions

The unions tie my hands. [Because of a negotiated labor contract] I can't hold more than one faculty meeting a month, and even then, it can't last more than an hour. If one of my teachers wants to help a kid after school or chaperon a dance or a ball game, he's got to get paid for it. If there's no money in the budget, the union won't let him do it, even if he wants to donate his time. . . . That's why I say unions are unprofessional. (Interview with a New York high school principal)

SELF-SERVING CLAIMS UNSUPPORTED BY RESEARCH

Officials of teachers' unions argue that when public monies are spent to improve working conditions for teachers, children are the ultimate beneficiaries. Their arguments are, no doubt, familiar: Public school students suffer because teachers are underpaid. The hard work of good teachers deserves greater compensation. Unless teachers are given higher salaries, not only will the current crop of teachers be discouraged, but the brightest college graduates will not go into education, and children will be taught by the less able. Similarly, union leaders argue, teachers should be given salary increases based on the number of hours of graduate credit they have taken and their years of seniority as teachers. Teachers, it is claimed, will not pursue advanced degrees without a financial reward, and students will not reap the benefits available only from better-educated teachers.

The logic of labor in these examples is simple: What is good for teachers is good for children. If the public wants better education for its children, the work of teachers' unions to improve education through increased remuneration for teachers should be supported, and collective bargaining practices, picket lines, and work stoppages (strikes!) should be considered ultimately beneficial to society.

Convincing? Not really. The public interest is not served by making schools good places for teachers. Schools are for children. The public's interest in education is not measured in teachers' job satisfaction but in the quality of learning provided to students. The implied causal link between increased teacher salaries and improved education has not been demonstrated by research. No experimental evidence exists to support the claim that giving teachers more money pays off in better schooling for students, or that teachers with master's degrees are more effective in the classroom than teachers with less academic training.

Despite the rhetoric, it has not yet been demonstrated that teachers' unions have a positive payoff for students. Research finds negligible differences in achievement between students in union and nonunion schools (Eberts and Stone, 1984). In fact, it is not at all possible to evaluate the impact unions have had on any specific school or on any single group of teachers or students. For example, it cannot be known with any certainty how a group of unionized teachers would have fared over time if they had not joined a union. Perhaps they would have done better in salary negotiations and in their treatment by the board of education, perhaps not. There is no way to know. At best, gains by a group of teachers can only be compared with average gains made by their colleagues across the state or nation. Similarly, the impact of compensation on teacher performance has produced no clear research findings (Johnson, 1988; Stern, 1986). The public has been forced to accept higher salaries for teachers as an article of faith, an emotional appeal from unions which cannot be supported by scientific findings, and which occasionally defies common sense. It is not likely, for example, that good teachers would become poor teachers without financial incentives, and it is fatuous to assume that financial rewards can improve the teaching skills of weak teachers.

MOVING FROM BREAD-AND-BUTTER TO POLICY ISSUES

Despite the absence of hard data, unions claim that they have improved teachers' salaries. They argue that the union-wage effect is actually in the neighborhood of 5 percent to 10 percent, not enough to make teachers wealthy, they admit, but enough to keep paying their union dues and more than enough to encourage unions to extend their influence in education beyond bread-and-butter issues* (Kerchner, 1986). Both the NEA and the AFT now want to

---

* "Bread-and-butter issues" typically refer to wages, hours, working conditions, fringe benefits, grievance procedures, organization rights, impasse resolutions, and such specific items as extra pay for extra duty. Policy issues include curriculum, personnel, class size, disciplinary procedures, textbook selection procedures, in-service training, and teacher transfer policies, among others.

participate in policy decisions. Under the familiar guise that collective negotiations will result in better education for children, union leaders argue for increased teacher participation in the decision-making and managerial aspects of schools. No matter how it is packaged, this would be destructive of community control of education.

In most communities, school board members are elected officials, voted into office on the basis of their personal qualifications and educational platforms. They typically work long hours, without pay, to ensure that appropriate education is delivered to the children of their friends and neighbors. The school board appoints the superintendent of schools to design local educational policies. On the recommendation of the superintendent, building principals are hired, a curriculum is developed, and teachers are recruited to implement the board's educational plan. School boards, as public employers, are given decision-making authority as a public trust, and this trust cannot be shared with those who are not directly responsible to the electorate. If the board fails to deliver the education it has promised, its members can be voted out of office, and the superintendent can be replaced.

The unions were not hired, and they may not represent the best teachers. They should not expect that using collective bargaining tactics will enable them to substitute their views of education for the judgment of the community. The unions are not suited to be district or school leaders, nor should they be given leadership authority. Over the years, teacher unions have become stronger, and teachers have increased their political power. While teachers were winning, parents and the community were losing (Baird, 1984; Friedman and Friedman, 1979). If unions were allowed to bargain collectively about issues of policy, schools would become less responsive to the community and more an agency of the unions.

Unfortunately, representatives of the NEA and the AFT have been trained to regard local communities with disdain and to treat school boards as the enemy. In their pursuit of hegemony over the schools, unions have been willing to ignore the interests of the community, and unionized teachers have been forced to disregard the needs, the aspirations, and the future of the children they teach (Braun, 1972). Educational policy should not be a matter of union concern. Policy issues, such as the selection of reading programs or school discipline procedures, should not be subject to collective negotiations. The district, through its elected board and board-appointed administrators, is held legally accountable to the public for the quality of education it provides. The unions have no such responsibility and they should defer to those who do.

APOLOGIZING FOR BAD TEACHERS

In many instances, unions have caused more problems than they have solved. Unions have become apologists for schools and an obstacle to school reform. They fail to admit that weak teachers may be a cause of many of the schools' shortcomings. Everyone familiar with public schools knows that the quality of classroom instruction varies widely. Nestled among the good teachers, the great teachers, and the marginally adequate are those who fail to convey enthusiasm for learning and, unfortunately, more than a few who have neither the skill nor the knowledge necessary to teach children. While the good teachers can whet students' appetites for academic achievement, bad teachers kill interest, leave students with enormous gaps of information, and tarnish the reputation of the profession.

Trade unionists in education are hard put to account for the numbers of poor teachers in their ranks. Typically, they place the blame either on weak university programs in teacher education or on public school administrators. The sad fact remains that too many schools have teachers who are not able to do the work expected of them. Unfortunately, because of unions and tenure laws, even the poorest teachers will probably stay on the job until retirement. The unions protect their members independent of the quality of their teaching.

Stories of barely literate teachers and teachers who tyrannize students force parents to recoil in horror. Although these accounts represent a tiny fraction of the nation's teachers, they are shocking not only in their perversity but in the union's behavior in defense of poor and, occasionally, dangerous teachers. For example, one case involved a teacher in New York City who was known to be mentally unstable. Responsible administrators sought to have him removed from the classroom and treated. However, because of union rules, he was not dismissed even after he physically attacked students. He eventually lost his job as a result of criminal proceedings that arose after he had fatally thrown a fellow subway passenger onto the tracks. In another case, a Chicago teacher was known to punish bright students because they made his work more difficult. His supervisors were alerted to the problem, but he was not fired. Under union rules, the teacher was allowed to transfer to another school (Freedman, 1987, p. 1).

The public believes that schools are designed to treat each child individually and to make judgments about those who should be rewarded and those who should fail. The public suspects that schools would benefit if similar judgments were made about teachers. Unions insist that all teachers should be treated the same. They resist merit pay for excellent teachers because it would promote dissension in the ranks, and they rush to the defense of any teacher whose job is threatened.

RESISTING CHANGE

Left to their own devices, it is unlikely that unions will rid the profession of bad teachers. The job of the union is not to improve the teaching profession but to protect teachers. Given this goal, the unions can hardly refuse to fight dismissals, even when the teacher involved is obviously incompetent. As a result, it is nearly impossible to fire a tenured teacher. It is estimated that a district would have to spend between $10,000 and $50,000 in legal fees to get rid of its worst teacher, a price few districts can afford (Lieberman, 1985, p.

343). Union opposition to culling incompetents from the classroom has forced school districts to decide whether to spend money on new books and programs or on litigation.

Unions and teaching do not fit together gracefully. Unions are more appropriate for industries, such as auto or steel production, where all workers perform similar tasks under much the same circumstances. The net effect of poor work or lazy workers is more destructive in teaching than it would be in factory work. One bad steelworker could make the job of coworkers more difficult, but he or she is unlikely to hurt the steel industry. A bad third-grade teacher almost certainly impedes the educational development of children.

Unions are educational anachronisms. They may have been necessary at one time, in the early days of public schooling, but they have become obstructionists, destructive of good education. Teachers should be treated individually, not collectively. Good teachers should be recognized for their professional competence and rewarded financially according to the level of their performance. Teachers and schools would be served better if unions got out of education. Teachers and administrators would be able to work cooperatively toward the solution of school problems and the design of better education. Good teachers could be rewarded. Weak teachers could be helped or weeded out, and labor negotiations would not consume the energies of teachers and administrators.

POSITION 2
For Teacher Unions

My principal says joining a union is the most unprofessional thing he can think of. I can think of things that are more unprofessional. How about low salaries, extra work for no extra pay, and no say in how this place is run? . . . When administrators call something "unprofessional," it means either that it will cost them money or it's a threat to their authority. (Interview with a high school teacher from New Jersey)

FORCING TEACHERS TO JOIN UNIONS

In the early part of this century, teachers were trained to believe that sacrifice was the essence of their profession. Over time, teachers came to realize that what they were being asked to give up in the name of professionalism was not good for them or their students, and that through collective action schools could be made better for everyone. In the early 1900s, teachers worked long hours; their classes often numbered fifty or more students; salaries were low, and schools were at times poorly heated, poorly ventilated, and unsanitary. Female teachers were not allowed to go out unescorted (except to attend church) or frequent places where liquor was served; and in many communities, when female teachers married, they were forced to resign from their jobs. In addition to living truncated social lives, teachers were assumed to serve at the whim of school boards without any promise of tenure, health, or retirement benefits. They did not participate in textbook selection, and were excluded from deliberations about the curriculum.

As school systems developed into large bureaucratic organizations, conditions worsened for teachers. School principals became administrators. Once principal or main teacher, the head of the school became a manager who shared few of the problems of teachers and none of their perspective. Most of the new school administrators were male; most of the classroom teachers were female. Reflecting the sexism of the nineteenth century, it was easy for administrators to regard teachers as inferior workers who needed be told what to do. The authority to run schools was vested in the men in the administrative offices, and their authority was assumed to be unchallengeable by the teachers.

Teachers were never eager to join unions; they were forced to because the culture of administrative managers was at odds with the culture of working teachers (Jessup, 1978; Urban, 1982). Teachers turned toward unions and collective bargaining to improve their working conditions and to gain a voice in the improvement of education. The following letter, typical of the calls for teachers to organize, was issued in 1913:

> On the ground that teachers do the every-day work of teaching and understand the conditions necessary for better teaching, we propose the following principles for the new organizations: Teachers should have a voice and a vote in determination of educational policies. The granting of legislative opportunity to the teachers would inevitably contribute to the development of a strong professioinal spirit, and the intelligent use of their experience in the interest of the public. We advocate the adoption of a plan that will permit all teachers to have a share in the administration of the affairs of their own school. In no more practical way could teachers prepare themselves for training children for citizenship in democracy. ("A Call to Organize," *American Teacher,* December 1912, p. 140, quoted in Eaton, 1975, pp. 13–14)

The decision to join the labor movement no doubt came hard to many teachers. Teachers typically tend to be politically conservative, first-generation college graduates who identify with management more than with labor (Aronowitz, 1973; Rosenthal, 1969; Zeigler, 1966). The fact that the union movement has succeeded in recruiting teachers speaks well for unions; that most teachers now belong to some sort of union, despite a decline in union membership in other fields and continued middle-class antipathy toward unions, is evidence of teachers' faith in unions.

PROTECTING TEACHERS' RIGHTS

Unions have been good for classroom teachers. The research literature indicates a positive union effect on teachers' working conditions. As a result of collective bargaining, teachers' salaries have increased, and teachers have gained protection against unreasonable treatment by management. Unlike the pre-union days, teachers cannot be dismissed simply because the principal does not like them or because they worked against a school board member in a local election campaign. Unions have also been good for education. They have put the faculty squarely in the front ranks of the battle for better schools and better education for children. Unions have allowed faculty to speak collectively about matters of curriculum and school policy.

Of course, teachers' unions have always gotten some bad press. Some of it is traditional antilabor rhetoric, and some of it is simply misinformed. No doubt, you have heard that unions are to blame for bad teachers, and that unions have hurt education by serving as protectors of weak teachers who deserve to be fired. This is not the case. In fact, it is mystifying when unions are blamed for weak teachers. Before teachers are awarded tenure, they must graduate from state-approved teacher education programs, convince administrators to hire them, and survive an extended probationary period, which typically varies from three to five years. Unions play virtually no part in any of these processes. Weak teachers may make it through the system, but they do so with no help from organized labor. Teachers' unions are embarrassed by poor teachers in the same way that the American Bar Association and the American Medical Association are shamed by weak, corrupt, or lazy members in their ranks. No responsible union wants to protect incompetent workers.

On the other hand, without union guarantees of due process, it is likely that many good teachers would be subject to dismissal for political or personal reasons. Therefore, unions have been very protective of all teachers' rights to a fair hearing before losing their jobs. Unions insist on protection for the due process rights of all teachers. Teachers should not be fired because of arbitrary or capricious behavior on the part of administrators or members of the board of education. Unions see an obligation to stand behind teachers to make sure that any dismissal is a result of demonstrable cause, not administrative whim, retribution, or discrimination. Union support guarantees fairness in the workplace.

You may have also heard that "those who are good teachers have no need for tenure, and those who have need for tenure are not good teachers." This is dangerous rhetoric. Tenure is essential for the freedom to teach, and unions are proud to support teachers' rights to tenure. Without the academic freedom guaranteed by tenure, teaching would be too chancy for all but the independently wealthy or the hopelessly foolish. Tenure is among the more misunderstood aspects of teaching. It is not designed to provide teachers with a sinecure, a lifetime job free from the threat of dismissal. Tenured teachers can be fired for incompetence, but they cannot be dismissed for criticizing school policy or for using a teaching strategy or an approach to reading that the principal does not like. Tenure is essential to freedom of thought and action. It guarantees that teachers can use appropriate teaching methods and take reasonable academic positions in classrooms without fear of administrative reprisals. Tenure is the cornerstone of a merit system of employment. The unions' support of tenure helps to staff the nation's classrooms with practitioners secure in the knowledge that they are free to teach, governed by the norms of academic responsibility and unfettered by political constraints. It also assures the public that schools will remain forums dedicated to democratic processes and open inquiry.

EXTENDING WORKPLACE DEMOCRACY

Most school boards now accept teachers' rights to bargain over working conditions, but many remain unconvinced of the legitimacy of labor's voice in policy issues. Some administrators argue that the traditional roles of school employees and employers must be preserved. Superintendents and principals should be the executives and managers; teachers should be the workers. They argue that policy-making is the rightful province of the former; implementation is the only job for the latter. Policy, they claim, should not be subject to the art of compromise, the democratic give-and-take of collective bargaining. Policy-making, they say, is not for teachers.

This is another foolish argument. Even if it were desirable to separate issues of policy from conditions of teachers' work, it is not possible. The concerns of teachers extend far beyond hours and wages. Classroom teachers are directly affected by a broad range of educational policy decisions. Restricting collective bargaining to bread-and-butter issues of working conditions, wages, and hours is naive to the ways in which schools function. Issues of school policy, from the adoption of new basal series to the recruitment of a new building principal, influence every teacher's work. How could a teacher's work fail to be influenced by changes in the materials he or she uses in class? Textbooks, curriculum packages, the assessment of students, the evaluation of teachers, and school disciplinary policies all affect the daily lives of teachers. Policies that affect the school's organization are central to teaching and must be considered as the rightful province of collective negotiations. The education of children will be better served when teachers are given a voice in shaping policy and in making decisions about curriculum and personnel (Maeroff, 1988).

Unions have insisted that teachers be given a voice in the reform of schooling, but in doing so they are not robbing administrators of their authority, they are simply, in the best democratic sense, extending decision making to a broader constituency. Research suggests that workplace democracy has positive pay-offs for schools. Collective bargaining about policy issues appears to produce a greater sense of professional efficacy in teachers; they feel better about their jobs, and they use their new authority to give more of themselves to the school (Johnson, 1988, p. 619).

UNIONS' STAKE IN EDUCATION REFORM

Unions have opened the door to teacher decision making, and teachers have used this right to join with management in the development of better schools. In education, labor and management are not necessarily adversaries; being pro-union does not automatically make teachers the enemies of administrators.

Today, union concerns go beyond the protection of teachers and the enhancement of their working conditions. Unions have always recognized their role in school reform, and they continue to insist that teachers be given a collective voice in bringing about better schooling. Teachers serve in the trenches of education. Their direct daily contact with students provides them with powerful data about those policies and programs that work and those that do not. Teachers know what should be done to improve schooling, and their unions want them to use their knowledge to solve school problems.

Unions also realize that unless teaching becomes a better job for practitioners, it will be increasingly difficult to keep good teachers in the classroom. A sad fact of teaching is that too often the best teachers leave the field after only a few years. Lured by more lucrative careers or seduced into administration, where they can effect change while being paid more, many of the most able teachers look for ways out of the classroom soon after landing their first teaching job.

The teacher union in Rochester, New York, has been trying to keep teachers in the classroom by granting them more authority to run the schools. Referred to as a "career ladder plan," the union-conceived model is designed to tap the knowledge of the best teachers. Senior teachers with at least ten years of teaching experience and five years in the district assume leadership functions in the school that combine administrative work with classroom instruction. The plan calls for selected teachers to spend half their time working in administrative or supervisory capacities and the other half teaching in the classroom. Their out-of-classroom work includes serving as mentors for new teachers and working as curriculum developers and consultants in specialty areas such as math, reading, and science. For their additional responsibility, and their eleven-month contracts, these lead teachers receive a 20 percent differential based on their regular salary.

The union model is designed to recognize exceptional teaching skills honed by years of experience. The most experienced teachers, like the most able surgeons and attorneys, should not only be the best paid; they should also be glad to take on the most challenging cases. The president of the Rochester union wants his lead teachers to assume a "Clint Eastwood" attitude. They should say, "I'm a good teacher. I've seen it all. Give me any student or program that is the toughest challenge and if I can't do it, it can't be done."

Such attitudes put teachers where they belong: designing policy for, and participating in, the fight for better schooling. Unions and unionized teachers are the keys to the future of education. In the past, unions have used their collective bargaining power to improve schools and to make teaching a better job. Unions are eager to continue the education reform agenda; they want to use their power to improve the quality of teaching and learning.

FOR DISCUSSION

1   Assume that you are a tenured teacher attending a meeting with other teachers from your school district to decide whether or not to unionize. What arguments could you

make to convince your colleagues to join a union? What arguments could you make that would discourage them from joining a union?

2 What do you think accounts for the steady decline in union membership in the United States? What do you think the future holds for unions in education? Will they be, as suggested in the introduction to this chapter, beneficial, harmful, or merely irrelevant to the quality of education?

3 Assume you had a choice of two jobs in adjacent school districts, each with similar student populations, working conditions, and salary schedules. The only major difference between the two jobs is that one is in a unionized district (AFT or NEA) with collective bargaining; the other is a nonunion district. Which job would you be more likely to accept?

4 In Japan, the Nikkyoso (Japan Teachers Union) enjoys general support from teachers, and the union plays a significant role in decisions involving education policy matters and bread-and-butter job issues. Although the union takes strong positions, it does not use confrontational tactics. The Japanese traditionally dislike confrontation, preferring instead decisions based on consensual agreements between labor and management. The writings of Prince Shotuku Taishi (604 A.D.) reflect the cultural traditions of harmony and shared decision-making:

Decisions on important matters should not be made by one person alone. They should be discussed with many. But small matters are of less consequence. It is unnecessary to consult a number of people. It is only in the case of weighty affairs, when there is a suspicion that something may miscarry, that one should arrange matters in concert with others, so as to arrive at the right conclusion.

Harmony is to be valued, and an avoidance of wanton opposition to be honored. . . . When those high above are harmonious and those below friendly, and there is concord in the discussion of business, right views of things gain acceptance. Then what is there which cannot be accomplished?*

Compare the cultural values reflected in these quotes with American values concerning leadership and followership in the workplace. Do you think shared harmonious decision-making could become part of the culture of American schools? What advantages and disadvantages would it offer?

REFERENCES

Aronowitz, S. (1973). *False Promises: The Shaping of American Working Class Consciousness*. New York: McGraw-Hill.

Baird, C. W. (1984). *Opportunity or Privilege: Labor Legislation in America*. Bowling Green, Ohio: Social Philosophy and Policy Center.

Braun, R. J. (1972). *Teachers and Power: The Story of the American Federation of Teachers*. New York: Simon & Schuster.

Eaton, W. E. (1975). *The American Federation of Teachers, 1916–1961: A History of the Movement*. Carbondale, Ill.: Southern Illinois University Press.

---

* Quoted in Duke, B. (1986), *The Japanese School: Lessons for Industrial America*. New York: Praeger, pp. 30–32.

Eberts, R. W., and Stone, J. A. (1984). *The Effects of Collective Bargaining on American Education*. Lexington, Mass.: Heath.

Freedman, M. (1987). "Difficulty of Firing Bad Teachers: Continuing Embarrassment for Schools." *ENS Special Report*. Employers Negotiating Service, May 20, 1987.

Friedman, M., and Friedman, R. (1979). *Free to Choose*. New York: Harcourt Brace Jovanovich.

Jessup, D. K. (1978). "Teacher Unionization: A Reassessment of Rank and File Education." *Sociology of Education*, **51**, 44–55.

Johnson, S. M. (1988). "Unionism and Collective Bargaining in the Public Schools." In *Handbook of Research on Educational Administration*, edited by N. J. Boyan. New York: Longman.

Kerchner, C. T. (1986). "Union-Made Teaching: Effects of Labor Relations." In *Review of Research in Education, vol. 13*, edited by E. Z. Rothkopf, pp. 317–349. Washington: American Educational Research Association.

Lieberman, M. "Teacher Unions and Educational Quality: Folklore by Finn." *Phi Delta Kappan*, **66**(5), 341–343.

Lieberman, M., and Moscow, M. H. (1966). *Collective Negotiations for Teachers: An Approach to School Administration*. Chicago: Rand McNally.

Maeroff, G. I. (1988): *The Empowerment of Teachers: Overcoming the Crisis of Confidence*. New York: Teachers College Press.

Rosenthal, A. (1969): *Pedagogues and Power: Teacher Groups in School Politics*. Syracuse: Syracuse University Press.

Stern, D. (1986). "Compensation for Teachers." In *Review of Research in Education*, edited by E. Z. Rothkopf. Washington: American Educational Research Association.

Urban, W. J. (1982). *Why Teachers Organized*. Detroit: Wayne State University Press.

Zeigler, H. (1966). *The Political World of the High School Teacher*. Eugene, Oreg.: University of Oregon.

HOW SHOULD EDUCATION BE EVALUATED?

The general theme of this section concerns the debate about the evaluation of education and the ways in which educational assessments ought to be conducted.

Evaluation is an assessment of value, a process for the determination of merit and worth (Stufflebeam and Webster, 1988). Many aspects of education are subject to evaluation. Universities may test prospective teachers to find out if they have the knowledge and skills necessary for success in the classroom. Schools test students to determine who merits special programs or scholarships, and to place students in one academic track or another. Schools also evaluate curriculum programs in order to measure their effectiveness. Given the limited resources available to schools, they are forced to evaluate their goals and to decide if it is better to support programs of excellence for the most talented students or general programs designed for all students. Arguments in this section also draw your attention to an evaluation of the public, a determination of whether or not public support for education matches the public's rhetoric of educational expectations.

The evaluation of education depends, in large measure, on the way in which schooling is viewed. For many years, the factory assembly line was among the most common metaphors used to depict education. Using the language of metaphoric comparison, schooling was described as a slow, thirteen-year crawl from raw material to finished product. Every year of schooling required that different parts be fitted to the product, each one enhancing its value. Along the way, measurements were made to ensure that prescribed growth was taking place. The product was regularly probed, poked, tested, and finally graduated. A few defective models were thrown out, but most were given the necessary correctives and they made it through.

The metaphor was, in some ways, very convenient, and useful. Most people were familiar with factories, even if they had never worked in them. They realized that some factories, such as those run by Honda and Mercedes Benz, turned out intelligently conceived, carefully crafted products. Other factories produced Yugos. The differences between the factories that turned out good products and those that manufactured bad products has never been entirely clear. It was suspected that the best products represented the most thoughtful designs and the highest assembly standards. Good factories evaluated the designs regularly to ensure that the products manufactured were those the public would buy. Good factories also had exacting standards, and at every point along the assembly line, they checked meticulously for quality.

The earliest evaluation models were wedded to this factory model (see Smith and Tyler, 1942). Evaluation was narrowly conceived as the process of determining student merit. Learning objectives were established for students. Students were put in competition with one another, and were graded and sorted according to the number of objectives they could achieve. The better students achieved more objectives; the best schools were those with the most students achieving the most objectives.

Despite its attractively straightforward reasoning, the production metaphor is no longer considered appropriate for education. The production model of education is now judged to have sacrificed individuality to accountability. The standardized outcomes prized by the manufacturing industry are not necessarily suitable for schools. No one assumes that a ton of steel, plastic, and rubber has the right to determine what it should be. Children are viewed differently. It is more than a bit disconcerting to think of them flowing along a conveyer belt being fitted with the same skills, habits, and dispositions, and denied any voice in how they should turn out or what is to become of them.

Today, educational evaluation means far more than the determination of whether objectives have been attained and the ordering of students in terms of who has achieved the most. Current evaluation practices raise questions about the appropriateness of objectives, the means by which objectives are established for students, and the ways in which students are examined. Evaluation is used not only to judge students but also to help administrators evaluate the worth and merit of programs, and to inform the public about the level of attainment of education goals.

The three chapters in Part Four are designed to reflect some of the current debate about education evaluation. All of the positions support evaluation; none argues that high-quality education is likely to occur by chance. Schools must evaluate themselves and their students to be accountable and to gather data required for good decision-making practices. However, reasonable questions can be asked about the gathering of evaluation data and the ways in which schools, teachers, and educational programs are asked to demonstrate their merit and worth.

Students planning for careers in education are, no doubt, aware that evaluation is playing a larger part in schooling than ever before, but they should know, too, that a great many questions have no generally agreed upon answers. We have tried to include several of these questions in this section. For example: How should students be asked to demonstrate what they know? To what extent should society be held accountable for the outcomes of public education? Is it possible or desirable to use standardized tests that are designed to compare students? Is it fair to evaluate schools simultaneously for their excellence and their equity? Should schools be evaluated by the excellence of education they provide to the most able, or should they be judged by the manner in which they are able to offer appropriate education to all students? As one educator puts it:

> The fundamental question that any theory of evaluation must address is not what can be evaluated, or how, or whether or not objectives have been achieved, but how it is that humans come to know in the first place. And in the second, how it is that they represent what they know to others. (Eisner, 1985, p. 229)

The information in this introduction is designed to provide you with background information necessary to consider the competing perspectives found in the chapters.

CHAPTER 15: RESTRICT OR EXPAND STANDARDIZED TESTING

> Educational and psychological testing represents one of the most important contributions of behavioral science to our society. It has provided fundamental and significant improvements over previous practices in industry, government and education. It has provided a tool for broader and more equitable access to education and employment. (AERA–APA–NCME, 1985. *Standards for Educational and Psychological Testing.* Final Review Draft. Washington, D.C.: American Psychological Association. Quoted in Mehrens and Lehmann, 1987, p. 4)

> . . . testing's effect on society extends far beyond the matter of who is admitted and who is rejected, of who is hired and who is not. Since what is tested directly influences what is taught, ETS's [Educational Testing Service] ubiquitous multiple-choice exams have an enormous impact on education and beyond, from kindergarten up through law school and beyond. And since what is taught influences how we live, the effect of these tests reverberates through society. (Owen, 1985, p. 261)

Too often, the public views evaluation narrowly, as a numerical indication of success or failure. Measures of achievement are confused with numbers, percentiles, ranks, reading levels, and the like. When asked about educational evaluation or the process of assessment, most people think of standardized tests, and for good reason. Standardized testing has become the most commonly used device to determine attainment and proficiency.

The first standardized tests were used in the Boston public schools in 1845 to measure students' knowledge of school subjects (Travers, 1983). Today, as many as 300 million standardized educational and psychological tests are administered every year in the United States, and most of them are given to public school students. A typical high school graduate will be subjected to six full batteries of standardized achievement tests in twelve years of schooling (Mehrens and Lehmann, 1987, p. 2). Test taking has become one of society's more commonly shared phenomena, and it is unusual to run into anyone who has not taken at least one standardized multiple-choice exam.

Proponents of standardized testing argue that machine-scored mutiple-choice testing instruments are the best available means for determining academic merit and assuring educational quality. Test advocates argue that well-designed tests, properly administered and interpreted, can provide schools with the information necessary to make curricular decisions and judgments about the cognitive growth of students. Test programs can inform educators about the effectiveness of teaching, the power of certain courses to affect students, and the extent to which students of one generation compare with students of other generations or with students in other school districts. Standardized testing can also be the vehicle through which school districts demonstrate that the money spent on education is being used prudently; it can justify expenditure on existing programs or indicate the need to increase or decrease spending levels in one area or another.

Opponents of standardized tests maintain that the tests are crude, imprecise measures that reward superficiality, ignore creativity, and penalize those test takers who read too much into the questions. Instead of informing the public, it is argued, test makers confuse people with test results shrouded in an aura of mathematical precision. Rather than offering accountability, testing mistakenly applies the simpleminded methods of cost accounting to the complexities of the teaching-learning process. To meet the demands for a large-scale testing program, test and measurement experts have had to design instruments that comport with a machine-scored, multiple-choice format. Critics of standardized testing claim that few things of significance can be reduced to discrete bits and measured in a series of short-answer questions.

Standardized tests are one of the most controversial applications of social science findings to education, and despite the extent to which they have permeated every level of school experience, they represent a relatively recent development in education. Civil service examinations were first administered centuries ago in China, but it was not until the last century that standardized exams became a common part of social and economic life. Nineteenth-century Britain, in the throes of an expanding domestic economy and an international empire, found that the demand for large numbers of middle-class managers could not be satisfied by the traditional practice of patronage appointments. Large numbers of administrators were needed in the far reaches of the empire, and vacancies could not be filled only be tapping privileged males—the sons of civil servants, members of Parliament, or others with wealth and connections. Competitive examinations were introduced in Britain to open the civil service to a broader range of educated males.

The United States also viewed testing as a means to democratize the selection of government workers. Political abuse was rampant in the late nineteenth century. Those who worked for the government often secured their positions through pull rather than merit, and every change in congressional leadership was accompanied by wholesale shifts in office holders, clerks, and cleaning women. Civil service reform began with the Pendelton Act of 1883, which established competitive examinations for prospective public employees. Civil service tests were intended to provide a means of filling public offices based on ability rather than party loyalty.

The original impulse for testing was meritocratic: to provide an objective measure of ability that would allow vacancies in public offices to be filled by the most qualified. Tests were to be used as a means of demonstrating ability and securing entry to successful careers. In many ways, performance on standardized tests still controls access to power in society. Test results help determine a student's acceptance into selective school programs and admission to higher education and into prized vocations (Eggleston, 1984).

Testing is controversial. If standardized exams can deliver fair, unbiased access to the limited rewards of society, they are socially important, essential to democratic societies, and their use should be encouraged in assessment designs. If, on the other hand, standardized examinations restrict access to power, and serve as agents of social control, their use is destructive to democratic ends and they should be abolished.

In Chapter 15, two competing perspectives of standardized testing in assessment are presented. The first position presents arguments against such testing. It contains arguments that little of real value lends itself to standardized testing. It represents a position that regards standardized testing as a biased mechanism for controlling access to education and employment that stifles student creativity and motivation while perpetuating social injustice (Broadfoot, 1984; Crouse and Trusheim, 1988). The second position, led by psychometricians and educational psychologists, contains arguments in support of standardized testing. It is argued that whatever is worthwhile educationally can and should be measured through formal, objective evaluations. In order for public education to be accountable, decisions must be made about the ways in which resources are allocated. Supporters of the psychometric approach conclude that standardized tests are the best single means for gathering the data needed to make educational decisions and demonstrating effectiveness.

CHAPTER 16: PUBLIC SUPPORT FOR OR RESISTANCE TO SCHOOLS

Applied to education, "evaluation" has typically come to refer to the assessment of student performance or the measurement of program effects. Chapter 16 directs attention to a different dimension of evaluation—the evaluation of the public—and it raises questions about whether or not the public has been adequately supporting its schools. In other words, the public has asked the schools to teach skills and values and to solve social problems ranging from drug abuse to racial discrimination, but has the public been willing to give schools the financial support and academic authority necessary to do the job? Does the public's support for education match its rhetoric?

Although the questions raised in this chapter may be difficult to answer, they are posed fairly. Educational evaluation is considered to be more than a technical process, a set of scientific skills with which to measure small, discrete bits of education (Scriven, 1983). Evaluators have been encouraged to see themselves in larger terms, as more than technicians. They have been urged to consider the social function of evaluation and to play a greater political role in the society (Cronbach et al., 1980; House, 1973). It is assumed that effective evaluation cannot be divorced from political and social ends. Evaluators must consider education as a political activity. The questions they ask and the ways in which they ask them rightfully link the schools to the people they serve.

Schools cannot be separated from the society which establishes them, and it is entirely appropriate to ask how well the public has been supporting the schools. If the society charges schools with a full portfolio of obligations, to what extent is the society responsible for providing the conditions that will allow the schools to discharge their duties? An evaluation of the public may be necessary to judge its intentions. Is the public charge to schools given honestly? Or, has the public entrusted schools with a social and educational agenda which it knows schools cannot discharge, but which it does not want to deal with more squarely?

The first position presents the argument that the public gets from schools only what it has been willing to pay for, and that is not very much. Schools, it contends, are publicly praised and privately patronized. The public may express great love for its schools, but it entrusts them with neither the money nor the power to bring about real educational or social change. The second position argues that the love affair between the public and the schools is the genuine article. Analyzing state and local statutes and data from public opinion polls, the second perspective finds much to praise in the public's record of support for its schools.

CHAPTER 17: EDUCATIONAL EXCELLENCE AS VISION OR SHAM

When schools are evaluated, questions naturally arise about the goals of schooling, and the extent to which the pursuit of some of them may exclude the realization of others. For example, can the schools be held accountable for delivering academic excellence while maintaining educational equity? Are the goals of excellence and equity so incompatible that, in the reform of public education, society is forced to choose one or the other?

"Excellence" typically refers to rigorous educational programs and high academic standards. Excellent schools are marked by the lofty expectations they set for students and the ways in which they encourage all students to reach them (Adler, 1982; National Commission on Excellence in Education, 1983). "Equity," on the other hand, refers to the role played by schools in providing social justice. Equity demands that schools provide appropriate educational opportunity and democratic advancement for all children independent of their academic ability (Aronowitz and Giroux, 1985; Bastian et al., 1986).

At first glance, it might appear that no conflict exists between excellence and equity; education should be able to help the less fortunate while, at the same time, contributing to the advancement of the most able (Glazer, 1987; Strike, 1985). If excellence is defined in such a way that anyone can become excellent, then everyone could be treated the same. All students could be given a similar education, and on the basis of merit, the best would achieve excellence, the rest varying degrees of adequacy.

Some critics argue that such a formula serves only to reinforce social inequities. Education for excellence, they claim, too often leads to schooling that is socially repressive. Students do not enter school with similar advantages. In kindergarten, the children of the poor perform at lower levels than the children of the wealthy, and the achievement gap between the two groups widens every year. Schools, it would seem, serve some children better than others. In the name of excellence, schools perpetuate social differences. Schools, these critics argue, should serve everyone, not just those who begin school with comparative advantages. Education for equity would put schools more squarely in the fight for social justice and an expanded democracy. Equity demands curricula that serve the career and personal needs of all students equally well (Aronowitz and Giroux, 1985; Friere, 1973).

Previous efforts to reform schools have been guided by the assumption that education could not allocate sufficient human or fiscal resources to provide both equity and excellence. Therefore, public education has alternately responded to the social tugs of competing camps. The 1950s was a decade of elitism for schools. Prompted by Soviet advances in space technology, American social policy demanded that schools meet the challenge with enhanced programs in the sciences. New money was poured into schools, labs were added, and institutes were established to train science teachers at federal expense. The investment in excellence paid off in measurable ways. Scores on science achievment tests went up; increasing numbers of students—mainly males—took science courses; and more students majored in science at college. The United States launched rockets, orbited satellites, and in 1969 a manned spacecraft landed on the moon and brought back samples of the lunar landscape.

The social upheavals of the 1960s caused other changes in schooling. The war in Vietnam, a renewed focus on poverty and civil rights, and demands for social justice were reflected in the school curriculum. Education was asked to become more inclusive. Students and faculty from varied cultural backgrounds demanded that the schools be excellent not only for the college-bound, but for everyone. Academic requirements were changed to reflect the schools' new constituents. The core curriculum all but disappeared, and requirements in math and science were replaced by courses that were broader, more flexible, and, it was assumed, more relevant to the diverse social concerns of the students (Fantini, 1986).

It is difficult to measure the relevance of the curriculum or its ability to provide greater numbers of students with a more appropriate education. The quality of schools is measured by scores on standardized tests, and it came as little surprise that during the 1970s and early 1980s SAT and ACT scores declined precipitously. Some saw this as a harbinger of doom; others were less shaken. It has been pointed out that most of the decline in test scores can be attributed to the performance of newly empowered groups—women, minorities, and the poor—who had previously been excluded from college. Lower scores may only be a temporary downward phenomenon, a reflection of new students not yet accustomed to this format for displaying knowledge. The lower scores may ultimately be a reflection of progress, a sign that education is becoming more open and democratic (Howe, 1987).

In 1983, a new excellence movement was born. The National Commission on Excellence in Education declared the schools to be in crisis (*A Nation at Risk*, 1983). The report said the nation's educational foundation was so badly eroded that the future of the society was threatened. In unequivocal language, it announced that "if an unfriendly power had attempted to impose on America the mediocre educational performance that exists today, we might have viewed it as an act of war."

The report was followed by several others, including those written or issued by Ernest Boyer (1983), the College Entrance Examination Board (1983), John Goodlad (1983), the National Science Foundation (1983), Theodore Sizer (1984), and the Twentieth Century Fund (1983). These reports, reminiscent of John Gardner (1961), argue that our educational system can provide students with both equality of opportunity and excellence in achievement. Many in education greeted the reports with cautious optimism, praising the potential complementariness of educational excellence and educational equity (Fantini, 1986; Glazer et al, 1987; Shanker, 1984).

Critics of the reports have been more skeptical, arguing that they are part of a neoconservative offensive in education. The endorsement of the reports by the political right (for example, The Heritage Foundation, Senators Orrin Hatch and Jesse Helms, former Secretary of Education William Bennett, the historian Diane Ravitch) have raised the suspicions of political liberals who see the latest round of school reform as an elitist program designed to promote the success of the few at the expense of the many (Altbach, Kelly, and Weiss, 1985; Aronowitz and Giroux, 1985; Bastian et al, 1986; Pincus, 1984).

Chapter 17 contains a debate over the excellence and equity goals of education. The first position argues that the primary purpose of education is to improve the lives of people through knowledge, and that the quality of education can be measured only by its excellence. However, the first position finds no inherent conflict between excellence and equity in planning for future school reform. The second position contains arguments that schools cannot be excellent and equitable at the same time. The new call for excellence, it argues, is a "sham," a smokescreen that promotes elitist and undemocratic goals in the name of reform. The second position denounces the excellence movement as a "restrictive and negative list of requirements that is likely to increase the gap between those who have and those who do not have economic advantage."

REFERENCES

Adler, M. (1982). *The Paideia Proposal*. New York: Macmillan.

Altbach, P. G., Kelly, G. P., and Weiss, L. (1985). *Excellence in Education: Perspectives on Policy and Practice*. Buffalo: Prometheus Books.

Aronowitz, S., and Giroux, H. A. (1985). *Education Under Siege: The Conservative, Liberal and Radical Debate Over Schooling*. South Hadley, Mass.: Bergin & Garvey.

Bastian, A., et al. (1986). *Choosing Equality: The Case for Democratic Schooling*. Philadelphia: Temple University Press.

Boyer, E. L. (1983). *High School: A Report on Secondary Education in America*. New York: Harper & Row.

Broadfoot, P., ed. (1984). *Selection, Certification and Control: Social Issues in Educational Assessment*. London: Falmer.

College Entrance Examination Board (1983). *Academic Preparation for College*. New York: College Entrance Examination Board.

Cronbach, L. J., et al. (1980). *Toward Reform of Program Evaluation*. San Francisco: Jossey-Bass.

Crouse, J., and Trusheim, D. (1988). *The Case Against the SAT*. Chicago: University of Chicago Press.

Eggleston, J. (1984). "School Examinations—Some Sociological Issues." In *Selection, Certification and Control*, edited by P. Broadfoot. London: Falmer.

Eisner, E. W. (1985). *The Art of Educational Evaluation: A Personal View*. London: Falmer.

Fantini, M. D. (1986). *Regaining Excellence in Education*. Columbus, Ohio: Merrill.

Freire, P. (1973). *Pedagogy of the Oppressed*. New York: Seabury Press.

Gardner, J. W. (1961). *Excellence: Can We Be Equal and Excellent Too?* New York: Harper.

Glazer, N., et al. (1987). "Equity and Excellence in Education." *Harvard Educational Review*, **57**, 196–199.

House, E. R. (1973). *School Evaluation: The Politics and the Process*. Berkeley: McCutchan.

Howe, H., II (1987). "Remarks on Equity and Excellence in Education." *Harvard Educational Review*, **57**(2), 199–202.

Mehrens, W. A., and Lehmann, I. J. (1987). *Using Standardized Tests in Education*, *4th ed*. New York: Longman.

National Association of Secondary School Principals (1988). *High School Leaders and their Schools*. Reston, Md.: NASSP.

National Commission on Excellence in Education (1983). *A Nation at Risk: The Imperative for Educational Reform*. Washington, D.C.: U.S. Government Printing Office.

National Science Foundation (1983). *Educating Americans for the 21st Century: A Plan of Action for Improving Mathematics, Science and Technology Education for all American Elementary and Secondary Students so that Their Achievement is the Best in the World by 1995: A Report to the American People and the National Science Board*. Washington, D.C.: National Science Foundation.

Owen, D. (1985). *None of the Above*. Boston: Houghton Mifflin.

Pincus, F. L. (1984). "From Equity to Excellence: The Rebirth of Educational Conservatism." *Social Policy*, **14**, 50–56.

Scriven, M. (1983). "Evaluation Ideologies." In *Evaluation Models*, edited by G. F. Madaus, M. Scriven, and D. L. Stufflebeam. Boston: Kluwer-Nijhoff.

Shanker, A. (1984). "Taking the Measure of American Education Reform: An Assessment of the Education Reports." *American Journal of Education,* **92,** 314–324.

Sizer, T. R. (1984). *Horace's Compromise: The Dilemma of the American High School.* Boston: Houghton Mifflin.

Smith, E. R., and Tyler, R. W. (1942). *Appraising and Recording Student Progress.* New York: Harper.

Strike, K. A. (1985). "Is There a Conflict between Equity and Excellence?" *Educational Evaluation and Policy Analysis,* **7,** 409–416.

Stufflebeam, D., and Webster, W. J. (1988). "Evaluation as an Administrative Function." In *Handbook of Research on Educational Administration,* edited by N. J. Boyan. New York: Longman.

Travers, R. M. W. (1983). *How Research Has Changed American Schools.* Kalamazoo, Mich.: Mythos.

Twentieth Century Fund (1983). *Making the Grade: Report of the Twentieth Century Fund Task Force on Federal Elementary and Secondary Education Policy.* New York: Twentieth Century Fund.

U.S. Department of Education (1987). *What's Happening in Teacher Testing: An Analysis of State Teacher Testing Practices.* Washington, D.C.: U.S. Government Printing Office.

CHAPTER 15

RESTRICT OR EXPAND STANDARDIZED TESTING

POSITION 1
For Restricting Testing

VEXED TESTS

In a witty attack on standardized testing, Banesh Hoffmann (1962) recounted a debate that was played out on the pages of the *Times* of London. A letter had been sent to the editor of that paper asking for help in solving a multiple-choice problem that was part of a battery of school tests taken by the letter writer's son. At first glance the question seemed to be straightforward and not uncommon to anyone who has attended public schools. It asked, "Which is the odd one out among cricket, football, billiards, and hockey?"

The letter writer believed that the answer must be billiards because it is the only one of the four games played indoors. He admitted to being less than sure of his answer, and he reported that there was no agreement among his acquaintances. One of his neighbors argued that the correct choice was cricket because in all of the other games the object was to put a ball in a net. The writer's son, apparently unfamiliar with games played on ice, chose hockey because it was the only one that was a "girl's game." The letter writer asked the *Times* for help.

Ensuing letters and arguments succeeded only in muddying the waters, as the logic supporting one choice was no more compelling than the logic of any other. For example, billiards could be considered the odd one out because it is the only one of the four games listed that is not a team game. It is the only one in which the color of the ball matters. It is the only one in which more than one ball is in play, and it is the only one played on a green cloth rather than a grass field. Unfortunately, equally convincing briefs could be submitted in behalf of the other choices.

Hoffmann fumed about the inherent cultural bias in the question. He assumed that the test was designed to measure reasoning ability and not knowledge of sports, but he argued that the test taker may be disadvantaged by either too much or too little experience with athletics. For example, not all students with good reasoning skills may know the manner in which cricket is played, and many working-class students may be more familiar with pool than with billiards. If test takers knew too much, they could choose hockey as the odd one out because it is really two different games that share the same name: in England and in several other countries, hockey is a game typically played on grass by players who receive no salary; elsewhere it is played on ice by professional athletes. Equally disadvantaged are Americans who may be tripped up by the language of test directions asking them to select the "odd-one-out" instead of the question stem more commonly found in the United States, "Which of the following does not belong?"

Test questions of this sort seem silly. There is no readily apparent "right answer," and no opportunity for test takers to demonstrate the thought processes that led them to their decisions. Multiple-choice questions are an unnatural problem-solving format that is discontinuous with the way in which real-life problems present themselves. Rarely are life's dilemmas accompanied by four answers, one of which is guaranteed to be correct. Good problem solvers in the real world are seldom locked away, deprived of books, computers, and human contact, and told to respond to a set of timed, multiple-choice questions that have no meaning for them or anyone else. As Hoffmann noted, "What sense is there in giving tests in which the candidate just picks answers, and is not allowed to give the reasons for his choice?" (1962, p. 20)

If multiple-choice questions, such as the one that vexed readers of the *Times*, were nothing more than parlor games, a form of Trivial Pursuit to amuse guests after dinner, there would be nothing wrong with them. However, as everyone knows, standardized testing is serious business. On the basis of results of standardized multiple-choice exams, decisions are made about placement in reading groups, about who should be admitted to the college-track programs in public high schools, who should go to elite colleges, who should be awarded scholarships, who should be admitted to medical and law schools, and who should be allowed to practice a profession or trade.

IF TESTING IS THE ANSWER, WHAT WAS THE QUESTION?

Standardized tests have an unsavory history. In the early twentieth century, defining something called "native intelligence" and attempting to measure it through the use of standardized examinations produced one of the most controversial legacies of the testing movement (Gould, 1981). Although attempts to measure mental capacities through standardized tests can be found in the work of twentieth-century Europeans, such as Galton and Binet (Cremin, 1961), widespread testing was first used by psychologists working for the United States during World War I. The army was interested in classifying all new recruits, with special attention given to two groups: those who were considered of exceptional ability and those unfit for military service. The tests used by Binet and others were individual IQ tests, not well suited to large scale testing, and under the direction of American psychologists, the army developed the first mass testing program in history (Gumbert and Spring, 1974, pp. 87–112).

The army used the tests to answer questions about the placement of soldiers: who would best fit where, and how the army could best use the varied talents and abilities recruits brought with them. After the war, when colleges and universities bought up large quantities of surplus exams, the language of the army tests required only slight modification for use in the schools. The original instructions given to soldiers read:

> Attention! The purpose of this examination is to see how well you can remember, think and carry out what you are told to do in the army. . . . Now in the army a man often has to listen to commands and carry them out exactly. I am going to give you these commands to see how well you carry them out.

In schools, these instructions were changed to read:

> Part of being a good student is your ability to follow directions. . . . When I call "Attention," stop instantly what you are doing and hold your pencil up—so. Don't put your pencil down on the paper until I say "Go." . . . Listen carefully to what I say. Do just as you are told to do. As soon as you are through, pencils up. Remember, wait for the word "Go." (Gumbert and Spring, 1974, p. 94)

The army used IQ tests to predict the ability of recruits to do well in the army. For many years, schools used IQ tests to measure a child's ability to perform well in school. However, according to self-reports of school administrators, fewer decisions are made on the basis of IQ scores today than in the past. In 1965, for example, 82 percent of high school administrators believed that grouping students by IQ was desirable. By 1987, only 57 percent thought that such grouping was desirable (NASSP, 1988). Decreased reliance on IQ scores has not meant that public schools have abandoned commercial testing. Standardized examinations are used to measure aptitude, achievement, the assessment of performance, interest, personality and attitude.

MISLEADING THE PUBLIC

Until the last few years, despite questions about the validity of individual test items on standardized tests (Crouse and Trusheim, 1988; Hoffmann, 1962; Nairn, 1980; Owen, 1985), test takers were neve able to see a list of the "right" answers after they had taken the exams. The Educational Testing Service (ETS) of Princeton, New Jersey, and other test developers published only a few sample questions, claiming that full disclosure would compromise the tests. In order to make the tests reliable, they argued, many items had to be repeated from year to year, and the answers therefore must be withheld from public scrutiny. ETS admitted that although it was possible to construct new equivalent exams every year, it would be an expensive process whose costs would ultimately be borne by the test takers.

Recognizing the power standardized exams have in the lives of individual test takers, New York and California, not persuaded by ETS's arguments, enacted legislation that allowed test takers to see the answers after they had taken the exams. Referred to as the "truth-in-testing laws," this legislation revealed ambiguities in test items and the possibility of two or more correct items. The truth-in-testing laws have cast doubt on the ability of tests to measure what they claim to measure.

In some states, the results of standardized tests have intentionally been used to mislead the public. Take the case of the "magic mean," uncovered by a physician in West Virginia. According to newspaper accounts, the students in the state were performing above the national average on standardized tests. This was intriguing, considering that West Virginia had one of the highest rates of illiteracy in the nation. Further checking by the physician revealed that no state using this test was reported to be below the mean. The test results made every test taker (and the school systems which bought them) appear to be above average. This result was obtained by using tests for which the norm data had been gathered on groups who had scored lower than the students in West Virginia. This, unfortunately, is not an isolated example (see Southern Regional Education Board, 1988). By the late 1980s, it was hard to find any school districts or states that scored below the mean on nationally normed standardized tests. These data have contributed to what has been termed "the Lake Wobegon Effect," after the mythical Minnesota town created by Garrison Keillor in which "the women are strong, the men are good looking, and all the children are above average" (Fiske, 1988).

The point is simply that for the past fifty years psychometricians and companies that market tests have convinced the public that short-answer tests are objective, scientific measures deserving of public confidence and faith, when in fact these tests suffer from vagueness, ambiguity, and imprecision. As David Owen points out, there is nothing objective about these items; they are written, tested, compiled and interpreted by highly subjective human beings (1985, p. 33).

BIAS AGAINST WOMEN AND THE POOR

The results of standardized testing too often are clouded by their bias against women and the poor. Take the example of the Scholastic Aptitude Exam (SAT), a test taken by college-bound high school students, ETS has encouraged colleges and universities to consider the SAT exam as a scientific predictor of students' freshman-year grades in college. Consequently, SAT scores are often part of the data used by colleges in making acceptance decisions. According to ETS, high school students with higher scores on the SAT exam should earn higher grades during their first year in college. One recent study, however, indicates that the SAT might be a gender-biased exam (Rosser, 1987). The gap between male and female scores on the test is 61 points. Female test takers scored 50 points lower on the math section and 11 points lower on the verbal section of the exam. If the SAT accurately predicted grade point average, males would have higher freshman grade point averages than female students. But this is not the case. Despite lower scores on the SAT, females earned higher grades than males. The SAT does not predict what it is supposed to predict: success in college. The numbers students get on SAT exams have less meaning than ETS has promised.

Standardized achievement tests are biased against women; standardized IQ tests have been shown to discriminate against the poor. In the United States, whites, on average, score more than 15 points higher than blacks on IQ tests. There is also a significant gap between the standardized test scores of whites and Mexican Americans and American Indians. Some educational psychologists believe that most of the difference in IQ scores is attributable to genetic endowment (Jensen, 1969). However, most anthropologists and educational sociologists argue that IQ is more reflective of the child's socioeconomic status than his or her native ability (Ogbu, 1978). For example, when the family background and academic experiences are held constant for white and minority children, the differences in achievement scores tend to disappear.

Standardized tests are terribly flawed, but despite their problems they are allowed to exert tremendous influence. Every teacher knows that testing drives the curriculum. What is tested is taught. No teacher wants his or her students to perform poorly on standardized achievement tests, and no school administrator wants his or her school to be ranked below others in the state. Everyone in education knows that, too often, the results of statewide testing are reported in newspapers in much the same way as basketball standings are reported. Headlines such as "We're Number One" or "County Schools Lowest in State" are not uncommon in many local newspapers. To avoid invidious comparisons, instruction is geared to the test. Over time, material not tested tends not to be taught. Teachers and administrators fall victim to test makers' promises and the public's misplaced faith in testing. In truth, IQ tests are of little value in making educational decisions about children. Nationally normed achievement tests are often no better, and there is no compelling reason to subject students to large-scale multiple-choice exams. Why should it be assumed that students in any given school ought to learn the same content, in the same way, as students in any other school? And why should all students be asked to demonstrate their level of academic achievement in the same way?

There is an antidote to standardized testing that does not sacrifice accountability. In every community, teachers, parents, and administrators should select appropriate content based on the students' interests, experiences, goals, and needs. Teachers should teach that content with all the skill at their command, and evaluate the extent of student learning with a wide variety of instruments. Students should be encouraged to demonstrate their ability to think through written exercises, verbal expression, and informal papers, and they should be given ample opportunity to demonstrate the reasons for their choices. The assessment of student learning requires educators to develop a broader, richer array of measures. Student achievement cannot be reduced to a single numerical score. Multiple-choice tests cannot tell the story of academic success. Standardized testing is deceitful and biased; standardized tests should be abolished. A student's record of school achievement should include a rich portfolio of papers, essays, videos, poems, photographs, drawings, and tape-recorded answers, not a series of test scores.

POSITION 2
For Expanding Testing

Education was "rediscovered" in the 1980s and carefully examined. Researchers, critics, and government officials raised many questions about the quality of teaching, student learning, and school leadership. Public education was rescued from decades of neglect, dusted off, and reassessed. It was no surprise that problems were discovered from the head to the tail of the academic procession. The schools, it was generally concluded, were again in need of reform.

Previous generations of education reformers had concerned themselves with making education available to the children of all classes and races, and to a large extent they were successful. By the 1980s, a higher percentage of students were completing twelve years of schooling than ever before. Instead of availability, the current generation of reformers is now forced to consider the quality of those school experiences. As Mortimer Adler (1982) argues, the legal mandates for education cannot be satisfied only by guaranteeing all children access to education. To satisfy the educational responsibilities of a democratic society, public education must demonstrate that each student is provided with adequate levels of skills and knowledge. Educational outcomes no longer can be measured only in quantity—years of schooling and the number of high school diplomas granted; schools must guarantee that education has a demonstrably positive effect on students. Schools must show that students benefit from their years of attendance, that increased investment in schooling can be measured in greater ability to read, write, and do mathematics, and that moving up the academic ladder from grade to grade is based on merit rather than social promotion.

The issue of educational quality raises a broad range of questions:

How good is the education provided students in grades K through 12?

How do the students of today compare with former students?

How do students in School A or District A or State A compare with those in the B, C, and D counterparts?

How can prospective employers be assured that students who have graduated from high school possess a minimum level of skills, knowledge, and ability?

How can the public know that the teachers who work in public schools are qualified to teach the subjects they are hired to teach?

How can taxpayers know that the dollars given over to public education are being well spent?

If changes are made in public education, how can it be determined that they have contributed positively to learning outcomes?

Answers to these questions must be based on hard data. Schools need quantifiable measures of student performance and teacher effectiveness if they hope to maintain public support. Intelligent policy decisions should be based on objective information, and although no single means of data collection is sufficient, the data generated by well-designed standardized tests are crucial to an understanding of school outcomes. Good tests and good testing programs permit schools to gather information about curricula, students, and teaching personnel that are not available to them by other means. Without these data, schools cannot make good decisions about the quality of the curriculum, the ability of the teachers, or the power of specific programs to produce academic learning by students.

Testing is the scientific base that supports decisions about the art of teaching. It is also the yardstick against which society charts the progress and shortcomings of education, and it is the form in which schools report the status of education to public officials and parents. Test and measurement experts are often at odds with others in education, and they have suffered abuse from critics who are concerned about the power of testing and testing agencies to influence public policy. The purpose here is not to answer the critics or to submit a brief in support of the Educational Testing Service or the National Assessment of Educational Progress. Instead, it will be argued that (1) standardized testing is an essential tool for examining the measurable dimensions of education, and (2) education has entered an era of accountability in which school officials must demonstrate that the money being spent for education is paying dividends in quality.

TESTING FOR THE GOOD OF SCHOOLS

Standardized testing is an essential element of rational curriculum work. The data generated by testing programs help curriculum planners determine whether or not the measured outcomes of a given set of instructional inputs match the intended goals. In other words, tests can help educators find out if a specific program is working the way it was designed to work. When taxpayers are asked to foot the bill for a new science program in the high school or a new math program in the elementary school, they should be informed of the likely effects of these programs. They should also have hard data by which to judge how well these programs have worked elsewhere. It is a simple question of cost accounting and fiscal responsibility.

Effective change does not occur by chance. Educational decisions must be made about the progress of the students, the rate of achievement of proximate goals, and the best choice among the competing paths to the next objective. Educational planners need to choose appropriate measures of student attainment. Impressionistic data are not sufficient; anecdotal evidence is not scientific. It is not enough that a program "seems to be working" or the teachers "claim to like" this method or that. Schools need to have better answers to direct curriculum questions. At what grade level are the students reading? What do diagnostic and prescriptive tests tell us about a child's performance in academic skill areas? How much of the required curricula have students mastered?

In order for schools to make rational decisions, they must have hard, sound, objective data. Standardized testing should not be viewed as a report card but as part of an assessment system that permits schools to make decisions about curriculum and instruction. Standardized achievement tests are objective measures of performance. They are not designed to provide apologies for ineffective programs, nor are they arbitrary standards of excellence. Standardized tests are designed to measure the consensual goals of education and determine the extent to which the nation is meeting its responsibilities to provide educational quality to all children.

SHOOTING THE MESSENGER

Determining educational quality across state boundary lines is especially difficult. The United States has no national curriculum, and although education is essentially an enterprise run by the individual states, Americans have a right to know how well their children are being educated when compared with the children of other states and regions. Since 1969, the federal government has financed an assessment program known as the National Assessment of Educational Progress (NAEP). NAEP has been gathering data about the knowledge, skills, and attitudes of students across ten subject areas: art, career and occupational development, citizenship, literature, mathematics, music, reading, science, social studies, and writing. Tests are given to four age groups (ages 9, 13, 17, and young adults), and they have been administered since 1983 by the Educational Testing Service of Princeton, New Jersey. Educational planners need to have this information in order to reform schools.

Unfortunately, much of the NAEP test data have been negative; schoolchildren appear to know less today than in previous periods in our history. Although these findings grab headlines and cause a great deal of collective hand-wringing, they are not an end in themselves. NAEP is designed to facilitate reconsideration of the quality of teaching and learning in public schools. Too often, the response to negative findings has been to blame the test makers instead of addressing the cause of poor scores. More energy has been expended in attacking the validity of standardized testing than in examining the conditions revealed by the tests. It seems that it is easier to shoot the messenger than to consider an unpopular message.

In 1985, a project funded by the National Endowment for the Humanities and administered by the staff of NAEP assessed students' knowledge of history and literature in a test called the National Assessment of History and Literature (NAHL) (Ravitch and Finn, 1987). The results were unequivocal: the eight thousand 17-year-olds who took this exam were, in the words of the authors, "ignorant of much of what they should know." The assessment group included an equal number of boys and girls drawn from a representative sample of the national population by geography and ethnicity. Among all test takers, only 20 percent could identify Joyce, Dostoevsky, Ellison, Conrad, or Ibsen; fewer than 25 percent were able to identify Henry James or Thomas Hardy; only one in three knew that Chaucer was the author of *The Canterbury Tales;* 65 percent did not know what *1984* or *Lord of the Flies* was about. Three-quarters of the students did not know when Lincoln was President; one-third were unfamiliar with the *Brown* decision; 70 percent could not identify the Magna Carta.

Critics screamed that the test was not valid; it did not measure knowledge of the history and literature students learn in school. This criticism cuts to the heart of testing. The goal of psychometric testing is to provide policy-makers with valid, reliable data on which to base decisions. Too often, criticisms of standardized tests come from people who are uninformed about the field of measurement, admittedly a technical area that seems to defy understanding by most of the general public and many educators.

The NAHL was certainly a valid exam. Written in cooperation with public school teachers, the major portion of the questions was drawn directly from the most important material covered in the textbooks and the curricula. Most of the questions were designed to cover fundamental material that students of this age might reasonably be expected to know. Citing a handful of the literature questions—such as biblical references—that covered content not typically taught in school, critics raged that certain students were put at a disadvantage.

The detractors of the NAHL were apparently unmindful of the goal of the exam: the NAHL was not designed to grade students in the hope that many could be failed. It was designed to determine what students knew so that the curriculum and the nature of instruction could be improved. The test did not try to identity individual or typical 17-year-olds. The sample was stratified for sex, race, ethnicity, geography, and private school attendance in order to reflect a national population. The test results were to be used as one body of objective data for considering what was learned in schools. The test was not meant to replace teacher tests or to substitute the judgments of state legislators or curriculum workers.

Standardized test results cannot be ignored. One of the goals of the NAHL was to provide baseline data for future assessments in history and literature. Relatively little is known about these fields of instruction other than enrollment statistics. It is, frankly, shocking that the test has been attacked so viciously. Although testing is far from a perfect science, at the present time there are no measures that can compete with standardized tests for gathering economical, valid, and reliable data about what children have learned in school.

The NAHL reported "large differences in achievement on both assessments (knowledge of history and knowledge of literature) among racial and ethnic groups" (1987, p. 132). Asian and white students performed significantly better than black, Hispanic, and American Indian students. Rather than claim that these differences are a function of biology, the authors suggest that geography and income are correlates of performance. For example, blacks in certain areas of the country lagged behind other blacks. More of the highest-achieving black students came from families with a history of college graduation, and they lived in homes in which there were computers. These are important data that reflect the power of social and school forces to influence academic performance independent of race.

Admittedly, standardized tests, as measures of educational achievement, are not without problems. Many of the goals of education are difficult to measure. The ability to communicate verbally and healthy self-concept are hard to determine with paper-and-pencil tests. It is also well known among test developers that minimums have a tendency to become maximums, and teachers tend to teach for the test. Not everything that is taught can be included on an exam, and material not tested has a tendency to disappear from the curriculum. Test writers do not want to dictate what should be taught, but schools and the public must realize that tests of minimum competencies cannot cover everything that is taught in schools. Despite the risk of skipping some learning outcomes that are significant, and of emphasizing others that may have lesser significance, standardized achievement tests can be recommended unequivocally as a cost-effective means of assuring educational quality. Instead of attacking the tests, those who do not like standardized testing should develop better measures of school achievement. So far, none exists.

Opponents of standardized tests argue that too often the use of these instruments has resulted in discrimination against minority groups. Indeed, standardized testing is designed to discriminate, to make distinctions about what is known and by whom. If there were no differences in test scores—that is, if they did not discriminate among categories of test takers—the tests would be worthless. It is not a question of whether or not tests discriminate, but rather of whether they discriminate unfairly, and whether the results of even the fairest tests are used for unfair purposes.

TESTING TEACHERS

A test can be unfair if members of minority groups (gender, race, or ethnicity, for example) score lower than others, and if the scores are unrelated to what the test purports to predict. For example, if a school district wanted to hire a kindergarten teacher, and used a test that measured knowledge of football trivia from the 1950s, you might guess that as a group, young, female applicants would do less well than middle-aged males. If the hiring decision were based on this test, it would be unfairly discriminatory because the knowledge being tapped would be unrelated to what was being predicted—success as a kindergarten teacher—and the test would tend to favor one group of test takers over others.

On the other hand, the use of scores on the National Teacher Examination (NTE) in making hiring decisions could be an example of discrimination that is fair. The NTE, a standardized test typically administered to students completing teacher education programs, has a distribution of scores that shows regional, racial, and ethnic variations. However, this differentiation alone does not make the test unfair. The NTE is constructed by experts in education who argue that the knowledge it tests is basic information about teaching which has been mastered by the more able teachers, and that those lacking such mastery are disadvantaged by their ignorance. By measuring knowledge that is central to good teaching, the NTE is related to job success. It may be useful in hiring decisions because it is an accurate predictor of who will succeed in the classroom.

Albert Shanker, president of the American Federation of Teachers, argues the post-baccalaureate examinations are common for lawyers, engineers, and other professionals, and they should be welcomed by teachers. Critics have claimed that these tests are not designed to tap teachers' ability to engage children in worthwhile activities, pique their curiosity, or encourage their intellectual growth, and they are right (see Department of Education, 1987). The NTE, which has been in use since 1939, is not a perfect exam, but it is useful because it will exclude from hiring considerations those candidates who have not minimally mastered the subjects they plan to teach. ETS has also announced that by 1992 a new form of the NTE will be on the market. Recognizing that paper-and-pencil tests have drawn sharp criticism, ETS has invested $2 million in the development of a multitiered test for prospective teachers. In addition to the traditional test of knowledge and reasoning, the new design calls for live exercises, computer simulations, teaching situations with real students, and other practical exercises in which teachers can demonstrate their ability to make decisions and exercise professional judgment.

No test is designed to stand alone as the sole criterion for hiring. To a certain extent, all standardized tests reflect environmental factors, including the education of the test taker's parents, parental income, geography, and the like. Intelligent use of the NTE in conjunction with subjective data sources (for example, interviews, recommendations from universities, and so on) has provided schools in thirty states with hiring data for the past fifty years. The new NTE will be even better. It will give more powerful reassurance to parents that the new teacher who meets their children at the classroom door in September scored well on a nationally normed test.

Minimal investment in standardized testing programs to assist in educational decision-making cannot help but pay dividends in better student evaluation and wiser selection of teachers. The intelligent use of testing provides educators with scientifically generated data that are not available by other means. Without standardized testing, what kind of evaluation system would we have? How would we know if schools are doing as well as we expect or if teachers have the knowledge and skills demanded of them?

FOR DISCUSSION

1   As an alternative to standardized testing, one university has proposed the following design to assess students' knowledge of the liberal arts core of the curriculum: A random sample of students would be examined. On a Friday, students would be given a series of essay questions from the sciences, the social sciences, and the humanities. Students would be allowed to work in groups of three. The library and the computer facility would be open to them. Students would be expected to turn in written answers to the questions by 8:00 A.M. on Monday morning.

What do you see as the advantages and disadvantages of this assessment design? What would it tell the university about its students? What could not be determined from this design? Would something like this be appropriate for the public schools?

2   In 1988, one court ruled that the Scholastic Aptitude Exam unfairly discriminated against women and could not be used to make college admission decisions. If all standardized short-answer tests were to disappear from American education, what would be the likely consequences? How could the American public be assured that schools were accountable without objective measurements?

3   Increasing numbers of states are using tests to screen prospective teachers. If you were to construct such a test, what knowledge would you expect a teacher candidate to possess? How would you ask the candidates to demonstrate that knowledge?

4   Harold Rugg, a noted educator of another generation, proposed a "yardstick" to be used as a means of evaluating schools. Several of the items from that yardstick are included here for your consideration. Compare them with contemporary school objectives established by states and local districts. To what extent does Rugg's list represent the concerns of contemporary schooling? Are Rugg's objectives quantifiable? Are they considered significant in an era concerned with skills, objectivity, and comparability?

Rugg's Key Questions to Be Asked of Any School*

1 Is the general relationship of students and teachers one of friendly comradeship, of mutual respect for others as persons? Is it one in which the teacher assumes the role of mature guide and the student the role of learner, that is being guided by one who knows—the whole enterprise approached in the spirit of sincere, questioning inquiry?

2 Are the parents and teachers and administrators developing a theory of American culture upon which to build the school program?

3 How far does the school practice the concept of equality and functional interpretation of freedom of thought and expression?

4 Does the school help students to analyze the potential of a mixed and expanding economy? Or does it preach "back to the normalcy" of private enterprise and laissez-faire? Or does it follow the line of least resistance and avoid the entire problem?

5 Does the school teach the implications of the interdependence of the peoples of the earth?

---

* Only selected excerpts are presented here. For the original yardstick see Harold Rugg, *Foundations for American Education.* Yonkers-on-Hudson: World Book Company, 1947, pp. 808–813.

6 Is the school confronting frankly its responsibility in the continuing battle for consent? Does it confront students with the current pitfalls in understanding social conditions and problems?

7 Does the school deal frankly and fully with the problems of propaganda and censorship?

8 Do the students understand that "he who owns the things that men must have, owns the men that must have them"?

9 Does the school invite in representatives of various points of view and sources of knowledge and thought to help students in the study of such issues as property, employment, government, race, and religion? Or are these studies merely from books and other materials, under the direction of the staff? Or are they ignored?

REFERENCES

Adler, M. J. (1982). *The Paideia Proposal: An Educational Manifesto.* New York: Macmillan.

Cremin, L. (1961). *The Transformation of the School: Progressivism in American Education, 1876–1957.* New York: Knopf.

Crouse, J., and Trusheim, D. (1988). *The Case against the SAT.* Chicago: University of Chicago Press.

Fiske, E. B. (1988). "America's Test Mania." *The New York Times, Education Life,* April 10.

Gould, S. J. (1981). *The Mismeasure of Man.* New York: Norton.

Gumbert, E. B., and Spring, J. H. (1974). *The Superschool and the Superstate: American Education in the Twentieth Century, 1918–1970.* New York: Wiley.

Hoffmann, B. (1962). *The Tyranny of Testing.* New York: Crowell-Collier.

Jensen, A. R. (1969). How Much Can We Boost IQ and Scholastic Achievement? *Harvard Educational Review,* **39,** 1–123.

Nairn, A., and associates (1980). *The Reign of ETS: The Corporation That Makes Up Minds.* Washington, D.C.: Nairn and Associates.

Ogbu, J. (1978). *Minority Education and Caste: The American System in Cross-cultural Perspective.* New York: Academic Press.

Owen, D. (1985). *None of the Above.* Boston: Houghton Mifflin.

Ravitch, D., and Finn, C. E., Jr. (1987). *What Do Our 17-Year-Olds Know?* New York: Harper and Row.

Rosser, P. (1987). *Sex Bias in College Admissions Testing: Why Women Lose Out,* 2d ed. Cambridge, Mass.: Fair Test.

Southern Regional Education Board (1988). *Measuring Student Learning.* Atlanta: Southern Regional Education Board.

U.S. Department of Education (1987). *What's Happening in Teacher Testing: An Analysis of State Teacher Testing Practices.* Washington, D.C.: U.S. Government Printing Office.

CHAPTER 16

PUBLIC SUPPORT FOR OR RESISTANCE TO SCHOOLS

POSITION 1
For a Bad Grade for Public Support

The public wears blinders when it comes to support for the schools. Education is something like old-fashioned motherhood. We profess great love and admiration, but continue to mistreat both. We expect mothers to sacrifice all for their children, and to demand little in return. Similarly, we expect schools to solve all social problems, but we are niggardly in our financial and personal support for them.

There are still people who don't expect mothers to take on independent careers and lives of their own, but to be loyal servants of the family. Mothers must humbly accept the blame when children misbehave or when families come apart. Schools are likewise expected to be places of social conformity and tradition, with teachers taking the role of loyal and quiet servants. And schools are expected to shoulder the blame willingly for a variety of educational and social problems, even when the schools can do little about them. Mothers' work is never done; and mothers' work is not even considered real work in the society. Teachers know that schoolwork never ends; and the public doesn't consider schooling to be real work for teachers or students, only preparation for work. Schools of today are what mothers of the past were expected to be, and still are by some people.

The public's attitude toward mothers and schools is symptomatic of a general lack of public support for children in American society. Though we still think of ourselves as a nation that prides itself on its vision for the future, we ignore or devalue the human resources which make that future possible. The generation of children just starting school should graduate from high school in the twenty-first century, but consider these indicators of public support: These children were born into a nation which ranks twenty-first in the world in the rate of infant death. About 30 percent of them will receive no or inadequate prenatal and early medical care. Almost 25 percent will not have basic immunization against controllable diseases by the age of 2. About 25 percent of the classes of 2000 to 2010 will have lived with the deprivation of poverty, but more than 20 percent of the eligible children will have been denied participation in Head Start programs which give some educational compensation for being born into poverty. Twenty percent are likely to become teenage parents; one-sixth will have no health insurance; and one out of seven will drop out of high school. Further, half will grow up in families where both parents work, but where there is only one available opening in a licensed day care facility for each twenty children (Oski, 1989, pp. 219–221).

Many more examples could be cited of the public's lack of real concern for children and for our future, but the point here is that the weakness of actual public support of schools fits into a bigger societal picture. The schools are not the only agencies that bear responsibilities for children and America's future, and that do not have adequate support. But they are the primary social agencies for assisting and inspiring young people who will someday lead the nation. The lack of public support is especially appalling in regard to schooling because schooling is the society's lifeline. We love schools, but do not want to pay for them in money, energy, or even respect. As Michael Kirst (1984) notes in a discussion of why there has been a significant decline of interest in becoming a teacher:

> One explanation for the diminished attractiveness of education as a career is the substantial erosion of public respect and support for teachers. . . . Parents are now discouraging their children from becoming teachers. A 1983 Gallup poll reveals that only 45 percent of parents polled thought teaching a desirable career for their children. Contrast this with the 75 percent who believed, only 14 years ago, that teaching was a good calling. (pp. 140, 141)

THE RHETORIC AND THE REALITY

Beneath the high-sounding public discourse about improving our schools, there is little commitment to making actual improvements. Most of the reform of the past decade has consisted of attempts simply to bring schools up to what should have been the national agenda for them during the previous two decades. Of the almost forty reports on school reform which have appeared since the 1983 publication of *A Nation at Risk,* nearly all have documented too little attention and too little support to the obvious problems of education in America (*Education Week,* 1988). A long tradition of insufficient financing, depending far too heavily on property taxation, and lack of general concern with the deteriorating conditions for schooling in America are what put this "nation at risk." Class size has been increasing; real income of teachers has declined while that of other professions improved; school building maintenance has been postponed; textbook life has been artificially extended to save money; schools have become the arena where social problems ignored by public officials (poverty, class and race bias, drugs, family dissolution) are manifested in student problems; and educators who have tried to bring these issues to the public forum have been seen merely as self-serving complainers. It is not the schools that create the problem; they are the victims. Now the victims are perceived as the perpetrators because they are an easy target for politicians, news media, and the public. There is a cynical, but realistic, view among educators that the current interest in school improvement will shortly abate, well before dramatic improvements have occurred, and that public concern for conditions of life in schools will again decline. This has been the historic pattern.

The smart politician holds forth on the importance of schools and then chastises them for failing to perform an educational miracle. This same politician will ignore the historic underfinancing of schools by politicians of both parties. The same one will speak to the taxpayers' association about keeping taxes low by keeping schools cheap, and will vote against a lower ratio of students to teachers or a substantial increase in state aid. And the same politician will gladly come to a school, if there are enough students and it is an election year, to talk to an assembly about how schools are good for you—but will not visit a variety of schools to see the problems and to find out what can be done to help teachers.

The politicians only reflect the public. The ambivalence among most citizens about schools shows itself in many ways. Many parents of children in a particular school give a lot of attention to that school for their child's sake. They want the best teacher, the best cafeteria food, the right curriculum, good textbooks, excellent experiences, high-quality physical and mental education, and the teacher's special focus for their child. These are natural desires, and needn't have negative effects. Often, however, parents' interest in their own child's education does not extend to a general interest in all schools, or in other children whose parents aren't as active or vocal. For these active parents, interest and support for school is very limited and is actually just self-interest in getting increased social advantage for their child. They will withdraw their support for the school when their children leave the system.

Public school teachers surveyed in a Gallup poll ranked parental lack of interest as the most serious problem in schools; but the general public, in the same poll, identified lax discipline, rampant drug use, poor curriculum, and low standards as the most important school problems (*Phi Delta Kappan,* 1984). The public also rated the schools much more negatively than did the teachers, and favored merit pay for teachers and standardized tests for students while teachers were significantly more skeptical about these measures. This disparity in views illustrates a continuing willingness by the public to blame teachers and schools for social failures, and to impose accountability systems to correct presumed defects. The perceived defects (discipline, drugs, standards) have not been demonstrated to be pervasive in schools, but often represent sensationalist news reporting, and the simplistic accountability measures do no more than expose teachers to more abuse and less respect. National tests of student achievement have been shown to be defective, culturally biased, and invalid, and the best colleges have become very cautious about using standardized test scores for student admission. Yet a 1988 Gallup Poll showed that 81 percent of the public trusted national tests of students which could be used to compare schools on the differences in student scores. Subject field tests for teachers have been severely criticized (*Mental Measurements Yearbook*) and are being completely revised by the test manufacturers, but the 1988 poll showed that 86 percent of the adults questioned wanted subject field competency tests for experienced teachers. The same poll showed that the primary source of information on schools was newspapers (*Phi Delta Kappan,* 1988, pp. 33–46). The public seems to want quick, easy, cheap, and unsophisticated information on schooling. This represents a basic indifference to improving the quality of life in schools.

Voting in school elections is another area of public disinterest. We have a traditional belief that schools are a basic part of the democratic society and that we need publicly elected school boards to run the schools. In some states the public is even given an opportunity to vote each year on the school budget, as though the electorate will thoughtfully examine and intelligently cast ballots on an educational spending plan. Of course, what occurs is that school budgeting becomes a taxpayer political issue that sacrifices long-term development for short-term votes. There is a myth that this voting on schools keeps the schools close to the community.

The United States has an extremely low voter turnout for all elections, compared to most other democracies, but the turnout is preposterously low in school elections. In the typical school election, for board members or budget items, less than 10 percent of the registered voters will cast ballots. That allows a very small proportion of the electorate—5 percent or so—to determine school policies, decide on school administrators and teachers, and control school finances. These elections can be manipulated by exceedingly small interest groups, such as landlords and senior citizens who want to keep property taxes low. As a result the school administrators are continually vulnerable to tiny special interests and individual vocal parents, and tend to blend into the background and to avoid advocating school improvements that cost money or are at all controversial. Also as a result, school boards become filled with people who have no strong concern for actual improvements in public education, but who want to keep schools cheap or to use the school board office as a stepping-stone to higher political office. There is little in this picture that suggests the great democratic tradition, or a close relationship between community and school.

Public ambivalence about schools is also demonstrated in such areas as teacher and administrator salaries, buildings, teaching materials, and equipment. While members of the public know about and accept high salaries in other areas, they resent and resist comparable salaries in education. Nearly everyone can cite the extraordinary incomes of movie stars and professional athletes. These are fairly rare salaries. However, newspapers carry stories every few months on the earnings of business executives, engineers, and employees in other occupations which require collegiate preparation.

In relatively modest businesses, with annual budgets of a few million dollars, executives earn $200,000 to $350,000 per year, plus bonsues and many perks, including free travel, a car, expense accounts, and tax advantages. Even businesses that are not doing well for their stockholders, and that may even have undergone bankruptcy, will still pay executives well. There is an American mystique that managers, including the incompetent ones, are much more valuable than other workers. In large corporations, the top executives make upwards of $1 million per year. Middle-management executives can earn $100,000 and more per year with additional bonuses and perks. And many supervisors and key employees earn $75,000 to $150,000. Even beginning-level professional employees, with degrees, start at $30,000, with plenty of opportunity to gain more.

For people in education, the very top salaries of the largest and most difficult administrative positions in the country will be only about $150,000, and that only in the school districts of the few biggest cities. The annual budgets in such districts will approximate $1 billion, and the school staff will number in the tens of thousands. The more typical situation is in middle-size districts where the school superintendent, managing a staff of several thousand and a budget of around $100 million, will earn $65,000 to $100,000. The very best teacher in that district cannot hope to earn nearly that much.

A teacher with both an undergraduate and a graduate degree and fifteen or more years' experience can expect to earn a top of about $35,000 in the high-paying districts, and less in most schools. Beginning teachers will start between $15,000 and $22,000 in most districts, with a few wealthy areas paying slightly higher salaries. As Theodore Sizer states the problem for a typical teacher named Horace, "the task [teaching] is already crushing, in reality a sixty-hour work week. For this, Horace is paid a wage enjoyed by age-mates in semiskilled and low-pressure blue-collar jobs and by novices, twenty-five years his junior, in some other white-collar professions" (p. 20).

The public does not seem to get aroused at high business salaries or excessive ones in sports and the arts, but they cannot comprehend comparable incomes in education. We fail to recognize that the public actually pays these private salaries in the long run, since the prices of goods, services, and tickets are increased to provide for executives and others. And taxpayers provide much of the money for private salaries because the government uses tax money to buy large quantities of supplies and equipment from business.

Government contracts for defense equipment, computers, paper, and other goods and services provide billions of dollars for corporations. These are taxpayers' dollars. Taxpayers have had to pay millions to rescue corporations which are threatened with failure, such as Chrysler and Lockheed, while high salaries are paid to the executives. We do not vote on the budgets of these corporations, nor do we elect boards to control their policies, yet they are heavily supported by taxes. Taxpayers have also footed the bill for excessive defense costs, for example, $500 toilet seats and multimillion-dollar cost over-runs by weapons manufacturers. The schools must operate within an annually balanced budget, and there are nowhere near the same financial scandals sur-rounding schools as there are surrounding the defense industry and the gov-ernment. Middle- and higher-level managers in business have high salaries, partially supported but uncontrolled by government. For some reason we do not see the need to give comparable salaries for public education, and as a result, we have difficulty in convincing the most highly qualified people to commit to careers in education in a society where income is very important.

THE PHYSICAL FACILITIES

The facilities where education is to take place have been in decline for a quarter century. New York City schools, for example, will require at least $15 billion to cover the costs of delayed maintenance and improvements to bring them up to minimal conditions. A task force that studied New York City schools re-ported that 83 percent of the public schools were deteriorating; "some are so overcrowded that classes are held in locker and store rooms." (*The New York Times,* 1989, p. B1) This sorry condition of schools is serious in older, urban centers, but it is also reflected throughout the nation in all but the wealthiest communities. School boards, administrators, and teachers do not desire to have unsatisfactory and potentially unsafe schools. School staff and students do not prefer to spend their school lives in such locations. But the public has not been adequately aroused, and has not been sufficiently interested to spend the money and time to respond to educators' requests.

School buildings, in most communities, have been built to be as efficient in the use of space as possible. As a result, they are not usually very inspiring: a series of square classrooms along a long hall, with a gym and cafeteria and some office space. Even in the more affluent towns, where the exterior of the school is embellished and handsome, the interior is often suited to mass seating and hall passing. Schools are usually painted and equipped with the most economical and durable materials, seldom fashionable or interesting. There are, of course, some very beautiful and expensive school buildings in wealthy areas. These are built as a monument to the town or a particular politician, and use vast resources in the building which could be applied to improving educational activities. These same wealthy areas will pay teachers and admin-istrators somewhat better salaries than poorer areas can afford, but these higher salaries will still fall well below the average incomes of families whose children are in the schools.

A teacher does not have an office, but only a desk in front of a classroom. Secretarial help for teachers is essentially nonexistent, and teachers are not permitted even individual telephones. The standard school will have a very plain "teachers' lounge," with a few cushioned chairs, a few tables, some school equipment for duplicating, and bathrooms on the side. When not on hall, cafeteria, library, or playing-field duty, teachers are expected to prepare lessons, mark papers, keep up with their profession, and arrange teaching materials for class. The duplicating and other equipment is often broken from overuse, there are not enough books or films, field trips are too expensive, and teachers often purchase needed materials themselves or construct makeshift substitutes. Teachers eat lunch, during the twenty to thirty minutes available in many schools, in the "lounge," in the classroom, or in the cafeteria. In some schools teachers are still required to use a punch-clock to keep track of their arrival and departure times. Compare that with the kinds of facilities, time available, offices, and general treatment of key professionals in businesses.

Schools also handle large numbers of children for long periods of time, with relatively few resources. The typical elementary school teacher will have direct responsibility for twenty-five to thirty students for seven hours a day, with a short break for lunch and a preparation interlude while the students have gym or music. A secondary school teacher will have twenty-five to thirty students per class for five to seven classes each day. Most parents are exhausted from dealing with two children for a day. Seven hours of keeping the attention of thirty elementary students or 150 secondary ones in forty-five minute segments, plus the added paperwork and "duties," is daunting. It is also a cheap way to handle lots of students.

Finances are not the only example of public shortsightedness in education. The general commitment to education in the society is only halfhearted. We have had cabinet-level secretaries in the federal government for such areas as agriculture, commerce, health, defense (formerly war), housing, and transportation for many years. These positions were to provide a national focus on that area, after considerable political visibility and advocacy, and undertake systematic management of issues in each cabinet area because they were considered significant in the society. Yet, it took massive lobbying by teacher associations over decades, and a commitment from presidential candidate Jimmy Carter, to establish the first secretary of education. Even so, President Reagan vowed to close the Department of Education, and he tried. If education were really considered to be as important as the rhetoric proclaims, the length of time it took to get to minimal national governmental attention would be incredible. Instead, it is merely another example of public ambivalence.

In these and other ways the public comes up short when evaluated in its actual support for schools. Despite the strong feelings about school expressed in politics and in local communities, there are few places where a concerted effort is made to provide the highest-quality schooling possible. These few examples occur in some of the poorest communities, where the local people make real sacrifices to give their children greater opportunities. The reluctance of the federal and state governments to provide sufficient resources to relieve these few districts of their excessive burden, and to enable them to shed their second-class status, is an unfortunate result of the tradition of treating education as a costly expense rather than an investment in the future. The report card evaluating the public on their support for education shows a B in rhetoric, a B-plus in good intentions, a C for effort, and a C-minus in achievement. None of these grades is good enough for America.

POSITION 2
For a Good Grade for Public Support

American society from the start has had a love affair with education. We continue to believe that through the schools the American dream can become reality. Through education all can achieve and the society will improve. America has led the world in providing free public schooling, in addition to private schools, for the whole population. Our record in education is extraordinary. Our broad, visible support and participation in schools make them the strongest of public activities. No other social activity involves such a large proportion of the population. Not only students and teachers, but also parents, public boards, publishers, businesses, libraries, and local, state, and national governments expend enormous amounts of time, energy, and money on schools.

We often recognize deficiencies in schools, as in any public enterprise, but in most communities the local schools are regarded with great pride. Schools are often the centers of community life. School colors and symbols are widely recognized and respected. School activities draw large numbers of local people. House prices, as real estate agents know, are directly related to the perceived quality of local schools. People want to live where schools are good. We make major efforts to correct and improve schools to provide better educational opportunities for each succeeding generation. Even with the problems that seem always to plague schools, the American people grant generally high marks to them.

For over twenty years Phi Delta Kappa has commissioned the Gallup Poll to conduct an annual public evaluation of education. Among other things, Gallup asks a systematically selected sample of the public to grade the schools. The public schools get high marks from the public, with over 40 percent grading the schools A or B. As one would expect, parents of children who attend private schools and citizens who have no children in school rate the public schools somewhat lower. But those who have the most at stake, the parents of children in public schools, rate public schools much higher, with about 55 percent giving grades of A or B. Further, people rate their local schools much higher than schools in general (Gallup and Elam, 1988, pp. 33–46).

Over the years there have been some fluctuations in these grades. For example, when there is public criticism of schooling, as in the school reform movement of the early 1980s, the level of public support declines somewhat, but still remains very strong. Interestingly, the public schools get better grades from those who are themselves better educated, are somewhat older, and have higher incomes.*

Gallup has also examined public perceptions of a variety of social institutions for a long time. The institution in which the public has had the most confidence for the past fifteen years is organized religion, followed by the military, the U.S. Supreme Court, and banks. The public schools have continued to rank fifth, just below banks in public confidence, and well above other institutions such as newspapers, television, and organized labor. Over 50 percent of those polled said they had "quite a lot" or "a great deal" of confidence in schools. The public also ranks teachers very high in comparison with people in other professions in their contribution to the general good and their prestige—third, just below clergymen and medical doctors. Teachers rank much higher than judges, bankers, lawyers, business executives, politicians, and others (Gallup Reports, 1981). The public also recognizes the pressure on teachers, ranking their jobs second only to that of medical doctors in stressfulness. Public support for schools and teachers has been, and remains, strong.

STRONG LEGAL SUPPORT:
THE SCHOOLS AND OTHER AGENCIES

Schools in America not only have strong support according to opinion polls; for a public service they enjoy an especially strong legal and financial structure. Of the many different agencies providing social services—welfare, highway construction, public health, and so on—no other enjoys the peculiar legal and budgetary support that the schools have.

The distinction between constitutional, statutory, and administrative regulations suggests the differences in strength of public agencies. Constitutionally based requirements are at the top. These are basic rights and conditions which are very difficult to modify. Statutory laws are more temporal, changeable by the formal actions of legislative bodies. Administrative regulations, by comparison, can be altered at virtually any time by the duly authorized agency. For example, highway construction is not covered under the U.S. Constitution or various state constitutions. Federal highways are broadly governed under some congressional acts and are technically governed through administrative regulations of the U.S. Department of Transportation. State highways, and state involvement in federal highways, are governed under state statutes and administrative regulations of the appropriate state agency.

In regard to schools, the U.S. Constitution does not specifically include education, or most other services, as an identified area of national concern because schools were already under state control at the time the Constitution was drafted. Except as they are covered under such broad terms as "provide for the public defense" and "general welfare," and the rights identified in the

---

* Gallup Poll results are drawn from reports in issues of several journals: *Gallup Reports, Phi Delta Kappan,* and *Newsweek.*

Bill of Rights (speech, religion, association, and so on), none of the standard public services are specified in the U.S. Constitution. Schooling, however, has been interpreted by the U.S. Supreme Court as falling within U.S. constitutional boundaries when cases arise on such matters as free speech, prayer in school, and segregation. There is, then, a constitutional context for education, and an increasing federal interest in schools. The U.S. Department of Education has become the initiator and evaluator of much of the current educational reform in America. Federal funds have been particularly useful as seed money to enable schools to experiment with effective school practices, and to stimulate good local schools.

At the state level, education is one of the primary concerns of most state constitutions. Schools are acknowledged to be a significant responsibility of the states. Their position in state constitutions conveys considerable strength to schools. Schooling is ingrained in the basic operations of the states. The constitutions of most states require free public education, and permit the legislature to develop laws to strengthen the schools.

An examination of statutory law in the several states will show that educational topics consume vast amounts of legislative time and energy. Because school law consumes so much legislative activity, separate categories and books of school law are found in many states. States also usually develop administrative regulations for schools. These are under state law, and delegate specific operational responsibilities to agencies such as the state board of education, the state department of education, and a state superintendent of schools. Laws and administrative regulations also govern local school operation to guarantee minimal quality and consistency throughout the state.

In cities and local communities, schools enjoy extensive support and participation. Local boards of education, citizens' committees, parent-teacher organizations, athletic and musical support groups, and other groups are involved in multitudes of school affairs each year. State laws generally delegate considerable power to local communities to govern their schools. It is at the local level that administrators and teachers are employed, that the school curriculum is implemented, that teaching materials are purchased, and that the variety of school activities is designed and operated. This local involvement helps to keep schools close to their client community. It is an American tradition, different from the way schools are set up in much of the rest of the world. In England and France, for example, the national and regional governments control much of the school structure and operation, and local parents have little direct involvement with schools. In the United States the local school is often the main community cultural center, with a variety of activities for all citizens. This has helped the schools maintain strong community support.

STRONG SCHOOL FINANCIAL SUPPORT

Although we may never have enough money to pay for everything we desire in schools, the American public has been very generous in its financial support for schools. The financing of schools is another indication of the broad support and participation of public bodies in education. In real dollars the federal government has increased its financial commitment to education over the past hundred years, and is currently spending over $20 billion annually to help schools of all levels. Included in this figure is federal money for model school programs, special education, cafeteria support, minority student development, scholarships, and educational research. In addition, states allocate very high proportions of their budgets to schools. In many states education is the largest single social service in the budget. The third tax support for public schools comes from local communities. Schools are the largest item in local budgets, far surpassing other municipal services.*

Since World War II we have committed vast tax resources to our schools and have made dramatic increases in the funding of our schools. Thirty-five years ago the total federal, state, and local expenditure for education at all levels in the United States was about $20 billion per year; it is now about $320 billion. For the elementary and secondary schools expenditures increased from $16 billion in 1960 to about $200 billion now—a thirteenfold increase in spending. Of this current spending for elementary and secondary public schools, about 9 percent comes from federal support, 45 percent from the state, 40 percent from local taxes, and the rest from other sources such as business.

The proportion of the Gross National Product which has been used for schooling in America has increased since 1949, when it was only 1.8 percent, to about 3.5 percent now (*Statistical Abstract of the United States,* 1988).

STRONG SOCIAL SUPPORT

In addition to the considerable legal and financial support for schools in America just discussed, there are many other indicators of the strong position of schools in the society. Among these factors are the increasing proportion of students who are staying longer in schools, the social recognition that increased education deserves increased income, general acceptance of the inconvenience and expense of having students in school longer, and the extensive coverage of schooling in the media.

We have had compulsory school laws across the country for the past seven decades, and have increased the legal age for leaving in most states to 16 or 17. That increase in minimum age could explain some increase in the proportion of students staying in school longer, but not all of it. Indeed, increases in the legal school-leaving age have been the result of a social recognition that more schooling is a good thing. But, beyond the legal requirement, students are also voluntarily staying longer in education. Completion of high school is not required by any state, only attainment of a certain age before leaving. To see

---

* Data about schools are drawn from government documents, including publications of the National Center for Education Statistics and the U.S. Bureau of the Census.

the increasing level of social acknowledgment of education it is helpful to examine the pattern of school attendance since the Depression.

In 1940, of those persons age 25 and over, 75 percent had not completed high school and the average years of school completed was only 8.6. By the census of 1980, however, of those age 25 years and over, about 75 percent *had* completed high school. Surprisingly, the average number of school years completed went beyond high school: 12.6 years. Further, in 1940 only 4.6 percent of the adult population had completed four years of college, but by 1980 over 12 percent had finished at least four years of college. That is amazing growth in a short time, and shows the generally high value placed on schooling in our society.

SCHOOL AND INCOME: SOCIAL RECOGNITION

The relation of education to income is another indicator of social support for schooling. If more education were not considered monetarily valuable in the society, there would be no systematic disparity in incomes according to the level of school completed. Although not everything we value can be measured in increased salary, a higher income does suggest social acknowledgment of value.

A simple comparison of incomes by school years completed shows that in 1939, the average annual income for a person who had completed high school was about 50 percent higher than the annual income of someone who had only completed elementary school. The college-educated person in the same period just before World War II earned about two and one-half times the annual income of someone with only elementary schooling. Currently, the average annual income for someone with four years of high school is twice that of someone with only elementary schooling. A college-educated person will make about three and one-fourth times the annual income of someone with only elementary school, and half again as much as someone who has completed high school. In lifetime earnings the disparity in income is remarkable: compared with a person with elementary schooling only, a high school graduate will earn about $250,000 more, and an average college-educated person will make about $450,000 more. Clearly, society values education in monetary terms.

There is a cost in money and inconvenience to having children stay in school, but families suffer these to provide their children as much educational opportunity as possible. This is another indicator of social support. Obviously, the more students there are in school, the more educational cost to taxpayers. There are other costs of longer time in school, however, that are borne by the individual families. These include payment for school expenses not covered by taxes, such as medical expenses for shots and health-related records, uniforms or special clothing, some supplies, memberships in school associations, athletics and arts productions, and special activities, as well as purchases of certain kinds of clothing and supplies due to school-based peer pressure.

Beyond high school, costs are spiraling for college tuition, books, and student fees. There is also an indirect cost to all of those families whose children are not a part of the income-producing work force while they are in school. Inconvenience to the family as a result of schooling includes the need to schedule family vacations around school calendars, school-required paperwork, and conformity to the school's daily schedule. These extra costs and inconveniences have not slowed the increase in social support for schools.

Few public services, outside of the government itself, get the amount of media coverage that schools do. People want to hear about school and schooling. Advertisers recognize this, and key their ads to the school calendar, with "back-to-school" ads and school-supply specials spaced out throughout the school year. School events are widely covered in rural weekly papers and big-city dailies. News about educational problems, proposed solutions, and results are common in the media. Many papers have reporters assigned to cover education.

There is something very American about our strong support for schools. A society built on the ideals of opportunity and progress would be expected to establish, revise, and revere social institutions that promote those values. Schools are a primary example of such institutions. They are the focus of opportunity and of progress. We may take them for granted sometimes, but that only underscores the general public support. We expect our schools to make continuing contributions to the well-being of the society, and when things are going well there is no reason to fuss over them. Complaints about schools never pose the idea of abolishing them; rather the usual theme is to keep improving them. The American public has given the schools a very high level of support in all areas.

FOR DISCUSSION

1 Evaluation presumes the setting of values. How much value does the American society give to schools? How can this be measured? What yardsticks can be used, and what comparisons can be made?

2 What would be the potential consequences, for other parts of the society, if the budgets made available to schools were doubled? From what sources could such funding come? What would be the likely consequences of that move?

3 If people were paid what they are worth in the improvement of our civilization, what alterations in salaries for differing occupations would need to occur? What effects would be expected from dramatic changes in salaries for these occupations?

4 The following table shows total expenditures and teacher salary averages for public education in the United States since 1910, with an estimate for 1990.

Year	Total expenditure (in $ millions)	Number of teachers	Average salary
1910	$ 525	523,000	$ 485
1920	1,036	680,000	871
1930	2,344	854,000	1,470
1940	2,344	875,000	1,441
1950	5,838	914,000	3,010
1960	15,613	1,387,000	5,174
1970	40,683	2,131,000	8,840
1980	103,100	2,211,000	16,000
1990	165,000	2,200,000	24,600

Source: Statistical Abstract of the United States (1988), U.S. Department of Commerce, Washington, D.C.: U.S. Government Printing Office; Historical Statistics of the United States: Colonial Times to 1970 (1975), U.S. Department of Commerce, Washington, D.C.: U.S. Government Printing Office.

A comparison among selected countries on educational expenditures in the mid-1980s, as a percentage of Gross National Product, shows the following:

Rank	Country	Percent of GNP spent for education
1	Sweden	8.5
2	Canada	8.0
3	Norway	7.0
4	U.S.S.R.	6.6
5	Hungary	5.8
6	United States	5.5
7	Thailand	3.9
8	Mexico	2.7
9	Nigeria	2.1

Source: A Vision for America's Future (1989). Washington, D.C.: Children's Defense Fund; UNESCO Statistical Yearbook.

These data do not account for inflation or other national expenditures. What factors seem to explain the changes and differences in each of the columns: Are these numbers sufficient to answer whether or not the public supports education and values teachers? What other information would be valuable in arriving at a conclusion?

REFERENCES

Children's Defense Fund (1989). *A Vision of America's Future*. Washington, D.C.: Children's Defense Fund.

Education Week (1988). April 27,

Kirst, M. K. (1984). *Who Controls Our Schools?* New York: Freeman.

Gallup, A., and Elam, S. M. (1988). "20th Annual Gallup Poll." *Phi Delta Kappan*, **70**, 33–46.

The Gallup Report (1981). p. 193.

The New York Times. (1989). "Master Plan Seeks $15 Billion for Schools." January 10, p. B1.

Oski, F. (1989). "How to Raise Money for the Class of 2000." *The Nation,* **248** (February 20), 217–221.

Sizer, T. (1983). *Horace's Compromise: The Dilemma of the American High School.* Boston: Houghton Mifflin.

Statistical Abstract of the United States (1988). Washington, D.C.: U.S. Government Printing Office.

CHAPTER 17

EDUCATIONAL EXCELLENCE AS VISION OR SHAM

POSITION 1
For Continuing the Excellence Movement

The primary purpose of education is to improve the lives of people through knowledge. That is also a fundamental purpose of any democratic and progressive society. To be satisfied with less is to move away from democracy and progress. Improvement is, therefore, the key to educational reform. Obviously, it does not make sense to advocate reforms which do not intend to improve on the way things are. Why would one want reform which made things worse?

But improvement is elusive without a sense of direction; and improvement may be so minor that it is virtually unmeasureable, or it may be very extensive. The issue, then, is to determine criteria against which to evaluate reforms. In effect, we should ask: How far should we go in reforms in education? And, how do we know which reforms are going in the right direction?

The answers to those questions need to be addressed in terms of our long-range goal. This goal sets the basic agenda, and allows us to plan the strategies and tactics which will change schools toward the achievement of that goal.

The goal we should use in education as the basis for planning, and as the main criterion against which to judge various reform efforts, is excellence. Excellence as a goal sets our vision high, but still provides an ideal which has the flexibility to change as conditions change. Excellence is the appropriate educational goal for a nation which has already achieved world recognition in democratic self-governance in science, in the arts, in literature, in business and industry, and in the protection of human rights. The Report of the National

Commission on Excellence in Education showed the shortcomings of our nation's schools and advocated reforms to set excellence as our goal. The report defines excellence as follows:

> At the level of the individual learner, it means performing on the boundary of individual ability in ways that test and push back individual limits, in school and in the workplace. Excellence characterizes a school or college that sets high expectations and goals for all learners, then tries in every way to help students reach them. Excellence characterizes a society that has adopted these policies, for it will then be prepared through the education and skill of its people to respond to the challenges of a rapidly changing world. (*A Nation at Risk,* 1983, p. 12)

For America, there can be no lesser goal for the schools. This would seem to be a goal over which there is no argument. Excellence, one would think, is what we all want. But there is dispute that needs review.

THE NAYSAYERS

Some people argue that America should not set excellence as the goal for schools because it makes the schools too rigorous, too "academic." They want the schools to be a place of free play for children, where little work is required. This may sound like a pleasant purpose for schools and for children, but it is misleadingly pleasant. Without struggle, little is gained. Freedom without purpose is really slavery to personal whims. The schools form the new generation of citizens in the society. We can't let them become playgrounds; if we do, America will suffer. Excellence requires effort and achievement. Our children deserve more credit and more challenge.

Other people don't want to change the schools because they fear the challenge of excellence. They are not accustomed to having their work reviewed, and they resent any intrusion that holds them responsible for good work. They have found a sanctuary in the bureaucracy and do not want exposure. For them, reform toward excellence threatens their jobs or their convenience. They do not want to be evaluated; they do not want to exert energy; they do not want to be accountable. Despite the evidence of weakness in the schools, they resist change. There is good reason to shake up this group. It is more than a question of mere job productivity; the resisting ones are holding back students, parents, and the society. School is too important to leave in the hands of those who are satisfied with less than excellence. Some of the resisters will respond when they see that the reforms are coming regardless. Others will begin to fade as their inadequacies are revealed by the reforms. Resisting change is a losing proposition for all concerned. It is a prescription for atrophy in schools and in society.

Some merely distrust excellence because it is an unknown. They have seen school fads come and go, without improvement. They argue that if the schools won't change, why try to force them? They have become accustomed to mediocre performance in schools, and do not know how to alter it. They have watched test scores drop. They know about graduates of high school who are illiterate. They have observed deficiencies in student knowledge of American history. And they know students who have trouble with simple math and scientific principles. They are frustrated with the state of the schools, but complacent. Complacency, especially in the face of declining quality, will simply speed the decline of the schools. Since change is always happening, these people stand against the tide. Standing still while everything else moves leaves you further behind. While this group may not like the decline of schools, they are unsure of what excellence would mean. This group is at least open to setting a new agenda for the schools.

A final group of naysayers believe that excellence in education is somehow undemocratic. This is a very substantial argument, since equality is popularly believed to be part of democracy. How can we have equality and still have excellence? Not everyone can be excellent, they claim, so using excellence as a criterion will only separate people, and then they will not be equal. That idea is interesting, and deserves fuller consideration than the objections of the other naysayers.

EXCELLENCE, EQUALITY, AND EQUITY

It is illogical to suggest that excellence and equality are opposites. Excellence does not automatically exclude equality. To be equal does not mean that we cannot be excellent. We do not have to choose one or the other. In fact, the democratic idea of excellence that is advocated as a goal for the schools actually improves equality. It is through the goal of excellence that everyone has the chance to develop. Excellence is defined as providing for all to be excellent. That is the best form of equality, an excellent society. Although this is an ideal, and is not yet achieved, it is an ideal worth keeping.

Excellence can occur in the daily work of individuals. A cabinetmaker who carefully fits together fine-surfaced pieces of wood exhibits a pride of workmanship that represents excellence. A stockbroker who examines company financial statements with care and diligence before making recommendations can also demonstrate excellence. Street sweepers who recognize their contributions to the beauty of a city and make special efforts to do a first-class job can be excellent. Store clerks, bankers, florists, computer mechanics, politicians, artists, hairdressers, librarians, and workers in all other occupations can show excellence in their work. Pride in going beyond the mediocre is as noticeable as the resulting product. The benefits accrue to the individual and to the society. Excellence becomes a great motivation, with intrinsic and extrinsic rewards. We feel better about our work, and we do better work.

FORMS OF EQUALITY AND EQUITY

Some of the dispute over excellence and equality occurs because of differences in the way equality is viewed. There are several ways to look at equality.

Equality of condition means that everyone has or gets an equal amount of things. If we had an apple pie to divide among eight people, we could cut eight equal slices so that each person would have equality of condition in regard to the pie.

There is also an equality of claim. This form of equality presumes that everyone has the same claim to equal portions of things, though not everyone exercises this claim. If we cut the pie into eight equal pieces, and one person gave his slice to another, we would no longer have equality of condition. One person would have two slices, another would have none. But we would have equality of claim. Each person could have claimed an equal piece of pie.

Equality of opportunity is similar to equality of claim. If we notified all eight people that the pie would be cut at 6:30, and only seven people showed up by that time, we could cut it into seven equal slices. The eighth person would get none, but did have the opportunity to get a slice. There was equal opportunity, but equal condition did not occur.

Equality determined by justification suggests that there are rational grounds to justify unequal conditions. There may be sound reasons to slice the pie into unequal parts. If one person is diabetic and can't eat the pie, this could be a good reason not to divide it equally among all eight persons. If one person does not like apple pie, that may alter the division. If one person cannot eat an equal slice, and another can eat much more, an unequal division is reasonable. If the group agrees to give half of the pie to two people who missed out on pie the last time, this is a justification for inequality in pie slices. This is the basic notion of equity, that things may be divided unequally if there is a reasonable justification for doing so.

It is equity that a democratic society can attempt to provide. Equity is based on fairness or justice. Equity permits inequality when it is fair to do so. There are times, as in our attempt to correct the racial discrimination of years ago, that we need to provide extra help for those who have been victimized. That extra help is unequal since not everyone gets the same amount of it. But it is considered the fair, or equitable, way to proceed. Programs of assistance in welfare, in tax relief for those with low incomes, in special college scholarships for disadvantaged minorities, and in many other unequal distributions of financial support are considered fair as examples of equity in society.

Equality of condition is something which has never occurred, and is unlikely ever to develop. Despite efforts in some socialistic countries, there is no example of completely equal treatment for all people of a society. Socialist governments attempt to make some things appear equal by requiring conformity and stifling individual initiative, but inequalities still occur. Commissars and internationally competitive athletes are treated better than typical workers. We are simply born unequal, and we grow unequally. We have inherently unequal mental and physical characteristics. Inequality is a natural condition. We can't manufacture equality of condition by dividing everything into equal portions.

Equality of claim, of opportunity, and of justification all permit some inequality. These views of equality can fit into the concept of equity. If we provide that all persons have a claim to equal treatment under the law, that is fair even though not everyone will necessarily have an equally sound case or an equal amount of time, lawyers, and speaking ability. If we provide equality of opportunity for everyone to succeed by giving free public education, special help for those who want to take advantage of it, and access to public information and assistance, that is fair even though not everyone will get, or want, an equal amount. If we give special assistance to some groups and individuals because there is social justification for such special treatment, that is fair even though not everyone will get an equal distribution.

SCHOOL REFORM FOR EXCELLENCE AND EQUITY

The promotion of excellence and equity at the same time in schools is difficult, but worth the effort. Essentially, there are two major premises for this approach to reform in education. One offers clear and open opportunity for all to achieve; the other sets standards for performance.

First, public schools need to remain open to all who can benefit from them, and should give special encouragement to those who make the most effort to do well in schoolwork. Schools should make this point very clear in their communication with the community and in their organization and operation. The schools must be places where all are welcome, but where learning is valued and disruption is not tolerated. Equality of opportunity occurs when everyone understands the focus of the school, and is able to take advantage of what it offers.

Second, the schools need to emphasize excellence in academic study. This should include giving extra help to those who have had difficulty, but who desire to succeed and show potential. It should also include extra help for those whose exceptional talents can be expanded and enriched. This latter group, sometimes called "gifted and talented," are the people who are likely to become the leading figures of society in adulthood. They deserve to have their abilities honed. And the society will reap the benefits in the future. It is a social and educational tragedy to have our brightest and best held back in their development because a school is misguided in its idea of equality. Glazer (1987) points out that "if effort is important—and I think it is—how do we encourage it? Not, I am sure, by saying, 'regardless of effort, it doesn't matter—all rewards are equally available to all, or may be equally available to all by lottery.'" Equality regardless of effort to achieve excellence is meaningless. Equity would suggest that our best need the best.

DEVELOPING EXCELLENCE

High-caliber students develop in the company of others of high quality. Excellent tennis players want to play with other excellent players because they improve their skills that way. Excellent carpenters want to work with excellent carpenters because it helps them learn and improve. But weak tennis players and carpenters learn more when they are with others who are only slightly better than they are. If there is too much difference between the levels of quality and talent, the weak ones become embarrassed and drop out, and the talented ones are restricted in their development because of the time spent with the weaker ones. The development of excellence in school requires some separation to maximize peer encouragement and initiative.

Excellent students must also have excellent teachers and administrators. That should not need to be said since it is so obvious. But, in many schools, high-ability students are not challenged by their teachers, and the school is run by administrators who impede their progress by requiring lockstep education. Reforms are needed in teacher and administrator education. We must provide adequate rewards for teaching and school administration, but we must expect high-quality performance. Further, we must give extra reward to truly exceptional teachers and administrators to sustain motivation for excellence in education. It is these excellent educators who serve as role models for the students who are academically talented and who put out the effort.

EFFORT AND EXCELLENCE

Innate intellectual superiority over other students and high social standing are unsuitable grounds for receiving educational advantages over other youths. High intelligence is not a sufficient basis for special treatment if the student does not work to develop his or her gifts. Similarly, the mere luck of being born into a family of high social class should not entitle a person to favored treatment in schools. We need to motivate and encourage students toward success in academic activities, but there may be some who forsake their talents or who rely primarily on family status to get them through. Neither of these choices is compatible with the movement toward excellence in education. And neither is consistent with the concept of equity in the distribution of special advantages in schools. Those who are intellectually lazy and those who believe that wealth deserves favor are not making the kind of contribution needed for the excellent society.

EXCELLENCE AND EQUITY IN SCHOOLING REFORM

The movement toward excellence in education includes school reforms which:

Provide access to schools for all who can benefit
Set high standards of performance
Hold schools accountable for their academic work
Reward merit in students, teachers, and administrators

Schools need to develop performance standards for students, teachers, administrators, and the school as a whole. These standards need to be rigorous and measurable to show when they have been achieved. And they will need revision upward as time goes on. Such adjustment will reflect the level of excellence expected in future periods. Those who achieve high standards, "the champions" noted by Peters and Waterman (1982), deserve public praise and recognition.

It is clear that excellence is the most appropriate goal for American society and its schools. Without such a goal, schools are adrift and will decline. It is to the general benefit of society that schools continually strive for excellence. That striving will require extra effort, and may involve some discontent. Some of the discontent can be easily dismissed, but the concern about equity is important. It is incumbent on the schools to demonstrate that the reforms leading toward excellence are also equitable, that they justify necessary inequalities.

Excellence and equity are very compatible when educational excellence offers equality of opportunity for all students to become high achievers. Further, some inequality of condition is fair and equitable because the whole society gains from the nurturing of the most talented. This helps America's search for excellence.

POSITION 2
For Exposing Sham in the Excellence Movement

It will come as no surprise to you that we are striving for excellence in the society and in our schools. Human society has been able to survive the agrarian and the industrial revolutions; we have gone beyond the paleolithic age, the stone age, and the atomic age; and we have endured Kafka, *Brave New World,* and *1984.* Can the age of excellence hold any fears?

Isn't excellence our new national motto? Is there a business, a university, or a school district remaining in the United States which has not used the word "excellence" to describe its efforts? But what is excellence? And why have we consumed most of this past decade of school reform so frenetically pursuing it? Could it be that we believe that repeating a word often enough makes it come true? We may be in the middle of another fairy tale, or mere dupes of the advertising world.

Unfortunately, the excellence movement in education is a sham and a deception, despite its popularity. There is a hidden agenda beneath the soft rhetoric that should make American citizens alarmed and angry. First, we will explore the nature of the excellence movement; then we will present a critique.

If you doubt that the word "excellence" is the key word of the 1980s school reform agenda, consider the evidence. The most prominent term used in coverage of the current school reform movement by most of the major newspapers and weekly news magazines is "excellence." *Education Week,* "American Education's Newspaper of Record," has devoted front-page space in many issues to the "excellence movement," and has chronicled, state by state, the several school reform activities identified as moving toward excellence. Even

Burger King, noted for its own concerns for quality, sponsors national awards for excellence in education.

The professional education literature has been filled with such stories. *Educational Leadership* and *Phi Delta Kappan* have devoted entire issues and many articles to "excellence." Most widely read publications in education have used or overused the term in the past two years.

A comparison of annual issues of *The Education Index*, an index which lists current articles each month in the most widely circulated journals on education, reveals the increasing overuse of the term in the 1980s. Near the end of the 1970s, from July 1977 to June 1978, there was no separate category "Excellence" under which to list articles. And of the thirty-four articles listed that year under the category "Education: aims and purposes," not one used that term in the article title. Five years later, in academic year 1982–1983, there also was no separate category "Exellence," and no articles under aims and purposes with "excellence" in the title. But the next year, 1983–1984, "Excellence" appeared as a category, and eleven of sixty-seven articles cited under aims and purposes of education used the word "excellence" in their titles. By the end of the decade, the category "Excellence" had become a fixture because the articles on that topic were so numerous, and about one-third of all articles cited under the category of aims and purposes used "excellence" in the article title.

A similar situation is seen in examining *Current Index to Journals in Education* (CIJE), another reference work to professional literature. Before June 1983, there was no separate category for articles on excellence. By December 1984, there were two categories: "Excellence," and "Excellence in Education." By the end of the decade a new, third category, "Excellence (Quality)," was added.

The year 1983 is important in this literature because that was the year of the widely publicized Report of the National Commission on Excellence in Education, *A Nation at Risk*. The risk to America, the report suggested, was a school crisis that threatened America's military and business competitiveness in the world. No significant evidence of the "crisis" was presented, but that politically important and volatile document contained the oft-quoted phrase about schools developing "a rising tide of mediocrity." The answer to the risk was excellence, even though the report did little to define excellence, or to explain how we would know it when we saw it.

Given all of this publicity, one would think that there actually was a massive excellence movement in education in America. Certainly, much is written on it. That might be taken to indicate some level of agreement on what excellence is and how we are moving toward it. Advocating excellence is easy. Without critical thought it sounds desirable, but determining what constitutes excellence as it appears in schools raises some critical questions about it. It is, after all, the "operational definitions" of excellence advocated for schools by policymakers that give us specific recommendations to judge.

WHAT CONSTITUTES THE EXCELLENCE MOVEMENT
IN EDUCATION

Current parameters of the excellence movement in education are illustrated by a list of "reform" regulations and activities that have been described in recent articles. These include:

Mandatory kindergarten
State-required tests for grade-to-grade promotion
Increased time in school day and school year
Emphasis on homework and mastery of skills
Limits on student extracurricular activities and time
Increased course and grade requirements for graduation
Expanded testing for statewide comparative school assessment
State-mandated exit tests for students before graduation
Increased college admission requirements
Increased state control of teacher education
State-required tests to obtain teacher licenses

There are several important points to note in this list. The excellence movement seems intent on making school a place of lifeless drudgery that focuses on a series of test hurdles and gates which separate students and label them for life. There is nothing on the excellence list which speaks of improving the quality of school life for students and teachers, for the encouragement of creativity, or for the joy of learning. There is nothing which speaks of the need to correct disadvantages among children, to equalize opportunities, or to bring minorities more fully into the American mainstream through education. It is mainly a restrictive and negative list of increasing requirements that are likely to increase the gap between those who already have and those who do not have economic advantage. No wonder we now face increasing student dropout rates, especially for minorities, and a decline in the number of minority candidates for teaching credentials. The excellence movement is taking its toll on our democracy.

Most of the items on the list are new state mandates, inserting the state bureaucracy more fully into control of the schools. This increasing centralization of control limits the possibilities of variation and flexibility among schools. In addition to the obvious conformity this entails, it further threatens school district autonomy and teacher academic freedom, because it enables the state more easily to exert control over curriculum and teacher methodology.

Also, the list shows increasing infatuation with simplistic numbers from test scores, rather than with the deeper quest for quality in education. Tests are establishing the curriculum, teacher activities, teacher evaluation, and school evaluation. Boards and administrators force teachers to teach to the test. Teachers drill students to score higher. If the tests were universally valid, actually showing what students know, there might be some grounds for more testing.

Instead, the tests are seriously limited and generally invalid; they are mainly devices that reduce schooling to a series of comparative numbers to make political, not educational, decisions easier.

State legislatures, which have underfunded education for decades, are escaping blame for school problems by now blaming the victims of this situation. Minorities and members of lower socioeconomic classes are being penalized by the shift in public policy from equity to excellence. Teachers are being deprofessionalized by state requirements that deal in quantity, not quality. Although there has been some effort at improving teacher salaries, the increase does not make up for years of neglect, and does not compensate for the restrictive and elitistic nature of most of the ''excellence'' agenda.

These examples of the excellence movement in schools pose serious questions in regard to the definition of the word, the direction of the movement, and the relative virtue of setting excellence as the school purpose in a society which aims to be free and democratic.

EXCELLENCE AND ELITISM

''Excellence'' is a word which separates people. To excel is to be superior to others, to stand above, to outdo. Excellence seems to require some form of elitism. It starts on the premise that some people are superior to others; and the only question then is how to measure those differences. The measure must separate people, labeling some ''excellent'' and others by other titles. We can then have categories of people: excellent, very good, good, poor, rotten failures. If you are in the excellent category, you might be happy to have the others below you. If you are in the poor one, you may not be so content. The elitism necessary to the term ''excellence'' may rest only on the desire of an elite group to maintain itself.

Assume that we are members of a foot fetish group, and what we are going to measure is the length of people's feet—the longer the better. That is easy to measure, and we can set the excellent category at those with feet of eighteen inches or longer. Very few will be excellent, but we have a clear though absurd measure. Those identified as excellent on this measure are likely to protest any effort to lower the requirement. If, as a result of some egalitarian concerns, we enlarge the category of excellent to include those with feet nine inches or longer, we have not added to the quality of the definition, only to the quantity of people who can now be called excellent. This approach gives the impression of precision in measurement and rigor in standards, but it is a facade with no real meaning in the complex workings of the society. The length of the foot does not describe the quality of either the foot or the human attached to it. Relative size of foot may be of great significance to shoe manufacturers, but has little to do with the broad context of everyday life.

Similarly, the measures we have of excellence in schooling are usually severely limited, weak, and simplistic symbols that convey impressions far more than is valid. Various state tests of ''achievement,'' SAT scores, grades, or other single-score indicators hide more knowledge of students than they reveal. These indicators are often biased in language, content, form, and intent. They typically show that those who have been born into the proper families and have the proper training do well, while those who are born into disadvantaged families and have more limited economic environments do more poorly. Excellence on these indicators is not excellence but luck. Worse, the measures become labels which separate and identify those who will succeed and those who will not. Even though the measures have little relationship to real life in a complex world, they become the stamps which society accepts and which individuals begin to believe. Those stamped as failures begin to see themselves that way and become failures. Those from the already elite groups remain elite because they control the images of success and failure. That means they must control the measures, the symbols, and the rituals which give power in the society. And they must utilize convoluted logic and language to try to convince a presumably democratic society that elitism is a way of moving toward the basic democratic values of justice and equality. This is the sham of the "excellence movement."

MYSTIFICATION IN EDUCATIONAL REFORM

The "excellence movement" is an example of mystification. Mystification is a process which uses vague and ambiguous terms, objective-appearing symbols, and politically dramatic rhetoric to confuse and hide real purposes. An inability or an unwillingness to clearly define adequate criteria for excellence, and attempts to argue that excellence and equality are easily compatible, are examples of vague and ambiguous use of language. Use of objective-appearing symbols includes overreliance on testing, despite questions as to their validity, and the separation and labeling of people by comparative test scores. Dramatic political rhetoric is easily represented by national reports which claim, without examining conflicting evidence, that the nation is "at risk" and subject to international decline because of schools.

Mystification serves the interests of those in the dominant class. It is a means to undergird and protect the power base of elites. Techniques of mystification are used to persuade the public that the ruling elite are naturally endowed and/or best suited to further the interests of the whole society. In hierarchical societies, most elite positions are reserved for those who claim a birthright monopoly on such terms as excellence, nobility, or refinement. The definition for excellence includes vague and mysterious qualities that the elites are already presumed to have. These qualities are not clear and open to all citizens equally, since the elites have early and continuous advantage. And the elites control the measures and the gates for admission. A democracy, however, is intended to provide more equality and justice in real opportunities for all. One should expect much more social mobility in a democracy, but that mobility is a threat to the elites. Mystification, in a democracy, uses terms which sound democratic, but which hide the latent purposes of elitism.

This is of particular importance, since the political rhetoric that surrounds necessarily elite terms like "excellence" either must boldly announce that the advantaged will get increased favoritism, or must tread very lightly on the required hierarchical separation. In a nominally democratic society, the goal of excellence requires subtle political expression to retain public support. It is theoretically possible to have justice, equality, and freedom for all. But how can excellence be attainable for all and still be excellence? The answer is that if all were excellent, then excellence would have no meaning. It is the essence of the term "excellence" to require elites.

MANIFEST AND LATENT GOALS OF EXCELLENCE

A manifest goal of an excellence movement is to achieve excellence, that is, to increase or enhance the separation among people(s) on some criteria identified as fitting a definition of "excellent." That goal may be stated in terms that attempt to incorporate large proportions of a society, like "better than we were" or "better than other contemporary societies." There is thus a necessary presumption that quality was lower in previous times or other places. A statement of goals for excellence may also appear as a separation among people for social benefit, as in the expression of support for special advantage for the best and brightest to assure excellent leadership.

Often, manifest goals are cloudy and disguise the potential consequences of separatist requirements, as when advocates of merit salary systems for teachers presume that we all agree on what merit is and how it is measured. Interestingly, the majority of current literature and the National Commission report do not refer to the previous excellence movement for schools following the launching of Sputnik in 1957. That movement contained much of the same mystification rhetoric, testing and dull routine in school life, and elite gate-controlling seen in the contemporary movement. It also suffered from the same inability to be clear, to expand democracy, to enhance opportunities, and to provide for quality in education. Latent goals of the excellence movement are based on such grounds as social-class interest, racism, free enterprise capitalism, and political power. These latent goals include:

Reassertion of social control
Preservation of the status quo
Maintenance of certain elites
Reversing a shift toward progressive egalitarianism
Reasserting the influence of business and industry

The current reform efforts, aimed at "excellence," are a collection of restrictions and requirements which will do little to improve democracy, justice, or equality. The previous excellence movement only reinforced gross inequalities in public tax money available for schools. Wealthy suburbs gained significantly, while poor urban schools suffered more. Excellent schools were arranged for the well-to-do, while deficient schools were provided the poor.

The drive for progressive equity in schools, drawing from ideas of the 1930s and 1940s, was slowed.

Current efforts appear to be repeating this phenomenon. The government restricts funds for equalizing opportunities, such as Head Start, Chapter 1, and higher education loans, while initiating projects to reward high test scores and "meritorious" students. Progressive equity policies expanded in the 1960s are the victims of efforts to provide elite support, under the banner of "excellence," in the 1980s. Is it the society, or the elites, that have chosen excellence over equity?

The sham of the excellence movement in education will become known as its dimensions are realized by an educated and critical public.

FOR DISCUSSION

1 What evidence and support is there that excellence is measurable and attainable in society and in schools?

2 If it is possible to be excellent at fascism, excellent at dictatorship, excellent at creating death and destruction, then being excellent is insufficient without some values to guide the purpose for excellence. What legitimate values should undergird the striving for excellence in American society? How are these values addressed in the current movement for excellence in schooling?

3 Being opposed to excellence sounds un-American. What case, in addition to the ones presented in the chapter, can be made that being against excellence is in the American tradition?

4 In what ways do the following data about the United States* show what excellence is in America? What does it mean to be excellent? What do these data show about equity?

Infant mortality. Ranks sixteenth among nations (lower than such nations as Spain, Ireland, Japan, Germany, France).

Prenatal care for mother. 25 percent do not or cannot receive it.

Immunization against polio. 20 percent are not immunized.

Health care insurance. Almost 40 percent of children have no coverage.

Poverty. 20 percent of all children under age 18 are poor. 33 percent of those with parents under 30 are poor.

Income gap. Gap between rich and poor is wider now than at any time since the Census Bureau started records (1947). Poorest 20 percent of population get only 3.8 percent of total American income.

Child abuse. Reported incidents increased 90 percent between 1981 and 1986.

School dropout rates. Among poor families, 28.5 percent. Among nonpoor families, 10.5 percent.

* *Sources: A Vision for America's Future* (1989), Washington, D.C.: Children's Defense Fund; Ruth Leger Sivard (1988), *World Military and Social Expenditures, 1987–8*, Washington, D.C.: World Priorities.

Military expenditures. Ranks first among 142 nations.
Nuclear reactors. Ranks first among nations.
Military aid to other countries. Ranks first among nations.
Population per physician. Ranks eighteenth among nations.
School-age children per teacher. Ranks twentieth among nations.

REFERENCES

Bridgman, A. (1985). "States Launching Barrage of Initiatives, Survey Finds," *Education Week,* **4**(20), February 6, 1, 31.

Carnoy, M. (1983). "Education, Democracy, and Social Conflict." *Harvard Educational Review,* **53**, 398–402.

Finkelstein, B. (1984). "Education and the Retreat from Democracy in the United States, 1979–198?" *Teachers College Record,* **86**, 275–82.

Finn, C. E. (1984). "The Excellence Backlash: Sources of Resistance to Educational Reform." *The American Spectator,* **17**, 10–16.

Gardner, J. W. (1961). *Excellence: Can We Be Equal and Excellent Too?* New York: Harper & Row.

Glazer, N. (1987). "Equity and Excellence in Education: A Commentary." *Harvard Educational Review,* **57**, 196–99.

Husen, T. (1985). "The School in the Achievement-Oriented Society: Crisis and Reform." *Phi Delta Kappan,* **66**, 398–402.

Lewis, J. (1986). *Achieving Excellence in Our Schools.* Westbury, N.Y.: Wilkerson Publishing.

McNett, I. (1984). *Charting a Course: A Guide to the Excellence Movement in Education.* Washington, D.C.: Council for Basic Education.

National Commission on Excellence in Education (1983). *A Nation at Risk.* Washington, D.C.: U.S. Government Printing Office.

Peters, T., and Waterman, R. H. (1982). *In Search of Excellence: Lessons from America's Best Run Corporations.* New York: Harper & Row.

INDEX

INDEX